# Mongolia

# *Other Places Travel Guides*

# Mongolia

## Nathan Chamberlain, Leslie Chamberlain, Ashlee Christian and Andrew Cullen

## Published by

# OTHER PLACES PUBLISHING

First edition

Published August 2012

*Mongolia*

**Other Places Travel Guide**

*Written by: Nathan Chamberlain, Leslie Chamberlain, Ashlee Christian and Andrew Cullen*

*Edited by: Benjamin Cook*


*Cover designed by: Carla Zetina-Yglesias*

*Cover photograph and back cover photograph of man with eagle by: Andrew Cullen*

*Back cover photograph of Arkhangai monastery gate by: Ashlee Christian*


*Published by:*

**Other Places Publishing**

www.otherplacespublishing.com


All text, illustrations and artwork copyright

© 2012 Other Places Publishing


ISBN 978-1-935850-02-1

# Acknowledgments

We are thankful for all the contributors who made this book possible! Mongolia is a sprawling country and we deeply appreciate the hard work of the following individuals: Aaron Swan, Alexander Lyddon, Alexandra Yang, Alison Boland, the American Center for Mongolian Studies , Ashlee Burt, Blain Logan, Brian H. Martin, Caitlin Monahan, Cameron Asam, Ch. Tuul, Cristiana Cassano, Crystal Pierce, Garrett Prendergast, Geoff Grecynski, Jamie May Ly, Jon Hetts, Julie Tate, Kara Estep, Kathleen Carnahan, Katie Holder, the Khovd Monglish group, Kiley Larson, Laura Godfrey, Leigh Wells, Leila Greenia, Lindsay Holmes, Mark Estep, Mike Loehlein, Nadra Marie Safi, Narangarav Jambaltseren, O. Nyamtaivan, Patrick Larsen Hamilton, Patrick Olson, Robert Figlock, Robin Rue, Robyn Gardner, Ryan Donnelly, Ryan McGibony, S. Enkhtsesteg, S. Oyuntugs, Scott Burt, Starlight Rainbow, Stephanie Hackbarth, Travis Hellstrom, Tugsbayar Bayanzul, Tysen Dauer, Wallace Good III, Zach Moore, and Zachary Wellman.

The expertise of the cycling, birding, and photography contributors was astounding: Andrew Neal, Alison Jarman, Jim Moulton, Leigh Wells, and Hyun Sang Kenneth Hwang. We are thankful for how they shared their passions with us.

Lastly, we are endlessly thankful for the love, care, and support of our American and Mongolian families and friends as well as our Mongolian colleagues and the staff of Peace Corps Mongolia.

# About the Book

The purpose of this guide is to give travelers a resource for finding the Mongolia that lies off the beaten path. Sure, the parts on the path are pretty fun and fascinating, and we give you a lot of information to help you discover them. But this guide is for the adventurer willing to be creative, resourceful, and patient.

The four main writers and the 30-plus contributors lived and worked in communities in some of Mongolia's most remote regions, and we have seen sides of Mongolian life that few travelers or travel writers have had the opportunity to experience. Our guide should help you find some of those places and some of the people we've met, with the aim of giving you the time of your life.

The first chunk of the book will give you background on Mongolian culture, including history, politics, art, sport, and everyday life. Take the time to brush up on some of the nuances because you will get a lot more out of your trip if you know why men flick their throats, where to sit in a *ger,* or what that symbol on the Mongolian flag is.

After giving you the background, we lead you directly into Ulaanbaatar, the capital and transportation hub. At some point you will come through the sprawling metropolis and you need to know where to find a cheap bed, a cultural site worth seeing, or a fun spot. We do our best to give you our recommendations, but you never know what new place has just sprung up, so keep your eyes and ears open to experience your own version of "UB."

To get you out into the countryside (generally anything that's not UB), we listed the *aimags* (provinces) in alphabetical order. As a rule of thumb, decide where you want to go first and travel to the nearest provincial capital. From there, arrange transportation to countryside sites as needed.

All roads lead to Ulaanbaatar and often do not link the *aimag* centers (provincial capitals) well, so it is usually fairly difficult to travel even to the neighboring *aimag* unless you've hired a private car, but the adventure is in navigating these areas of sparse transportation. Because all public traffic leads to Ulaanbaatar, plan your trip to go out as far away as you think you want to and then work your way back. Going the other way can lead to long delays in your travel.

In each *aimag* chapter, we profile individuals and organizations we know well to introduce you to typical Mongolians often doing extraordinary things. We also point out some ordinary folks who we feel represent the many different people you'll likely encounter. For the *aimags* you don't travel to, still check out those profiles. We think you'll like them.

Toward the end of the book, there's some survival language guides in Mongolian and Kazakh. There's also a glossary. We hope you find it useful, even if you just awkwardly point to words while you feign like you're trying to pronounce them correctly.

Good luck on your journey in the land of the blue sky. If you get lost, follow the power lines.

*– Nathan, Leslie, Andy and Ashlee*

# Contents

BULGAN AIMAG 184: Bulgan Soum, Uran-Togoo Tulga Uul Nature Reserve, Khugnu Khaan Uul Nature Reserve, Teshig Soum, Bugat Soum

DARKHAN-UUL AIMAG 192

DORNOD AIMAG 201: Choibalsan Soum, Toson Khulstai National Park, Khalkhgol Gol Soum, Sumber Soum,

DORNOGOVI AIMAG 212: Sainshand, Zamiin-Uud, Khantanbulag Soum,

DUNDGOVI AIMAG 222: Mandalgovi, Ulziit Soum, Adaatsag Soum, Deren Soum, Saikhan Ovoo Soum

GOVI-ALTAI AIMAG 229: Altai, Eej Khairkhan Uul, Great Gobi Strictly Protected Area

GOVISUMBER AIMAG 235: Choir

KHENTII AIMAG 237: Undurkhan, Dadal Soum, Binder Soum, Khukh Nuur, Khan Khentii Protected Area

KHOVD AIMAG 247: Khovd City, Munkhkhairkhan Soum, Tsambagarav Uul National Park, Khar Us Nuur National Park, Mankhan Soum, Durgun Soum, Khovd Soum, Buyant Soum, Must Soum

KHUVSGUL AIMAG 264: Murun Soum, Khatgal Soum, Khuvsgul Nuur National Park, Erdenebulgan Soum, Arbulag Soum, Tsagaan-Uur Soum, Chandmani-Undur

ORKHON AIMAG (Erdenet) 278

SELENGE AIMAG 287: Sukhbaatar Soum, Altanbulag Soum, Yeruu Soum, Shaamar Soum,

SUKHBAATAR AIMAG 298: Baruun Urt

TUV AIMAG 305: Zuunmod, Gorkhi-Terelj National Park, The Bogd Khan Mountain National Park, Khustain Nuruu National Park

UMNUGOVI AIMAG 314: Dalanzadgad, Gobi Gurvan Saikhan National Park

UVS AIMAG 325: Ulaangom, Uvs Nuur Basin Special Protected Area, Tarialan Soum

UVURKHANGAI AIMAG 333: Arvaikheer, Kharkhorin Soum, Khujirt Soum

ZAVKHAN AIMAG 350: Uliastai, Tosontsengel Soum

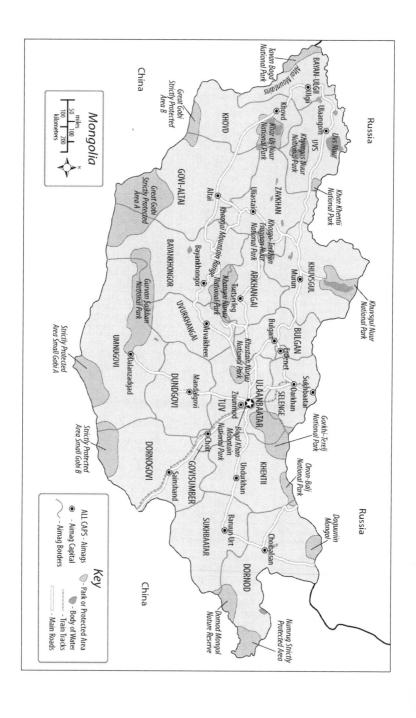

# About the Authors & Recommendations

## NATHAN CHAMBERLAIN

**Nathan Chamberlain** is the youngest of three brothers from Wilmington, Ohio, where he was bitten early on by the wanderlust bug as an Eagle Scout and family road-tripper. After graduating from Ohio University with a BA in International Studies, Nathan enjoyed non-profit management and fundraising in Philadelphia. Despite the comfortable life, Nathan and his wife packed nearly all their possessions into a storage unit, and the next thing they knew they were in Mongolia with the Peace Corps. For 27 months he was a business adviser in Bayankhongor Aimag for an international NGO and community organizations implementing micro-lending and other programs including tourism development.

Nathan has enjoyed traveling around the United States, Europe and parts of Asia with his wife and always looks forward to staying off the beaten path where the most important adventures take place when he least expects them.

### Nathan's Travel Recommendations

I like traveling because I enjoy connecting history and culture using my own experiences. That's why I loved my trip to **Uvurkhangai Aimag's Kharkhorin** to visit the **UNESCO World Heritage Site, the Orkhon Valley Cultural Landscape** (p343). I went expecting to see the ruins of the ancient imperial cities, but I found a whole lot more.

For this trip, I traveled by *purgon* from my home in Bayankhongor Aimag to Uvurkhangai's capital, Arvaikheer. I stayed overnight exploring the town before I went on to Kharkhorin the next afternoon by taxi from the market. When I arrived in the remote village, I laughed—not at what I saw, but what I didn't see. It certainly wasn't the ruins of Angkor Wat or the Coliseum or the palatial Forbidden City.

Being there in the wide open Orkhon Valley was so mysterious and big and wondrous, but there wasn't much there to see; only traces, hints, and clues. For me, standing in this unassuming pastureland in the middle of Mongolia from where storied civilizations had spread out far and wide, I instantly understood more about my Mongolian friends, and my perception of conversations with Mongolians before and after changed. Just being there made me rethink so many things about wealth, power, pride, history, progress, perception, sustainability, and legacy that I hadn't expected when I set out on a whim to Kharkhorin two days prior.

I returned to Arvaihkheer a few days later and hitchhiked on the afternoon bus on its way back to Bayankhongor. The trip ended much differently than it had begun, and it included the Erdene Zuu Khiid and many of the other attractions around Uvurkhangai. Along the way, I met inspiring Mongolians and interesting international travelers I'll never forget, but I also connected with the country, its people, and world history in an unexpected way, and I hope you do, too.

## LESLIE ANN SHAFFER CHAMBERLAIN

**Leslie Ann Shaffer Chamberlain** grew up in the small town in northeast Pennsylvania on Lake Erie. She's always been able to tell where she is based on the location of the closest body of water. She also is fine with cold weather as long as it is accompanied by heaps of snow. In an odd twist of fate, she went with the Peace Corps to a freezing cold, landlocked country entirely too dry to have heaps of any precipitation and near no major bodies of water. Nevertheless, she hasn't lost herself yet.

Leslie is a 2002 graduate of Ohio University with a BM in Music Therapy and a 2008 graduate of Temple University with a Masters in Music Therapy. She was a life skills adviser in the Community Youth Development (CYD) program working with the Bayankhongor Children's Center and Children's Temujin Theater. She thinks the countryside is the best part of Mongolia and is thrilled to be able to highlight it.

### Leslie's Travel Recommendations

It's not everyone's favorite, but one of my best trips in Mongolia was through **Khentii and Sukhbaatar** *aimags* (p237 and p298) You may recall the BBC Planet Earth series where they highlighted the Mongolian gazelle. The bus ride from Khentii's Undurkhaan (p238) to Sukhbaatar's Baruun Urt (p298) is one easy, cheap way to get where you need to go *and* see these majestic animals.

From Ulaanbaatar you can catch a morning bus at the Bayanzurkh bus station and get to Undurkhaan, the capital of Khentii, in roughly five hours. One friend of mine describes Undurkhaan as a glorified village, and I think that is a great part of its charm. Enjoying an afternoon by the river and munching on the tasty Khentii "fish bread" makes for a slow and relaxing summer day!

From Undurkhaan you can jump on the bus to Baruun Urt, Sukhbaatar by the Fourth School in the afternoon or arrange tickets at the bus office for the morning. This ride is really where the magic happens. The eastern steppe teems with wild white gazelles as you drive through the remote countryside. Once in Baruun Urt, you won't need to feel lost, as there are a growing number of community members who speak English. And Sukhbaatar Aimag offers exploration like no other in Dariganga Natural Park (p303), where the steppe meets the Gobi with its volcanoes, lakes, sand dunes, and sacred mountains above sweeping views of those galloping gazelles.

If you are interested in seeing Mongolia where comparatively few other tourists venture, make this Khentii/Sukhbaatar trip! I was welcomed in these communities like an old friend and instantly felt connected to the expansive natural glory of the Mongolian countryside.

## ASHLEE CHRISTIAN

**Ashlee Christian**, a small girl with big dreams from Chicago's north side, knew from a young age that she wanted to be an astronaut. After realizing that the pursuit of such a career would require math skills beyond addition and subtraction, she humbly hung up her space helmet and moved to Bowling Green, Ohio to pursue a degree in photography. Ashlee had also always been fascinated by other places and cultures, a fascination that manifested itself in the most extreme way possible when she moved to a felt tent in central Mongolia. After spending two years in the land of blue sky, Ashlee is now back in America resting her itchy feet and plotting her next adventure. She may or may not revisit the idea of going to space.

### Ashlee's Travel Recommendations

In terms of getting around Mongolia, the juice is worth the squeeze. And if you plot your course correctly, you can squeeze the most out of a limited amount of time and money. My perfect path would be **Arkhangai-Erdenet-Khuvsgul**. While these places may look relatively close to one another on a map, they take a bit of scheming to reach.

Start in UB and take the bus into Arkhangai (this is the easy part). While in Arkhangai (p152) make sure to give yourself some time in and around the *aimag* center as there is much to see and do. From Arkhangai you can catch a bus that will take you to Erdenet. The operators of this bus like to keep things somewhat mysterious, so it would be wise of you to ask someone at the Fairfield Café and Guesthouse when it will leave. That way you can claim a seat and then have the rest of your time to gallivant about Arkhangai.

On the mysterious bus to Erdenet, you will be transported to a lovely little city full of Russian foodstuffs and surrounded by beautiful scenery. You may only need a day in Erdenet (p278), but make sure you factor in a nice hike outside of the city. From Erdenet you can take a *purgon* to Khuvsgul (p264). They leave daily, usually in the afternoon whenever they fill up. This ride isn't for the faint of heart, but I can assure you, it is worth it. Khuvsgul is by far one of the most beautiful places in Mongolia and, I daresay, planet Earth. Going up to Khatgal Soum (p270) and taking a jaunt about the lake is an absolute must. If you had any desire to pitch a tent and catch thee some fish, this is the place to do it. From Murun (p265), Khuvsgul Aimag's capital, it's an easy (albeit long) bus ride back to UB. Voila!

## ANDREW CULLEN

**Andrew Cullen** grew up traveling to skateboard parks and punk rock shows throughout New England. He received a degree in journalism from Boston University, from which he took a semester off to study in Mongolia. After graduation, Peace Corps sent him to Bangladesh. When Peace Corps pulled out of the hot, tiny, crowded country due to security concerns, he suggested that Peace Corps send him back to frigid, sparsely populated, expansive Mongolia. They obliged, and he served as an English teacher in western Mongolia from 2006 to 2009. Following his service, he remained in Mongolia, working as a freelance photographer and journalist for a year, while also researching and writing this guide.

Andrew is a passionate observer of nomadic cultures, migration, and the relationships between people and their local environment. He seeks to place remote people and places into a global context with his writing and photography.

### Andy's Travel Recommendations
I always felt fortunate that Peace Corps placed me in Western Mongolia. The remoteness—a good 800 miles of unpaved, dirt track separated me from Ulaanbaatar—satisfied my perverse desire to "rough it," and the vaguely Martian landscape of red, craggy mountains was beautiful in a way that couldn't be compared with the gentle Appalachians of eastern America I was accustomed to.

One of the absolute best factors of living in the region, though, was that it was so easy to get to **Bayan Ulgii** (p172), the Kazakh-dominated province at Mongolia's western apex where the country meets both Russia and China. Because of its strong

Kazakh culture and Central-Asian feel, I always felt that Bayan Ulgii was like a special added bonus on the Mongolian adventure: one visa, two countries.

I went to Bayan Ulgii numerous times: for the fantastic eagle hunting festival in October, for the *Nauriz* celebration in March, and for the province's eightieth anniversary *Naadam* in 2010. Each time, the people of Bayan Ulgii were tremendously friendly and helpful, and the displays of Kazakh music, dance and their ability to communicate with their mighty golden eagles were endlessly fascinating.

But one of my favorite trips to the province was the one during which I had the least contact with the people: a camping trip at the foot of the country's tallest mountain, Altai Tavan Bogd (p181). Certainly, we met people who I'll remember for ages to come, like the park ranger whose house was tucked so deep into a mountain pass you would never know it was there if you weren't looking for it, or the Kazakh man with the Mongolian name who stopped his horse to chat after we stalled our Jeep in the middle of a snowmelt-engorged river and nearly had to swim out of it. But just as memorable was the place. The area, in the heart of the Altai Mountains, is absolutely beautiful: miles after miles of snow-capped peaks, glaciers, and turquoise high-altitude lakes. At the edge of the Mongolian wilds, it had never been easier to appreciate how small I was, how big the world was, and how right that ratio is.

## OTHER LIKELY ITINERARIES

Must-see holidays in Mongolia include July's **Naadam** festival (p51, hopefully outside of UB) and **Tsagaan Sar** (Lunar New Year, p57) celebrations in February. While Mongolian life has modernized, Mongolians take a little step back in time to celebrate their heritage during these holidays, and they are usually proud to share it with travelers.

If you are in Mongolia for just a few days and you want to stay on the beaten path, **Terelj National Park** (p305) in Tuv Aimag is a good option to get the quickest glimpse. You can and should go, though you don't necessarily need a tour company to do it. The park can get a bit "touristy" and kitschy. Another option is the close but somewhat less tourist-jammed **Khustain Nuruu National Park** (p312), home to a large herd of re-introduced Przewalksi's horses.

Instead of parks, you might take a bus or train to **Darkhan** (p192) or **Erdenet** (p278) to see how Mongolia's smaller cities operate—you can still stay in *ger* camps near either city for a taste of traditional Mongolia.

The most sought-after destination is the Gobi in **Umnugovi Aimag** (p314), where you will find plenty of tourist services and English-speakers as well as impressive natural wonders.

If you have a few weeks, you could see a combination of those things or venture well off the beaten path to farther reaches like beautiful **Bayankhongor Aimag** (p159), the "Rich Darling" of Mongolia. There, you can see a convergence of ecosystems at the foot of **Ikh Bogd Uul**. In one pinwheel turn, you can see steppe, forest, water, and desert, and you will have it all to yourself. Or head east to **Dornod Aimag** (p201) for fishing and superb birdwatching.

Whichever way you choose, you're likely to see something new, meet someone great, and eat something...interesting. Good luck, be patient, and just go with the flow.

# Introduction

Mongolia is an adventure travel destination. Though some luxury accommodations exist in the capital and some tourist hot spots have more Westerner-friendly accommodations, the most interesting things to see and do are outside **Ulaanbaatar (UB)** and other tourist-centered areas. In the countryside, travelers must be more creative, patient, and resourceful. The good news, though, is that your extra work pays off. Traveling in Mongolia can be the reward of a lifetime.

Mongolia stands in contrast with other Asian destinations that offer sandy beaches, fruity cocktails, and architectural remnants of European colonialism. Here, nomadic traditions have left little architecture or modern infrastructure, especially outside UB. While this may make traveling on your own challenging at times if you don't speak at least some Mongolian, it provides a great opportunity for you to see Mongolia as Mongolians see it. In our book, we highlight Mongolia's most unique aspects and interesting places for the intrepid, culturally curious, and low-budget traveler.

Since billions of development aid dollars began to pour into Mongolia in the early 1990s, noticeable changes have continued to develop yearly and even monthly. Despite many economic changes and challenges, everyday life in Mongolia is charmingly influenced by its pastoral history, even in UB.

One advantage to the lack of infrastructure is that every car is a taxi, and even if a car is full, it will probably pick you up and cram you in somewhere. An obvious disadvantage is that travel can often be uncomfortable when you have to stuff seven people in a car meant for five or twenty in a microbus meant for twelve. Mile for mile, though, transportation in Mongolia is relatively cheap, and every trip is an adventure.

As you search for horses and two-humped camels to ride, eagle hunters, overnight stays in authentic Mongolian yurts (or *gers*, pronounced like "gair") by the Gobi Desert, and swimming spots shared with curious livestock after a long hike in the middle of nowhere, take some time to meet Mongolians. Ask them about their day and life and try to connect one-on-one. Long after your aching backside recovers and blisters wear off or the *tugriks* you paid out have been spent on new jeans or new tires, that personal connection will remain for both of you—because after all isn't that what travel is all about?

The winters are harsh, unforgiving, and not for the faint of heart – even some of the bravest travelers may wither at -40° F, though tourists do come every February to witness the Lunar New Year celebrations, *Tsagaan Sar.* Instead, the best time to come to Mongolia is the summer between late May and late September. The peak is in July during the summer sports festival, *Naadam*, when the temperature is well into the upper 30s Centigrade (upper 90s Fahrenheit).

# About Mongolia

Mongolia is a landlocked country about the size of Alaska, one-fifth the size of Australia, and almost three times the size of France. It shares its northern border with Russia and is otherwise surrounded by China. Sometimes it is referred to as "Outer Mongolia" in contrast to the northern Chinese autonomous region of "Inner Mongolia," where a great number of the world's Mongolian speakers live thanks to a complicated past with China.

As you will quickly come to appreciate first-hand, Mongolia has one of the lowest population densities in the world at only 1.77 persons per square km (4.58 per square mile). Between a third and half of its roughly 3 million people live in the capital city, Ulaanbaatar (UB), which has seen an

> **Geography Statistics**
>
> **Land area:** 1,565,000 sq. km (972,446 sq. miles)
>
> **Population:** 3,086,000
>
> **Population Density:** 1.77 per square km (4.58 per square mile)
>
> **Borders:** Russia 3,000 km (1,864 miles) and China 4,670 km (2,902 miles)
>
> **Terrain:** Mostly mountainous with an average altitude of 1,580 m (5,184 feet) above sea level. Gobi Dessert across the south. Forested across the north.
>
> **Highest Peak:** Tavan Bogd in the Altai Mountains at 4,374 m (14,337 ft.)

influx of Mongolians as periodic winter weather disasters and the transitional economy have enticed job seekers. UB is also the main travel hub where most tourism services, infrastructure, and supplies are found. The city itself is like a different country—a cramped urban Mongolia jammed with automobiles and asphalt, restaurants, and modern glass and steel architecture.

Outside of UB, large population concentrations exist in each of the 21 provincial capitals or *aimag* centers. In all of these areas, Mongolians typically live in either Soviet-style high-rise apartment buildings connected to centralized hot water systems, or in patchwork neighborhoods of side-by-side wooden fences that contain *gers* and single family houses. These compounds are almost always without running water and are heated by wood stoves.

The rest of the population is spread across wide steppe, where families live the nomadic herding lifestyle romanticized in movies such as *The Cave of the Yellow Dog, Mongol,* and *The Story of the Weeping Camel.* This tends to be the more interesting Mongolia for visitors. Travel to most points of interest is often measured in days, but the difficulties of travel are made more tolerable by unobstructed views of the rolling semi-arid landscapes of the central and southern plains and the plush green pastures of the north, all of which sustain nearly 40 million head of sheep, cows, goats, yaks, and camels.

To travel independently, you will more often than not make your way to the *aimag* center by bus (or sometimes by train where it exists) and arrange private or shared transportation to the points of interest from there. Provincial capitals usually act as regional hubs linking all points of interest in the area. Travel between the provincial capitals is often impossible unless the destinations are on the same road network en route to UB, where cheap, reliable buses run to each capital and some points of interest.

From 1921 to 1991, Mongolia was resolutely aligned with the former Soviet Union, without actual membership in the USSR itself. During this time, literacy rates skyrocketed, especially for women, who now make up a large portion of the educated work force. You're likely to notice that many tour guides, tour coordinators, and English-speakers in general are women, though drivers and business owners are typically men. With Soviet aid, permanent infrastructure was built in a country previously based solely on the nomadic herding lifestyle characterized by the traditional, mobile *ger*. A *ger* or yurt is a round, wood-framed tent sheathed in felt that can easily be torn down and moved with all a family's worldly possessions in half a day. In lieu of hotels, there are over 450 registered and countless unregistered *ger* camps that often make up the rural accommodations for travelers. *Ger* camps have various degrees of amenities that might include running water, toilets, and a kitchen in a separate building, though many only have squat outhouses and lack running water, similar to the homes of most rural Mongolians. Usually the smaller and more rural the camp, the more authentic the feel.

Many *ger* camps are close to mineral springs and religious sites. For centuries before Communism and since its fall in the early 1990s, Mongolians have practiced a variation of Tibetan Buddhism and traditional shamanism, especially near the springs and sacred mountains. Most monks and monasteries did not survive the Stalinist purges of the 1930s, so religion went underground for much of the twentieth century just as it did all over the communist bloc. As religion reemerges, family rituals, traditions, superstitions, and modern lifestyles are mingled with modern practices. The country does boast several ornate yet humble monasteries that have survived or been restored in recent years and are interesting to explore, even if you know nothing of the religion. Mineral springs and energy centers across the country are claimed to possess certain healing properties.

Additionally, Mongolians tend to idolize Chinggis Khan (Ghengis Khan) as an ancestral deity of sorts, and in almost every home you are likely to find a portrait of him hanging on the wall in a prominent place. Anything with his likeness makes a good souvenir or gift for a welcoming host.

Though religion was squashed by the state, much modernization occurred during the planned economy era. With their role in helping to liberate Mongolia from feudal Chinese rulers and twentieth-century modernization still fresh in the minds of Mongolians, Russians are typically perceived favorably, as are Westerners in general. The main sources of revenue for the country still include gold and copper mining and cashmere exports, all industries started during the communist era. Mineral rights especially have been a hot political topic in recent years, fueling

## Mongolian Geopolitical Distinction

The Mongolian word for "province" is ***aimag* (аймар, pronounced "eye-mag")**. There are 21 independent *aimag*s in Mongolia, including several like Ulaanbaatar, Darkhan, and Erdenet which are little more than large urban centers. Every *aimag* has a capital city which serves as the administrative and commercial hub for the province. These cities are commonly referred to as the ***aimag* center (*aimagiin tov*, аймагийн төв)** or simply *aimag*. Each *aimag* is further divided into a number of ***soums* (сум, the vowels pronounced as in "soap")**, which act rather like counties or parishes, albeit very rural ones (the *aimag* center is also considered its own *soum*).

Generally speaking, a *soum* will have one permanent village that is home to its administrative center and provides services including schools, medical clinics, banks, and small shops. This is the ***soum* center**. The *soum*s are further divided into districts known as ***bags* (6ar, pronounced like "bahg")**. A *bag* is usually entirely rural, and its inhabitants tend to be full-time nomadic herders. When taking public transportation, vehicles leaving from Ulaanbaatar will always travel to the *aimag* center; shared taxis from *aimag* markets to the *soum*s will almost always make their final stop in the *soum* center.

speculation of government corruption and malfeasance. The cashmere markets have struggled to normalize since the early 1990s as well; so much of the cashmere wool raised in Mongolia is not processed there. This makes the price of cashmere a little higher within Mongolia than you might expect, though still a great bargain for Western travelers.

*Introduction*

## Concentric Countryside

Mongolians have a concentric concept of "countryside" depending on where they are. From Ulaanbaatar, everything is the countryside or *khudoo* (хөдөө), even Erdenet and Darkhan, the second and third largest cities. From an *aimag* center, everything surrounding that is countryside. From *soum* centers, everything surrounding that is considered countryside, and in the countryside, everything outside the vicinity of herder's *ger* is the countryside.

# Pastoral Nomads of Mongolia

Pastoral nomads, who move with their households in search of pasture for their animals, make up roughly one-quarter of the country's 3 million people and are the foundation of the Mongolian culture. The romantic idea of a nomad, a wandering free spirit with no fixed location, is part fiction and part reality in Mongolia. The industry is very important, but mother nature has made some serious readjustments to counteract overgrazing and overpopulation, including the 2009-2010 winter weather disaster (*dzud*) that left nearly 8 million animals starved and frozen.

## HERDING IN MONGOLIA

When you think of nomadic herding, it might conjure thoughts of great treks from region to region following animals as they wander the vast steppe in each direction looking for prime spots to graze. But, while their movement is seasonal and linked to rainfall and the availability of good forage for the animals, herds usually rotate on roughly the same swaths of land located close together. Herders depend on those lands to be free each year (both in price and availability), and though there are usually no formal agreements among them as to who may use what land or when, herders know the allowable spots. Even still, many herds overlap, which does not seem to bother most as it is a professional courtesy and code of the steppe to share and share alike.

Because this lifestyle takes them out onto the land and away from more permanent settlements, herder families are usually remotely separated. Herders are often hours from the villages where their children attend schools and live in dorms for part of the year.

Livestock production is the main source of income for Mongolians and involves about half the workforce of the country. But only half of those herders are nomadic. Others raise smaller numbers of livestock in or around villages, utilizing slat board barns with angled roofs that typically face south to protect against winds from the north. Their children go to school and live at home. These herders might also be taxi drivers, teachers, shop owners, or handicraft makers who supplement their income with herding. Additionally, some families own animals that friends or family members herd for them most of the year.

## OVERPOPULATION & OVERGRAZING

Since the introduction of democracy and the free-market system, herd sizes have grown and herding customs have changed. While greater herd numbers provide the opportunity for greater wealth accumulation, they have caused unintended environmental consequences, further exacerbated by decreasing rainfall.

Though the composition of small livestock herds was maintained at 70 percent sheep and 30 percent goat during Soviet times, the 2008 Official Yearbook of Mongolia shows that Mongolian herds are now composed of five animals: goats (45%), sheep (42%), cattle (6%), horses (5.5%), and Bactrian two-humped camels (less than 1%). Mongolians also raise yaks, which are considered to be cattle. The total number of livestock as of November 2009 was 44 million, up 10 percent from 2008, according to the United Nations Development Programme (UNDP). The previous decade had also seen double-digit yearly increases in livestock numbers.

The largest of these increases has been in goats because their hair is the coveted material used to make cashmere. In the mid-2000s, prices had dramatically risen, so many herders added large numbers of the animals to take advantage. Of course, this flooded the market and drove prices back down, but herders could still make a decent living. In the meantime, the goats, which can be very destructive to steppe grasses because they eat the plants down to their roots, damaged parts or all of previously arable pasturelands. This has had disastrous consequences for herds, meat prices, and the average Mongolian household who has a diet heavily based on meat and fat.

Overgrazing, combined with a trend of low rainfall and other signals of changing climate over the past decade, has informed predictions that as much as 75 percent of Mongolia will be desert by 2050. While this projection may be alarmist, it does call attention to the possibility that the future of pastoral herding in Mongolia could be in danger.

### All Roads Lead to UB

Because UB is the travel hub, you must usually return to UB if you want to travel by bus from province to province when traveling away from UB. Instead, it's best to start your trip by going out as far away as you want to go from UB and then work your way back by microbus or car.

# Mongolian History

The steppe—a vast, semiarid grassland—connects Mongolia to Asia and Europe (from China through Siberia and the Middle East into the Mediterranean). These regions have been connected for a long, long time not only by geography and climate but also by politics, economics, and especially culture. Though Mongolia is technically in Asia, you'll probably notice the Westward lean away from the Far East, though Mongolia maintains many links with the East as well.

There are over 500 deer stones (*balbal*) and man stones (*khunii chuluu*) that mark the graves of long-lost kings who ruled over the Mongolian countryside going back thousands of years. Without warning, you can wander upon Turkic relics that might be 5,000 years old or tread on the grounds of ancient empires in the Orkhon Valley Cultural Landscape, a UNESCO World Heritage site near modern-day Kharkhorin. Khovd Aimag boasts petroglyphs in the Gurvan Tsenkher Agui, and Bayankhongor Aimag even claims that the first Asians lived in and around its White Cave 750,000 years ago. Oddly, none of these sites are protected or preserved with formal markers, roped off, or otherwise acknowledged, making them both free and difficult to find at times.

The traditions of the steppe have been preserved by families through regional dress, ceremonies, herding methods, and spoken stories, many of which share common themes from across the Eurasian steppe. Travelers like Marco Polo and Flemish Franciscan monk William of Rubruck and historians like the Persian Rashid al-Din have left written accounts of the Mongols from their respective eras going back many hundreds of years. Discovering the convergence of empires and epochs in the people is part of the fun of coming to Mongolia.

First, though, you have to know what you're looking for.

## MONGOLS TO MONGOLIANS

Any member of the tribes that inhabited ancient Mongolia was a Mongol, but a citizen of the present-day parliamentary republic called Mongolia is "Mongolian" when we refer to them in English. Mongolians are almost always Mongols, but it would be too simple to assume that modern Mongolians are a homogenous group with a continuous past.

Mongols have been pastoral nomads in this area and across the steppe for many thousands of years, identifying themselves primarily within clans and tribes just as they have across Eurasia. This familial political structure pops up often in modern media while referring to remote parts of Afghanistan and Pakistan that still operate as they have for as long as anyone can remember.

By uniting in different groups and confederations, tribes have been conquering what consists of modern-day Mongolia and its surrounding borders since many generations before Christ. Groups that have seated their empires here included the Xiongnu or Hunnu (400-300 B.C.E.) whose raids in China forced the Qin Dynasty to connect and fortify the Great Wall to keep them out. The Xianbei or Tunghu, while under the rule of the Chinese Han Dynasty (207 B.C.E.–220 C.E.) became an important part of the burgeoning silk road across the steppe. The Rourans (330–555 C.E.) were the first people to use the titles "Khagan" and "Khan" for their emperors

## The Secret History of the Mongols

*The Secret History of the Mongols* is a three-part saga recounting the origins of the boy called Temujin who later became the great Chinggis Khan. It is the only source of information about Mongolian life during the medieval period written from a Mongolian perspective, and it is considered a treasure among Mongolians and social scientists. It was written by an unknown author using the Uighur letters that were eventually adapted as the vertical Mongolian script. The only version that has survived is a Chinese translation from the 1300s.

The first part reconstructs oral myths in a legend that describes the origins of the Mongolian people from a the union of a divine bluish wolf and a fallow doe. It is followed by an extensive genealogy of the Mongol khans of the Golden Line that became the basis for ancestral lineage and legitimacy after Chinggis's death in 1227.

The second part conveys more reliable historical data using the zodiac to date events in the history of the numerous Mongolian tribes and their unification into a single state in 1206. Chinggis Khan is portrayed as a great strategist, statesman, and tolerant ruler with an unrelenting iron will.

The final part, which is thought to be an addendum to the original text, recounts the reign of Chinggis' third son Uguudei who continued the expansion of the empire to its farthest reaches into the west by invading Europe.

If you're interested in the work, there's no need to buy a translated copy unless you enjoy single-function things like separate, phone, camera, calculator, watch, stopwatch, and paperweights. Instead, multi-purpose your purchase by picking up the 2004 book "*Genghis Khan and the Making of the Modern World*" by Jack Weatherford. It recites much of the *Secret History* in the beginning and goes on to provide relevant historical perspective. Audiophiles can find a copy of a 2010 radio performance, the "Secret History Radio Drama," in UB bookstores or contact the producer at javkha_ara@yahoo.com.

and kings. Finally, the Goturks or "Celestial Turks" (552–747 C.E.) were the first to write using the Orkhon script that can be seen on scattered relics. The Goturks were downed by the Uighurs (742–848 C.E.), who adapted the Orkhon script, which was later adopted and transformed into the traditional Mongolian script of Chinggis Khan around 1204.

Because of the mobility and vast reach of the tribes, it must have been hard to keep track of who was who. It seems Europeans were confused as to who was actually raiding and plundering them. For example, the Chinese name "Xiongnu" is the tribe that ruled over Mongolia in the third century B.C.E. They may be the same group or ancestors of the group that Westerners know as the Huns (or *Khunnu* to Mongolians). Hungary, actually populated by Magyars who share common roots with Finns and Estonians, is mistakenly named after them. Similarly, some groups in eastern Europe called the thirteenth-century Mongol invaders "Tartars," perhaps because the Mongolians looked like the once prominent Tatar tribe or because the Mongolians had folded the conquered Tatars into their invading armies. Europeans further confused the tribe name with Tartarus, a Greco-Roman hell, and linked the invaders to mythological retribution (and misspelled the name). Depending on the source, any of these groups can be generically referred to as "Mongols."

Today, roughly 80 percent of Mongolians are of Khalkh ancestry, the clan of Chinggis Khan. Indeed, though you may find it unbelievable, you can hardly find anyone in Mongolia who doesn't claim to be from that group, especially since it is considered the most prestigious lineage. In 2004, National Geographic reported that nearly "8 percent of the men living in the region of the former Mongol empire carry y-chromosomes that are nearly identical. That translates to 0.5 percent of the male population in the world, or roughly 16 million descendants living today." So, there is a good chance that most of Mongolia's 3 million people are somehow descendants of Chinggis. It is even a popular myth that anyone with a **blue spot** on their backsides during infancy is related to the historic khan, although there is no direct correlation.

## *"Mongoloid"*

The pejorative term "Mongoloid," which is an anthropological classification of skull features found mostly among Asians that means "resembling a Mongol," has nothing to do with genetic regression as John Langdon Down claimed in the mid-nineteenth century. The British doctor assumed that this congenital malady was an expression of recessive Asian features accompanied by mental retardation due to the race's supposed inferiority. But alas, Down's syndrome is actually caused by the duplication of the twenty-first chromosome and not thirteenth-century Mongol invasions.

There are minority groups, though. Among them there are the Dukha and Tsataan who herd reindeer and live in teepees near Khuvsgul Lake, the Buriats who hail from many areas along the Russian border and tend to look more Slavic, and the Khoton in Uvs Aimag, an ethnic group of Turkic origin who mainly speak and dress like Mongolians these days but continue to practice Islam. Western Mongolia is home to a number of minority Mongolian ethnic groups, like the Durvud, Uriankhai, and Zakhchin with their own dialects and customs.

Because Mongols do come from so many different places and ethnic groups across the steppe, you'll find faces in Mongolia that bear resemblance to their steppe-dwelling Uzbek, Kazakh, and Kyrgyz brethren, not to mention the Chinese, Japanese, Korean, and many other nationalities. After meeting the fearsome leader, historian Rashid al-Din wrote that Chinggis Khan himself had red hair and green eyes, characteristics more aligned with European ancestry than Asian.

Today in Mongolia, strong family ties are some of the last vestiges of the underlying clan culture, but little remains of that life as a political institution. The modern Mongolian state and its socialist-leaning politics are also undoubtedly affected by these roots as well.

## THE RISES & DEMISES OF THE MONGOL EMPIRES

**Chinggis Khan** (1162–1227), also known as "Genghis Khan," is considered the father of Mongolia because he unified the various regional Mongolian tribes under his empire in 1206 by conquering a number of lesser khans and their people. He unified these tribes through military conquest, intimidation, and alliances against common enemies. Then, he and his combined army took over, among others, the Naimans, Uighurs, and Tangut in the south and the Mergids, Tatars, and Tuvans in the north and west using the same tactics.

These different tribes express themselves latently now in the form of women's ceremonial headdresses or boot shapes and in minor herding practices like the placement of a camel's nose peg. Chinggis Khan was ethnically Khalkh, a tribe whose dialect is the root of the modern Mongolian language.

Chinggis continued to expand his sphere of control eastward until his death in 1227. Afterwards, the empire was divided into four parts. Chinggis' vast genetic imprint left the so-called "Golden Lineage" so watered down that after the collapse of the Yuan Dynasty in 1368, there was no clear successor. Civil war and tribal allegiances returned as the Oirat Tribe from western Mongolia achieved dominance in the region, even reaching as far as Beijing in 1449 in its quest to reclaim the empire.

But it was not to be, and in the wake of the 1455 death of the Oirat khan, the region slipped back into generations of tribal and civil war. By 1578, a descendant of **Khubilai Khan**, Altan Khan emerged as a central figure among the eastern tribes. He is best remembered for reestablishing ties to Tibetan Buddhism in Mongolia, which he used as a tool for political unification.

At its height, the Mongolian empire stretched from the Pacific Ocean to Eastern Europe and the Middle East. It covered Siberia in the north and stretched into the Indian subcontinent to the south. It was the largest contiguous empire in recorded history with over 120 million people spread across 22 percent of the earth's total land area.

Introduction

## Chinggis Khan Trivia

Chinggis Khan (Чингис Хаан) was arguably the most powerful and influential non-religious person ever—even Chaucer called him the greatest lord that ever lived. He was also responsible for the systematic destruction of towns, cultures, and people in some of the most vicious ways imaginable, all in the name of plundering, raping, and pillaging for the benefit of his own people. Though it was all but forbidden to talk of him favorably during the communist era, the most famous of the khans is a hero to the Mongolian people today. But what else did he do? He:

- Cried a lot as a child and was afraid of dogs.
- Killed his own brother in a power struggle when they were children.
- Was from the lowest tribe, and because of his humble roots built a system of ascension based on merit rather than nepotism, a system that held aristocrats in contempt. When he conquered cities, he would kill the richest because he felt they were worthless and dangerous.
- Was the son and husband of abducted women and consequently outlawed the common practice of abducting women to help prevent tribal in-fighting.
- Unified the silk road, encouraging free trade and commerce to connect people through and across continents.
- Built some of the first actual and diplomatic bridges between the East and West.
- Was tolerant of all religions in his empire, something novel considering it was during the time of the Crusades.
- Required tribute from his conquered lands but was not a totalitarian.
- Turned over much of his plunder to his people and never acquired much personal wealth.
- Exercised a rule of law that included unmolested passage for diplomats during a time when torture was common.
- Oversaw an army divided by decimals of men: 100,000 soldiers were divided into 10-men squads, in 100-men companies, in 1000 battalions, in 10 10,000-man armies, 100 percent of whom were cavalry and artillery. The system borrowed from the Mongol tradition was perfected under his reign, and remains a prevailing military structure today.

## Other Noteworthy Mongolians

**Uguudei Khan (Өгөөдэй хаан)** (1186-1241): Chinggis Khan's third son who inherited and expanded the empire to its greatest reaches, from Poland to Persia to the Korean Peninsula. He began a vast bureaucracy within the empire and set up his fortified, stationary palace at Karakorum, outside present-day Kharkhorin in Uvurkhangai Aimag. The imperial city included all religions, paper money backed by silver, and a postal system, and it was a major stop on the route connecting east and west on the Silk Road.

**Khubilai Khan (Хубилай хаан)** (1215-1294): Was not groomed to be the empire's heir apparent because he was seen as a bad administrator and a poor military leader, but he was able to take advantage of his charisma to be elected by the *khural* as the great khan after the empire was divided up amongst the heirs following the death of his uncle Uguudei Khan.

He spoke Chinese, was interested in Chinese culture, and quickly held favorable standing and power within his realm in China. While his brothers were far away from home trying to hold ties over far-flung reaches of the empire, Khubilai consolidated his power. Eventually, he was voted as the next emperor by the *khural*, which decided such matters in accordance with the *Ikh Zasag*, laws established by Chinggis Khan. Khubilai moved to Beijing to set up the Forbidden City, from which his line ruled Mongolia for generations. Here, Mongolians continued to live like the Mongolians of the steppe. In fact, every child was to be born in a *ger* and women greeted the morning by tossing milk into the air as an offering to the sky just as they still do in Mongolia.

Khubilai was the emperor who welcomed the famous Italian merchant and traveler Marco Polo and thus became a legend in Europe. His summer palace, Xanadu, a symbol of decadent retreat for generations around the world, was in what is now modern-day Inner Mongolia.

Khubilai and his palace at Xanadu have popped up in literature and the arts throughout the ages. A Broadway show and a movie called Xanadu starring Olivia Newton-John, Michael Beck, and Gene Kelly was inspired by the 1816 poem, "Kubla Khan, or, A Vision in a Dream: A Fragment" by Samuel Taylor Coleridge. Coleridge, who was addicted to opium, wrote the poem in a drugged state. In the poem, he attempted to present the supernatural as reality, playing off European fantasies of an exotic and luxurious Far East. While the trippy movie and Broadway show were also inspired by the poem and the real garden of pleasures at Xanadu, they were works of fantasy and have nothing to do with the actual Khubilai Khan or his palace.

**Undur Gegeen Zanabazar (Өндөр гэгээн занабазар; pronounced "dzahn-badzr")** (1635–1723): One of the most important cultural and spiritual figures in Mongolian history. He was the spiritual head of the Yellow Hat sect of Tibetan Buddhism in Mongolia as the first "Holy Venerable Lord" (Jebtsundamba Khutuktu) and a descendant of Chinggis Khan through the Golden Lineage in the Khalka Tribe. The title of *undur gegeen* can be translated as "high saint."

Called the "Michelangelo of Asia," Zanabazar brought artistic and scientific renaissance to the Mongols as well. One of his most lasting influences is the Soyombo symbol on the Mongolian flag, which was the first letter of his alphabet, which was used by Buddhists at the time.

There is a museum in UB named after Zanabazar on Tourist Street (Juulchin Chuluu). It contains a number of his finely-wrought statues and other works of art. For more information, please see page 131.

**The Bogd Khan (Богд хаан)** (1869-1924): Was born in eastern Tibet in what is now Sichuan Province in China. He was the third most important bodhisattva (Buddhist deity reincarnate) below the Dalai Lama and Panchen Lama. As the spiritual and national leader of Mongolia's Tibetan Buddhists, he reigned over the lands that make up most of modern-day Mongolia and was a proponent of Mongolian sovereignty. In December 1911, the Bogd Khan became emperor of Mongolia when he declared independence from the collapsed Manchurian-led Qing Dynasty.

Though he was married to another important and popular religious figure at the time, he was known to have had sexual contact with young boys and had relationships with men. With his death in 1924 of syphilis, the Mongolian Communist party, which had made public spectacles of the unsavory aspects of his lifestyle that also included excessive drinking and eating, decreed that he would be the final khan and that no more reincarnations would be found in Mongolia. His legacy is preserved in the Bogd Khan Winter Palace between the Peace Bridge and Zaisan Memorial in UB. For more information on the palace museum, please see page 129.

**Damdin Sukhbaatar (Дамдин Сүхбаатар)** (1893-1923): The "Axe Hero" was the main figurehead of the 1921 revolution and was later immortalized by an early death during the birth of the Mongolian People's Republic. He was one of the most important military leaders of the Bogd Khan's army that fought with the Russian Red Army for independence against the Chinese People's Republic, and he was a founding member of one of two groups that later went on to form the Mongolian People's Party. On March 18, 1921, Sukhbaatar's overmatched troops miraculously defeated the Chinese in Khiagt, Russia, across the border from Altanbulag in Selenge Aimag; this day is now celebrated as "Soldier's Day" and "Men's Day."

Though disputed, it is commonly believed that Sukhbaatar was killed by poisoning during a period of high alert for a suspected coup that would take place during February's *Tsagaan Sar* in 1923. To honor the revolutionary Sukhbaatar, Mongolian's capital city was renamed Ulaanbaatar or "Red Hero." The main government square is named after him and contains a large red statue of him atop a horse. Both an eastern aimag and Selenge Aimag's capital city are named after Sukhbaatar. He is also featured on all denominations of Mongolian paper money from the 10 *tugrik* note to the 100.

**Khorloogiin Choibalsan (Хорлоогийн Чойбалсан)** (1895-1952): Was a devoted student of Stalinist ideology and the head of the Communist party from 1936 until his death. With strong Soviet backing, he carried out the purges that gutted the intelligentsia, the aristocracy, political dissidents, and religious figures in Mongolia within three years of taking power. Ironically, he was poisoned to death in Moscow on Stalin's orders.

Choibalsan presided over monumental infrastructure development in Mongolia that revolutionized education and medicine. Many Mongolians believe he was merely a puppet of Stalin, incapable of defying the Soviet leader and thus not culpable for the mass murders. Others argue that he was a tyrant. Regardless, the capital of Dornod Aimag is named after him, and his statue stands in front of Mongolian National University.

**Sanjaasurengiin Zorig (Санжаасүрэнгийн Зориг)** (1962-1998): Was born to a Buriat father and a Russian-Mongolian mother. He attended Russian language schools in Ulaanbaatar, and in the early 1980s he studied philosophy in Moscow. He taught at the Mongolian State University, later founding the New Generation group whose aim was to break the single-party system in Mongolia through peaceful action.

Soon after the transition to democracy, he was elected to parliament and advocated for moderate free market reforms, eventually becoming the Minister of Infrastructure in 1998. Later that year, after Elbegdorj was forced to resign as the prime minister over the sale of a state-owned bank, a back room compromise was made to allow Zorig to replace him. Before the announcement could be made, Zorig was viciously stabbed and strangled in his apartment. The murder shocked the nation; the innocence of Mongolia's early democracy was brought brutally to an end. His sister Oyun was elected in his place and was named the minister of foreign affairs. Since then, she has run the Zorig Foundation, a non-profit that promotes civil discourse and democracy in honor of her late brother.

**Tsakhiagiin Elbegdorj (Цахиагийн Элбэгдорж)** (1963- ): Former two-time prime minister and elected president in 2009, just the second to hold the latter title without being a member of the communist MPRP or MPP. He was born in Khovd but finished secondary school in Erdenet, where he briefly worked as a machinist before a stint in the military. He studied journalism and Marxism-Leninism in Lviv, Ukraine, earned a diploma from the economic institute at the University of Colorado Boulder, and earned a Masters in Public Administration from Harvard. He was part of the democratic youth movement of the late 1980s and early 1990s along with Zorig.

## Yours, Mine, Ours

Mongolian and Chinese history overlapped extensively during parts of their histories, and both groups claim certain accomplishments as their own. If you've ever visited the Forbidden City in Beijing for example, you might be surprised to know that it was first constructed by the Mongolian Khubilai Khan during the Chinese Yuan Dynasty (though the original city was burned down and later rebuilt). The Yuan Dynasty also introduced paper money. Mongolians and Chinese often count these milestones as their own.

# POST-EMPIRE

In the mid-seventeenth century Ligden Khan, the last great khan, made one final attempt to reclaim the great empire by centralizing control over the various Mongol tribes, and he signed a treaty with the Ming Dynasty to protect the Chinese northern borders against the Manchurians for a fee. This alienated a number of eastern Mongolian tribes that eventually aligned with the Manchurians. By the end of the seventeenth century, the Manchurians brought down the Ming Dynasty of China and incorporated most of Mongolia into their Qing Dynasty. The Manchurians ruled until Mongolia's 1911 Independence Revolution.

During Manchurian rule, the Mongols were forcibly intermarried and controlled by military and economic policies. Regional Manchurian officials were installed in Ulaanbaatar (then called Ikh Khuree), Uliastai in Zavkhan Aimag, and Khovd, while the country was carved up into oppressive feudal and religious estates. Corrupt Mongolian lords, aggressive Chinese traders, and the collection of taxes in silver instead of animals contributed to poverty and anti-Chinese sentiments that continue to characterize Mongolian life today.

Following the establishment of the Yellow Sect of Tibetan Buddhism in the late sixteenth century and during the Manchurian reign of the Qing Dynasty (1644–1912), Buddhists leaders served as rulers of the Mongolian nation. Buddhist leaders were often found reincarnated in the families of the Mongolian nobles including **Zanabazar**, a top-ranking religious and political figure in the seventeenth and early eighteenth centuries. In 1758 the Qianlong Emperor decreed that all future reincarnations were to come from Tibet.

The last khan, the **Bogd Khan** or "sacred king," was himself born in what is now the Sichuan province in China, formerly part of Tibet. He was an important figure for the Mongols at the beginning of the twentieth century as an advocate of Mongolian autonomy. He was, however, an enemy of the Mongolian Communist party, which tried to discredit and disgrace him. As the Republic of China was established in 1911, the Bogd Khan declared his region, consisting of modern-day Mongolia, independent from China.

In 1919, Chinese troops again occupied Mongolia, but in October of the following year Russian troops arrived and ran the Chinese out within months. By July 1921, Mongolian revolutionaries like **Damadiin Sukhbaatar** supported by the Bolshevik army, declared Mongolian independence. After the death of the Bogd Khan in 1924, the Communist party declared that no more reincarnations were to be found and established the Mongolian People's Republic.

## RED RUSSIANS & MONGOLIAN INDEPENDENCE

With the help of the Russian Red Army in 1921, the Mongolians finally closed the door on Chinese occupation. In doing so, they opened a wide window for Russian influence and ideology. Tied closely with the new Russian brand of communism, Mongolia relied heavily on Russian influence to guide the country toward modernization, and Russians were considered friendly big brothers from the beginning. With their heavy-handed financial and technical help, Mongolia built roads, buildings, and electricity and plumbing grids. They funded schools and hospitals and brought medicine. The Russians also established a new writing system, encouraged literacy for both sexes, and planned manufacturing and agriculture, a system that left no one hungry. But with the advancements came many hardships that are evident even today.

In 1928, **Khorloogiin Choibalsan** rose to power as the leader of the Mongolian People's Revolutionary Party, a position he held with an iron fist until his death in 1952. As a staunch Stalinist, Choibalsan orchestrated the systematic murders of opposition voices among the intelligentsia, former aristocrats, Qing Dynasty sympathizers, and religious leaders. By the end of the 1930s, Choibalsan's government had raided the monasteries, killing no less than 30,000 monks and lamas (and perhaps as many as 100,000) and leveling nearly all the religious buildings across the country. Over 800 monasteries and more than 3,000 temples dating back as far as the 1500s were destroyed. Thus, they quelled an armed opposition uprising in the northwest that left more than 1,500 people dead, and they collectivized the economy.

The Russians helped build state-run factories and mines that guaranteed jobs in wheat, leather, textile, meat production, and mining of gold, coal, and copper. Farmers and herders were organized into cooperatives and given agricultural and livestock production quotas to fill. The products were distributed in Russia via train lines the Russians built to carry the raw materials and manufactured goods.

# Timeline: Chinese and Mongolian History

1211 Mongol campaign against Jin Dynasty

1214 China becomes a vassal state and the capital is moved from Beijing

1227 Beijing is burned to the ground by the Mongols

1233 Kaifeng, the new capital, is captured by Uguudei Khan, son of Chinggis. No clear ruler of China emerges.

1271 Khubilai Khan, grandson of Chinggis, founds the Yuan Dynasty and is called Emperor Shizu. The following emperors in his line all took both a Chinese name and a Mongolian name and lived a Mongolian lifestyle in the Forbidden City where every child was expected to be born in a *ger*.

1368 The Yuan Dynasty under Ukhaantu Khan (Emperor Huizong), who had begun his puppet reign at age 13, falls during the Bubonic Plague as trade routes diminished and ministers enacted extensive anti-Mongolian policies.

1644 The Qing Dynasty begins under Manchurian rule. (The Shun Dynasty had quickly collapsed the same year.) Feudal estates are set up in Mongolia and Tibetan Buddhist leaders like Zanabazar and Bogd Khan become important national figures.

1911 The Qing Dynasty in China dissolves. Bogd Khan declares Mongolian independence.

1919 Republic of China invades Mongolia

1921 Russian Bolshevik Army defeats Chinese forces. Mongolia reasserts independence.

1924 Bogd Khan dies. The Mongolian Communist government declares that no new Buddhist reincarnations will be found in Mongolia and establishes the People's Republic of Mongolia.

1936 Choibalsan begins purges of up to 100,000 intellectuals, political dissenters, and Buddhist monks.

1952 Yumjaagiin Tsedenbal takes power and distances himself from Choibalsan's personality cult while strengthening the alliance with the Soviet Union, relying on them for defense, education and economic support under the planned economy.

1989 Zorig leads protest of 200 to open the government. Soon protestors number in the thousands.

1990 The MPRP politburo resigns, ending one-party rule in Mongolia.

1993 New constitution provides for a free market system. Many companies collapse and unemployment forces many to herding.

1999 Three consecutive severe winters (*dzud*) kill 11 million livestock and hundreds of people.

2008 First violent protests against MPRP.

2009 Elbegdorj becomes second non-MPRP president.

2010 *Dzud* kills more than 8 million of Mongolia's 44 million animals, nearly 18 percent of the national total.

2010 MPRP drops "Revolutionary" from its Mongolian People's Party to become MPP.

The planned system ultimately proved unsustainable, though. Quotas on manufactured goods encouraged low quality standards on products meant only to achieve a number, not a real function. In the fields, cooperatives often had to fudge yield numbers if they were unable to meet quotas. Herders forced into artificial groups with unmotivated members often found the onus upon themselves to pick up the slack of the other members.

Today, as international aid groups pour development dollars into Mongolia, they often find these same practices carried on by local staff wanting to keep their jobs and by beneficiaries worried that their funding will be cut if they don't meet program goals. Moreover, teachers' income is based on student performance, so teachers have a reputation for giving artificially high marks. The legacy of the old system is strong, but things are changing.

## THE DEMOCRATIC TRANSITION 1991-PRESENT

By the end of 1989, Communism had begun to stumble globally. The Berlin Wall had fallen, and Gorbachev's perestroika and glasnost policies were leading to new freedoms and opportunities in the Soviet Union. In Mongolia, the head of state, Jambiin Batmunkh had tried with mixed success to institute economic reforms after replacing Yumjaagiin Tsendenbal as the country's leader in 1984. These factors set the scene for the rapid shake up that would turn Mongolia from Russia's first satellite state to a model of post-Soviet democracy.

Throughout 1989, groups of young Mongolians met secretly to discuss radical political and social reforms. Many of the reformers were educated in the great cities of the eastern USSR, Moscow, Prague, Kiev, and Berlin, and a number of them were the children of top ranking communist bureaucrats. These secret meetings gave way to a full-on protests calling for a multi-party state in December 1989.

By March of the next year, thousands of people were participating in marches on Sukhbaatar Square in Ulaanbaatar, demanding democracy. Sensing that reform could no longer be avoided, the ruling communist Mongolian People's Revolutionary Party (MPRP) adopted laws allowing alternative political parties to exist in Mongolia beginning in mid-March. After continued protest, the government announced in May that elections for a new *Khural* (Parliament) would be held in July 1990.

The MPRP quickly re-branded itself as a democratic institution. Aided by its 70 years of political experience and superior funding, it easily won a majority of parliament seats in the July elections, taking 357 of the 430 available seats. However, new faces replaced most of the old MPRP ministers and politburo hacks. Reform came quicker under the newly elected *Khural*. Within just a few years Mongolia had a new constitution protecting the recently instituted democratic system and freedom of speech, religion, and private property.

The new constitution, implemented on January 13, 1992, established Mongolia as a parliamentary democracy. The parliament, known as the State Great Khural (Ulsiin Ikh Khural, Улсийн Их Хурал), has 76 seats and is the main law-making body. The prime minister, typically the leader of the majority party in the *Khural*, is the head of government, while the president, elected in a popular vote, is the chief of state.

Many of the young political revolutionaries, including the beloved **Sanjaasurengiin Zorig**, who was later assassinated, had staged the hunger strikes and demonstrations that broke the single-party government and were elected into the new government. But although a National and Social Democratic Party candidate, P. Ochirbat, won the first presidential election in 1993, democratic dreams of the revolutionaries were not turned into reality as quickly as they had hoped.

The new faces for democracy were heavily favored and encouraged by international agencies like the IMF, World Bank, and Asian Development Bank, which guided the transition into an open market system with virtually no regulations. The effort to move away from a collapsing planned economy defined by its lack of competition and guaranteed markets would prove difficult at best.

The open market was supposed to allow foreign companies, especially from the West, to invest and compete on an even playing field, which would force competition and weed out weaker or redundant Mongolian companies, but there was little Western investment in Mongolian companies or Mongolian-made products. Instead, given the unstable domestic market, Mongolian producers of raw cashmere and other materials favored a sure payday in China. Because communication and transportation infrastructure was also lacking, herders often unknowingly took prices for their raw materials that were well below market value from Chinese traders.

Proponents of the market economy, both inside the Mongolian transitional government and among the international donor agencies guiding the transition, inadvertently created prime conditions for subsidized Chinese companies to buy raw materials from Mongolians and sell back processed goods to Mongolian markets cheaply. Not surprisingly, this undercut the struggling domestic producers. With no government disincentives to dissuade imports topped by slow development of transportation infrastructure and government corruption, the Mongolian private sector has consequently been slow to transition in many areas despite enormous amounts of international aid. In fact, entire industries like flour production, boot manufacturing, and milk processing that had existed during communist times were nearly wiped out. The Democratic Party has enjoyed only one stint in power from 1996 to 2000, during which they replaced the cabinet three times. They didn't quite represent the new direction Mongolians were looking for.

Since 1996, the Mongolian People's Revolutionary Party (MPRP) has dominated national politics. Remaining true to their communist roots, the MPRP favors a government welfare-based approach to improving the lives of the populace.

As industries collapsed, many were out of work and returned to the countryside to herd, relying on family connections to survive. After generations away, though, most didn't have the capital to invest in enough animals or lacked the experience to properly herd. The winters of 1999-2002 were particularly harsh as well, killing many livestock and herders in winter disasters called "*dzud*." For many families, the last hope has been a job in Ulaanbaatar or state support to remain in the countryside.

Because of this, the MPRP retains a power base in the countryside, although their support has slipped somewhat as more and more herders and rural students gravitate to the urban centers. The MPRP maintained their control over the country only through a power-sharing deal with the Democrats after the 2004 parliamentary elections left them with 50 seats in the *Khural*, one shy of a workable majority. As part of the deal, Democratic Party leader Ts. Elbegdorj was named Prime Minister, but when the defection of a Democratic Party parliamentarian to the MPRP gave them an outright majority, they replaced Elbegdorj with one of their own and scrapped the coalition.

In the June 2008 parliamentary elections, the MPRP again won a majority of seats. The Democratic Party cried foul and accused the MPRP of rigging the elections. On July 1, riots broke out on Sukhbaatar Square in Ulaanbaatar. Rioters moved to the nearby MPRP headquarters, which were torched along with a neighboring museum and cultural palace, resulting in the loss of unique artwork and primary texts. It was the first violent protest in Mongolia. Five people died and dozens were injured before President N. Enkhbayar instituted a curfew and state of emergency, more firsts for the nation. The following year, the Democratic Elbegdorj narrowly defeated the MPRP's Enkhbayar in the presidential election, a result that the MPRP had little choice but to accept unless they wanted a new round of rioting to begin.

Corruption has been on the rise, and in April 2010 successful protests across the country demanded that the government make good on promises they had made to give every citizen MNT1.5 million (about $1,100) during the 2008 parliamentary campaigns.

In late 2010, the MPRP dropped the word "Revolutionary" and reverted to its original name from the Sukhbaatar era, the "Mongolian People's Party" (MPP). In this latest step to distance themselves from their totalitarian past, MPP officials claim that the "revolutionary" title no longer fits their mission, and that their focus is no longer on revolution but on development and stability. Elections slated for summer 2012 have shaped up to be as contentious as any, with both major parties spending cash like never before to capture precious votes. The Democratic Party gained seats against the MPP in the elections, though neither gained a clear majority.

Today, Mongolia stands in a difficult position as a country still nursing a hangover from communist times. They desire to maintain independence and work closely with foreign governments and international aid organizations to develop their human capital, though faith in Mongolia's political class seems low and many feel that there is little difference between the MPP and the Democratic Party. Recent infrastructure investment has made life easier in many of the more remote areas by bringing reliable electricity, water, and affordable communication options. As the private sector has developed, it has benefited from and adapted to the changes in the Mongolian lifestyle to provide better services and higher quality products than ever before, and there have been many benefits to the tourism industry.

## Mongolian Mining

Mining and mineral exporting is Mongolia's biggest industry, generating a majority of the nation's exports and a healthy chunk of the overall GDP. About 4 percent of the workforce is employed in the mining industry. Mongolia has major gold, copper, coal, fluorspar, silver, uranium, and tungsten deposits. The joint Russian-Mongolia mine at Erdenet, an enormous pit operational for over 30 years, is one of the world's 10 largest copper mines.

After a downturn following the transition to democracy, the mining industry has grown in recent years, though not without some drama to propel the narrative. Several of the world's largest coal and mineral deposits sit waiting to be excavated, but Mongolians at every level of society have concerns about the complex issue of ensuring that Mongolia makes a fair profit from minerals mined by foreign companies.

After parliament instituted a 68 percent windfall profits tax on gold and copper in 2006, foreign investors grew skittish. Partly because of the tax, which was repealed in 2009 by President Elbegdorj, the international mining giants Ivanhoe and Rio Tinto spent years negotiating the terms of a deal to exploit the Oyu Tolgoi gold and copper deposit in the Gobi. The three parties finally reached a $5 billion agreement in late 2009, although many Mongolians consider the deal a sham which will have little to no impact on the average citizen, and Rio Tinto and Ivanhoe continue to bicker among themselves about the role of outside investors. Meanwhile, the mine, one of the absolute largest in the world, is scheduled to start production in 2013.

With the Oyu Tolgoi agreement finally in place, observers speculated that Mongolia's mining sector was poised to take off and other agreements were sure to follow. Instead, the government decided it wanted to keep some mineral rights exclusively within the country and withdrew a 50 percent stake in the giant Tavan Tolgoi coal mine from public auction, setting off a frenzy of activity within the Mongolian business community to grab a piece of the action. The government later decided to sell a 30 percent stake in Tavan Tolgoi to foreign companies.

If and when the government settles on a strategy for mineral investment that also appeases the international companies who will do most of the technical work, mining should propel the Mongolian economy forward at a breakneck clip. Commentators have compared Mongolia's growth potential to that of oil states like Kuwait and Dubai if the profits are invested back in the country properly.

## NINJA MINING

While legitimate mining is big business, there's another group digging for a payday. Driven by unemployment and winter disasters that robbed herders of their flocks, over 100,000 Mongolians have turned to small scale, un-mechanized gold mining to earn a living since the mid 1990s. Called "ninja miners" because the plastic basins they strap to their backs when they head to their mine sites make them look like the characters from the popular '90s Ninja Turtles cartoon show, these miners are technically illegal. However, they produce as much gold each year as the formal mining industry, and while much of the ninjas' gold gets smuggled to China, their contribution to the economy is so great that there is little the government can do to stop it.

Unfortunately, the gold rush and its economic contributions come with a price. The work is physically difficult, not to mention dangerous. Collapsed tunnels kill informal miners every year. The camps where ninja miners live and work are sometimes bastions of alcoholism, child labor, and crime.

The miner's methods also have a grave impact on local environments. Miners use harsh and poisonous chemicals, including cyanide and mercury, to separate gold from useless rock and soil and are rarely able to dispose of the chemicals properly. Ninja miners are also blamed for soil erosion, destruction of local flora, and unsustainable water use leading to dried up streams and rivers.

Some efforts to improve conditions at mine sites have been effective. A few camps have self-imposed sobriety rules, effectively barring alcohol from the premises. The Sustainable Artisanal Mining Project, funded by the Swiss Agency for Development and Cooperation (SDC) has made headway working with model mining communities to improve safety and environmental conditions.

Major ninja mine sites can be found in Uyanga Soum (Уянга сум) in Uvurkhangai Aimag, Sharyn Gol Soum (Шарын гол сум) in Darkhan-Uul Aimag, Boornuur Soum (Бор нүүр сум) in Tuv Aimag, and throughout Bayankhongor and Gov-Altai Aimags.

# Religions in Mongolia

Although Chinggis Khan was one of the first world leaders to encourage religious tolerance, his homeland has seen many changes in its religious landscape over the last few centuries due to the shifting political climate.

The Mongolian-ruled Yuan Dynasty of the thirteenth and fourteenth centuries was led by Tibetan Buddhist leaders beginning with Khubilai Khan, but Mongolians primarily went back to shamanism after that empire collapsed. Buddhism became a prime religion again during the sixteenth century and thereafter under Chinese rule. However, things changed dramatically again with the Russian-backed communist regimes during most of the twentieth century.

Traditional shamanism, based on reverence of nature, was tacitly allowed during Communism, but Buddhism was harshly squashed by the conservative regimes. In the early 1930s, Mongolia had at least 100,000 monks and lamas (teachers), over 800 Buddhist monastery centers, and more than 3,000 temples across the country, some dating back to the sixteenth century. By 1990, only **Gandan Monastery** in UB remained standing (though other monasteries enjoyed seclusion and anonymity far in the countryside), and only a small community of 100 monks were allowed to practice Buddhism in Mongolia. With the fall of Communism, the long period of control on religious practice ended and Mongolia's modern spiritual history started to be written.

Most families mix together long-held shamanistic traditions with Tibetan Buddhist traditions, particularly outside of Ulaanbaatar. The most notable spiritual practices include the morning ritual of stepping outside to throw spoonfuls of fresh milk to the sky, spinning small prayer wheels on family altars upon entering a home for the first time, or lighting small candles on special days during the month and year. Some of these traditions have been practiced within families for dozens of generations.

Many Mongolians continued to practice these rituals in secret, but with spiritual leaders all but extinct or deep underground, the religion was often centered around certain family rituals, traditions, and superstitions. Many children were still given Tibetan names like Suren (red Tibetan necklace), Davaa (Monday on the Tibetan calendar), and Lkhamaa (a pendant that represents the sky) as well as many others. Religious idols and images that were traditionally displayed in the sacred part of the *ger* (the north side opposite the door) were hidden away during Communism (and replaced with honorary certificates, commendations for work, and family pictures), but they were not thrown out.

Democratization has created space for cultural and religious rebirth, not only in the north part of the *ger*, but also in public. A very real spiritual reawakening has emerged since the early 1990s. Dozens of monasteries have been rebuilt, the number of monks and lamas continues to rise, and national pride in religious traditions is taking hold as more and more people openly discuss, join together, and share in their daily and yearly practices.

Especially in the last decade, several famous monasteries and sacred sites within Mongolia have either been renovated or completely rebuilt, and more restorations are planned throughout the country. Visiting these special sites in places like Kharkhorin (**Erdene Zuu Monastery,** p345) offers a wonderful view into the re-emerging spiritual landscape of Mongolia during this transformative time in history.

## AUSPICIOUS DAYS

Based on the ancient Tibetan calendar, which can be found tucked away in almost every Mongolian home, there are several "auspicious" or special days every month and a few very special days every year that are recognized throughout the entire country. These days are favorites for wedding celebrations, trips to the local monastery, and candle lighting ceremonies in large squares around the country, and foreigners are welcome to observe. Work and travel are not necessarily affected by the special days, though since the dates change all the time, travelers should ask a new Mongolian friend or travel company about upcoming events and whether it is possible to get involved to help make a vacation more of a cultural experience.

Mongolians are open to sharing their customs, so don't be shy in asking about something you don't understand. Keep in mind however that since Mongolians are new to rediscovering the religion and they may lack training in comparative religion, their answers aren't always entirely comprehensive, even at monasteries. By visiting, listening, and learning about Mongolian spiritual traditions, though, you have a chance to do more than just observe Mongolia, you can participate in their religious renaissance.

---

### "Dalai Lama" is Mongolian

The title of Dalai Lama traces its roots back to the Mongolian language where *dalai* means ocean and *lama* means teacher in Tibetan. *Altan Khan*, meeting Sonam Gyatso (the third Dalai Lama) for the first time in 1578, addressed him as "Dalai Lama" since *gyats* means ocean in Tibetan. As the histories of Tibet and Mongolia continued to be intertwined, the name stuck. The famous Tibetan spiritual leader and 1989 Nobel Peace Prize winner Tenzin Gyatso is currently the fourteenth Dalai Lama.

---

## MONASTERIES

If this is your first time in a Buddhist country and you know nothing about Buddhism but you still want to enjoy the artifacts in the monasteries, you're in good company. If you're not a comparative theologian, you will probably go to monasteries where the guides and scholars take for granted that your frame of reference on their topics is nearly non-existent. Still, guides often fleetingly highlight religious concepts without much explanation. You may find yourself left alone to look at a bunch of statues and paintings you don't know anything about repeating words you've never heard before. Obviously, these depictions warrant some serious explanation if you're only used to thinking about the world using the monotheistic concepts of Christianity, Judaism, and Islam. If you do find yourself in this situation while visiting a religious point of interest, hopefully this guide will help you understand what you're looking at. It is by no means comprehensive, but it should help make monastery trips more enjoyable. If you want comprehensive books with pictures, go to the **Bogd Khan Winter Palace** (p129) or **Choijin Lama Temple and Museum** (p129) gift shops.

## Mongolian Master of Art

**Zanabazar (1635–1723)** was a high saint and the first spiritual head of the Yellow Hat sect of Tibetan Buddhism practiced in Mongolia. He was called the "Michelangelo of Asia" because of his religious, artistic, and scientific contributions.

### Must-see Monasteries

There are monasteries all over UB and the rest the rest of the country. There are some in provincial capitals and even in rural villages. Some of these monasteries are very approachable and pleasantly ordinary, and even many of the newer ones look old. You could spend you whole time in Mongolia chasing monasteries, and if that's your goal, you'll probably have a fun time doing it. But, there are a few that are more noteworthy than the rest that you should see no matter what your interests are.

**Gandan Khiid (Гандан тэгчинлэн хийд)** in Ulaanbaatar is the largest and most important monastery. It reopened in 1944 with a skeleton staff after its closing in 1938 and was the only functioning monastery during the communist regime. It features a 26.5-meter-high statue of Migjid Janraisig built in the 1990s. p131

**Choijin Lama Temple and Museum** in Ulaanbaatar was completed in 1908 and was converted into a museum in 1938 by the Stalinist government. It was originally occupied by Choijin Lama Luvsankhaidav, the brother of Bogd Khan. English-speaking guides are very knowledgeable and thorough, and there is a great

## Buddhism in 350 Words or Less

Buddhism is a spiritual philosophy whose goal is to completely remove stresses through meditation and other behaviors to end a cycle of death and rebirth There is no such thing as a soul or "self" independent from the whole universe. Siddhartha Gautama, born in present-day Nepal, is commonly known as "The Buddha." He's revered as a great teacher, but is not a God. Anyone can be a Buddha, and there are many Buddhas.

There is a heaven and a hell, and deities with supernatural powers can affect and be affected by worldly events. These are called *devas*. Their stories are often depicted in monasteries along with multi-armed *bodhisattvas* (pronounced "bo-dee-sat-va"), beings that have almost attained the enlightenment of a Buddha but unselfishly stuck around to help the rest of us to enlightenment. They are depicted with many faces, arms, and apparatuses to show us the many ways we need help. Mongolians tend to refer to all *devas* and *bodhisattvas* generically as "gods" (бурхан).

There are many different schools of Buddhism that usually overlap with regional superstitions or rituals. Tibetan Buddhism, which in some ways incorporates the shamanistic Bon traditions of Tibet, dates back to between about 650 and 750 C.E. It became the state religion of the Chinese Yuan Dynasty founded by Khubilai Khan in the eleventh century.

Though Buddhism is complicated and can require years of study to uncover all its layers, the most important concepts to understand of the philosophy are that it is centered around altruism, living in the now, respect, and attaining nirvana, the perfect existence free of conflict and want. Many tenets are preserved through *thanka* and other artworks that can be as straightforward or complicated as you perceive them.

variety of books on sale in many languages. p129

**Erdene Zuu Khiid (Эрдэнэ зуу хийд)** in Kharkhorin, Uvurkhangai Aimag, was the first Buddhist monastery in Mongolia. It mainly functions now as a living museum. It's a tourist hot spot with antique souvenirs from other defunct monasteries, which we encourage all tourists not to buy. It's a highlight of the trip to the Orkhon Valley. p345

**Amarbayasgalant Khiid** (Амарбаясгалант хийд) in Selenge Aimag, accessible from Darkhan, is one the largest monasteries in Mongolia. It was originally built to house the remains of Zanabazar, who also designed it. Both Amarbysgalant's architecture and the secluded, river-crossed valley it lies in are stunning. p293

**Manzshir Khiid (Манзшир хийд)** in Tuv Aimag, outside of Zuunmod, is a living reminder of the communist purges. The rocky, terraced site once held 20 temples inhabited by 350 monks. Now the complex is in ruins, with only the restored main temple as a museum. It has a *ger* camp and could be a fine destination for a hike from UB. p309

**Khamariin Khiid and Shambala Energy Center (Хамарын хийд)** in Dornogovi are religious sites founded by Noyon Hutagt Danzanravjaa, a Mongolian intellectual and leader of the Red Hat Buddhism of the nineteenth century, who adapted a famous Tibetan play called *Saran Khukhuu* or "Moon Cuckoo" in 1830. The monastery's artifacts were preserved underground during Communism and were returned when the monastery reopened in 1990. Located two kilometers (1.24 miles) from Khamariin Khiid, Shambala, also known as the Energy Center, is a three-dimensional representation of the Sacred Land of Shambhala. The square of 108 ovoos has been rebuilt, along with three of the original four gateways and eight larger stupas. p213

**Tuvkhun Khiid (Төвхөн хийд)** is high in the mountains of the Khangai Nuruu National Park in Uvurkhangai, 60 kilometers (37 miles) from Kharkhorin. The retreat was founded by Zanabazar in 1653, and he lived there intermittently for 30 years. It was here that Mongolian Buddhism was truly developed, along with such innovations as the Soyombo script. Several pilgrimage sites have emerged around it, including the caves where you can supposedly see Zanabazar's boot imprint. p349

## Tibetan Buddhism

Tibetan Buddhism is a kind of polytheistic adaptation of traditional Buddhism that was incorporated into the shamanistic Bon traditions of Tibet in the eighth century by Padmasambhava, a Buddhist monk from India. For more information on Buddhism and Tibetan Buddhism, check out the book "Essential Buddhism" by Jack Maguire.

### Deciphering Art in Monasteries

**Deva:** Buddhism incorporates supernatural beings in the form of *devas*, many of which are discussed and passed on through scripture and in oral traditions. If Mongolians do not know the names of specific *devas* they may refer to them simply as "gods." The *devas* are not like omnipotent, omniscient gods that control creation, spiritual salvation, or punishments like the gods of the West. They are more like patron saints in the Catholic tradition that have the power to affect worldly events, similar to the way that humans can affect the world more than animals. *Devas* are more powerful than humans, but none holds absolute power, even within the realms they oversee. They have emotions that can be affected including jealousy, anger, delusion, sorrow, etc., which are often depicted in paintings on silk or through statues. Like humans, they continue through the *samsara* process of rebirth until they reach Nirvana, having lived the perfect existence.

**Bodhisattva:** Often portrayed with their many limbs, faces and objects, they teach or remind enlightenment seekers how to make their spiritual path. They have almost become Buddha themselves, but they chose not to take the final steps toward enlightenment. There are many different paths and stages of the *bodhisattvas,* so there are nearly limitless topics to be expressed through them in art.

Each has a name, and some are known in different languages by different names. Avalokitesvara is also known in Mongolian as *Migjid Janraisig* and is the most famous *bodhisattva*. The Dalai Lama is said to be his human incarnation. Before his death, he will give clues as to where to find him in the next life including geographic area and new parents. It is the job of other high monks, called a *tulku,* to track down the reborn *bodhisattva*.

**Heaven and Hell:** Heaven exists on a multi-layered plane above Earth. There are two types of hell, Cold Hell and Hot Hell, to punish offenders based on the severity of the offenses they have committed.

**Cold Hell:** Arbuda (Swelling), Nirarbuda (Shrinking), Atata (Chattering Teeth), Hahava (Shivering Tongue), Huhuva (Shuddering Mouth), Utpala (Blue lotus colored patches on the skin), Padma (Red lotus colored patches on the skin), Mahapadma (Big red lotus colored patches on the skin).

**Hot Hell:** Samjiva (Constant Repetition), Kalasutra (Black Wire), Samghata (Stone Slabs), Raurava (Lamentation), Maharaurava (Great Lamentation), Tapana (Scorching Heat), Pratapana (Fiercely Scorching Heat), Avici (Without Interruption).

**Rebirth:** Rebirth is ruled by karma, a law of cause and effect. After death, you might return in one of the many hells as a *Naraka,* a hungry ghost living among humans but invisible to most, as a *Preta,* an animal sharing space with humans but considered another life form, as a human capable of attaining nirvana, as a devilish anti-god or *Asura,* or as a god (*deva*). In fact, there are up to 31 levels.

## MINORITY RELIGIONS IN MONGOLIA

In the western part of Mongolian, there are about 150,000 Muslims, comprising five percent of Mongolia's total population. The vast majority are Kazakh-Mongolians in Bayan-Ulgii Aimag and the Khoton ethnic group of nearly 20,000 people residing mostly in Uvs Aimag. Islam is the nation's largest religious minority, but not by much.

Emerging from the vacuum of state-imposed atheism, Christianity is growing fast. In fact, around four percent of the country is Christian. Most Mongolian Christians are protestant, with a few (less than 1 percent) Roman Catholics and members of the Russian Orthodox Church. The Church of Latter Day Saints has had a large presence in the country for many years but their followers account for only around 9 percent of Christians.

Many of the big international aid organizations operating in Mongolia, including World Vision, the Norwegian Lutheran Mission, and ADRA (an Adventist NGO), are sponsored by Christian foundations. Most don't require religious affiliation to receive programming aid, training, or emergency assistance, but some Mongolians are drawn to the message of the workers and their examples, and some have been treated for alcohol abuse through 12-step programs that invite conversion. Some organizations do require workers to deliver a statement of faith in Christianity in order to gain employment, but because the high paying and stable jobs are coveted, many workers dedicate themselves to the statement, not the religion. Many grass-roots missionaries partner with local groups and Christian Mongolians, dotting the countryside towns with community centers and churches that teach life skills, agriculture, and other needed skills.

## Mongolian Education System

While intellectuals and most literate Mongolians were among the religious elite for many generations, the education system in Mongolia now reflects the equality of access to education during Communism that has produced an adult literacy rate of nearly 98 percent, among the best in the world.

Education up to ninth grade is mandatory, and the country has near universal enrollment for school-age children. Every provincial capital has a handful of secondary schools as well as kindergartens, which are more like daycare centers, enrolling children three years of age and older. Excepting the largest ones, village centers generally have just one secondary school and one kindergarten. Village schools often run dormitories, where children whose parents are full-time herders can stay during the school year. In order to match international standards and competition, Mongolia is in the process of expanding its secondary education system from an 11-year to a 12-year system.

While Ulaanbaatar has a number of international and private schools, very few areas outside of the capital have anything but public schools. Secondary schools typically cover first through eleventh (and now twelfth) grade. Public schools teach a wide range of subjects, from mathematics, chemistry, and biology to history, Mongolian language, and arts. Russian and English are mandatory foreign languages, and English is taught beginning in the fourth grade. Students have very few elective options and remain in the same classroom, with the same group of students, throughout their secondary education career. The universities operate on much the same system.

The system skews heavily towards theoretical knowledge, rather than practical skills, due in part, perhaps, to the widespread lack of resources. In many classrooms, 40 or more students may share just a few textbooks, and things like microscopes or chemistry equipment are unheard of. Most rural schools have a couple of cranky old computers, although various government programs have donated computer labs to select schools in recent years. The main motivation for students seems to come from competitions, like the annual nationwide academic Olympiad, and make-or-break standardized tests, like the Concourse exam, which determines which universities and majors a student is eligible for upon completing his or her final year of secondary school. While there are a handful of government sponsored colleges and universities scattered throughout the nation, the best are the public universities in Ulaanbaatar, and spots in these institutions are coveted.

# The Arts

Traditionally, Mongolian arts, including music, dance, contortion, painting, and photography are ritualized and often revolve around themes of nature while pure creative expression usually comes second. The performing arts are often used to help commemorate ceremonies, events, and holidays. If you're lucky, you'll be able catch an event on a rural town square or even on Sukhbaatar Square in Ulaanbaatar, where street vendors also sell paintings.

## MUSIC

Mongolia has a rich relationship with music. Its unique forms of traditional music date back to before the thirteenth century, to the time of the famous Chinggis Khan, and music remains important in many parts of Mongolian daily and ceremonial life. Much of it is connected to Mongolia's proud nomadic herding traditions. For example, Mongolians sing to their animals with a variety of lullabies to coax sheep to suckle their lambs, to order their horse in a given direction, to milk cows, to control goats, and even to imitate a camel's cry.

Traditional Mongolian vocal music encompasses two distinct singing styles, the *urtiin duu* (long song), which often resembles dramatic opera, and *khuumii* (throat singing). Both are remarkably difficult, composed of long sustained vocal lines to represent the vast, wide-open space of the Mongolian countryside while addressing Mongolian daily life and the beauty of the land. *Khuumii* is recognized worldwide for the large harmonic range of double or triple simultaneous tones it produces, including whistle tones and deep bass tones. Both of these vocal styles are registered on the World Heritage of Art and Cultural Objects list.

Traditional Mongolian instruments are often played alone or used to accompany a vocalist. This may not be surprising when you consider the low population density and the historically nomadic culture. The main Mongolian instruments consist of the *shanz* and *khuuchir* (three- and four-stringed instruments), the *bishguur, tsuur,* and *limbe* (three types of flute), and the two-stringed Mongolian national instrument, the *morin khuur* (horsehead fiddle).

All *morin khuur* are notable due to the distinctive decorative horse head carvings on the top of the neck of the instrument. According to a generations-old legend, the *morin khuur* was created by a herdsman to sing of the sorrow he felt over the death of his horse, from whose ribs and mane the instrument was first formed. It is considered by some musicologists as the father of the European string instruments.

All Mongolian events are marked by music. A traditional Mongolian wedding, for example, is mostly made up of the wedding attendees passing a single cup to each other one by one. When an attendee receives the cup, they must stand and sing a song for the couple. In most cases, the individual will lead the song and the rest of the attendants will join in after the first line. This makes up the bulk of the wedding and often goes on for hours. Office parties and other celebrations often take on the same characteristics.

Every Mongolian holiday celebration such as *Shine Jil* (New Years), Teacher's day, Soldier's day, *Tsagaan Sar* (White Moon, a Lunar New Year similar to the Chinese New Year), etc., involves people singing together to mark the occasion.

Modern Mongolian music is made up of some old and some new. There is a variety of genres in the country, from sentimental ballads to rock and roll, girl bands, boy bands, and hip hop. Young Mongolians listen to a lot of Western music, especially pop and music with heavy dance beats. With more advanced mobile phones, they have better access to popular music than ever before. Music is freely swapped between MP3 players, phones, and computers, though music shops that carry bootleg and legitimate cassette tapes and CDs exist in almost every market.

Ballads, especially about mothers and nature, are very popular with every generation. Javkhlant, Saraa, Ariunaa, and the duo Khishigbayar and Delgermaa are venerable favorites among twenty-somethings and elders for their keyboard-heavy ballads about mother's milk tea, seduction, first love, and longing. Each uses the undertones and metaphors of nature, often with engaging musical drama to tell stories you can feel without even knowing a word of the language. Even Mongolian hip hop's bad boy, "Ice Top," who spent time in jail for drug use (a rare and shocking offense in Mongolia), has a song called "Mother."

Hip hop artists in general, though, have left the politeness and themes of their parents behind in favor of political protest. Even so, there is an overt imitation (even direct copying) of the backing tracks, album covers, and wardrobes (baggy clothes,

## My Native Land

High stately mountains of Khentii, Khangai, and Soyon
Forest and stick-wooded ridges, the beauty of the North
The great Gobi Desert, the spaces of Menen, Sharga and Nomin
And the oceans of sand that dominate the South
This, this is my native land
A lovely country – my Mongolia
The crystal rivers of sacred Kherlen, Onon, and Tuul Brooks, streams and springs that bring health to all my people
The blue lakes of Khuvsgul, Uvs and Buir – deep and wide
Rivers and lakes where people and livestock quench their thirst
This, this is my native land
A lovely country – my Mongolia…

*Written by: Dashdorjiin Natsagdorj*
*Translated by: Odgoniin Nyamtaivan*

The translator, Odgoniin Nyamtaivan, is a high school student from Bayankhongor Aimag. As is common among many top students in Mongolia, Nyamtaivan dreamed of studying abroad. During the communist period, many top students and elite attended state schools, camps and universities in the Soviet Union in places like Moscow, Kiev and Prague. Students who study abroad today are typically among only the wealthy. Because Nyamtaivan's single mother was under employed and her adult sister lives with a mental illness, the possibilities of Nyamtaivan achieving that dream were nearly non-existent.

Fortunately, with private donations she was able to attend high school in St. Albans, Vermont, where she studied English, Spanish, German, civics and history. Due to its popularity and encompassing description of her native land, Nyamtaivan translated this poem in an essay introducing herself and Mongolia to her American host family. She hopes to attend a university abroad and return to Mongolia with her talents to help lead its future.

oversized jewelry, baseball caps) of Western hip hop artists among the artists and urban Mongolian youth. Tatar, Bold, and 2 Khuu are among the most popular acts of the last few years, and many others are constantly self-recording and producing their art to be played on the radio.

The alternative rock-pop group The Lemons writes fun and upbeat songs like "Minii Niislel" ("My Capital") that resemble American indie-pop. The Lemons are among the groups that regularly play sets in Ulaanbaatar restaurants and bars.

A favorite among foreigners, but less so among Mongolians, is Altan Urag. The group uses electrified traditional instruments like the *morin khuur* and throat singing in a folk rock style. Their music was the backdrop of the popular 2007 film "Mongol: The Rise of Genghis Khan." You also can see them play in UB, especially at Ikh Mongol. It's not a rock-and-roll atmosphere, exactly, but Altan Urag rips through the set every time, sounding something like Metallica playing 1,000 year-old instruments.

Just as with any other art form, Mongolian music continues to constantly evolve and reflect the culture as it changes. Be sure to check out local listings for live performances and discover what's hot while you're in the country.

## Music in Everyday Life
A 17-year-old student we know well was shocked to find out that people in the United States don't sing for weddings or other ceremonies. When we discussed all the events where Mongolians sing, he turned and said, "Even when we are just walking together, we sing."

# LITERATURE

Though most homegrown works of literature feature nature, Mongolia is also an importer of popular and historical books translated into Mongolian, including everything from Dickens to Dan Brown. In fact, former president Enkhbayar translated and published many of the classics from English and Russian into Mongolian.

Mongolian-born literature is a little harder to come by outside of religious texts, partly because literacy rates were extremely low until the twentieth century. Furthermore, the nomadic lifestyle does not encourage assembling a large personal library. Consequently, the tradition of literature in Mongolia is not robust. Besides the *Secret History of the Mongols*, little Mongolian literature is distributed outside of Mongolia.

Poetry, though, is alive and well with schoolchildren and adults alike. Young children learn popular poems and recite them impromptu and on holidays for friends and family, and adults often recite poems during holiday celebrations, talent shows, and ceremonies. Children also sometimes have poetry competitions where a group of students has a short time to write. After five or ten minutes, the students read their poems aloud with dramatic emphasis, and a winner is chosen.

One of the founding fathers of modern Mongolian literature, and probably the most well known Mongolian poet, is **Dashdorjiin Natsagdorj** (1906-1937), the son of a poor herder in Tuv Aimag. He was born during the last years of the feudal Qing Dynasty. His poems cover many topics including romance and the communist revolution, but he is most known and beloved for describing Mongolia with visceral pride. As travelers often come to appreciate, Mongolia's natural wonders are humble and subtle. There are no rainforests with plush canopies that house millions of animals. Nor are there vast sand dunes in the Gobi Desert, with a few isolated exceptions. Instead, the natural beauty of the country is found more in the landscape and how water draws life from the rocky and sandy soil high in the mountains down to the expansive plains. Natsagdorj beautifully portrays this beauty in "My Native Land," the most famous of his works.

The most famous Mongolian writer during the middle part of the twentieth century was Tsendiin Damdinsuren (1908-1986), whose prose was used for the Mongolian national anthem between 1950 and 1962 (and parts of the anthem after 1991). He was schooled in Leningrad and was a strong backer of Yumjaagiin Tsendenbal, the former prime minister and president from the 1950s until 1984. While imprisoned and after having been threatened with death, Damdinsuren backed the switch from the vertical Mongolian script to Cyrillic, which he later regretted. Translated copies of his short stories and other works, which are largely modern updates from the traditional oral stories, are available. One of his novels, *The Rejected Girl* was adapted into a popular film in the 1960s. His *Tales of an Old Lama*, (translated by Charles Bawden) showed a bygone era under the Manchurian-ruled Qing Dynasty through a set of interviews with an old lama from Urgoo, the old capital of Mongolia years. Damdinsuren also wrote the first comprehensive Russian-Mongolian dictionary.

## THE VISUAL ARTS

The arts have a long but non-traditional (in the Western sense) history on the Mongolian steppes. Visual arts date back to well before the Mongolian empire, gracing the grasslands in the form of stone monuments and mobile, utilitarian nomadic crafts for millennia.

The oldest forms of art found in Mongolia are the petroglyphs found on mountainsides and in caves across the nation. The cave paintings at Gurvan Tsenkheriin Agui in Khovd Aimag's Mankhan *soum*, depicting a menagerie of prehistoric animals, have been dated to at least 12,000 years ago and may be as much as 40,000 years old.

Sculpture came to the steppes somewhat later, but sculptures have been found dating back to the Bronze Age (around 3,000 B.C.E.) in the form of deer stones. These stone pillars, ornamented with relief carvings of animals, were scattered across the steppes, most likely marking burial sites. During the Turkish period from the fifth to seventh centuries A.D., stone monuments were again created and distributed across Mongolia en masse, this time carved to in human forms. Today, these are known as "people stones."

But nomadism doesn't provide a warm and supportive environment to develop things that don't move easily, like cities, pigs, fragile paintings, or heavy statues. Thus, none of these things were commonly found in the Mongolian home, or anywhere else in the country, until fairly recently. In the meantime, Mongolians demonstrated their creative vision in moveable, useable crafts. Notable examples include the intricately sculpted knife, chopstick, and flint sets carried in pouches hung from the waist of every Mongolian man's *deel*, silver-adorned Mongolian-style riding saddles, snuff bottles carved from colored stone, and the finely detailed, often geometric paintings on the tables, bureaus, and cupboards of Mongolian *gers*. The tradition of decorated, heirloom-quality snuff bottles, saddles, and *ger* furniture is continued to this day.

As Mongolian cities and monasteries became more established, the fine arts grew as well. In its prime as capital of the Mongol empire, Karakorum boasted a grand fountain: a life-sized silver tree that poured mare's milk, *airag*, mead, and wine. The great spiritual and political leader Zanabazar (1635-1724) was widely known for his exquisite bronzes of Buddhist deities and established an entire school of Mongolian sculpture. The golden era of Mongolian monasteries, coinciding with the 200-year Manchu reign, ushered in the beginning of long-lasting traditions of religious appliqué, *thangka* paintings, and architecture. Much of this religious art was heavily influenced by that of China and Tibet, from which it borrowed both visual aesthetics and materials such as silk.

Art in the Soviet era turned towards realism; would the communist leaders have had it any other way? Most of the classic works from this period, like Baldugiin

Sharav's painting *One Day in Mongolia*, celebrate Mongolia's landscape and pastoral culture.

Mongolian artists since the fall of Communism have opened themselves to more contemporary styles, although many still experiment with Western genres. Mongolia's artistic community is still very much influenced by themes of nature and nomadism, and hence you'll find a variety of contemporary painting styles featuring cubist horses or *ger* districts rendered in loose, illustrative styles.

For a tour of Mongolian art history in an afternoon, there is no better place to start than the Zanabazar Art Museum (p131).

# Sport

## THE THREE MANLY SPORTS OF NAADAM

*Naadam* (pronounced "Naaaadum") is the summer sports festival in July. Featuring Mongolian wrestling, horseracing, and archery, it really gets the national blood pumping. Each village and *aimag* has a round of games, and the main games, a spectacle orchestrated for the benefit of tourists as much as anyone else, take place in Ulaanbaatar.

Watch your wallet especially during this time because some people actually come in from the countryside to pickpocket Mongolians and travelers alike. If you can, your best bet is to avoid the UB *Naadam* altogether by finding a nice countryside *Naadam* weeks before the national event.

The Mongolian holiday lasts 3 days, but preparations begin days before. If they can, Mongolians will go to the countryside during *Naadam* to spend the time with family and friends.

### Wrestling

Mongolia regards its wrestlers with special esteem. This sport is seen not only as a physical endeavor but also as a somewhat spiritual one. Wrestlers are said to embody ancient ideals of nobility, strength, and chivalrous sportsmanship. The best wrestlers earn considerable respect in their communities.

Mongolian wrestling has no weight classes, no time limit, and no enclosed ring. Like sumo, in which Mongolians also perform at an extremely high level (Japan's last two *yokozunas* have been Mongolian), there is a set of ritual motions that wrestlers must do before and after each match, including a stylized dance that mimics the flight of a bird, performed in front of the judges and the community's flag and spirit banners. A cohort of elders serves as coaches to the wrestlers, overseeing one wrestler during each match, holding his hat, and offering encouragement, advice, and the occasional slap on the rump.

Mongolian wrestling is as much a trial of endurance as it is of strength. The first wrestler to touch the ground with anything other than a hand or foot loses. Matches between elite wrestlers can last a half hour or more as they grab hold of each other's arms or briefs, waiting for a mistake or moment of weakness to throw the other to the ground. On the other hand, a match between an experienced wrestler with some girth and a skinny novice, common during the early rounds, can be over in mere seconds.

Mongolian wrestling tournaments are single-elimination affairs. A loss in any round results in the end of a wrestler's day. There are typically eight or nine rounds in a competition, and every event starts with a legion of wrestlers in an exact multiple of eight; the national *Naadam* features 512 wrestlers. Wrestlers are ranked according to the number of consecutive matches they've won: winners of seven rounds gain the title *arslan,* lion; eight-round champions are called *zaan,* elephant.

The costumes have an interesting story. You'll notice that the tops are open in the front, baring the chest, but it wasn't always that way. As the story goes, one year a woman won the entire tournament, then stood up and bared her breasts reveling in her victory over all the men. In order to prevent this from happening in the future, a new regulation called for costumes that must reveal the chest.

### Horseracing

Horseracing goes back a long while in Mongolian tradition. What's interesting about races at *Naadam* is that only children ages 5-13 compete, usually bareback and without helmets. Each category includes not only riders of a certain age, but also horses of a certain age, both of which are awarded prizes. Mongolians have hundreds of words to distinguish the color and age of a horse, and as many as 1,000 horses can compete in the games. While only dedicated equestrians are well informed about all the breeds and characteristics of horses in the West, almost all Mongolians learn them from a very early age.

Depending on age, the horses walk 15 to 30 kilometers from the finish line, turn around, and race back to the finish. For spectators, much of the *Naadam* races is waiting. Attendees often play cards and carnival games, rest in the small pockets of shade cast by parked vehicles, or grab a *khuushuur* at a nearby stand. As they say, "If there's no *khuushuur,* there's no *Naadam.*" The moment the horses are spied on the horizon, however, the tension begins to increase. People rush to line up near the finish line, and a joyous pandemonium ensues as the first horses cross. Mongolians believe that rubbing the sweat off a winning horse garners good luck for the following year, and people virtually stampede, often against the orders and tazer guns of the police, to get a hand on a horse as it speeds by.

Others simply eat their *khuushuur* and watch the exciting races from home as the horses and jockeys are followed by SUVs with cameramen hanging from the windows.

### Archery

Once an important sport in the manly repertoire, archery has been nearly phased out of the *Naadam* festivals. Many *soum* festivals don't have it at all. Archers compete for long-range accuracy, aiming at a row of small baskets with rubber-tipped arrows, sometimes using traditional bows, sometimes using modern ones.

## OTHER POPULAR SPORTS

Besides the three manly sports, Mongolians enjoy playing team sports as well. Colleagues compete in weekly and weekend tournaments all around the country in several sports. Even if they are not very good, Mongolians love to just get out on the court and give it their best without being too self-conscious. This attitude is amazingly addictive.

Football (soccer), basketball, volleyball, and table tennis (ping-pong) are definitely the most played sports in Mongolia. School gymnasiums have pick-up games all year round, and when the weather permits, you'll see children and adults outside playing.

The rules are a little different in Mongolia than you might recognize, so if you join a game, be patient and observe. For example, every dead ball in volleyball is a

---

### The Myth of the Mongolian Blue Spot

Seen on the lower back of infants, the blue spot called "dermal melanocytosis" is the most common type of birthmark worldwide. It's caused by collections of pigment-producing cells in a deeper layer in the skin. A common anthropological myth is that if you have spot, you're related to Chinggis Khan.

However, just as Mongolian BBQ is neither Mongolian nor BBQ, the blue spot has nothing particularly to do with Mongolia. Unfortunately, it was just a little creative naming by German internist and anthropologist Erwin Baelz who observed the spots on Japanese children and made up the fanciful moniker. In fact, according to a study done by dermatologist Abdul-Ghani Kibbi of American University of Beirut Medical Center, those "blue-gray spots are seen in approximately 90 percent of blacks and Native Americans, roughly 80 percent of Asians, 70 percent of Hispanics, and between 5-10 percent of whites." Sorry Herr Doktor Baelz and our Mongolian friends, but there's just no clear connection between the blue spots and dear Chinggis or any other Mongolians.

point, not just on service. This is true for table tennis as well, a game most Mongolians call simply "tennis." Basketball games are always make-it, take-it, and don't bother calling a foul in the rebound mosh pit.

## MONGOLIAN GAMES

Perhaps the greatest way to break the ice and to get a foot into the *ger* door is through games. Mongolians are great to play games with. Every day you will encounter old men playing chess, taxi drivers playing cards, children playing *shagai* (anklebones), old women playing dominoes, and so much more. If you know how to play too, you can have a blast without even knowing the language.

### Shagai (Шагай) "Ankle Bones"

The word shagai refers to the ankle bone of a sheep or goat, but Mongolians also use this word to describe any game or fortunetelling where the ankle bones are used. Shagai games are most popular during *Naadam*, the national summer sport holiday. In all cases, the bones are rolled on the ground or on a table. The bones are said to have four sides that represent animals. The concave sides are the horse (морь) and sheep (хонь), while the convex sides are camel (тэмээ) and goat (ямаа). A "fifth side," cow (үнээ), is possible on uneven ground. If you buy a set, usually there are picture instructions inside to show which way is which, and you can ask almost anyone to show you.

There are several versions of games played using the shagai pieces. Depending on the game the anklebones may be tossed like dice, flicked like marbles, caught in the hands, or collected according to the roll of a die. There are even public tournaments held.

Full toss is one of the most common versions of shagai. In full toss, each of two to four players takes turns tossing all the pieces. Depending on the number of horses and/or camels landed, the player can collect pieces from the pool or has to add some. The winner is the player who has collected the most once the pool is empty.

In fortunetelling, four shagai are rolled on the ground or a table. The horse and sheep (the convex sides) are considered lucky, with horse being the luckiest. The sides with concave indents (goat and camel) are said to be unlucky. If you roll all four sides on one throw, congratulations!—you will have very good fortune.

### Khuzur (Хөзөр) "Cards"

The absolute undisputed, most popular game played throughout Mongolia is *Khuzur* (pronounced "Hoodzr"). In Mongolian, the word technically just means cards, but if anyone asks you to play cards, there's only one game they have in mind. Just pull out your cards or sit down and play with a group already at it, especially on a train.

*Rules:* It's a simple trump game, like hearts, but it is unique in many ways. One person leads a card, and then you have to beat that card with a higher card of the same suit or else pick up all the cards and add them to your hand. Throughout the game there is a designated trump that beats all other suits, which means the weakest card of the trump suit will beat the strongest card of a non-trump suit. Above the trump suit are the two jokers. They are the strongest cards and beat everything (the red joker is better than the black joker). If you understand up to this point, the rest is easy. Just always remember you need to play a higher card than the one that your opponent has played. This game is played without the 4s, 5s, and 6s of each suit. The cards in each suit are ranked from 7 to king, then 3, 2, ace, and joker. Thus, a 3 beats a king, a 2 beats a 3, and an ace beats a 2.

*The Deal and Trump Designation:* To begin, all players are dealt five cards (or seven if there are two to three players), and then one community card is turned over and placed in the center of the table designating the trump suit. If the red joker is flipped, trump is hearts. If the black joker is flipped, spades are trump. (Some Mongolians also play using a set order of trump cards, rotating each round: hearts, then diamonds, spades, and finally clubs.) Only higher trump cards will beat a lower trump card, and only a joker will beat the ace of the trump suit.

*Basic Game Play:* After the deal, the remaining cards are placed face down in a pile in the center. As long as there are cards remaining in the pile, no player can have less than five cards. So, if you successfully play a higher card than the person before you, you have to draw a card from this center pile. The first player to have no cards left wins the game. This cannot happen until all the cards have been drawn from the center pile.

First the leader plays, then the next person must play a better card, and so on around the table. This continues until a player cannot play a higher card and so picks up all the played cards or until each player has successfully played a higher card than the one previous. The cards are flipped over, placed in a discard pile, and the last player to play gets to lead a new round.

This continues until all the cards in the center have been taken and one player has successfully played all their cards to win.

The basic strategy is to have high strong cards remaining at the end. Without strong cards at the end it is almost impossible to win.

*Advanced Strategy:* The person leading can play from their hand any card or *combination of cards* they want. The leader has the option of playing a pair or a number of pairs (two cards of different suits but the same number) in addition to a single card. That said, a player must always play an odd number of cards. So if it is my turn to lead, I can play any of the following combinations:

A) 7c,7h,3h     B) 8d     C) Ad,Ah,2h     D) 10d,10h,9s,9d,Js

You can never play more cards than a player has in their hand. Five cards cannot be played until the center pile has been exhausted and every player has at least five cards in hand.

If a player plays a combination of a pair and a single card or few pairs and a single card before you, you don't need to play higher pairs to beat their play. As long as you can play a higher card on each of the cards they play, you can successfully play your turn.

With an even number of people, *khuzur* can also be played as a team game, with every other person playing for the same team (i.e., in a group of six, the first, third, and fifth people will form a team). In team competition, only one of the team's players must dispose of all their cards in order for the team to win. This changes the strategy somewhat, as some players may sacrifice their hand and actually pick up cards in order to give a teammate better opportunities to play their cards. During team play, Mongolians tolerate a great deal of "table talk."

As with all games, the more you play the better you will become.

| Spades | Гил | Gil | Jack | Боол | Bool |
|--------|-----|-----|------|------|------|
| Clubs | Цэцэг | Tsetseg | Queen | Хатан | Khatan |
| Diamonds | Дөрвөлжин | Durvuljin | King | Ноён | Noyen |
| Hearts | Бундан | Bundan | Ace | Тамга | Tamga |
| Trump | Дарах | Darakh | Joker | Хүн | Khun |
| Points | Оноо | Onoo | To play | тоглох | Toglokh |
| Pair | Хос | Khos | To win | хожих | Khojikh |
| Cards | Хөзөр | Khuzur | To lose | хожигдох | Khojigdokh |

## Shatar (Шатар) Chess

Chess is one of the oldest and most popular games throughout the world. It is a very popular past time in Mongolia, and you will be amazed at the skill that some of the youngest children bring to the game of kings. Through the short summer, old men can be found from early morning until dusk squatting over boards focusing on their next moves.

If you know how to play or you think you know how to play, just sit down and join a game. Don't be surprised if you lose really quickly.

| Pawn | Хүү | Khuu | Bishop | Тэмээ | Temee |
|------|-----|------|--------|-------|-------|
| Rook | Тэрэг | Tereg | King | Ноён | Noyen |
| Knight | Морь | Mor | Queen | Бэрс | Bers |

# Holidays

Although some of the following holidays (denoted with an asterisk) may not technically be official days off, they are often marked by organizations including schools, hospitals, local governments, and others with concerts, awards ceremonies, and banquets. You may be lucky to find these organizations operating as normal on these days, but then again, you may find them too busy preparing for a party to deal with your needs. It's best to plan around these holidays.

**January 1: New Year's (Shine Jil or Шинэ Жил)** is celebrated in much the same way as in America, but in the traditions of the Soviet Union, this holiday is filled with Christmas idols and imagery such as the "Shine Jil Tree," an evergreen with ornaments and tinsel, and "Grandfather Winter," a portly fellow with a red outfit and long white beard.

**January 13: Constitution Day\*** commemorates the signing of the new Constitution in 1992.

**January/February:** *Tsagaan Sar* (Цагаан Сар) is the lunar New Year festival. Dates change every year based on the Tibetan calendar and coincide roughly with the Chinese New Year. Celebrations can last from the official three days in Ulaanbaatar to several weeks in the countryside.

**March 8: International Women's Day\*** was popular throughout the communist bloc. It is often marked with concerts and award ceremonies.

**March 18: Soldier's Day\*** doubles as Men's Day in some regions, but is generally less of a big deal than Women's Day. It commemorates the defeat of the Chinese by Sukhbaatar's overmatched troops in Khiagt, Russia, across the border from Altanbulag in Selenge Aimag.

**June 1: Mother and Children's Day** marks the official end of the school year. The biggest celebrations are in Ulaanbaatar, although festivities can be found at the main squares of aimag centers across Mongolia.

**July 11-13:** *Naadam* (Наадам) is the annual sports festival and the social highlight of the summer. It also marks the break from Chinese rule in 1911 and the beginning of autumn for herders.

**Nov. 26: Independence Day\*** marks the creation of the communist Mongolian People's Republic in 1924 ending Chinese Rule in Mongolia but is still celebrated despite the rise of democracy.

## Tsagaan Sar

Besides *Naadam*, the other important holiday is the Lunar New Year celebration. The new year according to the lunar calendar in Mongolia is marked by *Tsagaan Sar*, which translates as the "White Month" or "White Moon." There are many opinions about the origin of the name, but Mongolians use white to symbolize happiness, purity, and an abundance of milk products.

The lunar calendar is thought to have been invented by the nomadic tribes of central Asia. A number of eastern and central Asian countries, including Mongolia, have followed the lunar calendar since ancient times. You might recognize the calendar's 12 years, 12 months, and 12 hours in a day (in the traditional Mongolian method of keeping time) marked by animals similar to the Zodiac, a Greek word meaning "circle of animals."

Nowadays there is occasionally an argument among Mongolian astrologers about the celebration date of *Tsagaan Sar* because depending on the phases of the moon and the calendar used, it falls anywhere between the end of January and early March. Some think they should follow the lunar calendar invented by Tibetans, while others prefer to follow the one used by the Chinese. The Lunar new year's eve in Mongolia is called *Bituun*, the last dinner of the old year.

Celebrants must eat all the traditional dishes on the evening of the holiday: boiled lamb or beef, a huge variety of milk products, *buuz* or *bansh* (large or small meat- and fat-filled steamed dumplings), and desserts. Many families have the tradition of placing coins inside the dumplings; whoever bites into the one with the coins will have good luck. At the end of the evening, everyone's stomach should be fully satisfied. The following morning everyone rises bright and early to walk outside of their house in the correct direction, which is indicated in their horoscope of the year and directed by the lamas. The path symbolizes that the destiny of each person is directed correctly for the upcoming year.

Then family members gather around the eldest in the family and greet each other by wishing a very happy new year. First, the youngest greets the eldest as the older person holds out their arms. The elder puts their hands palms down on the arms of the younger one and both pronounce traditional good wishes and rub cheeks while the older person sniffs on either side of the younger person's face, which is a tradi-

## Zodiac Animals of the Oriental Lunar Calendar

1. The Year of the Mouse promises good livestock productivity, especially in camels.
2. It snows heavily in the Year of the Cow and there is plenty of food and milk.
3. The Year of the Tiger is rather hard at the end.
4. The Year of the Hare is favorable at the beginning and spells disasters at the end.
5. The Year of the Dragon is rainy and floods may occur.
6. The Year of the Snake brings many disruptions and worries.
7. The Year of the Horse is also rather disturbing.
8. But the Year of the Sheep that follows it is favorable in all respects.
9. The Year of the Monkey, although cold and troublesome, brings in a bumper harvest.
10. The Year of the Cock is one of fertility and higher birth rate.
11. The Year of the Dog is severe at the beginning and kind towards the end.
12. The concluding Year of the Pig promises rich harvests, yet food shortages, should they occur, will hit hard.

tional Mongolian "kiss." Even if new year celebrations are over, friends and relatives meeting for the first time that year greet each other in this manner. In towns and cities, *Tsagaan Sar* is celebrated for one to three days, and in the countryside villages, the reveling continues for a week or more.

Guests may come and go at any time of the day and families serve guests with plenty of meals: dumplings and vodka in sets of three, salads, fruits, etc. The host also gives a small parting gift to guests. When the gift has been given, that's the signal for the guests to leave; guests may not leave sooner. Traditions and customs are different from place to place and from family to family. Even for Mongolians, it is impossible to follow every tradition, but by observing and practicing a few customs you can learn a lot.

# Ger Life

The *ger*, (pronounced "gair") or yurt, as it's often known outside Mongolia, is the traditional Mongolian home, made of felt covering a wooden lattice-work frame. Each section of lattice is called a *khaana* or "wall," and most *gers* have either four or five walls. A *ger* and its contents can typically be transported on two vehicles, traditionally large carts with wheels pulled by camels or horses. These days, trucks

---

## *Ger* Etiquette

**Don't...**

Step on the threshold.

Enter or exit a *ger* backwards.

Spread your arms across the doorway.

Whistle inside.

Cross the line between *ger* posts, including walking or handing things through.

Throw trash or salt in a fire (throwing trash in the metal tray underneath the fire is totally acceptable).

Sleep with your feet facing north or away from the door.

Roll up your sleeves because superstition says you might be asking to fight the host.

**Do...**

Move around the *ger* clockwise.

At least taste the soup or tea that is offered to you before putting it down.

Keep your hat ON when entering a *ger*, wait until you are shown a seat, then remove your hat with the open side facing down.

Make sure your sleeves are down when you receive food or drink.

Touch the bottom of a serving bowl with your right hand before taking something from it.

and Jeeps do most of the heavy work.

Because of the angle of the roof, there are certain demands on the furniture and interior design. Tables are small, usually more like Western coffee tables, and most people sit on small stools. The walls are lined with wool carpets with either colorful or traditional designs to match their style. *Gers* can have all sorts of modern furniture though, too, including desks, entertainment centers, lights, and a TV.

*Gers* are always situated with the door facing to the south, and are also arranged in a clockwise fashion according to custom. The left side of the *ger* is for children and guests. The floor or an extra bed on that side is where you will sleep if you are an overnight guest. You'll notice that the light first enters the *ger* there, politely waking you up and inviting you to start the process of leaving.

The right side where the pantry, cooking utensils, and dishes are kept is the women's half of the *ger*. Couples usually sleep together here if space allows. The rear part the *ger* opposite the door holds religious shrines, awards, and pictures.

## Customs & Culture

### SHARING

Something you're likely to notice immediately upon visiting Mongolia is how much Mongolians share. Mongolians are accustomed to sharing both their space and their food. Even small children offer around a bag of goodies before they take one themselves. The selfish phase we have in the West, the "terrible twos," just doesn't exist here. The Twix jingle, "two for me, none for you," seems simply crass after spending some time in Mongolia.

> **Etiquette Tip**
> If you finish your food or tea, you are asking for more. If you don't want more, don't finish what's offered to you – but do at least try some or risk offending your host. When you're done, you can place the bowl on the table or floor near the fire. Take your queue from them.

When you visit a home for the first time, you should bring a small present of candy, a box of chocolates, fruit, or even a beverage something you and they can share together. That means, if you're backpacking for a while and intend to meet Mongolians in *gers*, you should have something when you enter, not just cash when you leave. As you enter, give it to the host using both hands out in front of you. They'll likely smile and dive in right then, offering some to you, of course.

Similarly, if you want to make friends on a bus ride or at any other gathering, just pull out a bag of cookies, biscuits, candies, or chocolates and offer around. It really breaks the ice and helps make you one of the group, not just some crazy foreigner. You'll at least have the grace of a Mongolian child.

---

### They Fence the People In

In Mongolia, the livestock roam free while the people are fenced in. Without pasture fences, livestock meander through villages and towns as they forage. In contrast, nearly every family not settled in an apartment lives in a *khaashaa* (хаашаа), a fenced-in yard or compound that may include animal shelters, vehicle garages, summer kitchens, storage sheds, and the *gers* or houses of one of more families. Because of the superfluous fences, you should avoid making shortcuts wherever you are, including UB, and just stick to worn paths, that is, unless you like deliriously irate dogs, retracing your steps, and picking out splinters.

---

## MONGOLIAN CEREMONIES

If you're lucky enough to participate in a ceremony or rite of passage, you should know a few things first. Some things will be familiar, and some things may surprise you.

### Coupling

Couples almost always choose their own partner, often as teenagers or in their early 20s, as a lot of emphasis is placed on "first love." Traditionally, women are expected to have their first child in their early 20s, and though this trend is changing among more career-oriented woman, it is still expected that a woman at least have a child before age 30.

To formally ask for a father for his daughter's hand in marriage can take some time. As the tradition goes, they play a little cat and mouse game where the suitor must ask the father three different times on three different occasions if he can marry the daughter. The father must refuse the first two requests but oblige on the third. With little extra fanfare, they are said to be "sitting," a time during which couples consider themselves married and refer to each other as husband and wife but do not have the legal certification.

Marriage certificates and weddings are expensive, so couples may be considered socially married but not legally married. Couples with children are often considered married, and the conception of a child often marks the announcement of permanent commitment to the community and often each other. If couples are dating more than a few months, there are expectations of marriage by the family and the community, something many foreigners don't quite grasp when they date Mongolians. In Ulaanbaatar, things can be a bit different, but the rumor mills still churn.

Wedding ceremonies are usually held on special Buddhist days as advised by the lamas, which means that everyone who has been waiting to get married usually marries within the same few days each year. If you are invited, you will be asked to drink various beverages such as *airag*, Mongolian vodka (distilled from milk), vodka, juices, yogurt, and milk. Participants sit in concentric rings around the inside of a *ger* with the couple in the center, and all take turns leading the group in song, one-by-one. If you don't know a Mongolian song, go with something from the Beatles.

In Ulaanbaatar, the Big White Wedding Palace near Choijin Lama monastery is the place more modern folks tie the knot. They may wear tuxedos and white wedding dresses or come dressed in their finest Mongolian traditional garb. Singing and drinking are still a part of the ceremony, but singing might be accompanied by disco, karaoke, and dancing.

Unfortunately, splitting up is pretty common among couples. It is often proceeded by infidelity by one or both of the partners (Mongolians often joke about *nuuts amarag* or "secret lovers" but it can be a painful reality), alcoholism, spousal abuse, and just growing apart.

Because of this, single-parent households run by women and mixed families are very common. Often, children are raised by the grandparents while young parents work. In fact, the average household in Mongolia consists of five people and often includes three generations. It is rude to call a spouse's child from another relationship as a "step child" as it shows disrespect, so to avoid being rude, don't ask too many questions about the parentage of a child.

For the first few years of life, Mongolian parents allow the hair of both boys and girls to grow until a special hair cutting ceremony, usually around the age of three. For this ceremony family and friends each cut a lock off the child's head and enjoy a little feast.

## Death

Death rituals in Mongolia can be far different than in the West. It's unlikely you will find yourself invited to participate in one, but if you do, there are few things you should know.

You can visit with the family and eat, but Mongolians don't give cards or bring food to the grieving family. They also don't give flowers because as one man said, "What can I do with these? I'm not a goat!" You shouldn't talk much when visiting, and especially avoid saying *uuchlarai* (sorry) to the grievers as an act of condolence because it translates as taking responsibility for the death, not sympathy. Also, avoid greetings such as "*Sain bain uu?*" ("Are you good?"). Just sit in silence or ask if you can do something practical like chop wood or get water.

Mongolians do not take much joy or pride in preparing or visiting gravesites, and they will find it not only weird, but often offensive, if you visit gravesites. If you do wander upon one, it's best not to loiter long.

## TRADITIONAL MONGOLIAN CLOTHING

The main traditional garment of Mongolia is the *deel* (pronounced "dell") consisting of a silk or wool robe with long sleeves that fall far below the hands. Different occasions call for different kinds of *deels*. The ornamented silk material is typically filled with repeating patterns that carry significance and can be worn by women and men, though patterns with flowers are typically only worn by women. Wool and sometimes cotton *deels* are more everyday herding garments for men or women, and depending on region and ancient tribal roots, the styles vary. With over 20 historic tribes in Mongolia, employing countless interpretations, the variations are limitless.

As you might expect, ceremonial garments are flashier and employ more accessories than the everyday wear. Each year in preparation for the lunar new year celebrations, *Tsagaan Sar*, most people will buy a new *deel* or add to their costumes. On the first day of the multi-day celebration, celebrants sport fresh haircuts to go with their fresh clothes, and they ring in the new year with their new hats, boots, belts, and snuff bottles, usually corresponding with their region's or family's cultural heritage dating back hundreds to thousands of years. In modern times, a *khantaaz* or vest can be worn to work by women with a pair of jeans and high boots with heels or it can be worn on top of the *deel* by men and women to complete a formal ceremonial outfit.

Boots or *gutal* (pronounced "go-tl") can vary by region and ethnic group as well. Of the traditional varieties worn by older generations, the most common ones worn

### What's in a Name?

Genghis, Ghengis, Chinggis, Chinggiss, Chingis, Dschinghis, Tschinghis, Chinguz, Chingiz, Chingidz, Jengiz Chan, Kan, Qan, Khaan, Khan. The man, the legend, the leader of the Mongols goes by many names these days.

In most English-speaking parts of the world he is known as Genghis Khan, with a "g" as in "gargoyle," owing to transliterations from Asian languages and Marco Polo, an Italian who wrote in French. The original pronunciation of his writing would have been with a soft "g" as in "generous," which would have been closer to the Mongolian Chinggis. Russians gave it their best shot too, with Чингиз or Chingidz.

In English we have adopted the word "khan" and use it with the hard "k" as in "ketchup," but Mongolians have a different sound more like the Scottish "loch" or German "Bach" to begin the title. It is more correct to use that sound, but you can also get away with thinking of the "h" standing alone, like the name of the cowboy-like Star Wars character "*Han* Solo."

by herders are flat and wide with an upturned pointed toe. They come in various shades of dark blue, black, brown, or green and have colorful accents and patterns along the sides and openings. They are accompanied by a complimentary felt insert called *oims*. They are really hard to walk in and don't prove much use on slippery, snow-covered walkways. Young people typically only wear these during ceremonies.

Another popular ethnic boot is the plain Buriat boot that usually comes in black or dark blue with a flat rounded toe that makes walking a little easier. The boot is seen most often around the countryside, though drivers, herders, and all sorts of regular fellas on the street wear the black, mid-calf Russian boot every day. No matter what boot or who wears them, pants are always tucked inside to show it off and to keep pants clean.

Hats, or *malgai*, really top off any Mongolian costume and show off the heritage of the region or wearer. If you've ever seen the character Queen Amidala from the Star Wars movies, you might recognize her "galaxy far, far away" headdress with swooping arches of hair among the many Mongolian costumes. Similarly, all hats that have white beads down the sides are for women. Men's hats might be furry with ear flaps and topped with a large knot in the middle (these hats are typically worn by wrestlers). You might also recognize this style of hat as the one worn by Sukhbaatar in Ulaanbaatar's main square.

Though you will certainly see variations of these costumes in the countryside no matter where you go or when, in UB most modern Mongolians only wear traditional garb during the holidays, if at all. Western clothes are the norm, and even in the countryside most people wear Western-style clothing imported from China. Professional men often wear suits without ties or other forms of business casual, and they often pay keen attention to the shine of their shoes. Women wear jeans and high heels of some sort almost all year round and for almost any occasion, even volleyball competitions! Especially in winter, superstition dictates that if a women's heels touch the ground, her eggs will freeze and leave her infertile.

## Little Horse in the Hat

As legend goes, each person has a special protective horse, known as *khii mor*, that lives underneath their hat. When you turn their hat upside-down, the horse flies away. This sounds like bad luck, so keep the open-side down when not wearing headgear.

# Traveling in Mongolia

## Visa Information

Citizens of the United States must have a valid passport to visit Mongolia. A visa is not required if you are visiting for fewer than 90 days. If you plan to stay in Mongolia for more than 30 days you must register with the Office of Immigration, Naturalization, and Foreign Citizens in Ulaanbaatar within 7 days of arriving in Mongolia and pay an application fee. If you do not register and you stay longer than 30 days, even for reasons beyond your control, you will be stopped at departure, not allowed to exit, and have to pay a fine of $100 or more depending on the circumstances.

Visitors who have been in Mongolia for more than 90 days must obtain an exit visa – if it is not already included in the entrance visa – to leave the country. The exit visa is obtained from the Office of Immigration and usually takes 10 days to process. You can obtain an exit visa by going to the immigration office located near the airport. Take the number 11 bus (Нисэх) and get off just after the large round sport hall (on the left as you travel away from the city) before the archway gate over the road. The immigration office is half a kilometer down a side road on the left and is hard to miss; it's set apart and is the biggest thing between the sport hall and the airport. It is open from 9:00 a.m. to 6:00 p.m., except for Wednesday and weekends, when it works on an abbreviated schedule of 9:00 a.m. to 4:00 p.m. The visa application form you'll need is written in both English and Mongolian. The staff will break for lunch and kick everyone out, so make sure you get there early, or you will have to start over again after lunch.

If you have already been in the country past the seven days, you can still stay longer by going to the office and filling out the same extension application. You will have to pay a penalty of about MNT150,000 and sign a piece of paper admitting that you violated the visa laws. Who knows what the implications of that are, especially if you come back to Mongolia in the future, but it doesn't sound good. Your only other option is to leave the country and come back, refreshing your 30 day visa. Don't try to skirt these rules, because they will keep you in the country until you pay up.

For citizens of the UK, Canada, Australia, and European Union, entry and exit visa are required and can be obtained from travel companies, consulates, or embassies and are valid for three months from the date of issue. If you are traveling with an organized tour, visas can be obtained through tourism companies or travel agencies. A group visa in the name of the tour leader is valid for all tourists on the list attached, provided relevant details (nationality, sex, date of birth, passport numbers, and dates of issue and expiry) are given at the time of application. Entry and exit visa: £40 (single-entry, 30 days); £55 (double-entry, 30 days per visit); £70 (multiple entry). Entry visa: £35 (single-entry, 90 days). Transit visa: £35 (single-entry); £55 (double entry). Prolongation of visas costs £15 upon request.

Citizens of New Zealand have a slightly more complicated procedure. Consulate-issued tourist visas are typically for 30 days (NZD95). For a tourist visa you must have a copy of your travel itinerary or, if you are with an organized tour, a copy of a letter from the tour company indicating the dates of the tour and a contact address while in Mongolia. This can be your first hotel or local tour company and is required so that if for any reason the authorities need to contact

> **Mongolian Immigration Agency**
> Service Hall 1882, Buyant-Ukhaa, 10th Khoroo, Khan-Uul District, Ulaanbaatar, Mongolia (Chinggis Khaan International Airport), 1170110481, (fax) 1170133448; info@immigration.gov.mn; www.immigration.gov.mn

you while you are in Mongolia, they have a starting point. Double-entry tourists visas are permitted (NZD120) but only for small trips when returning to Mongolia within a short time as part of one journey. A double-entry visa cannot be used to make two separate trips to Mongolia. Transit visas (NZD76) are for train travelers who are passing straight through Mongolia to Russia or China, and those passengers are not permitted to leave the train while in Mongolia.

You can purchase a single entry visa upon arrival but only at the Chinggis Khaan (Ulaanbaatar) Airport. There is an extra rapid transit fee of $50 plus a service fee of $3 (prices are subject to change without notice). This service is only intended for travelers who cannot normally obtain a visa at their originating point or who are traveling on very short notice. They are not available at any other border point of entry to Mongolia. All visas are valid for 90 days from the date of issue.

## OBTRAINING A CHINESE TRAVEL VISA

Getting to China from Mongolia is as easy as yi, er, san! All you need is the proper documents, some cash, and perhaps a bit of patience. Visas are processed within four working days; however, an express visa may be obtained within 2-3 working days for an extra $20.

In order to obtain a Chinese visa you need the following documents:

✓ A passport with at least six months of remaining validity and at least one blank visa page

✓ A completed visa application (which you can pick up and fill out at the embassy)

✓ One recent passport sized photo (3.5 x 4.5 cm)

✓ Your tickets in and out of China (This can be the tricky part, especially if you haven't planned that far in advance. Unfortunately, this is a must have because it will determine how many days you get on your visa.)

✓ In addition to a final destination ticket you must be sure to have a valid visa for that country.

✓ Information about where you are staying (e.g., hostel, couch surfer's address, random combination of numbers and Chinese characters). This may be just a formality, but they'll ask for it anyway.

✓ American dollars. (Yes, it's true.) The prices are:
  – American: Single/Double entry visa: $140
  – Serbian: Single/Double entry visa: $60
  – Others: Single: $30.00, Double: $60

The Chinese embassy (Хятадын элчин сайдын яам, 320955; 323940; 311903) is located in Ulaanbaaatar on the corner of the Small Ring Road (Бага тойруу) and Youth Avenue (Залуучуудын өргөн чөлөө), which is a quick walk from Sukhbaatar Square and МУБИС or a MNT1,000 taxi ride from the State Department Store. It is open from 9:30 a.m. to 12:00 p.m. Monday, Wednesday, and Friday.

## Obtaining a Russian Visa

If you didn't get your Russian visa before traveling to Mongolia, you should allow some time in your trip to spend window hopping in the vast bureaucracy that is the Russian-visa-getting process. If you need some help discovering what you need, the Legend Tour Company (http://www.legendtour.ru/eng/index.shtml) has made a name for itself as being the go-to agency for help in acquiring Russian visas.

# Travel Companies

Almost all tour companies are in UB, though their services take you far into the countryside. Many travel companies have themed tours for monasteries, birdwatching, the Gobi Desert, horse trekking; there's a tour for nearly every interest. These tours can be a fun way to meet other travelers with similar interests and get a view of the tourist sites you might want to see. On the other hand, they can really lighten your purse when travel to some of the same destinations can be self-guided if you have a sense of adventure and a little patience. To get to remote places, though, you will probably need a little hired help, especially if time is a factor.

Unless you come during the week of *Naadam* in mid-July, you can wait to arrange all travel and lodging at the last minute.

Just about every guesthouse, hotel, outfitter, and travel company in UB can plan a chaperoned tour of nearby countryside destinations such as Terelj National Park and neighboring provinces for about $35 to $150 per day, all inclusive. Tours with companies near the bigger deep-countryside tourist destinations like Khuvsgul tend to be more luxury resort-style experiences, though still rugged to some degree.

What you pay for with a tour company is a translator and the convenience of planned meals and lodging. If your time is limited, money is not much of an object, and you're interested in quickly checking sites off your travel list, a tour company is a sure bet. Most sites, however, are located in or around provincial capitals and UB where you can buy cheap bus tickets or hire a local driver at a lower cost by yourself if you don't mind a little miming and negotiating.

If you can buy a bus ticket from the Dragon Center, Bayanzurkh Tovchoo, or Teveerin Tovchoo to the province you want to see and find the local market or taxi area with map in hand showing where you want to go, you can make some pretty interesting things happen on your own. Look for hosts on www.couchsurfing.com for help finding local English-speakers or a floor to crash on. Remember that UB is the transport hub, so once you get outside the city, inter-provincial travel is more difficult. (See Domestic Travel on page 85.)

Some of the top companies offer prepackaged tours you might be interested in. Many will make custom tours, so look for what's best for you. You don't have to book a tour company for your whole visit. If you want to get your feet wet by taking a three-day trip to the Gobi and then make your own trek north, do it.

Though we don't endorse any of these specifically, here is a list of some of the most respected and dependable tour companies:

www.nomadicexpeditions.com

www.discovermongolia.mn

www.mongoliantravel.com

www.selenatravel.com

www.nomadstours.com

www.juulchin.com

www.bluemongolia.com

www.gertoger.org

www.travelgobimongolia.com

www.tripsmongolia.com

www.happycamel.com

www.boerte-nomads.com

www.legendtour.ru

www.mongolianbirdstour.com

## Don't Over Pay for a Tour

Most tours close to UB are standard, rinse-and-repeat, copy-cat tours involving the same sights, food, and general accommodations, so there is often little difference among the top and bottom prices except for the company of your fellow travelers. Don't be afraid to go cheap, especially through a guesthouse. Breakdowns, delays, and itinerary misunderstandings can happen regardless of how much you pay. Usually the cheaper you go, the more quaint and less rehearsed the experience.

# Accommodations

There are several different options, levels, and prices of accommodations in UB and some provincial capitals. According to the Ministry of Nature and Tourism there are over 3,750 hotels, most of which have at least a one-star rating. Most in UB are in the one- to two-star range with a few luxury options like the Chinggis Khaan and Kempinski that top out at the four-star level.

Unless you travel to the cities of Erdenet, Darkhan, and UB or to Khuvsgul, it may be slightly difficult to find hotels with showers or comfortable beds. Instead, you are most likely to find budget hotels that could barely meet a one-star rating, some of which have outhouses in lieu of a loo and a shared shower, if any. Some are better than others, and some are worse than others. Inspect the room before you agree to stay. If you don't like it, move on.

Outside most provincial capitals and places of interest such as sand dunes, oases, hot springs, Terelj National Park, and Khuvsgul Lake, you can usually stay at one of Mongolia's 250 registered *ger* camps, a group of *gers* set up for domestic and foreign tourists. They generally sleep between four and six adults and include at least a meal or two. Because they usually require a drive, *ger* camps are often much harder to locate unless you have booked through a tour with a company.

Camping is almost always an option in Mongolia and is about as regulation-free as you're going to find. If you want a guaranteed place to sleep, a tent is the perfect thing to bring along. If you don't bring one with you, you can rent them from a number of UB hostels and outfitters. Outside any town, village, or city, you can put up a tent and sleep. In Terelj National Park, you will be asked to pay a small fee of about MNT5,000 per night if you register or a ranger approaches you. Other than that, there are no regulations, one benefit of state-owned public land and a pastoral nomadic culture. If you are hiking, cycling, or riding a horse in the countryside, you might want to plan a hotel stay in a provincial capital every few days for a shower and a good meal. When camping near *aimag* centers, it is best to set up a kilometer or two from the edge of town. And any time there are *gers* nearby, you may want to ask if they mind your presence.

# Preparation

Because Mongolia is a pretty rugged place, rolling luggage is not your best bet. You'll end up carrying it much of the time, and fitting it in shared transport is tricky. Backpacks work best because they are easy to carry and store away. A second, smaller bag to keep fragile or expensive items safe during bus trips is a good idea. You will have few opportunities to bathe so you don't need many toiletries.

## Things to Bring

- ✓ Sleeping bag
- ✓ Flashlight
- ✓ Layerable clothing
- ✓ Dramamine for motion sickness
- ✓ Anti-diarrhea medication
- ✓ Good shoes/boots
- ✓ Camera
- ✓ Toilet paper
- ✓ Sunglasses
- ✓ Hat
- ✓ Sunscreen
- ✓ ATM card

## Things not to Bring

- ✓ Radio
- ✓ Big toiletries
- ✓ Too many clothes
- ✓ Traveler's cheques

## Things to Consider

**Tents:** Unless you plan to camp all the time, you can always find cheap lodging or rent tents in UB for short treks. If you're going to be traveling for a while, a tent may be useful. Camping is definitely the cheapest option.

**Contact Lenses:** It can get very dusty and windy, and you may not be able to clean your hands often. Definitely bring glasses as a backup. Contact solution is only available in UB.

**Laptop Computers:** "Notebooks," as they are called in Mongolia, should have good virus protection or better yet, don't plug in flash drives. Most guesthouses have internet for free and computers you can rent very cheaply. All provincial capitals have internet cafés. They aren't always fast, but travel is hard on electronics, so bring yours only if you must.

**Electricity:** You can find electric adapters almost anywhere, especially in the countryside. Mongolia runs on thick 2-pronged 220 V. Voltage converters are virtually non-existent. Most new appliances and computers come equipped with their own. Most coffee shops and businesses have power strips that accommodate every sized plug.

**GPS:** If you have it, bring it. Many roads and landmarks are not well marked, and it's easy to get lost. Planning your costs per kilometer is much easier and accurate, too.

**Mobile phone:** You can buy SIM cards and cell phones cheaply. If you plan to arrange travel via a shared vehicle, it is a good idea to have a phone. That way the driver can call you as he or she leaves town and you do not have to wait around all day waiting to leave.

# Money

Mongolian national *tugrik* (MNT or ₮) notes come in 1, 5, 10, 20, 50, 100, 1000, 5000, 10000, and 20000. There are plenty of ATMs in Ulaanbaatar at Khan Bank and Trade and Development Bank branches, where you can usually pull *tugriks* (pronounced "too-grk") from your home bank account (depending on your bank). Khan Bank, which has branches in every *aimag* center, is the best bet to find an ATM outside of UB.

Banks in Ulaanbaatar and the province capitals can often change your money and will sometimes cash traveler's cheques (which are not recommended) into *tugriks*, but it may be safest to change your money in Ulaanbaatar if you plan to be in remote areas. Most guesthouses and tours in Ulaanbaatar quote prices in USD, but outside Ulaanbaatar, you will not be able to use dollars. Though coins are no longer in circulation, money is generically referred to as "silver" or *mungu* (pronounced "moonk").

Even in some fancier establishments, making change is not a favorite Mongolian pastime. Especially in small stores and Mongolian restaurants, don't expect to give a 20,000 note for half a kilo of *aaruul* totaling MNT2,500. Smaller bills are always better to carry around with you because Mongolians often expect you to give almost exact change. Shop owners typically round off to the nearest 50 *tugriks* or give a piece of gum or box of matches instead of 10 or 20 *tugrik* notes, which few stores use.

There is no tipping in restaurants or taxis. Upscale restaurants may add a VAT that you are obliged to pay, which may or may not go to the server. You will have few opportunities to use credit cards except in some restaurants, hotels, and souvenir shops in UB. Plan to carry cash.

## Press Your Buck

Unless your dollar bills are in pristine condition, looking like they just came off the press, you may have a hard time exchanging them at banks. Banks often only prefer to exchange larger notes and typically will not exchange anything lower than $20. Many notes are denied simply because they've been folded in half.

At the time of publishing, MNT1,335 were equal to $1. Regardless of any small fluctuations in pricing, bear in mind that for the most part goods purchased inside the capital and other major transportation hubs are going to be less expensive than goods purchased in smaller cities and villages. Additionally, while there have been some minor fluctuations in the exchange rate it has stayed fairly steady between MNT1,200 and MNT1,400 to the U.S. dollar.

## Small Notes

The smallest denominations, 1 and 5, are not often seen or used outside of Buddhist temples where they are left as altar donations. If you plan on visiting several monasteries, it's a good idea to pick up 1 and 5 *tugrik* notes at a bank or in a Buddhist store. They are also beautiful to look at and make nice, cheap gifts for friends and family when you come home.

# Budgeting

If you take the bus and use a tent, you can keep your costs down to an average of about $25-35 per day depending on how far you travel. Guesthouses and *ger* camps will add about $15-20 to your daily budget in the countryside.

You can survive in UB on $10-15 per day if you eat in *guanzes*, stay in guesthouse dorm beds, and avoid alcohol. Most guesthouses have kitchens, and packets of ramen go for less than a dollar at grocery stores. Head to **Merkuri Market** by the Circus for deals on fresh produce, dry and canned goods, and fresh meat if you're in UB. In the countryside, hit up the local *delguurs* (shops) and outdoor markets while you travel.

## Guanzes

Referred to as "Mongolian fast food," a *guanz* is a small restaurant synonymous with a café (кафе), tea house (цайны газар) or bistro (зуушны газар). Expect instant coffee in sugary packets and tea as either Mongolian milk tea by the cup or individual bags of black tea. *Guanzes* also sell typical Mongolian fare – like fruit, huushuur, tsuivan, and salads (see p76 for descriptions of typical Mongolian food items) – at very modest prices.

If you want a mid-range experience, you'll probably spend up to $115 a day by staying in *ger* camps, eating in some Westerner-oriented restaurants, and sleeping in some hotels. You can get away with drinking beer and pick up some nice copper and felt souvenirs. You can take taxis and hire private drivers from province capitals to sights further afield, but you won't be able to fly anywhere.

Lastly, the posh traveler can spend from $150 to as much $500 a day with organized luxury tours. You'll be flown around the country to cherry pick the best sights and skip most of the harsher overland travel. You will have plenty of food, and it will usually be recognizable. Your guide will speak English really well, but you will just be along for the ride won't interact much with regular people. Also remember that more money spent does not make you immune to Mongolian travel hassles like bad roads, flat tires, or food poisoning.

## Inflation

While we tried to be as precise as possible when it came to prices in Mongolia, we are at the mercy of a rapidly expanding economy as well as a historically high inflation rate, between ten and twenty percent for 2011. The prices were accurate at the time of authorship, so please excuse us if the prices quoted in this book have changed.

# Souvenirs

From trinkets to traditional tables, Mongolian handicrafts reflect the intersection of the Eurasian steppe and the Far East. In many of the shops in UB you will find typical Mongolian and Kazakh steppe patterns on felt and fabric and silk textiles used for making clothing, and you will no doubt see some cashmere. What you choose to buy and what you pay for it depends on where you go and who made it.

Some things that make for good keepsakes are felt slippers (*tavchig*), ankle bones game (*shagai*), traditional hats (*malgai*), Kazakh bags (*Kazakh tsunkh*), a snuff bottle (*huuraga*) or a copper bowl (*zesin aiyag*).

**Slippers** are in European sizes up to about 36 (US 12). The patterns are typical of traditional Mongolian designs that may or may not have a particular meaning. Mongolians don't usually wear these, preferring cheap plastic sandals, but they do usually wear house shoes of some sort indoors. Grab some to wear during your trip.

**Ankle bones** or *shagai* can be found in most souvenir shops with directions in English, though the instructions are often hard to decipher. When you buy a small set, it is usually just a fortune telling set with only four pieces, but if you buy more, you can play a real game. See more about the game in the Mongolian Games section (p54).

**Kazakh bags** and wall hangings have bright patterns and are time-consuming to make, which means you should expect to pay a little more for them than for other souvenirs, though you're probably not going to break the bank. If you go to the Kazakh regions (Khovd, Bayan Ulgii), you'll find better deals.

**Snuff bottles** are something all Mongolian men and many women have. They're made from stone and precious metals like coral, jade, nephrite, chalcedony, onyx, aventurine, rock-crystal, porcelain, glass, silver, copper, etc. In the past they used to take months and even years to make, but nowadays the process is a lot quicker. They are classified as small (5-6 cm), medium (6-9 cm), and large (8-10 cm) and according to whether they are polished inside and out. The most expensive ones will be made of the rarest materials and polished inside. If you're going to be around for *Tsagaan Sar*, get one because you'll get a lot of use out of it.

**Copper bowls** are a must-have for any Mongolian household. During ceremonies and special events, they are passed around so each person can take a drink, much like communion. Shop around for the best deal because some are more intricately adorned than others. To clean them if they tarnish, Mongolians suggest using a little Comet or similar detergent.

**Traditional Mongolian clothing,** including the *deel* and *khantaz*, can be made to order in a few days. Pre-made versions are also available in the markets for about the same price. If you buy one made to order, you'll be measured and then have to return for a fitting or two. You usually have to pay for the fabric, which can often be purchased from the tailor themselves, as well as the service.

Boots come in a few different styles and sizes up to about European size 36 (US 12). Pairs with upturned toes look really cool, but they're hard to walk in. The more practical Buriat boots are dark colored with rounded toes and more traction on the soles but have little ornamentation. Depending on your personal style, you might be able to pull off some of these looks back home.

**Cashmere** is cheaper in Mongolia, but it's still expensive. The two most notable Mongolian companies are Goyo and Altai. They have sweaters, dresses, hats, and sometimes yarn, which is pretty hard to come by in Mongolia since most raw cashmere goes directly to China for processing.

## Food

Mongolian food consists mainly of meat, fat, flour, and rice adorned by potatoes, carrots, cabbage, sweet peppers (capsicum), and turnips. Despite the variety of goods that came to Mongolia during various points in history, not many spices fell off the wagons, and they haven't found their way into the Mongolian dinner bowls either. The main flavorings found in Mongolian cooking are salt, which is used excessively, and onion and garlic, which are used sparingly. Garlic and black pepper are often unappealing to Mongolians and described as too hot, but they can be readily found in grocery stores, even in the countryside. Ketchup and soy sauce are also easy to find and can save a bland dish, though not an entire cuisine.

To say simply that Mongolian food is bland is a little misleading, however. Mongolians tend not to use many extra flavorings in their dishes, but that's not to say that their food doesn't have flavor. In fact, the meat and dairy products in Mongolia often have a pungent flavor unique to their food because of the animals' diets. Many of the foods taste similar, though, so the food can seem monotonous if you prefer a lot of variety or a diet rich in vegetables.

You won't find corporate farms and slaughterhouses in Mongolia. Mongolian herders only raise their animals on free range grasses and humanely kill and slaughter their animals. For this reason, you might notice that the animals seem smaller and a little leaner than you are probably used to seeing.

One Mongolian meal you won't likely find on a restaurant menu is *khorhog*, but it's perhaps the finest culinary achievement in the land. Using a large, sealable metal container typically used for storing milk or water, raw meat and vegetables are slow cooked to delicious, mouth-watering perfection using hot rocks. The rocks are put in the fire while the animal is skinned and cleaned so they are plenty warm. The potatoes, carrots, onions, and garlic are placed in the jerry can with the meat and some water. Then the hot rocks get dumped in, the top is sealed, and the whole thing is placed on the fire's smoldering ashes. It takes about 4 hours to prep and cook, so it is usually prepared for gatherings and picnics. This is the true Mongolian feast.

*Traveling in Mongolia*

## Mongolian BBQ is neither Mongolian nor Barbeque

Sorry, but Mongolian BBQ is neither Mongolian nor barbeque. Thought up by Taiwanese marketing folks, this term is as authentic as chicken Kiev, a dish born from the brains of New York chefs and designed to sound exotic but which you will not find in Kiev. American chain restaurants have gone a step further by creating a silly origin story about Chinggis Khan and his thundering hordes taking a break from a long day of pillaging to grill some meat on their swords and other such nonsense. From the spices to the sauces to piles of vegetables, you'll quickly find out that there's nothing Mongolian about it.

But, if you do find yourself in UB at BD's or the cheaper Mongolian-owned Altai, do take a peek at the griddle top and see if you can guess which pile of food belongs to a Mongolian and which belongs to a Westerner. Don't forget to have some sheep fat, too!

# TYPICAL FOODS IN RESTAURANTS & GROCERY STORES

## Items at a Restaurant or Café

| | | |
|---|---|---|
| Цуйван | Tsuivan | Fresh, flat, handmade noodles with bits of meat, fat, and vegetables |
| Бууз | Buuz | Steamed dumplings filled with meat and fat, usually mutton |
| Банш | Bansh | Small dumplings. Usually part of a soup or steamed. |
| Хуушуур | Khuushuur | Fried unleavened bread pocket filled with meat |
| Пирошки | Peroshki | Fried leavened bread pocket filled with meat and rice |
| Шөл | Shul | Soup. Always has meat and fat (e.g., vegetable soup is soup with meat and vegetables). |
| Салат | Salat | Salad (pronounced "sal-AT"). Usually with a dressing of mayonnaise or vinegar. |
| Хуурга | Khuurga | Dish of food. Almost always bits of meat with a stir-fried vegetable. Sometimes served on a cast iron hot plate. (Exception: *Budaatai huurga* is like *tsuivan* with rice instead of flat noodles.) |
| Хормог | Khormog | Mixture |
| Тефтель | Teftel | Meatballs |
| Цагаан Хол | Tsagaan Khool | White food or vegetarian food |
| Цагаан Идээ | Tsagaan Idee | Dairy products |

## Drink

| | | |
|---|---|---|
| Уундаа | Uundaa | Beverage or sometimes carbonated beverage like soda |
| Ус | Us | Water (pronounced "oh-s") |
| Жуус | Juus | Juice |
| Кола | Kola | Cola |
| Пиво | Piv | Beer |
| Архи | Arkhi | Vodka (most know the word "vodka," too) |
| Айраг | Airag | Koumiss. Fermented mare's milk. |
| (Сүүтэй Сүүтэй) Цай | (Suutei) Tsai | (Milk) Tea |
| Кофе | Kofe | Coffee (sometimes pronounced "copy") |

## Condiments

| | | |
|---|---|---|
| Давс | Dowse | Salt |
| Перец | Perets | Pepper |
| Кечуп | Kechup | Ketchup |
| Цуу | Tsuu | Soy sauce |

## Vegetables

| | | |
|---|---|---|
| Байцаа | Baitsaa | Cabbage |
| Лууван | Luuwun | Carrot |
| Чинжүү | Chinjuu | Capsicum, bell peppers |
| Помидор | Pomidor | Tomato |
| Сонгино | Songino | Onion |
| Сармис | Sarmis | Garlic |
| Манжин | Manjin | Turnip |

## Grains

| | | |
|---|---|---|
| Будаа | Budaa | Rice |
| Гурил | Guril | Flour |
| Талх | Talkh | Bread |
| Боов | Boov | Pastry, usually fried, sometimes lightly sweetened |
| Гоймон | Goimon | Noodles |

## Sweets

| | | |
|---|---|---|
| Саахар /Чихэр | Saakhar | Sugar |
| Чихэр | Chikher | Candy, sugar, sweet |
| Шоколад | Shokolad | Chocolate |

## Milk Products

| | | |
|---|---|---|
| Сүү | Suu | Milk |
| Тараг | Tarag | Yogurt |
| Зайрмаг | Zairmag | Ice cream |
| Масло | Masil | Butter |
| Бяслаг | Byaslag | Cheese |

## Meat

| | | |
|---|---|---|
| Мах | Makh | Meat |
| Хонины мах | Khonni makh | Sheep meat, mutton (not lamb) |
| Ямааны мах | Yamaani makh | Goat meat |
| Үхрийн мах | Ukhriin makh | Cow meat, beef |
| Шарбуурцгийн Мах | Shar Buurtsgiin Makh | Soy meat |
| Өөх | Uukh | Fat |
| Хям | Khyam | Sausage, usually fatty and naturally flavored |

### Airag

*Airag* is fermented mare's milk and is drunk not only by Mongolians but also peoples from Siberia to Turkey who sometimes use cow milk instead. In fact, in Turkish it's called *koumiss*, a word we also use in English to describe the drink, and the Russians call it *kef*. It has a sour taste unlike almost anything else. Decide for yourself what you think it tastes like.

Traditionally, the milk is put into a special hide, often the stomach of a cow, and thoroughly agitated. The bag is then hung for a few weeks during which it is smacked on the sides with a special stick to help mix the fermenting milk with the enzymes. After two weeks, it is tasted, and if the mix is right, it is served as is. It is important to be careful because if the fermentation is too short, it can cause your digestive system to back up. If it's too long, it can cause the opposite for a day or so.

Some regions, like Arkhangai Aimag, are known for their great tasting brew. Nowadays, their *airag* is shipped around and used as starter cultures. Using a starter culture requires far less time and can be done in a recycled Coke bottle instead of cow stomach. Really, any *airag* can be added to a container of milk, and in a few days it's ready to drink.

---

### Throat Flicking to Show Intoxication

In the West, a hand gesture we might use to imply someone is intoxicated is to hold an imaginary glass in our hand and mockingly tip it toward our faces. In Mongolia, it's a flick of the middle finger to the throat.

---

## EATING VEGETARIAN

For years, vegetarians, vegans, and others with an aversion to all-meat-all-the-time eating habits have been warned to stay away from Mongolia.

Unlike Buddhism elsewhere in Asia, Mongolia's unique brand of Buddhism does not emphasize sparing the lives of animals for food, probably out of pragmatism. The country's dry, mountainous landscape and nomadic culture mean that people have historically ignored agriculture and depended instead on meat and dairy products for sustenance.

This high-protein diet fueled Chinggis Khan's hordes as they swept across the known world some 800 years ago. Historians have noted that Mongolian soldiers could ride for days at a time, reputedly drinking blood from their horses' necks for nourishment on the go. Even more than meat, the traditional Mongolian diet depends on dairy products: milk tea, fermented milk, yogurt, cheeses, creams, curds, and more. Milk is viewed as sacred; each morning, women in the countryside and in urban apartment blocks make offerings to the sky, throwing ladles of the day's first milk tea in the four cardinal directions.

Fortunately for vegetarians and vegans, an unlikely vegetarian movement has taken root in Mongolia in recent years. The first vegetarian restaurant in Mongolia, Ananda's Café, opened in 2006 and today more than 20 vegetarian and vegan restaurants dot Ulaanbaatar. Vegetarian restaurants are increasingly easy to find in the *aimag* centers as well; cities as near as Darkhan and as far as Khovd play host to meat-free eateries. In smaller cities like Ulaangom, restaurants that cater to tourists and traveling Mongolians now include meatless options on their menus. Eating in is getting easier too, as tofu, gluten, and dehydrated soy products spread to finer *aimag* supermarkets.

The trend is driven in part by the growing economy and telecommunications industries, which make it easier for people to find information on health and nutrition. A more obvious influence is the religious revival in post-communist Mongolia; religious groups or their adherents own nearly all of the country's vegetarian restaurants.

In Ulaanbaatar, vegetarian menus differ by location. At the original meat-free spot, Ananda's Café, fresh vegetables like cauliflower, eggplant, and zucchini get the spotlight, starring in vegetable medleys that change daily. Perhaps the most popular veggie restaurant, Luna Blanca features an imaginative menu, heavy on meat substitutes and with a distinct south Asian influence. The Loving Hut chain, an international franchise with a half dozen or more locations in UB, is run by disciples of the intriguing quasi-Buddhist spiritual leader known as the Supreme Master Ching Hai. These restaurants serve stir fry dishes with a vague nod to Chinese food. Most of the smaller, independent vegetarian restaurants, like Erkhem Ayalguu near Gandan monastery, simply replace the meaty bits of Mongolian standards like *buuz* and *tsuivan* with soy.

Exciting as the availability of vegetarian fare in the capital and *aimag* centers may be, you'll still need to pack all your own food to the countryside if you intend to avoid meat completely. And, sadly, by eating vegetarian or vegan, you'll find it almost impossible to enjoy the legendary hospitality of rural Mongolia. It may be worthwhile to consider that Mongolian meat is almost always free range, grass-fed, and antibiotic free-before you decide to pass up a plate of *buuz* offered to you by a Mongolian host.

Traveling in Mongolia

## Humane Slaughter in Mongolia

Smaller animals in Mongolian are turned off from the inside. To kill a sheep or goat, an incision is made on its underside while it lays on its back alive. The butcher reaches inside to pinch a main artery, and the animal quickly expires.

# Time

Most of Mongolia shares the same time as Beijing (GMT+8). Khovd, Bayan Ulgii, and Uvs aimags are in a different time zone, one hour behind the big city and the rest of the country. Summer days begin in the middle of the night and the light remains until after 9:00 p.m. In the dead of winter, the sun comes up by 9:00 a.m. and goes back down by around 4:00 p.m.

Time is relatively fluid all over the country. Start times for meetings, concerts, and social events are generally suggestions rather than certainties. Before the advent of mechanized clocks, the story goes, Mongolians separated the day into twelve roughly two-hour blocks, determined by the placement of the sun and named after the same animals as the years in the lunar calendar. Thus, "in the time of the horse" could mean anytime within a relatively lengthy period. Add the facts that travel in Mongolia was subject to the elements and your horse's mood that day, and you get a culture with a flexible interpretation of punctuality.

Outside of UB, expect to wait for services with no sense of urgency. Greetings of tea and candy eat into appointments, so try to plan that into your itinerary. If you're a person that needs to be scheduled to the minute to have a good time, Mongolia might be frustrating for you. Just try to relax and go with the flow.

# Transportation

## BY AIR

International flights to and from Mongolia go through Moscow, Beijing, Berlin, Tokyo, and Seoul, and less reliably through Almaty via Uskemen, Kazakhstan. You won't need to worry about travel visas for connecting flights through these countries as long as you are just there for a layover and are not planning to leave the airport. If you're flying Aeroflot, be prepared for the possibility of lost luggage. Air China is the cheapest, but it is prone to delays and cancellations. MIAT Mongolian Airlines, the national carrier, flies to a handful of international destinations, but you may not find tickets available from outside the country. Korean Air is posh and comfortable with the best service. Our recommendation: if you have the choice, pay the extra $100 or so and fly Korean Air. There are very few visa requirements for visitors entering

Mongolia up to 30 days, but be aware that if you want to stay longer, you must register that plan within the first 7 days or risk exit delays and penalties when you try to leave. You can register only in UB. Please, see more about visa requirements on page 65.

To and from Kazakhstan there is one flight a week between Ulgii and Almaty (Алматы), with a stop in Uskemen (Өскемен), Kazakhstan. This flight, on the Kazakhstani airline SCAT, is not the most reliable and is extremely difficult to plan for. The airline's website's font does not format correctly on many computers, and you can only buy tickets, which cost about MNT320,000 ($240) one way to Uskemen and MNT450,000 ($330) to Almata in Ulgii. One of the Ulgii-based travel agencies may be able to help you acquire a ticket in advance. To buy a ticket yourself, go to the Ulgii Air (Өлгий Эйр) office on the first floor of the government building and turn left at the front desk.

The customs agents in charge of the whole affair do not see many non-Kazakh or non-Mongolian travelers on this flight, so be prepared for bureaucratic headaches going and coming.

If you are short on time and have the money, flying domestically could be your best bet to catch many sites all around the country. EZnis Airways (www.eznisairways.com) has been around for a few years now. EZnis flies to Altai, Bayankhongor, Choibalsan, Dalanzadgad, Donoi (Zavkhan), Khovd, Murun, Ovoot, Oyu Tolgoi, Tavan Tolgoi, Ulaangom, and Ulgii (as well as Ulan-Ude in Russia and Hailar in China). There are separate prices for foreigners, but if you want to visit locations out west, you can save yourself several days of travel. EZnis is safe and comfortable.

Aero Mongolia (www.aeromongolia.mn) flies to fewer locations than EZnis, and you'll have a harder time finding information about them in English. They travel to Altai, Dalanzadgad, Khovd, Ulgii, and Ulaangom. If you have a couple hundred dollars to spend, flying will save you more on comfort and time than you can even imagine.

Mongolian Airlines Group (www.mongolianairlines.com) is the newest domestic carrier. Their fleet is a mere two planes, and three of their ten destinations are mine sites (Tavan Tolgoi, Oyu Tolgoi, and Ovoot). Of more interest to tourists are their flights to Byankhongor, Dornod, Khovsgul, Khovd, Omnogovi, and Ovorkhangai aimags. All flights originate from and return to Ulaanbaatar, naturally. Mongolian Airlines Group began flights very recently, and the authors cannot vouch for the quality of its service. Ticket prices were not available on their website at the time of writing.

Traveling in Mongolia

# BY BUS

In Ulaanbaatar the two main bus stations for domestic travel are the Dragon Tuv (pronounced "dargon"), which runs all the buses traveling to the west, and the Bayanzurkh Tovchoo (pronounced "buy-in-zurkh"), which runs all the buses to the east. Be sure to buy your tickets at least a day in advance for most destinations, and buy them in the morning to ensure a seat for the next day. During the *Tsagaan Sar* (Lunar New Year) and *Naadam* (summer sports festival), you should purchase tickets two days in advance if possible. Buses leave around the scheduled departure time (especially for closer destinations), unlike any other shared vehicles in Mongolia.

There are many pros and cons to traveling by bus, though most foreigners prefer buses over other shared transportation options because they can purchase an

## Overland Travel Expectations

Traveling overland via public transportation in Mongolia may be one of the greatest tests of patience a Western tourist will ever endure. Any, or all, of the following inconveniences are likely to occur during a standard long-distance road trip:

- ✓ The vehicle will likely leave several hours later than advertised, so there's usually no need to panic. The longer the trip, the later the departure time will be.
- ✓ The vehicle might suffer a flat tire.
- ✓ The driver may stop at any number of random *gers* for tea.
- ✓ The vehicle might suffer engine trouble.
- ✓ Between the 23 passengers, excess cargo, and the goat, you will have approximately one quarter of a seat, which might be a lap, to yourself.
- ✓ Fellow passengers will happily use you as a pillow. Or as a bed.
- ✓ Children (and some adults) will vomit, repeatedly.
- ✓ The vehicle will suffer a second flat tire.
- ✓ Unpaved roads and cramped quarters will make it nearly impossible to sleep, even on a 45-hour ride.
- ✓ Your fellow passengers might be drunk. This will make them incessantly inquisitive, aggressive, or happy to use you as a pillow.
- ✓ The vehicle will suffer a third flat tire.

Fortunately, there are some upsides to overland travel. For one thing, if you can make it to Khovd or Bayan-Ulgii in an overloaded bus, you'll be hard pressed to find a more sanity-challenging experience in Mongolia or anywhere. You'll be basically invincible. Buses and *purgons* are also a good place to make friends if you can keep your spirits up, and people who traveled with you will remember you if you see them again after you've reached your destination. Best of all, road trips are a guaranteed venue to hear true Mongolian folk singing. There is something entirely magical about cruising across the Gobi under a full moon with a car full of Mongolians singing the slow, sweet songs of the steppes.

individual seat, not merely the opportunity to be in the vehicle. Buses, because they are so large, can make the long bumpy hauls more tolerable, and they are relatively safe. Even so, they are still pretty uncomfortable by most Western standards, especially if you're not a small person. Some have air-conditioning, and some have better heat than others. If you are at all prone to motion sickness, be sure to pack Dramamine.

> You will not be able to book Trans-Mongolian tickets from anywhere in Mongolia other than Ulaanbaatar.

Luggage gets packed under the bus, on overhead shelves, under seats, and in the aisles. There will be a spot somewhere for your luggage even if it doesn't look like it. This may mean your luggage will be under the bus, leaving your bags very dusty and dirty by the end of the trip. If not, you will most likely want your bag to be something malleable, so that it can fit into a real-life game of Tetris played in the middle aisle. Put anything fragile in a smaller bag to go overhead.

Paved roads to most destinations, especially the west, are more likely to be non-existent the further you travel from UB. Some trips west are scheduled for multiple days with multiple drivers, and sometimes breakdowns turn a trip of hours into one of days. There are scheduled food and bathroom stops along the way, but long distance drivers never stop to sleep. If you feel you absolutely cannot sleep on a bus, you may want to reconsider how you travel out west, although you'll probably be in a fatigue-induced state of semi-consciousness after the first 24 hours anyway.

International routes come in from Erlian, China and Naushki and Tashanta, Russia. All are almost always destined for UB, though some go to Bayan-Ulgii or Khovd from Astana and Almata, Kazakhstan via Russia.

## International Buses from China

Zamiin-Uud is the only border crossing for international travelers. Its counterpart on the Mongolian side is Erlian. **From Erlian to Beijing**, you can book a 12-hour sleeper bus (with beds instead of seats—sorry tall guys) from the bus station (around the corner from the train station) for around RMB200. **From Beijing to Erlian**, take the overnight bus from Beijing's Luili Qiao bus station or the local train to Erlian (RMB100-200, 12 hours). The train leaves Mongolia's Zamiin-Uud (MNT20,000; 14 hours) at 5:50 p.m. every day and arrives the next morning at 8:00 a.m. in Ulaanbaatar.

Taking the creative alternatives instead of the direct train from Ulaanbaatar to Beijing or vice versa can take you an extra day including accommodation (RMB10-30 in Erlian, close to the rail station), and it can be a hassle—especially since the train arrives in Erlian overnight. It can save you some money, though.

Traveling in Mongolia

## The Chinese Border Train/Bus/Microbus/Train Scenario Fair Warning

On both ends of the China-Mongolia border crossing, some travelers choose to take a bus from the train station to the border and then a microbus or Jeep while trying to save perhaps ten dollars on their trip toward Ulaanbaatar. You, however, will not do this because you are far smarter than that and realize that saving ten hypothetical dollars isn't worth the hassle in the middle of the night, the language barriers, and the likely rip-off you will encounter at some point from a taxi driver, bus driver, or border guard. You will stay on the comfortable, safe, reliable train nearly undisturbed. If you're on a tight budget and want to substitute bus for train travel to or from Erlian and Beijing, you can save money by taking the bus from Erlian on the Chinese border to Beijing and a direct bus from Ulan Ude, Russia to Ulaanbaatar.

## To & from Russia

The border at Tsagaan Nuur Soum (Цагаан нүүр сум) in Bayan-Ulgii and its Russian counterpart Tashanta, Russia, is one of a very few Mongolian land border crossings open to foreigners. This is a common place of entry for cars participating in the Mongol Rally. However, there is no public transportation across the border, and Tsagaan Nuur itself is a poor and sad-looking district despite its location on the border. To get into Russia without a car of your own, ask around the market in Ulgii. You might find a merchant making a run up to re-stock their shop, but there is no guarantee.

At Naushki, Russia, the counterpart to Mongolia's Sukhbaatar in Selenge Aimag, you can take a bus over the border and then arrange transportation to Ulaanbaatar. Buses from Ulan-Ude in Russia can be booked straight through to Ulaanbaatar, an 11-hour trip.

## To & from Kazakhstan

Buses and the occasional *purgon* or *mikr* (Russian and Korean-made minibuses respectively) will leave from Ulgii's market headed for Astana and Almata with a few other stops on the way. Depending on the vehicle, seat prices will range from about MNT100,000 to MNT120,000 to Astana and MNT120,000 and up to Almata. Mongolia does not border Kazakhstan, so it is necessary to travel briefly through Russia on the way. Check visa requirements for your nationality; American passport holders will need a Russian transit visa in addition to a visa for Kazakhstan. Visas cannot be obtained in Ulgii, but both Russia and Kazakhstan have embassies in Ulaanbaatar, although you may want to go through a travel agency to get the Russian visa (Legend Tours is recommended).

## Protect your Twinkie!

People will pack over, sit, or step on your luggage throughout the trip if it's inside the bus. Think of your bag as a Twinkie. Your most important possessions in your bag are the creamy filling. To ensure the creamy filling will be there later when you want to enjoy it, protect your Twinkie!

# Domestic Travel

## SHARED TRANSPORTATION

There are a few options for shared and private transportation, but they often cost more than buses. These can be your best and only options outside of UB, especially if you choose to travel outside provincial capitals or between provinces. They leave when they are full, not necessarily when the driver says. This is usually several hours later than planned. Arrange the day of or in advance, usually at the market. If you have a phone, you can leave your number and the driver will pick you up. Passengers typically pay drivers together at the first gas station before heading out of town. Shared transportation out of Ulaanbaatar to most destinations can be found at Narantuul, the large black market on UB's south side.

**Furgons (*purgon* or Фургон):** Bare-bones, flat-grey Russian minivans with four-wheel drive, which drivers are not afraid to use. Even on luxury tours, this is the vehicle most drivers choose for the long haul. They have seats for 11 but usually travel with at least 15 and as many 25 or more. Not a bad way to travel, but it is cramped. If you get car sick, don't face backwards or else take Dramamine.

**Mikr or Microbus (Микр or Микробүс):** Vans with seating for 12 to 15. These Korean- or Japanese-made vehicles are more comfortable than *purgons* because they have softer seats, the windows open, and there is a little more leg room. They're not rugged 4x4 vehicles though, so they are more prone to breakdowns. Often, luggage is strapped to the top.

**Car, Mashin (Машин), Taxi (Такси):** Often the most crowded from of shared transportation. Intercity rides are not very comfortable because these small 4-door Hyundais or Nissans are usually packed with at least five passengers, sometimes a few more. This means lap sitting or one-cheeking it for hours at a time. Cars usually cost a little more, but they have more freedom to leave on time than the larger shared rides and make pretty good time. For more leg room and to leave more quickly, you can pay for extra seats or negotiate for day-trips as a private hire.

*Make Strangers Into Friends with Candy*

When you first hop into a vehicle, offer candy, crackers, or other small sharable food items to everyone. Not only will it break the ice, your new friends will be more likely to look out for you if the need arises. The less anonymous you are, the better.

Traveling in Mongolia

## PRIVATE HIRE

You can book a private car through a guesthouse or travel agency. They almost always come with a driver for whom you may have to provide food and accommodations, but this form of

> **Car rental companies**
> www.sixt.com
> www.offroad.mn
> www.4x4offroadmongolia.com

transportation will give you the most freedom to set your itinerary. If you've ever wondered where they film those ridiculous off-road commercials for Jeeps and SUVs, you won't find them so absurd after you've driven across Mongolia in one, but you'll probably wonder why they don't film the ads in Mongolia where every feature of the vehicle is put to the test.

**Russian Jeep (Жийп or Жаран ес or "69"):** Usually grey with a soft black top and bare on the inside, these Jeeps can go almost anywhere, albeit uncomfortably. Even if it breaks down, it has been such a ubiquitous utility vehicle for so long that spare parts can be found in even the remotest villages. The 69 or *jarin yos* (pronounced "jar-in-use") should be a last resort for shared transport, but it is a good option for private use.

**SUV, Landcruiser (Ланд or "Land"):** The most expensive but most rugged transportation option you'll find. You know you're riding in style if you find yourself in one of these. It's not the budget option by any means, but it's by far the best way to travel if you have the money. The vehicles are usually fairly new, have seat belts, and can make what would be a 15-hour bus trip in closer to 8 hours. If you've rented the whole vehicle, you can plan your own itinerary. Some companies like, Sixt.com, let you pay with a credit card. You will pay by the day and the kilometer.

### Carcass Cargo
Don't be surprised if your bench seat partner used to be on the hoof. Mongolians travel with carcasses, raw meat, and furs on their way to or from market. If you're uncomfortable, just speak up (or gesture). Someone will likely switch with you, or they'll move the offending merchandise if you show you don't like it.

## INTERCITY BUS TRAVEL

Intercity bus travel is by either via bus, coach, microbus, or pugon. The **bus**, also known as "Post Bus," brings the mail. It is fairly reliable and you will have your own seat. Traveling by **micro** or **purgon**, also known as "an unpleasant way to travel," is unreliable as they breakdown often. Plus, you may or may not be sharing a seat with a goat. Avoid if possible.

The following schedules are provided by the Ministry of Transportation. All travel times, prices, and modes of transportation are subject to change without notice. Travel times may vary.

| Destination | Departure Day | Departure Time | Station | Form of Transport |
|---|---|---|---|---|
| Arkhangai | Daily | 8:00 a.m. | Dragon Center | Bus or coach |
| | Tue, Sat | 9:00 a.m. | | |
| Bayan-Ulgii | Daily | 3:00- 8:00 p.m. | Dragon Center | Microbus or purgon |
| Bayankhongor | Daily | 8:00 a.m. | Dragon Center | Bus or coach |
| Bulgan | Mon, Wed, Fri | 8:00 a.m. | Dragon Center | Bus or coach |
| | Tue, Thu, Sat | 10:00 a.m. | | |
| Darkhan | Daily | Every hour between 10:00 a.m. and 7:00 p.m. | Dragon Center | Bus or coach |
| | Daily | 9:00 a.m.-9:00 p.m. | | Microbus or purgon |
| Dornod | Daily | 8:00 a.m. | Bayanzurkh Tovchoo | Bus or coach |
| | Daily | 9:00-10:00 a.m. | | Microbus or purgon |
| Dundgobi | Daily | 8:00 a.m. | Dragon Center | Bus or coach |

| Destination | Departure Day | Departure Time | Station | Form of Transport |
|---|---|---|---|---|
| Erdenet | Daily | Every hour between 10:00 a.m. and 4:00 p.m. | Dragon Center | Bus or coach |
| Gobi-Altai | Tue, Wed, Fri, Sun | 10:00 a.m. | Dragon Center | Bus or coach |
| | Daily | 11:00 a.m.-2:00 p.m. | | Microbus or purgon |
| Gobisumber | Daily (except Tues) | 3:00 p.m. | Narantuul Market | Bus or coach |
| | Tue | | Bayanzrkh Tovchoo | |
| Kharkhorin (Uvur.) | Daily | 12:00 noon-3:00 p.m. | Dragon Center | Bus or coach |
| Khentii | Daily | 8:00 a.m. | Bayanzurkh Tovchoo | Bus or coach |
| Khovd | Mon, Wed, Fri, Sun | 4:00 p.m. | Dragon Center | Bus or coach |
| | Daily | 3:00-8:00 p.m. | Narantuul Market | Microbus or purgon |
| Khujirt (Uvur.) | Daily | 8:00 a.m. | Dragon Center | Bus or coach |
| Khuvsgul | Daily | 3:00 p.m. | Dragon Center | Bus or coach |
| | Daily | 2:00-4:00 p.m. | Tevriin Tovchoo | Microbus or purgon |

| Destination | Departure Day | Departure Time | Station | Form of Transport |
|---|---|---|---|---|
| Sukhbaatar | Daily | 8:00 a.m. | Bayanzurkh Tovchoo | Bus or coach |
| Tuv | Daily | Every hour between 7:30 a.m. and 8:30 p.m. | Tevriin Tovchoo | Microbus or purgon |
| Umnugovi | Daily | 8:00 a.m. | Bayanzurkh Tovchoo | Bus or coach |
| Uvs | Wed, Fri, Sun | 3:00 p.m. | Dragon Center | Bus or coach |
| | Daily | 3:00-8:00 p.m. | Narantuul Market | Microbus or purgon |
| Uvurkhangai | Daily (except Sun) | 8:00 a.m., 2:00 p.m. | Dragon Center | Bus or coach |
| | Daily | 2:00-4:00 p.m. | Narantuul Market | Microbus or purgon |
| Zavkhan | Mon, Wed, Fri | 12:00 noon | Dragon Center | Bus or coach |
| | Daily | 3:00-8:00 p.m. | Narantuul Market | Microbus or purgon |

Traveling in Mongolia

## TRAIN TRANSPORT

Trains come into Mongolia via Russia in the north and China in the southeast. While there are various stops along the Trans-Mongolian line of the Trans-Siberian railway within Mongolia, there is only one point of entry at either border.

Trains coming from Russia enter through Naushki, Russia and trains from China enter though Erlian, China. Unless you have another destination along the line in mind, it would be best to purchase tickets from wherever you are in Russia or China directly to Ulaanbaatar.

Obtaining train tickets to either Russia or China from Mongolia is a different process than in-country travel. These tickets are purchased at the Mongolian Rail (MTZ) building across the street from the train station and to your left if you are facing away from the train station.

---

### Let the Guesthouses Buy Your Tickets and Arrange Visas

If you are lucky enough to experience the cheap and convenient treasure that is a guesthouse in Ulaanbaatar, pay them to buy your international train ticket and visas out of Mongolia because it's really, really worth it. (You will have to give them your passport, but don't worry, they'll give it back.) They'll stand in long lines for you and make sure you get what you're looking for. The language barrier is as great as the distance from Mongolia to Beijing and Moscow, and customer service isn't a priority in most train stations. Trust us: you would much rather be relaxing and exploring Mongolia instead of seething inside a train station for two hours attempting to buy a ticket to Beijing only to leave with a slip of paper that says you *intend* to buy a train ticket in the future.

---

You can purchase tickets or *billet* (билет) for trains within Mongolia at the Ulaanbaatar Train Station known as either Вокзал (*vokzal* in Russian) or Галт тэрэгний буудал (*galt teregnii buudal* in Mongolian). To purchase the tickets, find the building on the left as you're facing the station. The lounge and restaurants are in the building on the right.

Traveling around Mongolia by train can be one of the most interesting and stress-free ways to visit places. It's also the safest. Unfortunately, the routes are limited to north and south, pretty much confined to the path that the Trans-Mongolian takes from Russia to China, and they are slow. Nevertheless, they run on time, and there are some great places to see along the way. The main stops through Mongolia are Sukhbaatar (northern border), Darkhan, Erdenet, Choir, Ulaanbaatar, Sainshand, and Zamiid-Uud (southern border).

There are three classes of train compartments, reflecting the level of privacy and comfort you can expect in the old Russian-style wagons. If you aren't traveling for a long distance (i.e., UB to Beijing), getting a first class private coupe isn't really worth

---

## I Choo-Choo-Choose You, Train!

So you wanna ride the train, eh? Brilliant. You should. If you are starting your journey from either Russia or China (or eventually using these countries as points of entry), there are some things to consider including price, convenience, and time.

There are many confusing and often erroneous train and bus time tables, even displayed on the walls of the ticket booth you're standing at. While the actual days and times are likely to change throughout the year without notice, one thing is for sure: the time printed on your ticket, is the time you leave. Be there a half an hour before to board. Then again, don't be entirely surprised if you have to wait for some unexplained reason.

the extra money considering that second class is much cheaper and still pretty comfortable. Because the ride is so long, you might be better off taking a *purgon* or bus if third class is your only option, unless you're up for an adventure. However, if you're traveling the 30 hours from UB to Beijing, do it in style; splurge for the coupe.

**First class** or "coupe" (купэ) compartments are closed cabins with soft bench seats that double as beds. Benches above fold down to accommodate a total of four passengers. Coupe (pronounced "coop-ay") tickets give you your own comfy bed in a private cabin, but unless you are traveling with three other people, there is a solid chance you will be in a private cabin full of strangers who might have different bathing habits than you. This can be a fun way to interact with new folks by playing card games, drinking, singing, and showing pictures. Or it can be a stinking holding cell with drunks who won't stop playing cards and forcing you to repeatedly look at pictures of people you don't know in places you'd rather not see.

**Second class** or "half coupe" (*hagas coupe*, хагас купэ) are open compartments nearly identical to the coupe but without a door, making them airier. They are a fine choice if you have ear plugs. If you're tall, your legs will hang off the end, and you will be bumped awake constantly unless you assume the fetal position. Despite some drawbacks, second class is the best deal for comfort and price.

**Third class** goes by many names including hard sleeper, public car (*obshii vagon*, обший вагон), and third class (*guruv dugaar zereg*, гурув дүгаар зэрэг). This is the most economical way to travel, but third class cars don't offer nearly the comfort you might crave. There tends to be a much more social atmosphere here. (Read: it might be smoky, and you're almost guaranteed encounters with unwanted drunks looking to make a new best friend.)

Traveling in Mongolia

---

## Russia to Mongolia: Pick the Right Mongolian Destination

In summer, there are daily trains from Irkutsk, Russia, to Ulaanbaatar ($85). Along this train line there are a few stops of interest, namely Sukhbaatar (Selenge Aimag) and Darkhan, so you may choose to purchase tickets to one of these destinations and then continue on to UB from there. And if you only want to go to Khuvsgul Aimag to see the lake, you can get there from Darkhan without reaching UB by bus (MNT30,000; 24 hours).

If you do book a bus to cross the border into Mongolia from Naushki (the last Russian stop), make sure it's to Sukhbaatar, not Altanbulag. The same goes for buses from Ulan Ude. Don't book a bus to Kyakhta. You'll have to get to Altanbulag in Mongolia and then find transportation to Sukhbaatar before continuing on your journey. Also, you can't always buy tickets from Naushki to Ulaanbaatar.

You can pretty much bet that there will be a train from Ulaanbaatar into Beijing ($250, 31 hours) every Thursday and Sunday and from Ulaanbaatar into Moscow ($450, 4 days) every Thursday as well as every Tuesday and Friday from May through September.

All of the important information on the ticket is in the upper right hand corner. The first line indicates the train number and departure date. The second line is the carriage number followed by your seat number. The third line is the departure date. Finally, the fourth line is the departure time. It is important to take note of the departure time because unlike most other forms of Mongolian travel, trains leave on time.

The M20 bus and the T4 trolley will take you between the train station and Sukhbaatar Square, and the M24 goes to and from the Dragon Center bus station. From Teeverin Tovchoo transportation center, take the 41 bus. The bus marked "Ботаник" will take you from Sukhbaatar Square to Bayanzurkh bus station.

## Know Your Visa Entrance & Exit Requirements and Plan Ahead

Most foreign visitors will require a visa prior to arriving in Mongolia. US residents can stay in the country up to 90 days without a visa, but must register within seven days that they intend to stay more than 30 days or face many exiting problems and fines. (For more, see page 65.)

## International Train Schedule

| Train | From | To | Depart Day | Depart Time | Arrival Day | Arrival Time | 1st Class | 2nd Class |
|-------|------|-----|------------|-------------|-------------|--------------|-----------|-----------|
| #5 | UB | Moscow | Tues | 13:50 | Sat | 2:28 p.m. | $465 | $325 |
| #6 | Moscow | UB | Wed | 21:35 | Monday | 7:30 a.m. | $465 | $325 |
| #24 | UB | Beijing | Thurs | 08:05 | Friday | 2:35 p.m. | $235 | $185 |
| #23 | Beijing | UB | Sat | 07:40 | Sat | 1:20 p.m. | $235 | $185 |
| #363 | UB | Irkutsk | Daily | 18:46 | 2 Days Later | 7:58 a.m. | - | $85 |
| #364 | Irkutsk | UB | Daily | 21:00 | 2 Days Later | 7:00 a.m. | - | $85 |

# HORSE TREKKING

Riding a horse is an absolute must for any traveler in Mongolia. However, if you choose to ride across a large portion of Mongolia there are a fair few things to keep in mind. If you plan on taking a tour, then some horseback riding will most likely be included in the package. However, if you are one of those intrepid adventurers that marches to the beat of your own drummer, then there are some things to keep in mind.

First, don't attempt riding a horse by yourself in winter. You will die. If you plan on going in the summer for more than a week, you are going to want two horses; one for riding, and one for carrying your things. Mongolian horses are not used to being alone, so having a pack horse or riding with other people and their horses is strongly recommended. Keep in mind that each horse will cost the same, even if one has been broken for riding and one hasn't. Due to harsh conditions in previous winters, the price of animals has increased. Many herders may not be willing to part with their horses. Normal horse prices can be anywhere between MNT250,000 and MNT300,000 (without saddles and other equipment).

The idea of a "broken horse" is a relative concept in Mongolia. Mongolians can pretty much ride horses as soon as they can walk, so when they break horses, they break them with the understanding that the riders have extensive riding experience. With that being said, these horses may not respond to Western riders in the way you might expect. In addition to that, traditional Mongolian riding gear doesn't allow for full control of the gait, and more often than not the horse will decide on its own pace of travel. Remember, Mongolian horses are generally broken for two purposes: herding and racing. Be patient with your horse and keep in mind that it may be confused as to why it is not involved in either of those activities.

Have a plan, and stick to that plan. The Mongolian countryside is no place for whimsy. It is harsh, it is sparsely populated, and it does not take kindly to lost souls. Many travelers set out into the open steppe with a sort of romanticized idea of a land scattered with gers (i.e., with people who could potentially help them in a pinch). Unfortunately, you will not find this to be the case. While the land is scattered with gers, they are few and incredibly far between.

As with cycling, know your route. This cannot be emphasized enough. It may seem like cheating to have a GPS, but trust me, nobody will think you are any less awesome if you carry one. You should know where the towns are, where the mountains and rivers are, and most importantly where you are, at all times. While much of Mongolia isn't mapped out as extensively as other places, there is still a fair bit of information available.

Bring gifts for people who you may encounter. If you are lucky enough to find a ger, and perhaps to be fed and/or housed, make sure that you bring an offering of gratitude. It may seem silly to pack extra things for hypothetical people, but money is easy to carry and it is much appreciated by the countryside dweller. Anywhere between MNT5,000 and MNT10,000 will be a generous thank you gift. If the host seems reluctant to accept cash, don't assume they wouldn't be happy to have it; they may simply be too proud to take money for performing basic acts of steppe hospitality. Give the money to one of the children instead.

For some more helpful tips and routing information along the same vein, please, refer to the "Cycling" section.

---

### Have Some Horse Sense

Plan as if you will not see another human being during your entire trip because that may be the case. This means bring enough provisions for you and your horse and then some. If possible, travel along rivers to take advantage of water supplies and fish. But pack gifts or cash in case you are invited into a Mongolian home.

---

## CYCLING

To the adventure cyclist, Mongolia remains one of the final frontiers. There is something rugged, remote, and challenging about this country. It is cyclist vs. steppe. The scenery afforded to those willing to pedal this wild terrain is spectacular, and the campsites are truly breathtaking. Yet the untouched views come at a price. This is the least densely populated country in the world. Winds can be soul-destroying, sand and corrugations relentless, and villages few and far between.

Battling the elements as you scour the landscape for food, water, and campsites on your own nomadic trek gives you an incredible insight into the challenge of survival that local Mongolian families face every day. However, as asphalt gradually stretches across the country, adventurers will have to start cycling soon before it all gets a bit too easy . . . and where's the fun in that?

If you're a would-be cycle tourist, there should be enough information here to help you carry out small trips and the resources to start the preparations for the longer treks that will prove you are an adventurer *par excellence*. You will likely be dedicating weeks of research into your cargo. For a complete list of equipment, examine carefully what others have taken in the blogs listed below. Only you can decide what you need and want to bring.

Your options lie with either a mountain bike or a dedicated touring bike and there are entire forums dedicated to the pros and cons of each. Factors to consider include: minimizing the parts that can break (aim for few "moving parts," no shocks, etc.), customizing with sturdy components (i.e., triple butted spokes, durable racks), and keeping rims to a standard 26 inch. A steel frame, although heavier than aluminum, is more robust and can be welded (Гагнуур) if required. These choices will help reduce the chance of a trip-ending mechanical issue.

For short trips, **Seven Summits** across from the Central Post Office in UB rents mountain bikes.

## Specific Bike Gear Considerations

Waterproof panniers are much more suitable than a trailer, especially if you choose mountainous routes. If planning a long journey, you will need to accommodate for the additional 15 kilograms (33 pounds) of food and water per person you may be carrying at times. Tires need to be stoic, but still take a spare. Be comfortable with your saddle before you go because you will have to cross many miles of corrugated dirt track before finding a replacement. Tracking distance with a bike computer in the unmarked steppe is nearly essential. Become intimate with your extensive tool kit and never underestimate the utility of gaffer tape and heavy duty cable ties.

Basic repair kits can be found from Seven Summits and cheap Chinese bike components can be found in the Narantuul Market. You will also be able to find allen wrenches and other standard tools.

## Routes

With sufficient time, determination, and equipment, almost any route in Mongolia is possible. Your limiting factors will be road conditions, weather, and availability of water. Expect to travel very slowly on the unsealed sections, often less than 10 kilometers per hour (6 miles per hour).

Popular destinations among cyclists include:

**Terelj National Park:** 60 kilometers (37 miles) east of UB

**Murun and Khovsgul Nuur in Khuvsgul:** 670 kilometers (416 miles) northwest of UB

**Kharkhorin in Uvurkhangai:** 365 kilometers (227 miles) west of UB

**Tsetserleg in Arkhangai:** 450 kilometers (280 miles) west of UB

**Tariat/Tsagaan Nuur:** 620 kilometers (385 miles) west of UB

**UB to Ulgii "The Trans-Mongolian":** Approximately 1750 kilometers (1,087 miles)

The Trans-Mongolian route is becoming an increasingly popular leg among adventure cyclists. It was cycled by Andrew and Ali, contributors to this section, in April-May 2010. At that point, the highway from UB to Tsetserleg was asphalt, but then the "road" became a collection of Jeep tracks that wound through the steppe.

The major towns to aim for are: Kharkhorin, Tsetserleg, Tariat, Tosontsengel, Ulaangom, and Ulgii. The finer points of your route will require much planning. Maps and GPS waypoints can only give you so much guidance. It will be the experiences of previous cyclists, widely available on the web, that should shape your decisions and guide you to the most scenic and safe route.

Traveling in Mongolia

Expect the Trans-Mongolian to spoil you with winding glacial rivers, dramatic 4,000-meter (13,123-foot) snow capped peaks, mountain passes upwards of 2,500 meters (8,202 feet) in altitude, surreal expansive steppe, vast inland lakes, and challenging semi-arid desert stretches. Although it has been completed in 21 cycling days, you should probably allow for about 30 days plus rests.

## Navigation

When the asphalt stops, the fun really starts. In places up to 15 different tracks, across the breadth of a kilometer, snake the steppe in their independent paths, often crossing like spaghetti. While electricity poles allude to the route, often the horizon is rather bare. If you find yourself hopelessly lost, you can follow the poles until you reach civilization.

**The Mongolian Road Atlas** (1:1000000), widely available in UB, lists small villages, rivers (some of which are dry), springs, and the most unlikely of roads. It is essential. Using **GPS** and having a pre-planned "route" with useful waypoints is also incredibly helpful. Download previous cyclists' paths and important waypoints from the websites listed. Two previous cyclists, Simon and Isabelle, have written a kilometer-by-kilometer guide from UB to Ulgii, which is available on their website (see

## Cycling Tips

Tip#1: *Cycling stuff for the bike nerd.* Consider a dynamo hub complete with an E-werk to convert your kinetic energy into juice for your GPS, smart-phone, bike lights, and MP3 player (*www.bumm.de*).

Tip #2: *Camping cargo.* The essentials to help you survive the steppe include: a four-season tunnel tent, a stove capable of burning low-grade petrol (the only fuel available), and a water purification device (ceramic-based).

Tip #3: *Camping strategies.* Plan your prospective hideaway 10-15 kilometers (6-10 miles) in advance near approaching dunes, hills, or ridges that offer cover from the road and elements. Expect to be within monocular sight of a friendly herder. It's recommended to camp away from villages.

## Cycling Hazards

Hazard #1: *Dogs.* When the family *ger* dog gets territorial, you may have problems. Keep a rock handy, stop to face the dog, and shout "Yawj oh!" Be confident, be masculine! If this fails, throw the rock.

Hazard #2: *Wind.* Expect westerly winds to predominate. On sandy stretches they can produce dust storms that will bring you to a halt. A face scarf is a useful defense.

Hazard #3: *Young boys* will be eager to surround you when you stop and touch everything, especially bells. Although these boys are usually just friendly and curious, cyclists have had loose items stolen from their bikes in the past.

below). And you'll need a bit of good ol' fashioned asking for directions. Along the way, a nomadic herder, passing motorcyclist, or family's *ger* is never too far way. These are invaluable sources of local geographical information. If you need to, continue to ask until you are comfortable that you have found your way as the recommendations you receive may vary from person to person.

## Food & Water

To maintain an appropriate level of food and fluid intake, once again careful planning is required. Most small towns have a *guanz* and a small store that carries at minimum chocolate, hard candies, and biscuits (sweet, animal cracker-like cookies). Only the very smallest will not have staples such as flour, rice, noodles (ramen and instant), oil, onions, and potatoes. Bread (though often stale) is widely available, but only in larger centers can you find luxuries like dried fruit, salami, and fresh vegetables. Often you will have to comb every store in town to get your full shopping list.

Water will be available in every town, either via the well (худаг, *khudag*) or nearby river, but you should purify it regardless and aim for a carrying capacity of 10 liters (2.5 gallons) per person. Filling up from freshwater lakes, streams, and springs will be required on certain routes. While the water may look clean and the locals may drink from it, don't take that chance. Always boil, filter, or both before drinking water in the countryside.

## Cycling Resources

There are plenty of folks who have made these treks, and they like sharing their triumphs and miseries. Check out www.crazyguyonabike.com, the ultimate resource, which includes over 4000 cycle tour journals and forums on every aspect of cycle touring.

The most handy **books** are *Zinn and the Art of Mountain Bike Maintenance* for beginners and *Barnett's Manual* for professionals. Digital versions are available.

You can also check out **personal blogs:**

http://www.hk-to-uk.blogspot.com (includes kilometer-by-kilometer Trans-Mongolian road diaries)

http://www.8bagsfull.blogspot.com

http://sainyavaarai.blogspot.com;

http://www.crazyguyonabike.com/doc/bikingbarkleys

http://www.mikenjencycleasia.blogspot.com

http://www.mountainbike-expedition-team.de/Mongolia/mongo_info.html

# Climate

## LAND OF THE LONG WINTER & THE SUMMER OF DAYS

Because it is landlocked, Mongolia has a continental climate prone to extreme temperature swings. It's not unheard of to wake up freezing in a blustering snow storm wearing all your clothes, and then find yourself stripped down, sweating through your T-shirt by lunchtime.

Mongolians say Mongolia has four seasons: summer, autumn, winter, and spring. Western expats joke that Mongolia has four seasons, alright: June, July, August, and winter. Because spring and autumn seem so short (noted as a few weeks without long underwear and then a few weeks after shorts but before long underwear) it can seem like Mongolia really only has two seasons.

With the two main holidays, Mongolian herders mark the shift in the major seasons, and they begin preparing their animals and resources accordingly. *Tsagaan Sar* in late February to mid-March marks the end of winter, though freezing temperatures can continue into June. At this time herders will begin preparations to rotate their herds into the spring and summer pastures, usually on higher ground. *Naadam* in mid-July signals the end of summer, so while temperatures may still be blazing into September, herders will begin preparing fodder, making and drying milk products or meat for winter storage, and bringing their herds down to hunker through the long winter.

In many places around the world, spring is a time of rebirth as plants and animals emerge from their cloistered winter hideouts and longer days of sunshine fill people with hopeful euphoria. In Mongolia, spring is the dreaded sandstorm season filled with fear as unannounced walls of painful dirt pellets wash over entire towns, filling *gers*, shops, and hairdos with their torturous wrath. Autumn is much more peaceful as temperatures quickly drop below freezing and deciduous trees seem to lose their colorful bouquets overnight.

Also, you can't mention Mongolia without mentioning the big blue sky. It even has the moniker "Land of the Blue Sky," and shamanism is centered around worshiping the sky. But although 260 days of the year will have clear blue skies, about 95 days of the year will be cloudy. Most precipitation comes in the summer, a popular time for tourism. Mongolians do tend to love rain, and the infrequent, short-lived sprinkles and summer thunderstorms are generally a delight, not least because Mongolia's wide-open expanses make rainbows astoundingly common.

# FOUR CLIMATE ZONES

There are four general climate zones in Mongolia that cut across the country from east to west, dipping toward the south like stacked soup bowls. They overlap and are affected by elevation and resulting rainfall.

The northernmost zone is **forest steppe**, which is partly mountainous with pockets of taiga or boreal forests. It is often compared to Switzerland. The floor of this taiga region is covered in permafrost that has been receding due to changing climate. Poor drainage leaves the summer ground mushy, and the over-saturated ground poses a health threat to trees and the regional ecosystem.

Surrounding the taiga to the south is the **grassland steppe**, home to graminaceous grasses like wormwoods. Pine trees run up the flat sides of hills, and birch trees gather near waterways. You can also find shrubs like potentilla and berry bushes like sea buckthorn, black currant, and blueberry. Grasses here are plush, sometimes reaching waist high, and support herds well, especially high consumers like cattle.

The central part of the country is an **arid desert steppe** where the grasses are typically short and thin and are suited to supporting goats and even yaks in the transitional zones. Birch trees can grow here with great care and cultivation but are not necessarily suited for it.

## 2010 Winter Weather Disaster (Dzud)

Mongolia's continental climate with its extreme and sharply fluctuating temperatures can be difficult for herders to weather, and the 2009-2010 winter proved particularly harsh. According to the United Nations Development Programme (UNDP), the bitter and long winter, which followed a dry summer, killed an estimated 8 million of Mongolia's 44 million animals (nearly 20 percent), about a million more livestock than the previous worst winter of 1944. These conditions, known in Mongolian as "dzud", also wreaked havoc from 1999-2002 when Mongolians lost an estimated 11 million head over three winters, according to the Adventist Development and Relief Agency (ADRA), an international NGO that has been operating in Mongolia since the early 1990s. ADRA and other aid agencies try to help herders prepare winter fodder and, provide disaster relief in many forms. Even still, these extreme conditions often prove too difficult for aid groups or the government to stay ahead of.

In 2003, the dzud (pronounced like "mood") conditions caused an urban migration as herders and those supported by herding income scrambled to find work. After this recent disaster, the price of meat doubled in some places, making imported chicken cheaper than domestic red meat.

There is no telling how this disaster will ultimately affect herding or Mongolians as a whole, but they have a way of taking care of each other and persevering that has allowed them to continue this lifestyle for thousands of years.

The **Gobi Desert** comprises the lower level of the country. It is situated between the Altai Mountains to the north and the North China Plain in the southeast, but it's not exactly what you might think of when you picture a desert. The Gobi differs from many deserts in that it is not an ocean of sand dunes. Instead, it is more like a dry, shrubby landscape covered with rock

> The word *govi* means "desert steppe" in Mongolian. The "i" is silent. When translated, Gobi Desert is a little redundant, so Mongolians just call it "gov."

outcroppings and isolated sand dunes in certain areas with some important oases strewn about. It gets cold in winter, sometimes as low as -40° C (-40° F), but don't think that it's always cold because, after all, Mongolia is a country of extremes. In summer, which is also the "rainy" season —average seasonal rainfall of about 7 centimeters (2.8 inches)—temperatures can reach over 40° C (105° F). There are wide temperature swings, so evenings and even days can be quite chilly, even during summer.

# Fauna

Antelopes, gazelles and wild horses can be seen wandering the open steppe, especially in Dornod and Sukhbaatar Aimags. In the Gobi Desert along the southern border with China, you can find the Asiatic wild ass (*khulan*) with some very diligent searching. To see reindeer and the teepee-dwelling Dukha who raise them, head north to Khuvsgul Aimag.

Along with wild herd animals, Mongolia supports a wide range of animals that burrow. Foxes, rabbits, squirrels, and badgers dig the ground or sand along with marmots, a Mongolian delicacy. Though it is illegal to hunt or eat marmots many are poached every autumn and enjoyed without remorse by everyone from herders to

## The Gobi Stats

World's fifth largest desert behind the Sahara, Arabian, Antarctic, and Arctic.

Cuts across: Bayankhongor, Dornogovi, Dundgovi, Govi-Altai, Govisumber, Umnugovi, Sukhbaatar.

The Himalaya Mountain Range blocks rain-carrying clouds from reaching the Gobi.

Just over 1,500 meters above sea level.

Ten percent of Mongolians (roughly 300,000 people) live in area about the size of France.

Home to various animals like gazelles, antelopes, two-humped Bactrian camels, wild horses, wild ass (*khulan*), and the rare Gobi bear (*mazaalai*).

government workers who prize their fatty, oily meat.

Other animals prove much more elusive. While wolves can be found almost anywhere in the country, it is unlikely to spot one during the summer. Similarly, Mongolia is host to the Argali sheep, Mazalai or Gobi bear, lynx, jerboa, and snow leopard, but it is unlikely that you will see any of these unless you head into the foreboding Altai Mountains in Alag Khairkhan Natural or Great Gobi Strictly Protected Area (both in Govi-Altai) and know exactly where to look.

**Khustai Nuruu National Park** in Tuv Aimag is home to the Takhi or Przewalski horse. It was considered extinct in the wild for 40 years, but it was successfully reintroduced to Mongolia after the Foundation for the Preservation and Protection of the Przewalski Horse was founded in the Netherlands in the late 1970s. The program mixed populations from Munich and Prague zoos to avoid inbreeding, and in 1993, 15 horses were reintroduced to the park. Since then, they have reproduced successfully in the wild, earning an upgrade from extinct to critically endangered status.

## FISH & FISHING

Mongolia has over 4000 rivers and more than 30 lakes. Since Mongolians don't do much fishing themselves, the pickins are aplenty. You can employ your fly fishing skills to catch and release taimen in the northeast in Khentii and Dornod Aimags' Onon-Balj National Park. If you're more of a pedestrian fisher, you can grab even the most rudimentary gear, head to almost any river or lake and try your hand at pulling out Siberian white fish, Siberian grayling, lenok, umber, baikal, omul, and river perch.

---

### Gobi Worm

Known by many names, the Gobi Worm—or Mongolian Death Worm, "Large Intestine Worm," or *Olgoi-khorkhoi* (олгой-хорхой)—is a mythical man-eating worm. At 60-150 centimeters long (2-5 feet) and 5 centimeters thick (2 inches), the Gobi Worm is said to look like a blood-red cow intestine with spikes on the ends. The natural habitat for the beast is in under the sand of the southern Gobi Desert where it kills its prey from a distance by spraying an acid or electrical discharge. It only emerges when the ground is wet after a soaking rain.

First introduced to the West in the mid-1920s by Roy Chapman Andrews, an American naturalist, few (if any) have ever actually seen the Gobi Worm. British, Belgian, New Zealand, Czech, Mongolian, and American zoologists, cryptozoologists, explorers, writers, and several recent TV programs have attempted to track the creature and presented tales of the slithering burrower that supposedly has a sweet tooth for *goyo,* a local plant that normally causes paralysis when eaten.

If you encounter the *Olgoi-khorkhoi,* take a picture and collect your millions.

---

Selenge Aimag is known for its smoked fish, so if you don't end up catching any yourself, pick some up Selenge Sukhbaatar's market pair it with a slice of Selenge's large loaf Buriat bread. Khuvsgul Lake is a popular destination for backpackers carrying rudimentary rods, so pack one if you think you'd like to take your chances on a fresh catch dinner.

You can find cheap fishing equipment in the Naraantuul Black Market. For more expert gear and kayaks, try Seven Summits (just south across the street from the Central Post Office, on the side of the Air Market building). If you're an avid angler or fly fishing fanatic looking to make fishing the focus of your trip to Mongolia, you may want to consider hiring a guide or tour company to help you find the prime spots.

## DINOSAURS

Dinosaurs don't still live in Mongolia, but they used to. More than 50 kinds of fossilized bones and eggs, mostly from the Cretaceous period, have been found, particularly in Umnugovi Aimag. Among them are many smaller and medium-sized species such as the Gobiderma, Goyocephale, Khaan, Oviraptor, Saurornithoides, and Velociraptor.

The fossils laid on the surface of the desert for tens of millions of years, mostly undisturbed and uncollected until 1922. Often, herders believed that these fossils were dragons' bones and held a superstition against disturbing them. These days, local museums and international researchers remove, protect, study, and display their finds.

The eggs and bones of Bulgan Soum in Umnugovi Aimag are known worldwide and are displayed in the Natural History Museum in Ulaanbaatar. The site, called Bayanzag (Баянзаг), is 550 kilometers (342 miles) from UB and 100 kilometers (62 miles) from the center of Umnugobi Aimag. The area, also called the "Flaming Cliffs" has an otherworldly quality reminiscent of Mars and is characterized by its red sand. It was so named by adventurer Roy Chapman Andrews, who also brought the myth of the Gobi Worm to the West. For more information, see Umnugovi Aimag on page 314.

Even though the most famous site is the Flaming Cliffs, fossil hunters can still find what they're looking for all across the desert, especially in Umnugovi Aimag, though most fossils have been picked through and picked up by locals and tourists. Regardless, it is ill-advised, not to mention illegal, to take dinosaur bones out of

Mongolia, so if you do find a rare paleontological treasure, please, make sure it finds its way to the Natural History Museum in Ulaanbaatar.

---

### The Almas

The Almas is Mongolia's version of the yeti, a large, hairy wildman with characteristics of both humans and apes. Sightings of the Almas by Westerners go back to the 15th century, and surely Mongolian tales of the creature date back much further. The Almas's Mongolian range appears to be confined to the Altai mountains in the west. First-, and even second- and third-hand accounts of almas sightings are far fewer in eastern Mongolia, and parents there are much less likely to threaten to give their children away to the almas when they misbehave.

---

## BIRDWATCHING IN MONGOLIA

You might be a little unsure about the birdwatching prospects in Mongolia because the dry climate and sparse vegetation of Mongolia couldn't possibly hold much variety, especially if you have visions of the birding jungles in Southeast Asia. Fortunately, Mongolia is a bird seeker's paradise, especially if you know where to go and what you're looking at. The wide open sky provides a great backdrop for soaring birds of prey, and even Ulaanbaatar plays host to birds of interest. To see the migratory birds, you need to go out a little further, though. With time and dedication, it is possible to see over 400 bird species in Mongolia, 23 of which are listed globally as threatened. There are many interesting varieties, and the tranquility of the Mongolian countryside makes discovering them a lovely experience.

Birdwatching in Mongolia is not just for ornithologists; it can be an important part of an environmentally sustainable future. Done responsibly, the act of observing wildlife often contributes to wildlife survival. Showing one's appreciation for the life of other creatures can lead people to sustain these beings. Observation and conservation go hand-in-hand.

If you're primarily interested in birdwatching in Mongolia, you would be very smart to arrange for an English-speaking guide. Having a knowledgeable advocate is priceless. There are lots of good translators, but locating someone who knows birds takes a little more effort. There are a couple of tour companies like Discover Mongolia and Birding Pal that will take you to some quality sites and have good naturalists. But if you're just an enthusiastic birder doubling as poor Mongolian language speaker, you can plan your own travel. Learn this vital request: "*zogsoroi*" or "please stop!"

Before you travel, you can identify and contact environmental and natural resource management organizations that are presently working outside Ulaanbaatar. As an English-speaker, you may be able to assist organizations like the Wildlife

Conservation Society and the Nature Conservancy, and these organizations may be able to help you. Find out how you can help them. These organizations will know a great deal about the habitats they work in and may help you learn the best way to locate, enjoy, and benefit from their respective sites.

Though poaching and overhunting are constant obstacles to naturalists, some Mongolians are keenly interested in and work toward maintaining healthy populations of declining native species. They are interested in the quality of life benefits that can come from supporting wildlife observation activities. They also understand that there are benefits to practices such as reducing the crippling trade in endangered Saker falcons, hunting at sustainable rates, and limiting goat herds.

## Best Birding Sites

During winter in **Ulaanbaatar**, red-billed choughs, and corvids abound with flocks of Eurasian jackdaws, carrion crows, rooks, and ravens watching over the city. But you can start birdwatching when you get off the plane.

Before you leave UB, see if you can catch a ride to the Tuul River near Peace Bridge. This riparian area is on the southern route out of the city, and it often features azure and penduline tit, Siberian rubythroat, Daurian redstart, and the beautiful azure-winged magpie.

Because of its close proximity to UB, **Terelj National Park** is the most common birding location. This is a region of modest mountains and an open transitional habitat of lovely white birch and extensive taiga larch forests that host the Eurasian jay, Palla's bunting, and thick-billed warbler. It is more challenging to locate the sought-after Ural and long-eared owl, Eurasian eagle owl, black capercaillie, hazel grouse, and numerous woodpecker species, but it's fun when you do.

**The Gobi/Gurvan Saikhan National Park** and Umnugovi in general can be excellent. Most people visit the Red Cliffs for the fossil hounding. Birders go targeting the saxaul sparrow, an unassuming denizen of the saxaul "forest." The habitat is a barren isolated stand of low growing, wind-gnarled trees stretching above the sand. It is a strange and peaceful place with various vulture species and other great finds, while the peculiar wallcreeper is the coolest Mongolian treasure.

**Boon Tsagaan Nuur** in Bayankhongor Aimag is a popular destination with dedicated birders for its relative accessibility and variety of species including vulnerable Dalmatian pelican and relict gull. Birders visit this area for the high quality and diversity of northern Asian water fowl, marsh birds, and shorebirds found on the lake and neighboring wetlands. **The Khangai Mountains** to Bayankhongor's north has Hodgson's bushchat, Altai snowcock, and Daurian partridge in the upper reaches as well.

**Bayan Ulgii and Khovd aimags** are known outside the birdwatching community as home to the "Eagle Hunters." Kazakh-Mongolian men have passed down the tradition of wolf, fox, and rabbit hunting with their Golden Eagles for centuries.

For birding in this area, look for Axel Braunlich's blog. He lived in Khovd for a couple years, and he talks about many encounters with numerous species including Daurian partridge, White's thrush, white-crowned penduline tit, Evermann's and Guldenstadt's redstarts, Siberian chiffchaff, rosy starling, booted warbler, Hume's leaf warbler, masked wagtail, Palla's long-tailed and red-mantled rosefinch, and Ortolan bunting.

**The Eastern Steppe** lacks a great deal of habitat diversity, though spring and fall migration offer some good opportunities for birders. Climate change and overgrazing are accelerating the pace of desertification, and wetland habitats are decreasing. While under intense threat, there are still some places for the cranes to drop in on passage or to breed.

There is generally wonderful birding in the steppe with its prolific grassland species, but birdwatchers often seek out the cranes. Demoiselle cranes are succeeding throughout the country. You'll likely see them on any land excursions, perhaps even on your way to see common or white-naped cranes breeding at **Gun-Galuut Nature Reserve, Mongol Daguur SPA** along the Ulz Gol. The endangered Siberian and red-crowned cranes along with the hooded crane are real possibilities, and plenty of other birds migrating from Russia to China can be found during late summer and early autumn.

### Birding Resources

As of publication there is no English language field guide to Mongolia's birds. While there is a rumor that an edition is forthcoming, there are a few helpful alternatives. Considering China's proximity, you can refer to Mackinnon and Phillipps' *A Field Guide to the Birds of China*. While it lacks Mongolia-specific range maps, the guide served as a good companion to Peterson's *Birds of Britain and Europe* and Grimmett, Inskipp, and Inskipp's *Birds of the Indian Subcontinent.*

On the web, excellent photo collections can be found at www.orientalbirdclub.org. There is also a blog by Axel Braunlich who is working on a Mongolia bird field guide. He has provided a fine primer called "Birding in Central Asia: an introduction to Mongolia," which can be found at www.qwerty.ch/birdingmongolia or www.birdsmongolia.blogspot.com.

Traveling in Mongolia

A good resource for studying Mongolian bird species lists is www.avibase.bsc-eoc.org. Also look at these sites: www.surfbirds.com, www.fatbirder.com, www.worldtwitch.com. Check out the resource, gallery, and forum pages with particular attention to the trip reports by Mark Beaman (May 21-June 8, 2006) and Mark Van Biers (May 23-June 12, 2010).

# Other Activities

## HIKING & BACKPACKING

There are various mountain ranges throughout the country. While some ranges are forested and well stocked with lakes, springs, and rivers, others contain desolate stretches of desert and semi-desert. You can save money by bypassing tour companies for these types of trips to the countryside and taking buses to the *aimag* centers you most want to explore. From the *aimag* center, arrange transportation to the mountains. You can often stay in *gers* with random herders, and if you have your own tent, you can camp almost anywhere.

Most backpackers tend to plan their hikes in stretches either between *soums* and *aimag* centers or within certain parks like the **Terelj National Park** in Tuv Aimag, which merges with the **Khan Khentii National Park** in Khentii Aimag. In the northeast part of that *aimag*, the **Onon-Balj National Park** contains many historical sites surrounding Chinggis Khan legends, including his birth and undiscovered burial grounds.

Other trips involve more intrepid sojourns through the **Altai Mountain Range** that cuts across the western portion of the country from Bayankhongor Aimag all the way to Bayan-Ulgii Aimag. The **Khangai Mountain Range** from Bayankhongor Aimag to Khuvsgul Aimag is popular among motorcyclists, bicyclists, and hikers because it is generally passable and many roads zig-zag toward various destinations making last-minute hitchhiking more possible in a pinch.

The route less traveled by is **Khugnu Khan Uul National Park** at the border area of Bulgan, Uvurkhangai, and Tuv aimags, which is accessible by the Ulaanbaatar-Uvurkhangai bus and *mikr* (microbus) routes.

A popular day hike is over the **Bogd Khan Uul** just south of Ulaanbaatar to neighboring Tuv Aimag's Zuunmod. The trip takes about 10 hours and winds through heavily forested mountains to or from the Manzshir Khiid. Other day hikes are possible in the hills and mountains surrounding almost every single *aimag* center. These hikes provide cheap thrills with enormous panoramas over towns and villages.

Remember that if you're out on a trek, you'll need a decent topographical map and compass at the very least, but take a GPS if you have it. If you get lost, it can be days before you see another soul. Also, the temperatures can change dramatically without warning, even in the summer and especially at higher elevations. If you're a relative novice, there's no shame in working with a tour company to hire a guide. In fact, getting to know your guide will probably be the best part of your trip.

## SKIING

In 2009, the first ski resort opened in Mongolia in the Khurkhree Valley of sacred Bogd Khan Mountain, 13 kilometers (8 miles) southeast of UB. Mongolia's **Sky Resort** (11320341; www.skyresort.mn) has seven ski runs for skiers of all skills and is served by two chairlifts. The lifts and runs are located between 1379 meters (4,523 feet) and 1570 meters (5,150 feet), giving it a 191-meter (626-foot) vertical elevation.

The runs are almost completely covered by artificial snow because the area is extremely dry with only 20 centimeters (7.8 inches) of snow between November and February.

## GOLF

If you're really itching to play golf, there are two golf courses in Tuv Aimag's Terelj National Park, the Chinggis Khaan Country Club and the course at the UB Hotel. Neither course is really great, but both rent clubs, and there's something interesting about playing golf on the steppe. The fairways are just rolling fields, and the tees and greens are artificial turf. They are fun to play, though in a different way than you're probably used to. It will cost you around MNT60,000 for the round at each and another MNT10,000 for the clubs.

# What to Expect

## WATER

There is running hot and cold water in UB all year, but in most provincial capitals, they turn hot water off April through October. Shower houses always have hot water.

Although Mongolians might drink straight from rivers, freshwater lakes, and the tap, it's not advisable for tourists, even if the water looks and smells clean. Boil drinking water or otherwise treat it. All bottled water is safe to drink and relatively inexpensive.

Springs and aquifers may offer supposed health benefits to those who choose to drink from them, but drink at your own risk.

Ice for drinks can only be found in more upscale UB restaurants, and is usually filtered. If you want some, just ask for some "moose" (мөс) at no extra charge. It is doubtful you will find ice outside of UB except on a mountaintop.

## TOILETS

In provincial capitals, you will find any combination of porcelain flush toilets ranging from squat to Western-style with (or, sometimes, without) seats. In the countryside, you may relieve yourself almost anywhere you choose as you travel. Outhouses are the squat variety, usually with just a board missing in the slat floor. Bring your own paper everywhere. Seriously. Everywhere.

## CELL PHONES

While traveling through Mongolia, it would be a good idea to get yourself a SIM card. They are cheap, easy to reload, and will definitely come in handy. Though mobile phones have been around less than 10 years, Mongolians are now very much married to them.

Texting is very cheap and is now the main form of telecommunication in the country. Most Mongolians text using Latin characters, creating a whole new (and not yet universal) alphabet in the process. Callers are only charged for outgoing calls that connect, so receiving a call and being hung up on is an invitation for you to call that person back because they probably don't have many units. Incoming calls are not charged.

The main cell phone providers in Mongolia are: MobiCom, Skytel, G-mobile, and Unitel. Each phone company has varying coverage and plans. Some offer in-network bonuses like free talking or texting, which has led many people to carry multiple phones with multiple phone numbers on multiple SIM cards.

There are some restrictions on which domestically purchased phones allow which SIM cards. Your safest bet would probably be MobiCom because they offer the most coverage throughout the country. They also have a conveniently located main office in Ulaanbaatar with some English-speaking staff who will be able to meet your cell phone needs. The MobiCom-TEDY Center is located in the Chingeltei District on Sambuu Street between the State Department Store and Tengiis Movie Theatre.

To purchase a SIM card, you will need a valid passport and an internationally equipped cell phone. The card will cost MNT10,000 and is loaded with 5,000 units. If you do not have a cell phone that is enabled for international usage, you can purchase a cheap used cell phone upstairs in the TEDY Center, above the main MobiCom office.

Units can be purchased at most shops throughout the country. It would be helpful to know how to say your phone number in Mongolian, but you can also just write it down and show it to the shopkeeper or enter your number as a contact and show them. Numbers are spoken in pairs. For example 95292857 would be expressed as: 95-29-28-57 (ninety-five, twenty-nine, etc.). They will ask you your number and how many units you would like to purchase. MobiCom units come in packages of 1,000, 2,500, 5,000, 10;000, 20,000, and 30,000. There are bonuses if you purchase more units at a time. Usually if you buy 10,000, you get an extra 1,000 free, and 30,000 gets you an extra 5,000. Units will either be given in the form of a card with a scratch-off back that reveals a secret code, or they will be electronically transferred to the phone by the shopkeeper.

Unit costs for talk time are about MNT70 per minute within network and MNT100 per minute to other networks. Text messages or SMS are MNT19 within network and MNT40 to other networks. The country code for Mongolia is +976. If you have trouble dialing a land line number (usually starting with 1 or 2) put a 0 before it.

### Useful Phone Phrases & Words

| English | Cyrillic | Transliteration | Sounds-like survival guide |
|---|---|---|---|
| SIM card | Сим Карт | *sim kart* | "sim kart" |
| hand phone (mobile) | Гар Утас | *gar utas* | "gar utas" |
| unit(s) | Нэгж | *negj* | "niggij" |
| I would like to purchase a new sim card. | Би шинэ сим карт авмаар байна. | *Bi shine sim kart avmaar baina.* | "Be shin sim kart awmaar ban." |
| Do you have MobiCom Units? | Мобиком нэгж байгаа юу? | *MobiCom negj baigaa you?* | "MobiCom nigij bag-uh you?" |
| What is your number? | Утасний дугаар хэд вэ? | *Utasnii dugaar khed ve?* | "Otis-knee doogaar hid way?" |
| Hello. (Are you there?) | Байна уу? | *Baina uu?* | "BAN-o?" |

## INTERNET

In UB, many restaurants, pubs, coffee shops, and guesthouses offer free wireless internet, and some have computers. In the countryside, you have fewer options. Each capital has a post office communication center with an internet café inside. Look for the building with all the antennae and satellite dishes. Internet cafés typically charge MNT500-800 per hour.

If you'll be in Mongolia for a while and need a regular and reliable internet service, several mobile phone companies, including G Mobil and MobiCom, now sell USB port wireless modems. The modems, which use SIM cards to connect, cost about $100 and up. The more you pay, the faster the modem. Monthly service fees are less than $20 a month for plans with the lowest byte transfer allowance.

## ELECTRICITY

The electricity is 220 V, 50 Hz, and the outlets accept the European-style 2-pin plugs, though most businesses, homes, and guesthouses have power strips that will accept any prong configuration. Wiring in most places is inadequate and electrical fires are not uncommon. Nonetheless, the power supply in each of the *aimag* centers is now mostly reliable and only subject to occasional blackouts. Most *soums* except the most remote have some electricity supplemented by solar panels and generators. The electricity is especially reliable in Ulaanbaatar. With its dusty air, Mongolia loves to eat computers and hard drives, so be sure to keep your electronics covered when you're not using them.

# Safety & Security

Pickpockets and bag slashers lurk between the state department store and the central post office and inside the Narantuul Market, but no area is completely free from thieves. Don't put your money, phone, camera, or wallet in outside pockets, and get in the habit of holding an arm over purses and backpacks while you shop. Buses get very crowded, so watch your pockets diligently here too.

> **The 3 A's**
> Alcohol, alone, at night. Most safety incidents happen when all three are involved, so, as always, be cautious about how festive you get, bring a buddy, and come in early.

In UB, areas where foreigners tend to gather are often protected by private security and are safe. However, walking to and from these places is less safe, as it may involve many dark and obstructed views. UB is a very walkable city, but at night it can be dangerous.

Bars and clubs are generally supposed to close at midnight with few exceptions. Often police are bribed to stay away after 12:00 midnight, so if you get into trouble, you are on your own. It's best to enjoy the pubs earlier in the evening and save the night for sleeping.

# FOREIGNERS IN MONGOLIA

Xenophobia has become a real problem in Mongolia as nationalism grows, especially against Korean and Chinese people and people of Korean or Chinese decent regardless of citizenship. This is especially a problem during *Naadam*. Attackers can target victims based solely on their ethnicity or perceived foreign nationality without being provoked or without robbery as the motivation. Caucasian tourists are generally better received, but that doesn't necessarily make them immune to violence. In Ulaanbaatar, you should exercise caution walking the streets at all times, particularly avoiding groups of young men.

In the countryside, tourists are less likely to encounter problems and are often greeted graciously. In provincial capitals, some tourists have been spit on or insulted, but there is little physical violence, especially without provocation.

## Watch Your Language in Public

Though native speakers know this word is multifaceted and quite flexible, using the word "fuck" too close to the word "Mongolia" can get foreigners into a lot of unwanted trouble, no matter how many words are in between. Keep it clean to keep safe. In general, speaking loudly and disparagingly about Mongolia in cafés or pubs frequented by foreigners, and therefore staffed by Mongolians with proficient English-speaking skill, is disrespectful and unlikely to win you friends.

# LGBT TRAVELERS

In Mongolia there is a general failure to understand lesbian, gay, bisexual, and transgendered people. The number-one concern for LGBT travelers is safety, which Robyn, the executive director of the LGBT Centre in Ulaanbaatar, emphasizes heavily.

In an attempt to keep safe, underground parties in UB are always in different places and mostly arranged by word of mouth. They are rarely attended by non-Mongolians, and even in those cases usually only by long-term expats. Because there have been major acts of violence against members of the LGBT community in Mongolia, it is unfortunately unwise to advertise yourself as LGBT. Also, be aware of your surroundings. There are several ultranationalist movements, the largest being Dayar Mongol, that have been responsible for violence toward members of the LGBT community. There have been several accounts of violence where police and hospitals have facilitated victimization by refusing service to injured persons, giving poor service, or refusing to report incidents. If you are attacked due to your sexual orientation, it is best not to report this to hospitals or the police. Instead, you should contact the LGBT Centre for help (99800339; www.lgbtcentre.mn).

Many thousands of foreign volunteers, expats, and tourists who count themselves among the LGBT community have lived, worked, and traveled very happily and safely in Mongolia, and you should also feel welcome to visit. Though these acts of violence happen, they are not the representative of most of Mongolian society. As long as travelers keep in mind basic safety tips, they should have a great vacation with no problems.

# Health

Since Mongolia is a remote place, sometimes access to basic health care and medical supplies can be limited or non-existent. It is a good idea to have a small medical kit on hand with the following supplies:

- ✓ Antibiotics for the following: travelers' diarrhea, skin infection, and respiratory infection
- ✓ Drugs for motion sickness (Mongolian transport is no place for faint of heart or the weak of stomach.)
- ✓ Sleeping pills (another handy accessory if you plan on taking long bus rides that you would rather not remember)
- ✓ Anti-inflammatory drugs like ibuprofen
- ✓ Antibacterial ointment
- ✓ Bandages
- ✓ Tampons or sanitary napkins (Sanitary napkins are available throughout the country, but tampons are only available in the bigger cities and are limited in selection.)
- ✓ Oral rehydration salts
- ✓ Water purification tablets
- ✓ Insect repellent
- ✓ Condoms (STDs are prevalent throughout Mongolia.)

If you happen upon any unfortunate situations that cannot be treated with a few bandages and some ibuprofen, then you may need to seek out further medical assistance. The two best hospitals in Ulaanbaatar for foreigners are SOS Medica Mongolia and the SongDo Hospital.

**SOS Medical Mongolia** (4a Building, Big Ring Road, 15th Micro District, 7th Khoroo, Bayanzurkh District;+976 1146-4325) is by far the most modern medical facility in Mongolia. It has an all-English speaking staff and offers emergency services; however, they do not perform major surgical operations. It is a membership-based clinic. Non-members are treated for $90 for a local physician and $195 for an international physician. (These prices are for basic exams, and may be more depending on treatments and medicine.)

**SongDo** (Choldog Street -5, 1st Micro District, Sukhbaatar District; 70239000) is a Korean hospital that was opened in 2007. Doctors are both Korean and Mongolian, and most have a basic knowledge of English. This hospital offers modern facilities but does not provide emergency care. The cost for a doctor's examination is MNT6,000.

## RECOMMENDED VACCINES

Before traveling anywhere it is certainly wise to be informed about the health dangers as well as making sure that you are properly vaccinated to protect yourself from any and all relevant disease risks. Mongolia is no exception to this rule. Four to eight weeks prior to your departure for Mongolia, you should see your physician or a travel health clinic to receive the following vaccinations:

**Hepatitis A and B:** Recommended for all travelers as these diseases are prevalent in Mongolia.

**Typhoid:** Recommended for all travelers, especially if you plan on visiting China as well.

**Japanese encephalitis:** Recommended for travelers who are planning to spend a good deal of their visit in rural areas.

**Meningococcal:** Recommended for those who plan on staying for long periods of time.

**Rabies:** If you only plan on being in Mongolia for two minutes, get a rabies vaccination. The rabies vaccination is typically a series of three shots, so plan this process accordingly with your physician.

## FOOD & WATER SAFETY

Water-borne parasites are extremely common in Mongolia, especially giardia. Many people in developing countries who have had exposure to this type of parasite their entire lives are immune to its destructive properties. You, however, are not. Giardia is your kryptonite, and you were never Superman to begin with (so take off that cape, you look ridiculous). However, you can defend yourself against our protozoan enemies by following a few simple rules:

- It's a good idea not to drink tap, well, or river water unless it has been boiled, filtered, or chemically disinfected through the use of chlorine or iodine tablets.
- In the capital, most touristy spots are wise to the paranoia of foreigners and would never serve you ice that comes from untreated water. However, if you want to be super safe, you should avoid ice as well.

- Try to avoid eating fruits or vegetables that have not been either peeled or cooked.
- Avoid cooked foods that appear to have been left at room temperature or are not piping hot.
- Unpasteurized dairy products should be avoided. (But most Mongolian milk products have been through at least one flash pasteurization so you should be safe with those. Basically, this is only an issue if someone milks a yak into a cup and hands it to you.)
- Do not eat any meat or fish that is raw or appears to be undercooked.
- Marmot, while technically illegal to hunt is a delicacy in the countryside. Some say it is delicious; we say it's a greasy, plague-infested rodent. If you must try this, make sure that you have absolutely no contact with the fur (or that the fur has been blowtorched to oblivion), because fleas on the fur can and do carry the bubonic plague. Bubonic plague is treatable these days, by the way. It might even seem like the kind of thing that would make for a great story after returning home ("I went to Mongolia, and all I got was the black death!"), but come on now—there's really nothing fun about coming down with a case of the plague in the middle of your vacation.

In the unfortunate event that you come into contact with a parasite or experience just a good old case of traveler's diarrhea, there are some remedies and treatments for the symptom.

Powdered Gatorade and rehydration salts are great for recovering from a bout of diarrhea. The salts are for your stomach; the Gatorade is for your happiness. Diarrhea and vomiting can dehydrate your body and make you feel 100 times worse than you already do. So as soon as sickness hits, dissolve one packet of rehydration salts in a liter of water. 10-15 milligrams or a couple tablespoons of table salt might do in a pinch. If you are able to find powdered Gatorade anywhere (perhaps at a bike shop), it can also be added in the same ratio as the salts to the water. It not only makes it taste way better, but it aids in the rehydration process.

You should have an anti-diarrheal drug on hand, but only take it if you are in a situation where diarrhea is most inconvenient. Otherwise, it's best to let things run their course. Diarrhea is typically defined as three or more watery or loose stools in an eight-hour period. It is also good to carry antibiotics, such as levofloxacin (Levaguin), rifaximin (Xifaxan), ciprofloxacin (Cipro), or azithromycin (Zithromax). But antibiotics aren't to be fooled around with, so make sure you talk to a doctor before you venture off.

Fortunately, giardia is pretty easy to self diagnose as it come with foul-smelling sulfur gas (from both ends). Tinidazole is a common antibiotic that is used to treat giardia, and it can be purchased over the counter at most Mongolian pharmacies, although since it is a prescription drug elsewhere it may be better to try and get a few boxes from a physician prior to your arrival in Mongolia.

# Travel Volunteerism

A simple Google search will offer you many opportunities for volunteering while traveling through Mongolia. The costs vary from place to place, sometimes as high as $3000 for travel, room, board, and program fees. Granted, there are some remarkable opportunities with reputable programs. Yet, we recommend that you not limit yourself to the opportunities you find online in a quick search. Why not look outside the box? As food and accommodations in Mongolia are generally quite inexpensive, why not directly look up organizations you would be interested in giving your time to? With an email or phone call you would be surprised how many organizations are looking for enthusiastic warm bodies to help out with day-to-day activities with no cost to you at all.

During the summer, nearly every *aimag* offers children's camps, usually through the *aimag* children's center. English is an official second language of Mongolia, so summer camps are always looking for English teachers. In addition to those summer camps, there are environmental researchers, international NGOs, and religious organizations that might welcome your help and input. Volunteering in Mongolia can be a very rewarding way to travel.

**The Lotus Center:** One of our favorite organizations in Ulaanbaatar. They work with vulnerable children and families to provide the basic human rights of shelter, food, and education for up to 150 abused, orphaned, and abandoned children at any given time. The center also has a beautiful guesthouse for reasonable prices as well as a fantastic vegetarian café, Ananda's, both of which can be found on Baga Toiruu, north of Sukhbaatar Square. The application process is simple, you can feel great about the work you are doing, and you won't have to break your piggy bank to do it. *11325967, 11325967; lotusguest@gmail.com; www.lotuschild.org*

**Projects Abroad in Mongolia:** Projects are carried out year-round and last from two weeks to a year. Volunteers are needed in teaching, care, culture and community, sports, medicine, journalism, business, and veterinary medicine. Participants should be 16 years or older and be able to pay fees for travel and accommodations starting at around $1,800. *US Toll-free (888) 839-3535, (888) 839-3535; info@projects-abroad.org; www.projects-abroad.org*

**Ecovolunteer in Mongolia:** Przewalski's horse research and re-introduction program in Khustai Nuruu National Park. The program is partnered with Samar Tours for a reasonable $80-85 per day depending on how long you stay. You find your own way to Ulaanbaatar, and a representative from the organization will meet you at the train, bus, or plane. You will stay in a *ger* and receive two meals a day with ample free time in the evenings. Coordinators will prepare you for the fieldwork and for the living conditions. Must be 18 years or older and speak English. *11311051; samartours@magicnet.mn www.ecovolunteer.org*

**New Choice Mongolian Volunteer Organization:** NGO that arranges short- and long-term placements for volunteers to teach English, renovate buildings, etc. Fees from $495 to $1,950. *Ikh Toiruu, Building-15, Room-405, Ulaanbaatar, Mongolia; 11314577; info@volunteer.org.mn; www.volunteer.org.mn/new/index.html*

**Volunteers for Peace (VFP), Volunteer Camps in Mongolia:** Services include providing consultation and a placement for camp hosts and volunteers and linking people with programs. Programs foster international education, voluntary service, and friendship. In the last 22 years over 22,000 volunteers have been placed in international camps world-wide. *www.vfp.org (search for Mongolia)*

**Eastern Mongolia Protected Area Administration (EMPAA):** Located in Dornod Aimag's Choilbolsan. Delgermaa and Odmaa would like to work with you to protect wildlife in the area. The organization often has research projects and other ways you can help on a short-term and long-term basis. *delgermaab@yahoo.com, choi_aodm56@hotmail.com*

**World Conservation Society:** The local group concentrates on protecting gazelles in the eastern region. *11323719; sbolortsetseg@gmail.com (speak to Boloroo), wcsmongolia@wcs.org; http://www.wcs.org*

**The Nature Conservancy:** Partnered with national and regional governments, other conservation organizations, and local people in creating a lasting natural legacy. The Conservancy is involved in the protection of Toson Khulstai, a national nature reserve of almost a million acres. It tests protected area and buffer zone strategies and creates partnerships with local and national stakeholders, including the Mongolia Ministry of Nature. Lessons learned from this endeavor will guide their strategies and priorities across Mongolia and can be replicated for other protected and mixed use conservation areas. *eoidov@tnc.org (speak to Enkhtuya Oidov, Mongolia Country Director); www.nature.org/wherewework/asiapacific/mongolia, www.nature.org/wherewework/asiapacific/mongolia/*

**Mongolian Ornithological Society:** If you're really into birding, this organization would love to have your help and/or organize a tour for you. Contact Dr. Gombobaatar Sundev and Mr. Amartuvshin Purevdorj. *11323970, 11462333, 99180148; gombobaatar@biology.num.edu.mn, info@mos.mn; http://www.mos.mn*

**The Sun Child Orphanage:** A Japanese-funded center in Darkhan for about 55 children displaced by poverty, abuse, or lack of family. The orphanage runs traditional Mongolian arts, culture, and crafts programs and a summer camp. If you would like to stop by to meet with the children, buy some handicrafts, or volunteer your time, summer is best because free time is aplenty. *sunschild.happychild@gmail.com*

**Human Development Center:** Erdenet's Human Development Center provides training and support services for local children and adults. The center operates groups, including a technical club where kids learn engineering concepts and build model vehicles, a family counseling center, a library and internet access room, Eternal Springs café and youth center, which offers various dance and music lessons, Mongol Designer, which offers classes on clothing design and other textile skills, and the Eye of Wisdom school, which features classes in English, mathematics, and computers. Contact Chingee. *95959598, 0135225821; chimgee_eyeofwisdom@yahoo.com*

# The Guide

## Ulaanbaatar (Улаанбаатар)

Ulaanbaatar (pronounced "oh-LAWN-BAHtr"), also referred to simply as "UB" (pronounced "you-be"), is the capital of Mongolia, and in almost every single way possible, life in UB contrasts with traditional countryside nomadic life. In fact, many Mongolians refer to it as simply *khot*, "the city." It's the transportation hub, it's the only place with an extensive grid of paved roads and traffic lights, it's where the NGOs and the international corporations are, and it has some good things to see and eat. You probably didn't drag yourself all the way to Mongolia to see a congested developing city full of cars and chain restaurants, but since you have to go there anyway, we have some hints on how to plan your excursions, shop responsibly, get a hot shower, and experience what this half of Mongolia has to offer.

The food in UB is plentiful and pulls from the many international influences that have become a part of the modern capital. If you're interested in trying Mongolian food, there's no reason to spend much money, so do not get your *tsuivan*, *buuz*, or *khuushuur* from one of the Modern Nomads chain restaurants or any other international chain. Try the Khaan Buuz, or better yet, any hole-in-the-wall *guanz* for just a few hundred to a few thousand *tugriks*, not the MNT7,000-10,000 you might pay in a fancy place for the same food. Besides, when you go to the countryside (and you absolutely should), you're likely to eat little else. Instead, look for the Mongolian twist on things you already know like pizza (with mutton fat), burgers (free range, grass-fed beef that tastes a little like mutton), or a *shorlog* (meaty kebabs).

Most of the action for tourists is in the center of town between the **State Department Store** and **Sukhbaatar Square** (west to east), and **Tengis Theater** to **Seoul Street** (north to south). The best shopping, restaurants, and guesthouses are in and around this area, and everything is within walking distance. You want to avoid taking taxis if you can because they not only get trapped in the congested streets, but they can needlessly drain your pockets. Moreover, some drivers take advantage of foreigners.

The Guide

There is a little something for everyone in UB, whether it's nature, nightlife, cuisine, or culture you're after. For monastery seekers, the **Gandan Khiid** should be on your list, while history buffs should check out the **Bogd Khaan Winter Palace** and if you like both, you'll love the **Choijin Lama Monastery Museum**. Dinosaur hunters should be happy to visit the **Natural History Museum**. For ethnography enthusiasts, the **National Museum of Mongolia** paints a great portrait of the many different tribes and influences in Mongolia through its long history, and if you're in for a mental challenge and a quirky time, think about visiting the **International Intellectual Museum**. The prices for all of these are low (around MNT2,000), so you're not likely to blow your budget learning. However, be aware that some of the exhibits aren't translated or are translated imperfectly. For outdoor excursions, check out the monuments on **Sukhbaatar Square** or take a walk up to **Zaisan** if you want the best view of the city.

## ORIENTATION

Ulaanbaatar is divided into many different districts, but you really only need to know a few. Most things you want or need to see and do are contained within the fifth and sixth districts inside the **Ikh Toiruu (Их тойруу or "Large Ring Road")** and Narnii Zam (Нарны зам or "Sun Road") to the south. You should know, though, that Mongolians do not use the names of roads or streets but rather landmarks. You'll have a hard time even finding street signs, and almost no one knows the names of the streets in English.

There are, however, four exceptions to the general failure to use street names.

---

### Naming the Capital

The capital of contemporary Mongolia has moved around perhaps as many as 25 times since 1639. Even Ulaanbaatar, or "Red Hero," was known by two different monikers before 1924 when it was finally named for Damadiin Sukhbaatar, the charismatic leader of the Mongolian communist revolution.

In 1639, Urgoo (Residence) was a mobile capital within the Orkhon Valley. Later, after the turn of the century under the Manchurian Qing Dynasty, it was called simply Khuree (Camp). In 1778, the capital moved one final time to rest in its current location and became known as Ikh Khuree (Great Camp). As the political, religious, and cultural center of the territory, Mongolian *gers* were nestled here beside Chinese and Tibetan religious buildings, the first permanent structures in the capital of 15,000 to 20,000 residents. The Qing Dynasty ultimately crumbled under civil war, and in 1911 the Bogd Khan declared Mongolian independence in his new capital, Niislel Khuree (Capital Camp). In its current incarnation, the capital is centered around Sukhbaatar Square, a Soviet-style parade ground laid out in front of the national government building.

**Enk Taivani Urguun Chuluu (Энх тайваны өргөн чөлөө or "Peace Avenue")** is the main west to east road, stretching all the way from the Dragon Center near the west edge of town to the Bayanzurkh Tovchoo bus station on the eastern side. It runs past the State Department Store, Flower Center and Sukhbaatar Square, and it is just north of the Wrestling Palace and Narantuul Market. You should use this as your main orientation point with Sukhbaatar Square as the center of the city. The roads are gridded in this area and surrounded by concentric curved roads in the north.

**Suliin Gudamj (Сөлийн гудамж or "Seoul Street")** runs parallel to Peace Avenue from Sukhbaatar Square to the Large Ring Road past the Circus and just south of the Beatles Statue Park. Here, you'll find most of the foreigner hangouts, chain restaurants, microbreweries, and some fancier fine dining as well as a shopping center for cutting edge electronics and the offices for EZnis Airways.

**The Large Ring Road** is the very outer border of the center and acts almost as a bypass around it, but the **Baga Toiruu (Бага тойруу or "Small Ring Road")** is as far north as you'll ever need to walk for food, drink, and tourist sites.

## GETTING THERE

All roads lead to UB. If you parachuted into the middle of nowhere, found a road, and stood there long enough, you could hitch a direct ride to Ulaanbaatar.

### By Air

EZnis Airways and AeroMongolia have service from most western *aimag* centers, operating various days of the week. The prices vary by season and destination but the fares are standard, meaning you can buy a ticket the day of the flight for the same price as you would booking it in advance. If you want to go out west to Khovd or Bayan Ulgii at all, you might do best to book a flight there and work your way back on the northern route through Zavkhan and Arkhangai or the southern route through Govi-Altai and Bayankhongor. Similarly, if you get stuck out west due to travel delays, you can hop on a plane and be back in UB in a few hours instead of a few days.

### By Bus & Shared Transport

Buses are usually the best way to get around. Often buses will arrive late into the evening and overnight from the farther reaches of the countryside. From the two bus stations, Dragon Center (western) and Bayanzurkh Tovchoo (eastern), you can find daytime buses to and from the center of town for MNT300. If you arrive overnight, you can take a taxi to your guesthouse. Also, some guesthouses will pick you.

The Guide

## By Train

Trains arrive and depart from Ulaanbaatar's only train station, known as either Вокзал (*vokzal*) in Russian or галт тэрэгний буудал (*galt teregnii buudal*) in Mongolian. Taxis or buses may be found directly outside of the train station. If you don't want to be hustled by taxis who may want to get an extra thousand *tugriks* out of you, it is wise to walk to the main street in front of the station and hail a car from there. Taxis from the train station to the area around the State Department store shouldn't cost more than MNT3,000. Always remember to negotiate a price upon entering a car. For comprehensive information about purchasing train tickets and the different seating classes, see page 89.

# GETTING AROUND

You can get around mostly on foot, and that should be your strategy unless you're crossing from the extreme of one side of the city to the other. Every site is reachable by foot within 30 minutes of Sukhbaatar Square, including the Zaisan Monument.

There's no subway, there are no streetcars, and there are few marked "legitimate" taxis. Buses are a pretty decent option because they are really cheap, but the routes are cryptic and since they're so crowded, they are good spots for pickpockets.

## By Taxi

Though every car is a taxi and you can almost always find a ride, you're going to get ripped off four out of five times, especially since you don't speak the language.

If your guesthouse is near the State Department Store, tell your driver you're going to "Ikh Delguur." When you get close, you can give him more precise directions or get out at the store and walk the rest of the way.

## By Bus & Trolley

The bus routes and fleet continue to improve, and buses will take you anywhere you need to go. They sure are crowded, though, and the drivers don't announce stops. A single fare anywhere in the city is only MNT300, however, meaning you can go pretty far for about a quarter of a dollar. You can even go all the way to the airport, which costs MNT15,000 by taxi and sometimes $15-20 from guesthouses. The buses don't start running until 6:00 a.m., and they make their final loops beginning around 9:00 p.m., which makes it difficult to take a bus if you are catching an early international flight or arriving late at the airport.

Unfortunately, the route plans are not easily accessible, even to Mongolians, and they aren't in English. The main stops to concern yourself with are Sukhbaatar Square, Tengis Theater, Ard Kino Theater (the former site of this theater just north of the Flower Center), MUBC (National University just north of Sukhbaatar Square), and Bayangol Hotel (just south of Sukhbaatar Square). All major routes come to and from these stops. When you get on a bus you can say the name of your destination to the ticket takers with a questioning tone, or point to it in the book. Look for the body language or listen for the "*tiim*" or "*ugui*." (Also don't forget that often an affirmative response in Mongolian is to say the word back to you.)

## BEEP and EEP and a Greener UB

If you're in UB during the winter, you know that the smog is choking most days. Some people even walk the streets with cloth masks, black around their mouths. The city looks like London during the birth of industrialization when the "London fog" would belch out of smokestacks and squelch visibility to mere meters ahead. In Mongolia, urban migration has brought job seekers from the far countryside to the outskirts of the nation's already crowded and sprawling city. They bring with them their *gers* and the stoves that heat them.

Some of these communities or "*ger* districts," used to be countryside villages that have now morphed seamlessly into the megalopolis. Like countryside towns, they are row upon row of side-by-side wooden fences. Inside, several families share each compound, often in one or more *gers* or wooden and plaster homes with corrugated roofs. The compounds generally lack sewage, running water, and garbage removal and are part of a patchwork of electric grids.

Aimed at increasing the air quality in Ulaanbaatar, the UNDP Building Energy Efficiency Project (BEEP) and the MCA Energy and Environment Project (EEP) are working to develop and provide access to a slew of new green technologies and education programs.

While apartment buildings inside the center of the city are linked together with a municipal hot water grid, the *ger* districts are filled with tens of thousands of homes burning wood and coal to stay warm and cook their food through the brutal winters, which accounts for up to 90 percent of Ulaanbaatar's greenhouse gas emissions. Though *gers* are perfectly suited for nomadic herding because they are extremely mobile, and while wooden homes are less drafty than felt-covered lattice, there are many opportunities to improve on the designs. To minimize heat loss, BEEP and EEP are working to develop insulation systems for *gers* and wooden houses, subsidizing mortgages for newly built energy efficient homes, overseeing the construction of such homes, and helping to redesign building codes to ensure tougher requirements for efficiency. They have also worked to create centers to support the testing and certification of energy efficient systems and dwellings to make it easier for Mongolians to find and guarantee that the products they buy are energy efficient.

The organizations aim to raise more awareness about the benefits of energy efficiency as well. In the winter and often through the summer, stoves inside homes are used for both cooking and heating. A small round hole on the top of rectangular or square stoves can be removed and a half-domed metal pot dropped in its place. These stoves have been useful and are extremely inexpensive to make (as low as MNT35,000), but they are inefficient. BEEP and EEP have developed high efficiency stoves that use a fraction of the fuel, though they cost several times more. One of the challenges of the program is to convince community members that the fuel savings in two seasons can make up for the added initial cost. Their outreach also supports technical education programs to develop new curricula that include energy efficiency.

## Useful Bus & Trolley Numbers

### To Dragon Center Bus Station (western destinations)

M22 – from the airport to Tengis movie theater

M26 – from Tengis and Sukhbaatar Square

M27 – from Sukhbaatar Square

M28 – from Urgoo movie theater

M41 – from Bayanzurkh Bus Station

T2 – from Bayanzurkh Bus Station

### To Bayanzurkh (eastern destinations)

M1 – from Sukhbaatar Square

M13 – from Sukhbaatar Square

M27 – from Sukhbaatar Square

M41 – from Dragon Center Bus Station

M46 – from Gandan Khiid

T2 – from the Dragon Center Bus Station

T4 – from Sukhbaatar Square

T6 – from Sukhbaatar Square

### To the Train Station

M20 – from Sukhbaatar Square

M24 – from the Dragon Center Bus Station

T4 – from Sukhbaatar Square

### To Teeverin Tovchoo

M4 – from Urgoo movie theater

M5 – from Tengis movie theater and Sukhbaatar Square

M23 – from Sukhbaatar Square

M31 – from Urgoo movie theater

M35 – from Tengis movie theater

M36 – from Sukhbaatar Square

M41 – from the train station

M46 – from Urgoo, Gandan Khiid

### To Airport and Immigration Office

M11 – from Ard Theater and Bayangol Hotel

M22 – from Tengis movie theater

The Guide

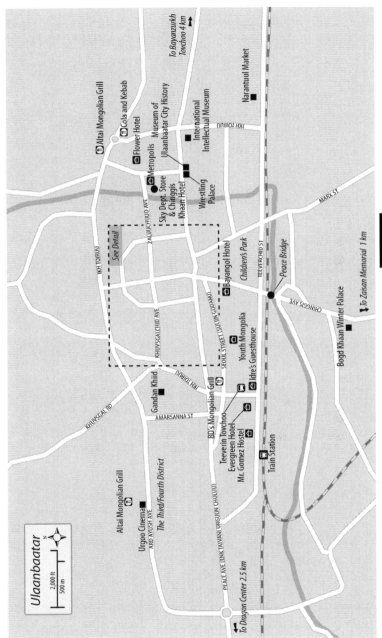

Ulaanbaatar

2,000 ft
500 m

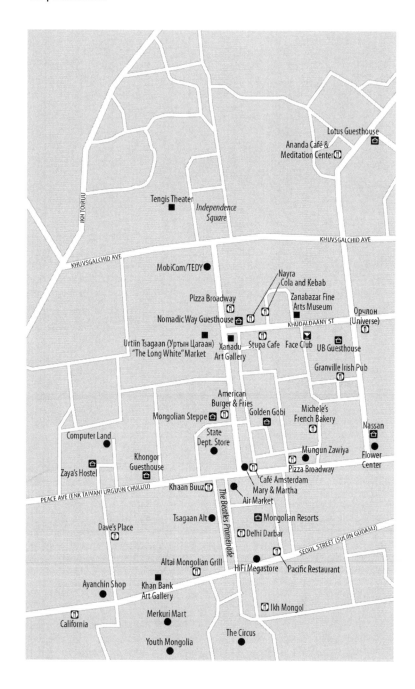

The Guide

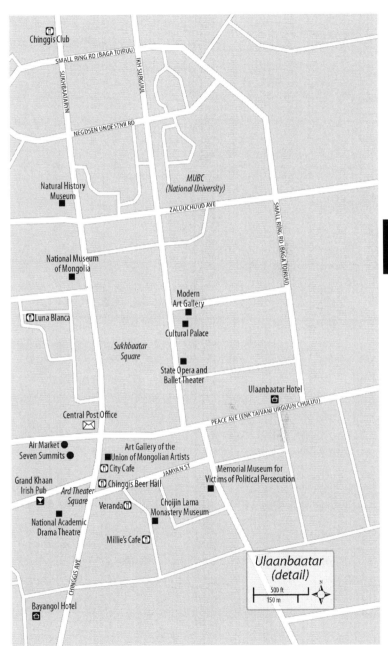

Chinggis Club

SMALL RING RD (BAGA TOIRUU)

SUKHBAATARYN

IKH SURGUUL

NEGDSEN UNDESTNII RD

Natural History
Museum

MUBC
(National University)

ZALUUCHUUD AVE

SMALL RING RD (BAGA TOIRUU)

National Museum
of Mongolia

Modern
Art Gallery

Luna Blanca

Cultural Palace

Sukhbaatar
Square

State Opera and
Ballet Theater

Ulaanbaatar Hotel

PEACE AVE (ENK TAIVANI URGUUN CHULUU)

Central Post Office

Air Market
Seven Summits

Art Gallery of the
Union of Mongolian Artists

City Cafe

JAMYAN ST

Memorial Museum for
Victims of Political Persecution

Grand Khaan
Irish Pub

Ard Theater
Square

Chinggis Beer Hall

Veranda

Choijin Lama
Monastery Museum

National Academic
Drama Theatre

Millie's Cafe

CHINGGIS AVE

Ulaanbaatar
(detail)

500 ft
150 m

N

Bayangol Hotel

# WHAT TO DO

## History Museums

The **National Museum of Mongolia** (MNT2,500 for adults, MNT1,200 for students; open daily 10:00 a.m.-4:30 p.m.) is located one block northwest of Sukhbaatar Square. Perhaps the best museum in the country, the National Museum guides you through Mongolia's past, from the Paleolithic to the present. The journey through time begins in prehistory with the museum's excellent collection of ancient artifacts. The first few halls are devoted to the earliest inhabitants of what is now Mongolia, before Chinggis united the Mongol tribes: the Khunnu, who roamed the steppes over 2,000 years ago, the shamanic Hianbe, the Jujan, who ruled from 402 to 552 C.E. and are the first group considered ethnically Mongolian, the Turks, who gave way to a likely pre-Islamic Uighur regime in 840 A.D., and finally the Khidan, who ultimately fell to Chinggis and his hordes.

Bronze-age bridles and swords adorned with ram's heads in this section shed some light on the region's inhabitants' long, close relationship with horses and livestock. This section also explains the only vestiges of truly ancient, pre-Mongolian society that you're likely to see during your trip: the "deer stones," which date to the Bronze Age, and the "man stones" from the Turkish period.

From there, the museum makes its own attempt at collecting the Mongol tribes in the form of a hall of *deels* and hats representing the country's ethnic minorities. Besides displaying some beautiful and incredibly detailed costumes, the hall points out some of the ethnic minority groups that make largely heterogeneous Mongolia somewhat more diverse, including the Khotons, who are Mongolized Uighurs, the Myangad, a mixed Turkish-Mongolian group, and the Uzemchin, the "grape people" of eastern Mongolia.

Some of the museum is a tad underwhelming. The Mongol Empire period feels choppy and underdeveloped despite being the pinnacle of Mongolian society, and there is scarcely any information on the Manchurian period, perhaps out of a desire to forget that the whole period of subservience to the Chinese ever happened. The hall devoted to the communist period should be fascinating but is largely untranslated and reflects the marginal imaginative capabilities of the period's leaders. But the museum ends on another high note with an exhibition on the democratic revolution and the years since. Fittingly, the contemporary era's exhibition, including some multimedia installations, is the most modern and energetic.

The **Natural History Museum** (MNT2,500 for adults, MNT1,200 for students; open daily 10:00 a.m.-4:30 p.m.) is located one block northwest of Sukhbaatar

Square. Mongolia has no shortage of impressive natural history from which to pull materials for a first-class museum. And while the Natural History Museum isn't the Smithsonian by any stretch of the imagination, it does have a wide range of objects, some awe-inspiring, others just a little silly, on exhibit.

This museum is a bit of a labyrinth. Start your tour at the hall heading right from the main lobby, and you should be on the right track. You'll move through exhibits detailing the plants, insects, minerals, and animal life found in Mongolia as well as the occasional intergalactic interloper in the form of some fabulous meteorites.

However, most people come for the fossils, which are found on the second floor. The main hall, a darkened cave where photography is not allowed, displays several nearly complete skeletons of fearsome beasts long since extinct. A sauropod pelvis, as large as a car, puts our own position at the top of the food chain in perspective, but not quite so much as the huge (really, absolutely massive) deinocheirus arms.

Beyond the big guys, there is an excellent collection of dinosaur eggs, fossils of ancient turtles and smaller dinosaurs, including the famous fighting dinosaurs, locked together in eternal combat by some unexpected force of nature millions of years ago. The fighting dinosaurs, as famed as they are, have not been put in any sort of special spotlight and are somewhat easily missed if you're not paying attention. On our last visit to the museum, they seemed to be missing entirely, hopefully just for some routine restoration and upkeep.

The **Choijin Lama Monastery Museum** (MNT2,500 for adults, MNT1,000 for students; open daily 9:00 a.m.-5:30 p.m.) is south of Sukhbaatar Square behind the big blue sail-shaped building. For those interested in Buddhist art and architecture, this museum is not to be missed. Housed in a small complex of once active temples, Choijin Lama ceased to function as a monastery during the purges of the1930s, but it has been open as a museum nearly ever since. Like most monasteries of historic importance, this one is exhaustively detailed in its décor; *thankga* paintings, *tsam* dance masks, Zanabazar statues, and other artifacts populate the rooms. There is also a highly interesting map of pre-Soviet Ulaanbaatar as it looked in the first decade of the twentieth century next to the ticket window.

The **Winter Palace of the Bogd Khan** (MNT2,500; open daily 9:00 a.m.-5:00 p.m.) is on the road to Zaisan; walk or take any Zaisan bus (M33 from Ard theater or Bayangol Hotel, M43 from Urgoo, Ard, or Bayangol Hotel, or M7 from Bayangol Hotel). A home of Mongolia's religious and political leader for the dozen years between the end of the Manchu period and the beginning of Communism, the eighth Jebtsundamba Khutugt, also known as the Bogd Khan, the Winter Palace is full of artifacts that attest to the leader's broad interests. Unfortunately, perusing his collection of exotic animals (a live menagerie in his time, now stuffed), luxurious furs and jewelry, carriages, cars, and other Western novelties is not quite as exciting as it must have been to actually hold court with the Bogd Khan, who was infamous for his alcoholic binges, lust for men and women of all ages, and thirst for power and influence, which he attained by any means necessary. Of course, we do not feel that we are missing out on the dose of poison that concluded a diplomatic visit to the White Palace for many foreign visitors.

The **Memorial Museum for Victims of Political Persecution** (MNT3,000; open Monday-Friday 9:00 a.m.-5:00 p.m.) is two blocks south of Sukhbaatar Square. Small and somber, this museum is devoted to the political purges carried out during the late 1930s at the demand of then-Prime Minister Khorloogiin Choibalsan. The Stalinist measures sought to scatter and destroy those considered a threat to Mongolia's planned economy and atheist communist government. Like elsewhere in the Soviet bloc, these purges were especially harsh on intellectuals and Buddhist lamas; nearly 750 monasteries were destroyed during this time, and an estimated 30,000 people died.

The daughter of Peljidiin Genden, Mongolia's Prime Minister from 1932 to 1936 established the museum. Genden was perhaps the first victim of the purges, assassinated in Russia after being charged of spying for Russia. (The next Prime Minister, Anandiin Amar, suffered the same fate in 1939. Choibalsan took the position next and began the purges in earnest.) Genden's office is still set up as part of the museum, which is located in his former home. You could sit at his desk and pick up his telephone if you were inclined to imagine yourself as the doomed leader.

Unfortunately, very little of the museum's information has been translated into English, and it is difficult to distinguish between who was a victim and who was a perpetrator. If you are truly interested in the time period, bring a translator and a healthy dose of patience.

For a jarring experience, visit the Zanabazar Fine Arts Museum before coming here and compare the famous painting *One Day in Mongolia* at the former with the painting (unofficially named) *One Day of the Purges* at the latter.

The **International Intellectual Museum** (MNT3,000; open Monday-Saturday 10:00 a.m.-6:00 p.m.) is located on the west side of the north-south road that runs from Peace Avenue to Narantuul. This museum towards the east end of Ulaanbaatar is an odd collection of dolls and toys from across the world (some may be familiar to visiting tourists from their own childhoods) as well as games, puzzles, and other brain teasers. The traditional Mongolian carved wooden 3D puzzles are decidedly highlights. The operator of this museum takes his games and toys very seriously and demands your undivided attention to them, so if you take a guided tour (and you may not have a choice) be prepared for your intellect to be challenged, tested, and stretched.

The **Museum of Ulaanbaatar City History** (MNT1,500; open daily 9:00 a.m.-6:00 p.m.) is found off Peace Avenue, 1.3 kilometers (0.8 miles) from Sukhbaatar Square near the Wrestling Palace. This very small museum is housed in one of the city's older buildings, a long, low Siberian-esque cabin. The museum has little English information, but for those keen on getting a better idea of how rapidly Ulaanbaatar has developed over the years, the visuals should do the trick.

**Gandan Khiid** (Гандан тэгчинлэн хийд) was one of only a few Buddhist houses of worship to remain after the communist purges of the 1930s. Originally opened in 1835, Gandan was closed for a brief period between 1938 and 1944 but remained open thereafter as the only sanctioned Buddhist monastery in the country until 1990. Once the center of Tibetan Buddhism in Mongolia, the grounds were maintained by a small staff of monks as a museum signifying the long cultural history of Mongolia. Now home to over 150 monks, Gandan also houses an impressive 26.5-meter-tall (87 feet) gilded and bejeweled Migjid Janraisig statue that was rebuilt from private funds in 1996 as an enhanced replica of the original copper statue that had been destroyed by Russian troops in 1938. It remains the most important monastery in Mongolia and a favorite destination for visitors, both foreign and domestic. You can get there by bus M46, or walk west from Sukhbaatar Square for 2.5 km (1.5 miles).

## Art Museums

The **Zanabazar Fine Arts Museum** and the **Red Ger Art Gallery** (MNT2,500; open daily 9:00 a.m.-6:00 p.m. in the summer, 10:00 a.m.-5:00 p.m. in the winter) are located on Juulchin Chuluu a block east of the Urtiin Tsagaan Market. It is one of the finest museums in Ulaanbaatar or anywhere in Mongolia. Named after the Bogd Gegeen Zanabazar, a seventeenth century spiritual and political leader and an accomplished artist who specialized in bronze sculpture, the museum is largely devoted to Buddhist art and traditional Mongolian mediums. Aside from Zanabazar's own intricate sculptures of Buddhist deities, highlights include an excellent collection of pre-Mongolian Bronze Age carvings and artifacts, better even than the National Museum's.

The rest of the museum takes you through exhibits of detailed Buddhist *thangka* paintings, cloth appliqué, *tsam* dance masks, and ritual instruments, some made of bone. Finally, there is a hall of somewhat more contemporary paintings with secular themes. *One Day in Mongolia*, by Balduugiin Sharav, is probably the most iconic Mongolian painting around. Ironically, Sharav later became a commercial and propaganda artist for the Communist Party, leaving his more creative work behind.

The first floor of the museum is composed of private galleries of modern painting, the best one being the Red Ger Art Gallery. Run by the Union of Mongolian Artists, it has an ever-changing selection of modern art by some of the country's brightest artists for sale. Entry is free and the opportunity to see some newer work shouldn't be passed up.

The **Modern Art Gallery** (MNT2,000; open daily 9:00 a.m.-5:00 p.m.) is inside the Cultural Palace on the east side of Sukhbaatar Square. The Modern Art Gallery has a large permanent collection of paintings and other works by Mongolian artists. As its name suggests, the museum trends towards newer works without the religious themes of Zanabazar of Choijin Lama, although modern Mongolian art still has a significant emphasis on the Mongolian; paintings of horses, mountains, mothers, and nature scenes, rendered in cubist styles or more abstractly than the older Soviet realist paintings, are common. The museum also has a space for temporary exhibits.

Some of the museum's holdings, including one-of-a-kind works of art and irreplaceable primary texts, were damaged or destroyed in the fire and looting of the July 2008 upheavals.

The **Art Gallery of the Union of Mongolian Artists** (open daily 10:00 a.m.-6:00 p.m.; free admission) is next to the Bangkok Restaurant on the second floor of a shopping center located conveniently across the street from Sukhbaatar Square. This one-room gallery features temporary exhibitions of contemporary art, generally paintings. If you wander in during a solo show, you may even have the chance to meet the artist. Exhibits rotate every few weeks or so.

The **Khan Bank Art Gallery** (open Monday-Friday 9:00 a.m.-5:00 p.m.; free admission), located at Khan Bank Center, Seoul Street 25, shows temporary exhibits of modern Mongolian art.

## UB Squares, Parks & Nature

Ulaanbaatar is troublesomely short on green space, but like any Soviet-designed city worth its hammer and sickle, there are plenty of public squares. The main ones are all within a few blocks of one another, but each has a distinct character. For first class people watching, drop in to any of them.

**Zaisan Memorial (Зайсан)**, a perennially popular spot, features a monument to Russian-Mongolia military cooperation through the years. Set on a hill at the edge of the Bogd Khan Mountain Range, the memorial is dominated by an immense, 360-degree mosaic featuring Mongolian and Russian soldiers, cosmonauts, nurses, and common-folk working together to rid the country of the White Russians, and later, fascist threats during World War II. From the hilltop, there is a nearly unimpeded view across the whole of Ulaanbaatar, giving you a sense of the true scope of the city and of the pace of its growth. Ulaanbaatar can feel small at times, but the reality is that the city center and the *ger* districts that surround it dominate the entire valley, creeping up the hillsides to the north. There is a large statue of a standing Buddha in the park next to Zaisan, along with a ritual drum and bell that you can take a swing at.

To get to Zaisan, take any south-bound bus marked Зайсан from the Ard Theater square or the bus stop near the Bayangol Hotel (numbers 33, 43, 7).

**Sukhbaatar Square (Сүхбаатарын талбай)** is the political heart and soul of Ulaanbaatar. The square is like a cyclorama of Mongolian history. At the north end is an enormous bronze statue of Chinggis Khan, which perhaps owes something to Washington D.C.'s Lincoln Memorial. Behind Chinggis's throne sits the Parliament building, where Mongolia's lawmakers meet. The square itself was a major tactical point for Damadiin Sukhbaatar and his Red Army allies when they pushed out the Chinese once and for all in 1921, hence the square's name. Later, pro-democracy activists used the square to stage the protests and hunger-strikes that led to the current multi-party era. Sukhbaatar Square remains the go-to spot for political dissenters looking to air their grievances, but it is also the venue for countless celebrations and cultural events throughout the year, including New Year's Eve fireworks and free, outdoor summer concerts.

The square's eastern side is shored up by the Democratic Party's headquarters and the stolid-looking but very active Cultural Palace, which features an art museum and performance halls. Turn around and look to the western side and you'll see that Mongolia's first major private banks have set up shop as has the Mongolian Stock Exchange. The Central Post Office sports a huge neon Coca-Cola billboard, an indication of inescapable globalization and international capitalism. Across Peace Avenue from the soft-drink adorned building, there is a small park with a statue of the much beloved and greatly missed "grandfather" of Mongolian democracy, Sanjaasuren Zorig. Finally, look towards the southeastern corner to get a glimpse of where Mongolia's burgeoning capitalist economy is headed—or hopes to be headed,

The Guide

at least. There, the Shangri-la Center houses boutiques from global fashion elites like Louis Vuitton and Burberry as well as a swanky nightclub on the 17th floor. There is a small park between Shangri-La Center and Peace Avenue with a fine fountain and a number of benches on paths that cut through well-groomed grass.

Sukhbaatar Square is active at nearly any time of day or night. During daylight hours, and especially in summer, you'll find a number of small-time entrepreneurs renting out inline skates, tandem bicycles, or go-karts, and curious passer-bys pay to take a spin around the square. There is also a small horde of licensed photographers present who take photos of Mongolians visiting the city in front of the statues and run to develop them at the photo centers nearby. In this age of cheap digital cameras and mobile phone cameras, these guys probably won't be in business for much longer.

**Independence Square**, which until recently was known as Victory Square, is a few blocks north of the State Department Store. Like Sukhbaatar Square, it holds an important place in Mongolian history. It was a prominent meeting place for revolutionaries in the 1920s, when Sukhbaatar's forces met the Red Army here before moving to Sukhbaatar square, as well as in the 1990s. Today, Independence Square's main point of interest is the Tengis movie theater, one of Ulaanbaatar's premier cinema experiences.

Independence Square was renovated in the summer of 2010, transforming it from obscurity as an empty concrete block to a legitimate public gathering place, complete with a well-lit fountain.

**The Beatles Promenade** (not the park's official name) is a series of non-functioning fountains that stretches the distance between the State Department Store and the Circus. The main attraction is the fairly inexplicable piece of public art memorializing the Beatles found at the northern end. Certainly, the Fab Four are as popular now as ever in Mongolia (if you're ever called upon to sing a tune, and you will be, you can't go wrong with "Yesterday"), but the statue appears almost out of nowhere. However, if you're in need of a spot to sit and think, you might as well do it with John, Paul, George, and Ringo.

**Ard Theater Square**, formerly the People's Theater, has a unique windowed façade. However, it is no longer a theater but rather a bank, and there isn't much noteworthy about this square. Still, it is in a high-traffic area, and there is always a crowd of people waiting for the bus—you can catch one towards Zaisan or the airport from here—or selling cigarettes and candy from the street-side benches. There are several excellent restaurants on the north side of this small square.

**Children's Park**, located south of the Choijin Lama Monastery, was partially renovated in 2010. This is about as close to an amusement park as anything in Mongolia; the attractions include a Ferris wheel, merry-go-round, and bumper cars, among other rides. The park itself is free. However, to tempt fate and go on the rides, you'll need to buy tickets for each go at a cost of MNT2,000-2,500. This park will be of most interest to those who fall squarely into the category of children.

## Birdwatching in UB

You can begin birdwatching when the plane taxis to the gate upon arrival at the airport in UB or your train squeaks into the station. While cities generally are not the best habitat, there are often a few prizes to be had. In winter, Red-billed Choughs and corvids abound with flocks of Eurasian Jackdaws, Carrion Crows, Rooks, and Ravens watching over the city. Catch a ride, walk, or take bus 7 or 47 (toward Zaisan) to the Tuul River near Peace Bridge. This riparian area is on the southern route out of the city and probably the best section within the city limits to see Azure and Penduline Tit, Siberian Rubythroat, Daurian Redstart, and the beautiful Azure-winged Magpie. It's on the way to the airport and if you plan well, you can make the convenient stop on the way to Zaisan Monument, to the Bogd Khan Palace, or out of the country.

## Entertainment

**Tengis Movie Theater** is just up the street from the State Department Store and the TEDY building. The theater has three screens and may or may not have movies in English. This is a really fun place to catch a Mongolian film or a film in English with Mongolian subtitles. The building also contains a really nice restaurant and an arcade. Check the website (www.tengis.mn) for movies and times. Though the website is not in English, it is easy to understand what the movies are and when they are showing.

**Urgoo Cinema (Өргөө)** is the largest Ulaanbaatar movie theater as it has five screens. From most guesthouses and hotels, you can take a cab or you can catch the bus or trolley (M28, M31, M43, M45, M46, T5). If you give yourself some time, it is worth walking to the third and fourth district to see the views of the city and peek in at where average Mongolians do their boutique shopping. Typically, there is at least one movie in English (with subtitles) and sometimes more. You can check the website (www.urgoo.mn) for movies and times, but like the website for Tengis, it is not available in English.

The **State Opera and Ballet Theater** is easy to find. Just look east for the salmon colored building next to Sukhbaatar Square. With a board outside the theatre listing the shows for the current month in English, it is also easy to find out whether there is a performance that you would be interested in. The box office is open 10:00 a.m.-1:00 p.m. and 2:00 p.m.-5:00 p.m. Wednesday through Sunday. You may not need to buy tickets too far in advance, depending on the popularity of the show, but it is best to be safe. It is a state-funded theater so the prices are beyond cheap. The most expensive seats in the house are MNT8,000. However, seats on the far ends of the balcony require you to lean really far forward, and you will a miss a chunk of the show. Honestly, the performances are far from perfect and nowhere near Western standards of opera and ballet, but for the price, it's worth the trip (but probably only once).

The **National Academic Drama Theatre** has performances throughout most of the year. The theater is hosted in the ostentatious red building next to the Grand Khaan Irish Pub. Productions by Mongolian playwrights as well as English-speaking playwrights are within the repertoire. There are only between six and ten performances every month, and schedules are sporadic. Show listings are available in the UB Post, which you can find at any newspaper stand. You can buy tickets in advance at the booking office in the theater.

## WHERE TO STAY

You'll have numerous options for lodging in Ulaanbaatar, but you don't need to spend a lot of money to get a decent night's sleep. To make the decision easier, we've made recommendations of our favorite places to stay in the city.

If you don't mind sharing a little space, guesthouses are perfectly suitable, especially for backpackers. Most of the guesthouses are in the best locations, and they have kitchens, hot water, clean sheets, dorms, and private rooms available all for great prices. Unless you're looking for a posh place with a doorman and a mint, or you're a little older and you just can't stand those darn kids and all that racket, it doesn't seem necessary to pay hotel prices unless you need to use a credit card. Guesthouses are more fun, the staff is more interesting and can help you book your countryside treks, and meeting the other guests is part of your adventure as well.

### Guesthouses

**Mongolian Steppe** A favorite not only because it's the cheapest, but that helps. If you are looking to meet some Americans who live and volunteer in the countryside, this may be your best stop. The owner, Eiggy (pronounced "Eggy"), is one of the sweetest women in the city. She grew up in the countryside of Sukhbaatar Aimag but now lives the big city life, often moonlighting as an English teacher. She can arrange nearly anything for you, and her English is fantastic. The guesthouse has a kitchen, shower, luggage storage, book exchange, visa services, airport transfers, car parking, laundry services, wireless internet, computer, and tours. If you are looking for someone to make you traditional clothes like a *deel* or a shirt, she can arrange that for you as well. Eiggy doesn't hover around all the time, but she comes in to clean every day. Dorm beds are $5 per person per night, double rooms $7, and single rooms $12 per person per night. They can arrange for you to stay with herders in Ulaanbaatar, Tuv Aimag (Terelj National Park), Sukhbaatar Aimag, and elsewhere at $5 per person per night. *11322100, 99162771; http://mongoliansteppe.mine.nu/index.php*

**Khongor Guesthouse** Just west of the State Department Store and a short walk to Sukhbaatar Square, Khongor has dormitory beds and private rooms. It's also a favorite for many volunteers. Like most other guesthouses, it offers kitchen facilities, hot showers, luggage storage, a book exchange, visa services, airport transfers, car parking, laundry services, internet, and tours. The staff can also pick you up from the train station and airport. Additionally, there is a safety box with every dorm bed, curtains, electricity, and light. Some interesting offers include bicycle rental and custom-made *deels* and *morin khuur*s. Dorm beds are $5 per person per night, a single room is $10, double room $12, and two-bedroom apartment with kitchen and shower $25 per night. There are discounts for stays of more than seven continuous days. *11316415, 99252599, 99199233; khongor@mongol.net; www.mandarinmedia.com/projects/khongor/*

**Lotus Guesthouse** Accessible through the courtyard of an apartment complex on Small Ring Road. This is a place where you can feel great about staying. If you are interested in volunteer tourism, this is your place. Proceeds from the guesthouse and its delightful vegetarian restaurant provide money for the children at an orphanage center, where you can volunteer short and long term. Since the guesthouse caters especially to expat professionals and international volunteers with disposable income, you have a good opportunity to learn about projects that the organization is working on and maybe offer your help, too. It is a bit more upscale and more expensive, but not by too much, and the atmosphere is calmer than you would expect from a guesthouse. The cheapest bed is around $10. Lower bunks in the eight-bed dorm can be transformed into couches making it the ideal place for small groups wanting to share a room and have some privacy. The bedding includes traditional quilts, which gives the room a comfortable home feeling. The double room ($20 per person per night) has a bed and a small cupboard perfect for a couple or a single person wanting some privacy. The Traditional Room ($15 per person per night) is decorated in traditional Mongolian style and has plenty of space for the weary traveler. There are four rooms equipped like a *ger*. All the typical guesthouse accoutrements are available including wireless internet. *Office open 10:00 a.m.-6:00 p.m. daily; reception is open 24-hours. Check-in after 12:00 noon. 11325967, 95137365; lotusguest@gmail.com; http://www.lotuschild.org*

**UB Guesthouse** The most well known and reliable of all the guesthouses, and a venerable favorite. The guesthouse has been seen and reviewed in countless books and magazines, and it deserves acclaim. Mr. Kim and his staff are all kind and willing to make your time Mongolia the best it can be. They've been doing this for a while, so they know how everything runs and they're good at it. The place is busy

The Guide

almost all year round, and if you want to meet other travelers from every part of the world, this is your best bet. There is a relaxed atmosphere, kitchen facilities, hot showers, luggage storage, book exchange, visa services, airport transfers, car parking, laundry services, wireless internet, and multiple tours. Any service you need, the staff can handle, including arranging a place to stay in Moscow if you are taking the Trans-Siberian Railway. Lodging comes with free breakfast. Dorm beds are $6 per person per night, a twin room (with bunk beds) $16 per room, double room (with one big bed) $18 per room, and single room $15 per person per night. Apartments and hotels can be booked through UB Guesthouse at a discounted price. *11311037, 91199859; ubguest@yahoo.com; http://www.ubguest.com/*

**Golden Gobi** Looks like it might be a former MTV Real World house. It has brightly colored walls, a large bar and kitchen area, and a comfy TV room with satellite in the basement filled with movies and huge couches. The guesthouse has a great location near the State Department Store (just east in the courtyard behind Peace Avenue). There are shared showers for dorm rooms, luggage storage, book exchange, visa services, airport transfers, car parking, laundry services, and tours. Dorm Beds are $6 per person per night, double room with private bath and king bed $23 per room, double room with shared bath $19 per room, and a single room is $19 per person per night. Watch for the rate of the dollar to change if you plan to pay with *tugriks*, especially if you stay for a couple of nights. If the dollar loses, you lose. *Chingeltei District, 1st Subdistrict, 1-40000, Building 13; 11322632, 96654496; golden_gobi@yahoo.com; www.goldengobi.com*

**Nassan** This guesthouse is just three minutes from Sukhbaatar Square next to the Flower Center. It offers a dorm and double and twin rooms as well as an apartment. Dorm beds are $7, and private rooms are $10. Like most guesthouses they offer visa services (extension of Mongolian visa, Chinese visa), airline or train ticket ordering, laundry, luggage storage, free internet, various tours, and transportation (free pick up from train station). The staff will also pick you up or drop you off at the airport for $10. *99197466; www.nassantours.com/contact/*

**Mr. Gomez Hostel** It is located near the train station. This 13-bed guesthouse is a little more expensive than your average Ulaanbaatar stop at $10 for a dorm bed and $11 for a private room. Services include airport pickup ($20) and free train station pick up. The guesthouse accepts credit cards and offers complimentary breakfast, a restaurant, guest kitchen, laundry, internet, free towels, and money exchange. Pets are allowed, and smoking as well as non-smoking rooms are available. If you have pets with you, this is one of very few choices. *Building #16, Door 3, Bayangol duureg, I Khoroo; 11311051; info@samarmagictours.com*

**Zaya's Hostel** Four minutes from State Department Store, this guesthouse offers two locations. They have triple ($12), double ($15), and single rooms ($25). All the standard services are included, such as free wireless internet, kitchen, complimentary breakfast, luggage storage, and tours. Check their excellent website for more details. *Apartment 10,11,12 1st fl., Building 63, Tserendorj Street or #2 Apartment 5, 3rd fl., Building 25/4, Peace Avenue; 11331575; www.zayahostel.com*

**Mongolian Resorts** This huge guesthouse has 46 beds, and at the height of the season it can house up to 60 people. If you have a large group, this is your best bet! Dorm rooms are $8, and double rooms are $16. The guesthouse offers visa services, free wireless internet, kitchen, laundry, free train station pick up, airport transport, and tours. You'll find this guesthouse on the corner of Seoul Street between the Circus and State Department Store. *info@mongolianresorts.com; www.travels-mongolia.com*

**Idre's Guesthouse** This guesthouse is near the train station in the Byangol District, 1st Micro District, Building 22. It has dorms and private doubles available at $6 for a dorm bed and $18 for a private double. It has a kitchen, internet, laundry, luggage storage, tours, complimentary breakfast, and a common room. Additionally, the guesthouse offers many options for tours. You can check the website for more detailed information. *99112575, 11325241; idrehouse@yahoo.com; www.idretour.com.*

**Youth Mongolia** This small guesthouse has a four- to eight-person dorm room at $10 per person per night. Located just west of the Circus, this guesthouse offers internet, 24-hour reception, tours, kitchen, and a common room. *88111774; youthmongolia@yahoo.com.*

## Hotels

**Flower Hotel (Цэцэг зочин буудал)** Located further away from shopping, entertainment, and tourist areas. However, this hotel offers some lovely views of the city and comfortable room options. There are three onsite restaurants that offer Chinese, European, and Japanese as well as Mongolian cuisines. Do yourself a favor and sit outside and enjoy the *shorlog* (kebab) and a cold draft beer. It's even worth the walk to the hotel if you aren't staying there. Free high-speed internet access in rooms. You can also enjoy a massage and sing your lungs out with some karaoke! A single room is $32 a night. The rest of the rooms range from $36-110. *Zaluuchuud Avenue 18; 11458330; flowerhotel@magic.mn; www.flower-hotel.com*

**Evergreen Hotel** The place to stay if you want a more Mongolian experience while still staying in a Holiday Inn-style hotel. It is really clean, and the beds are comfortable. The location is in a slightly residential area, which is a little sketchy to walk through at night. However, it's pretty close to Dave's Place (British expat hang out) and the festivities of Seoul Street. If you are interested in visiting Zuunmood (Tuv Aimag capital), the hotel is just around the corner from the Teeveriin Tovchoo (transportation depot) to get you there, and it's also pretty close to the train station. Free high-speed internet is available in rooms along with cable TV. A standard single is $45; most other rooms are $55-75. *Teeverchidiin Street 6, Bayangol district; 21242135, 242525, 11325744, 99081494; info@evergreen.mn; www.evergreen.mn*

**Chinggis Khaan Hotel** A beautiful four-star hotel located in the business and cultural district of Ulaanbaatar. What does that mean for you? Well, it is not particularly close to anything. But, if you are interested in a more luxurious vacation, you most definitely want to stay here. Each room has high-speed internet access and satellite television. The hotel contains restaurants with Mongolian, Indian, Chinese, and European food along with a pub. For relaxing, there is an indoor swimming pool, a sauna, massage services, and a fitness center. If you want

The Guide

help with your flight or future flights, you can arrange it through the Korean Air and Air Market offices located in the building. One large point of interest about the Chinggis Khaan Hotel is that it shares a building with the Sky shopping center. Many expats prefer this shopping experience because of the wide selection of Western food and beverages. In addition, you can find antiques and cashmere in the shopping center, though you will pay a price for them! A standard room with a single bed ranges from $110-142, and the standard with a twin bed is $132-166. A one-bedroom suite is $187-228, a two bedroom is $259-309, and, of course, there is the Presidential suite, which is $599-689. *Tokyo Street 10, Ulaanbaatar 49; 11313380, 11312788; www.chinggis-hotel.com*

**Ulaanbaatar Hotel (Улаанбаатар зочин буудал)** Has the best location of any hotel in Ulaanbaatar. It is situated just east of Sukhbaatar Square, incredibly close to the opera, museums, shopping, and several restaurants. However, it hasn't been updated in years, and many believe it isn't worth the price you pay. The hotel offers high-speed internet, sauna, massage, and a fitness center. There is a small store with souvenirs, but with its excellent location, you are better off walking down the street to find the same thing at a lower price. There is a decent Indian restaurant in the hotel called Taj Mahal, but Dehli Darbar has a better atmosphere and better food. The standard single room is $100-105, and the standard twin room is $120-127 with single bed and $160-169 with two beds. There are also superior, deluxe, and suite rooms from $147-317. The Presidential Suite is $1,200-1,267, but for that price you could stay in a better hotel for double the time. *Sukhbaatar Square 14; 11320620, 70116688; reservations@ubhotel.mn; www.ubhotel.mn*

# WHERE TO EAT

Restaurants are always coming and going in Mongolia, but these have been some of our venerable favorites. In the center of town, it's easy to walk down the street and find something that looks interesting. Don't be afraid to try a restaurant if it isn't listed here. The likely places to

| Food Price Key |
| --- |
| Prices in MNT |
| ₮ – 0 – 3,000 |
| ₮₮ – 3,001-10,000 |
| ₮₮₮ – 10,001-20,000 |
| ₮₮₮₮ – 20,000 + |

look for good food are on Peace Avenue between Sukhbaatar Square and the State Department Store, Seoul Street, and the Small Ring Road.

**American Burger and Fries (AB&F)** Just what you think it is. Are you tired of rice, noodles, and mutton fat and just want a juicy burger with fries? AB&F has the best burger for the price in UB. The restaurant has also recently rolled the former Sub'baatar Sandwich Shop's menu into their own. You can't beat the location, especially if you are staying at one of the many close guesthouses. The owner, Robert, is a very friendly American, though the cooks are Mongolian. The restaurant sometimes hosts English conversation events and tries to help raise money for several pet projects. ₮₮

**Ananda Café & Meditation Center** A must-visit location. Not only does it offer different vegetarian meals every day, it also runs programs, including Yoga, meditation, philosophy, and vegetarian cooking classes. It's a great organization. Stop by and see what is available to eat and do that day. *http://www.anandacenter.org/* ₮

**Café Amsterdam** The perfect place to start your morning people watching on Peace Avenue with a small snack and a brewed coffee or an espresso beverage. The prices are a little high, but it is worth it for the location. Wireless internet and couches could have you there until lunch. ₮₮

**California** Casual fine dining (think T.G.I.Fridays) on the higher end as far as prices go. The menu is strongly anchored by Buffalo wings, salads, sandwiches, and hearty entrees. The pizzas are delicious, and they come out with the cheese baked dark brown. It is probably the best place to get a really good (and huge) Long Island Iced Tea for the price, and the front patio is a nice place to enjoy it. ₮₮₮

**Chinggis Club** A brewery that dates back to 1997. It is run by a German master brewer, and it serves his native cuisine. Chinggis Club has a thirst-quenching light pilsner that goes down easy and a sweet dark beer. The food is decent and includes sausages and other typical Germanic meat and potatoes. ₮₮/₮₮₮

## Mongolian Barbeque

As previously stated, Mongolian barbeque is neither Mongolian nor barbeque. It is a stir-fried dish from Taiwanese restaurants that was first conceived in the 1970s. The food is comprised of meat and vegetables cooked on large, round, solid iron griddles at temperatures of up to 300° C (572° F).

The first Mongolian Barbecue restaurant, Gengis Khan Mongolian BBQ, opened in downtown Taipei, Taiwan in 1976. The idea for the name came from the images evoked of Mongolian soldiers cooking in the countryside on large open surfaces. The preparation derives from Japanese-style *teppanyaki*, which was popular in Taiwan in the 1970s. American restaurants such as HuHot Mongolian Grill and BD's Mongolian Barbeque claim that soldiers of the Mongol Empire gathered large quantities of meats, prepared them with their swords, and cooked them on their overturned shields over a large fire. Is this true? Who knows! But, it is a fun concept. Once you've spent time in the countryside without many vegetables, you'll love the idea regardless.

There are two chains that serve Mongolian barbeque in Ulaanbaatar. The first one is the popular American restaurant **BD's Mongolian Grill**. It is on Seoul Street, a short walk from the Circus and near the Teeverin Tovchoo. The kitsch is evident, but the food is great. One special touch that you will only see in the Mongolian location is the addition of sheep fat (өөх) on the buffet. You may not notice any foreigners picking it up, but the Mongolians eat it proudly. (When you bring your food to the griddle, see if you can pick which piles of grilling food belongs to Mongolians and which ones belong to foreigners.)

Surprisingly, BD's is more expensive than most fine dining restaurants in Ulaanbaatar. Expect to spend at least MNT15,000 for one meal. It is all you can eat, so it might be worth it if you are extremely hungry! **Altai Mongolian Grill** has a few locations around town, but the one closest to the action is east on Seoul from BD's, across the street from the Circus. Much like BD's, it is a pretty expensive meal, but it is slightly cheaper. The atmosphere is also less kitschy than BD's but not by much. You can use a credit card at both, and both have special lunch prices.

*The Guide*

**Chinggis Beer Hall** A part of the Chinggis Beer franchise. It's a little closer to the action than the Club and has a fun atmosphere. Bring a large group and have some fun—it's a beer hall, after all! ₮₮

**City Café** One of the best places to find *shorlog* (kebabs) in the city! On a nice summer day, sit outside and enjoy the smell of roasting meat. Get mellow and people watch at the busy intersection near Sukhbaatar Square while enjoying a GEM draft. Oh, and the rest of the menu is good, too. ₮₮

**Cola and Kebab** A budget chain with several locations all around the city. Don't say the name too fast or it might come out "Colon Kebab," and no one wants to eat there. The kebabs are not on skewers; they are more like gyros. It's cheap. It's fast. And it fills you up. ₮

**Dave's Place** An English pub near Brau Haus between Peace Avenue and Seoul Street. Expats and travelers trudge there every Thursday evening for the trivia competition at 8:30 p.m. (MNT1,000). The trivia host rotates each week among the Australian, Irish, British, American, and Canadian regulars, and the winning team walks away with the pot. This is the second incarnation of the Place during Dave's tenure in Mongolia. If you're knackered, the cold draught beer is the dog's bollocks, the food should leave you chuffed without nicking you too bad, and you might find a footie on the telly. ₮₮₮

**Delhi Darbar** An excellent choice for Indian food in Mongolia due to its wonderful menu and perfect location. The food here rivals any Indian restaurant you would encounter anywhere in the Western world. It is on the expensive side, but is well worth the price. It is a short walk south of State Department by the Beatles statue. Grab your friends and family and share a great meal after a day of souvenir shopping. ₮₮₮

**Grand Khaan Irish Pub** Located on Seoul Street near Sukhbaatar Square. A bit of a luxurious place where you're likely to find expat miners, your parents, and members of the Mongolian "upper crust." There is an extensive menu with both American (huge gourmet burgers) and British (surprisingly decent fish and chips) food as well as Guinness on draft. Live Mongolian pop and alternative rock musicians fill the small stage a few nights a week, though the local talent usually only plays one short set. The deck and secondary seating can be a boatload of fun on a summer evening. If you have cash to throw around, give it a shot. ₮₮₮

**Granville Irish Pub** Huge menu and a great choice if you are looking for American-style casual fine dining with huge portions at a good price. It occasionally has buy two, get one free drink specials. If you are staying at a guesthouse, it is just a heartbeat away. Look for it just north of the Ard Theater bus stop courtyard and fountain. ₮₮

**Ikh Mongol** Near the Circus, just off Seoul Street. Wide-open beer hall with huge portions of food and beer. It's nearly impossible to find a table in the summer evenings due to the daily live music performances. The beer isn't the cheapest around, but it is a fun hangout and a perfect choice for a group of people looking for a good time. It takes credit cards, too. ₮₮

**Khaan Buuz (Хаан бууз)** The largest Mongolian food chain in the country, ergo, the world! You'll see them around. The food is cheap and authentic. You can go here to get a typical Mongolian meal, but you might want to save those meals for the countryside. ₮

**Luna Blanca** On Juulchin Chuluu, 150 meters west of the National Museum of Mongolia. Excellent for travelers looking for vegan and vegetarian examples of Mongolian food as well as non-Mongolian salads and teas. One of the better restaurants based on the teachings of Supreme Master Ching Hai, the self-appointed founder and spiritual teacher of the Quan Yin Method. Choose Luna Blanca for lunch or dinner after a day at the museums, Sukhbaatar Square, or the opera. If you are staying at a guesthouse and want to save some cash, be sure to pick up some pre-made vegan *mantuu buuz* (yeast dumplings) to heat up in your guesthouse kitchen. ₮₮

**Michele's French Bakery** This is a favorite for breakfast. Sure, it isn't directly on Peace Avenue (just a block behind the Mungun Zawiya), but it is easy enough to find. Go there for the mouth-watering French pastries, excellent brewed coffee and espresso beverages, and gloriously fluffy crêpes. There is a deck outside if you want to enjoy the sun, but don't expect much as far as the view goes since it is in the alley. ₮₮

**Millie's Café** The perfect stop after a visit to the Choijin Lama Monastery Museum, directly across the way. Millie, a charming Ethiopian-American, and her Cuban business partner Daniel have anchored the neighborhood expat hangout with quality food and personal attention for more than a decade. Large sandwiches and mouth-watering desserts will really fill you up (and should for the high price). The coffee is good as is the breakfast. It shares the ground floor with an art gallery, and there are lovely photos and paintings on the wall. However, the best feature of the sunny café is the air-conditioning to cool you off on a blazing hot Mongolian summer day. ₮₮/₮₮₮

**Nayra** This is our favorite because the food is yummy (sloppy Dorj, chicken burrito), the location is great (on Juulchin Chuluu, near the Urtiin Tsagaan), the atmosphere is fun (wireless, armchairs, café tables), prices are reasonable (breakfast is the biggest steal at MNT1,200-2,000), and the English-speaking staff is friendly and warm. The pizza isn't perfect, but for the price you can't beat the thin crust selection, especially the petite size that is still big enough to share. If you are looking to meet other foreigners and learn more about the city, be sure to stop here. On your way out the door, take away something from the small bakery/convenience store downstairs. ₮₮

**Орчлон (Universe)** Next to the big, blue glass bank building a block up from Juulchin Chuluu. It's a reasonably priced Chinese restaurant good for groups of people who want to share a meal family style. The atmosphere is nothing fancy, but it will fit your needs if you are looking for Chinese food. ₮₮

**Pacific Restaurant** On the second floor of a two-story restaurant on Seoul Street between the Circus and Grand Khaan Irish Pub. The first floor, Pacific Fast Food, serves decent takeaway, both American- and Japanese-style. The second story restaurant is Japanese. There is a nice bar with a relaxed atmosphere and a kitchen that is open later than most. The sushi is decent but by no means excellent. Rarely, if ever, will you find all the items on the menu, so be sure to ask before you order. Also, though it does have a credit card machine, be prepared with cash. ₮₮/₮₮₮

**Pizza Broadway** Has two convenient locations in the center of town (on Seoul Street next to Mungun Zawiya and across from the MobiCom TEDY building) as well as another location in the third and fourth district. Not only are there several pizzas on the menu, but the restaurant also has salads and other options. It's not the best Italian food, but the pizza is hearty and will fill you up. And you can get a milkshake! The atmosphere is good at both locations, albeit dark. The price is good for what you get. ₮₮/₮₮₮

**Stupa Café** Across from Nayra on Tourist Street. It's a delightful little place filled with English-language books and magazines. It is a quiet and comfortable place to enjoy a sandwich, coffee, or tea. Stupa Café is part of the FPMT Buddhist centre, and profits go toward supporting the restoration of Buddhism in Mongolia. Have a brownie or a tasty seasonal treat and chat with a monk. ₮

**Veranda** Oh-so-expensive but oh-so-good. You may spot a Mongolian celebrity or politician if you know who you're looking for, and you'll likely run into expat bankers and NGO executives. This excellent Italian restaurant has all the typical Italian favorites—the ravioli and pizza are pretty good—in smaller portions than you might expect served on bigger plates than you might expect. Find it right across from the Choijin Lama Museum Monastery. ₮₮₮

# SHOPPING

Souvenir shopping all over Mongolia is a matter of taste and price. If you're in the countryside and you see something you like, buy it there. Not only will you get the best deal, but you'll have given all your money directly to the shop or themselves. But if you're in UB and you want to go trolling for trinkets, there are a few areas to find what you're looking for, some areas you might want to avoid, and some things you to look for that you didn't know you couldn't live without. Slippers and Kazakh bags come to mind.

Bargaining occurs in the outdoor markets, but in small retail shops and malls, there is usually little to no wiggle room. Keep in mind, they may drop a thousand *tugriks* here or there, but do you really want to haggle pennies back and forth with someone who could probably use them a lot more than you?

**The State Department Store** (Их дэлгүүр), Mongolia's oldest mall, has undergone a series of renovations in recent years, and it is looking impressively shiny and new these days. It has electronics, household appliances, camping gear, clothes, shoes, and more—pretty much everything you're looking for. But there's a catch. It draws a lot of English-speakers looking for a quick and easy place to shop, and the pickpockets know that, too. Besides the Narantuul Market, this is one of the top places to have things stolen in Ulaanbaatar. In fact, pickpockets are so good at stealing your stuff, the store's only defense is making the prices so high that you'll leave nothing for the thieves. Feel free to peruse if you have your belongings close to you and you are on guard, being especially careful near the doors and throughout the entire first floor because these guys are dressed well and are very good at concealing what they do. Avoid using the elevator to get to the fifth-floor ATMs unless you have nothing on you or you are very diligent. The stairs and fancy new escalators are usually faster anyhow.

On the top floor, there is nearly every Mongolian item you could possibly want for a souvenir or gift. With a little work, though, you can almost always find these

## Shopping with a Conscience

Quite a lot of international aid money and support has been entering Mongolia since 1991. With the help of this aid many Mongolians have been able to perfect their talents through training in trades. They often undervalue or don't value their time in creating their crafts, frequently selling handicrafts at cost, or only slightly above, to remain competitive or because they can't transport finished products to markets that pay what they really need. If you buy something and it seems too cheap, that's because it probably is too cheap. To combat this, two stand-out retailers sell fair trade goods at prices that allow their artisans to make a living wage.

**Tsagaan Alt** (just south of the State Department Store on the west side, near the Beatles statue) is a non-profit felt handicraft store used as a distributor for many artisans in Selenge Aimag and Darkhan. Employees at the store speak English and are exceedingly helpful. Though there are several products in the store, the Mongolian slippers (товчик, *towchik*) are of good quality and are must-have souvenirs. This is also the best place to find beautiful felt jewelry and felt animals. The animals make great gifts for children or even adults and are very reasonably priced. While you are there, take a minute to watch the informational video shown on the large television in the middle of the store. You can see how the products are made and who made them.

**Mary & Martha** (Peace Avenue just east of the State Department store and to the left of Café Amsterdam) is an adorable basement shop, and the best place to find many interesting things, but most notably, Kazak bags and wall hangings. The people on staff here are some of the best and most informed folks in town. All Mongolian staff members speak English, and if you come at the right time, you can meet Bill and Irene Manley, the investors. They work closely with their artists, know them well, and care about their lives. They are also sticklers for good quality, so you can be comfortable knowing you've bought the best products in town. One of their artists now designs necklaces and bracelets made from *deel* buttons. They are gorgeous, and you are not likely to find anything like them anywhere else.

Other small shops are still better than the State Department Store and other malls. If you buy from a small shop, don't worry that you're undercutting the artisans, because they get paid about the same in either place. In the smaller shop, though, you just won't be paying for as much overhead. In fact, you'll be helping the entrepreneur even though their prices are lower, and you save money, too.

items at better prices elsewhere. It's a good place to go without your money and identification to look around and see what items interest you, since the store has such a great selection.

The only thing you may find here that isn't found many other places is the huge variety of original, affordable artwork. Students and professional artists offer their work here in a range of styles, formats, subjects, and prices. Even still, if you are looking for just a simple hand painted note card or a watercolor landscape, walk on down to Sukhbaatar Square and negotiate with the artists peddling there. You can easily get a nice piece at a third of the price you would pay at the State Department Store, and the money goes directly to the artist. If you buy a large piece of art and you need a hard container to roll it up in, check the art store near the corner of Juulchin Chuluu at the intersection with the Urtiin Tsagaan Market.

To find almost any souvenirs you could want, try shopping in the area along Peace Avenue between the State Department Store and Sukhbaatar Square. You've seen the wide variety and high prices from State Department; now it's time to find those items cheaper. This is where your State Department window shopping comes in handy.

Start from the State Department Store and work your way east toward the square. Leaving State Department from the front, take a left. You will pass a few cafés as well as Mary & Martha, a highly recommended store selling free trade merchandise. Soon after the Amsterdam Café, you will hit the never-ending gauntlet of souvenir shops. If you are looking for jewelry and silver or copper bowls, head into the Mungun Zawiya (Мөнгөн завья) on the next block. This metalwork outlet has a huge variety of vendors who are willing to bargain. Sports equipment is the basement.

Continuing east, past the Mungun Zawiya, you will begin to see many stores that carry cashmere products. But don't feel you need to buy there; you can find more cashmere across the street from the State Department at several stores surrounding the park with the Beatles monument. Duck in, though, to get a browse, and come back if you want.

The Flower Center has a great selection of items upstairs you will want to look at. If you're looking for a **khadag**, the silk Tibetan scarf common throughout the country, this is the place. You can get one for a few hundred *tugriks*. Take your *khadag* to the countryside and tie one on an *ovoo* or take one home and display it in a high spot in your home. On the street facing Peace Avenue is another souvenir shop.

Once you get to the street crossing in front of the Central Post Office (Төв шуудан) near Sukhbaatar Square, cross at the light to the south side of Peace Avenue and walk back toward the State Department Store. After a couple blocks you will be back onto a souvenir shop region. The first souvenir shop you will find on the corner also has a great selection, but head toward the back for the best items.

When you reach a small boulevard that runs south, perpendicular to the State Department, take a left and walk along the small park with the huge flashing billboard and Beatles statue to pop into the cashmere shops. Don't expect to get some remarkable deal on cashmere, though. You'll notice it's expensive in Mongolia, too! The goats are raised in Mongolia, but the yarn is usually processed in China and then sent back to Mongolia. In most cases, the quality is very high, so don't feel too reluctant about buying it. It's important to note also that camel hair products, usually brown or tan colored, are often stocked next to the cashmere. Read the tag before you buy to make sure you know what you are getting. Camel-wool sweaters are pretty awesome as well as very warm, so pick up one if you're not into cashmere.

On the opposite side of the Beatles monument is a fantastic store called Tsagaan Alt, whose fare trade wares come from cooperatives in Selenge Aimag and elsewhere.

Your choices are fewer and farther between going west from the State Department Store, except for Computer Land tucked behind the black, glass-blocked Canon building. It has bootlegged media and software, first-hand and second-hand computer hardware, mobile phones, cameras, etc. It's a great place to find replacement electronics if you're in a pinch. Hardware is not especially cheap, but the software is. Beware the viruses attached.

**Narantuul Market (Нарантуул зах or "Black Market")** is a huge indoor/outdoor bazaar, one of the biggest in Asia. In summer, up to 60,000 people per day squeeze inside, paying a MNT50 entrance fee. (The market is closed on Tuesdays and Mongolian holidays, so be sure to check that it is open before you make the trip all the way out there.) It's big, scary, crowded, and a pickpocket's paradise. Yet, if you are careful and know what you want, it can be one of the best places to get that special souvenir or gear at a price that can't be beat. You can buy cheap camping and fishing accoutrements, among other things, but the real reason to visit is to marvel at this mammoth bizarre bazaar.

The covered area has a decent selection of clothes and leather boots but usually only in smaller sizes. In any given stall, for example, don't expect to find many shoes over a European size 35 (US 8) for women and a European size 46 (US 12) for men. This is also one of the cheapest places to get traditional Mongolian clothes like a *deel*

The Guide

or camel hair sweaters that Mongolians wear for ceremonies and everyday winter use. You might find some cashmere as well. If you have done the leg work to track down a seamstress who will make you a traditional *deel*, shirt, or vest, this is one of the best places to get your fabric. Bargaining is not only recommended but necessary. Take the time to shop around and compare prices. The fabric with the velour symbols on it can run you as much as MNT15,000 per meter. But you can find great fabrics for as little as MNT1,500 per meter.

Speak to your seamstress first to find out exactly how much you need and what additional fabric you will need for trim and buttons. Seamstresses can make repairs, too, so if you've torn your favorite pair of pants climbing a superfluous fence, ripped your sleeve on a jagged car door, or popped a zipper on your bag, they can fix you up for just a few hundred to a few thousand *tugriks*. If you need a seamstress, find one by talking to your guesthouse staff.

## Surviving Narantuul in Four Easy Steps

Many expats pride themselves on never having been to Narantuul. People fear the pickpockets, bag slashing, high pressure, and high prices the taxi drivers charge Mongolians and foreigners alike. Even still, Narantuul can provide many cheaper options for souvenirs, so with a few pointers, you should be able to maneuver Narantuul without harm.

**Step one:** Leave your passport, phone, and bags behind. If you have one of those nifty under-the-clothes money belts, this is a good time to use it. Leslie's grandmother has always preferred the "money in the bra" method. If you're a grandmother, or like taking advice from grandmothers like we do, do your best Jan Brady impression and go up a cup. It has always worked well for us.

**Step two:** Do not take a taxi to or from the market. Taxis in Ulaanbaaatar are notorious for drastically overcharging, especially foreigners and especially to and from Narantuul. Instead, you can take the M4, M6, or M21 buses to and from Sukhbaatar Square. You will get out near the back of the market and follow the crowd to an entrance.

**Step three:** Keep moving. It's very common for Mongolians to push and shove to get where they want to go, especially older woman. First, try to quickly walk around people. If that doesn't work, it is okay to gently maneuver people to the side so you can get through. A nice *uuchalaarai* or "sorry" is never wrong.

**Step four:** Bargain. In a perfect world, vendors would give you a fair price, you'd pay it, and then you'd go on with your life. In a parallel perfect world, it'd be great if you looked Mongolian, spoke perfect Mongolian, and could bargain to the perfect price with nearly no hassle. Since neither world exists, you'll have to work for the best price. We recommend you bring along a Mongolian friend to do the bargaining for you while you aren't standing there, if that's possible. If you're on your own, use the vendor's calculator to punch in your offer and be prepared to and walk away. If you find something you like at one stall, chances are you can find it at another.

For jewelry, walk two blocks north on past the Urtiin Tsagaan and MobiCom/TEDY building on your left and turn right at the dead end into the boulevard. You will find a plethora of jewelry and metal shops with some great deals. This is an especially great place to compare prices on copper bowls.

**Urtiin Tsagaan (Уртын Цагаан or "The Long White" Market)** is a semi-permanent outdoor flea market with white metal storage units and a few tents by the TEDY building where Juulchin Chuluu dead ends. It has metal works, leatherworks, felt handicrafts, art work, antiques, and more. The hours are sporadic, especially around holidays and weekends, and can vary from one stall to the next. Not all the stalls have great items, but you can find some diamonds in the rough there (sometimes, literally). Have a walk through and pick up something nice.

**The Third and Fourth District** is a popular area of town where many Mongolians shop, mostly for good deals on cheap clothes and other imports from China. This area of town isn't your best choice for buying souvenirs, but it's a decent place to shop for low priced clothes, electronics, and sundries—but don't expect the best quality. Several buses go to this area of town (M28, M31, M43,M45, M46 and anything with Urgoo on the front), but it is a nice 35-minute walk from Peace Avenue if you feel like you would like the exercise. There is no perfect or preferred place to start, though a good marker may be the Urgoo Movie Theater (www.urgoo.mn). If you feel like you need a break, this movie theater is new and often has movies in English with Mongolian subtitles at a good price. Plus, it's air-conditioned. Feel free to walk around and shop during the day, but this is not a place for foreigners in the evenings.

*The Guide*

## Avoiding Pickpockets

A great place for a thief is a crowded group of people who cannot move, such as buses, Narantuul, State Department, post offices, banks, watching street performers, etc. One recommendation, then, is to never stop moving. Push and maneuver your way around in a crowd, especially if you feel uncomfortable. You won't offend anyone because Mongolians do it, too. If you have a bag with you, carry it in front of you with an arm over it. Even an empty bag or purse could be slashed beside you or behind you, so if you like your bag and plan to use it in the future, your best move is not to bring it with you. Hide your money inside your clothes, not in a front pocket, not in a wallet in your back pocket, and especially not in a bag. The lighter you travel, the better your chances of keeping everything you brought.

## Outdoor Gear

The best value for adventure gear shopping is at **Seven Summits**, across from the Central Post Office (between Peace Avenue and Seoul Street), on the side of the Air Market offices (www.activemongolia.com). Seven Summits stocks German-made

Vaude gear, GPS units, maps, travel books, and accessories. It organizes tours, as well. You can also rent tents, sleeping bags, gas stoves, mountain bikes, and inflatable kayaks among other things. The staff is kind, knowledgeable, and helpful, and they speak English and German. If you are in a real pinch, you can also find some of these items at the State Department Store, Computer Land, or Narantuul Market but at a higher price and lower quality. Seven Summits is open 10:00 a.m. to 6:00 p.m., and it is closed Sundays.

**Ayanchin Shop** (Seoul Street 21) is another nice choice for outdoor needs. It lays claim to being Mongolia's first specialized outdoor retailer. It's still a good place to buy outdoor gear for camping, fishing, GPS, and all the adventure accoutrement.

### Music

If you are a music lover and want to stock up on some Mongolian music before you leave, head over to **HiFi Megastore** on Seoul Avenue, near the Ikh Mongol (Их монгол) restaurant. This fairly large place stocks all Mongolian genres of music including hip-hop, rap, pop, rock, and traditional folk. It also stocks a lot of legitimate Western music CDs and film DVDs. There is a selection of Russian MP3 CDs, some of which include an artist's entire back catalogue on a single CD. It's definitely worth a stop in. The State Department Department's fifth floor also has a good collection.

## NIGHTLIFE

While UB is admittedly no Tokyo or Las Vegas, it certainly has plenty of opportunities for a good time, with a wide variety of bars and dance clubs to suit whichever particular scene you roll with. Most places worth going to are in the Chingeltei and Sukhbaatar Districts (around the State Department Store). There are some places off the beaten path that offer a good time as well, although these places are a bit riskier.

Bars are supposed to close at midnight by law, but many stay open later by paying off local police. If anything goes wrong, you're not going to be able to call the police, so this would be a "play at your own risk" situation. Hot spots, by nature, tend to move, so keep your eyes and ears open for the new "it" places.

**Grand Khaan Irish Pub** Located on Seoul Street, just south of Sukhbaatar Square, this place is known to locals simply as "Irish Pub," and while there are "Irish Pubs" aplenty in UB, this one is the biggest and best. You'll almost forget you're in a developing country as you stare at a wide array of cocktails and beers as well as a large food menu of Western pub fare. This establishment is extremely foreigner friendly, and this is a favorite of locals and expats alike. It's also one of the most expensive places, and you will be paying a service VAT. ₮₮₮

**Ikh Mongol** On Seoul Street, just east of the State Circus, is another favorite of both expats and deep-pocketed locals. This lively beer garden offers its own delicious home brewed beer in sizable and affordable portions. Ikh Mongol is especially wonderful in the summer months when the outdoor patio is open and in the winter months while there is outdoor seating in the form of a bar made of ice—sit at your own risk, but taking pictures is a must. Nightly live music features all the hottest local acts. ₮₮

**Face Club** On Juulchin Chuluu between the Urtiin Tsagaan and the Small Ring Road, this is one of the best and most conveniently located dance clubs in UB. It offers a pretty decent selection of hip-hop and techno music, and it is a very foreigner-friendly establishment. Things don't usually get going until around 10:00 p.m. However, once it gets going there is no slowing down until the wee hours. This is one of those mysterious places that is open past midnight. The closing time is up to the discretion of the owners, but it has been known to go until 4:00 a.m. Drink selections are fairly limited, and hard liquor can get expensive. It may be a good place to go after you have gotten your liter or two of beer on at Ikh Mongol. Dress is casual, but you wouldn't be out of place if you felt like gussying up. Cover is MNT5,000. ₮₮

**Metropolis** Near Chinggis Hotel and Sky Department Store, it is about as "swanky" as one can get in UB. It is a favorite among the young, hip scene of Mongolians and is frequented by many foreigners as well. It boasts impressive decor as well as a large selection of well-known DJs from around the world. This is one of those places that you make a night out of considering it isn't all too easy to get to. However, it is well worth it if you are looking for a legitimate clubbing experience. Cover is MNT5,000. ₮₮₮

The Guide

## Going Out on the Town in UB

All bars, by law, close at midnight. If you're out past midnight, keep in mind this is a "play at your own risk" situation.

Depending on the establishment, foreign presence may not be appreciated. Exercise caution when dealing with drunk men and Mongolian women who may be accompanied by drunk men.

Drunk men may want to fight you, and you may want to fight back. However, it would be in your best interest to steer clear of any and all situations that involve fisticuffs. (After all, wrestling is a national pastime.)

The three A's: Alone, Alcohol, At night. These three A's should be kept in mind at all times. It isn't wise to gallivant alone, under the influence, or in an unfamiliar setting. Always know where you are, know where you are going, and go out with people you know.

# Arkhangai Aimag (Архангай аймаг)

Arkhangai, with its heavily forested hills, rivers, and meadows, is one of the most beautiful *aimags*. It is located just west of the center of Mongolia and lies on the northern slopes of the **Khangai Mountain Range**. It's a somewhat popular getaway spot because of the many hot springs, so many tours with domestic and international passengers make their way through here. The capital of the *aimag* was established in 1931 at the site of the **Zaya Khuree Khiid**, founded in 1586.

Arkhangai is known for its white foods, and its economy rests primarily on the backs of its nearly two million livestock. The *airag* from **Khotont Soum** is renowned throughout the country as some of the best and is copied widely using samples of matured Khotont *airag*. Arkhangai *aarul* sells well in UB's Merkuri Market.

The most famous mountain in the *aimag* is **Khorgo Uul**, which is an extinct volcano and part of the **Khorgo-Terkhiin Tsagaan Nuur National Park**. **Kharlagtai Peak** is the highest point in Arkhangai at 3,529 meters (11,578 feet). The **Orkhon Gol**, the longest river in Mongolia, also passes through the eastern part of Arkhangai and reaches the *aimag*'s lowest point where it meets the **Tamir Gol** flowing from the Khangai Mountain Range.

Arkhangai covers 55,313 square kilometers (21,357 square miles) and has roughly 90,000 citizens who live throughout the 19 districts and 99 sub-districts. It shares

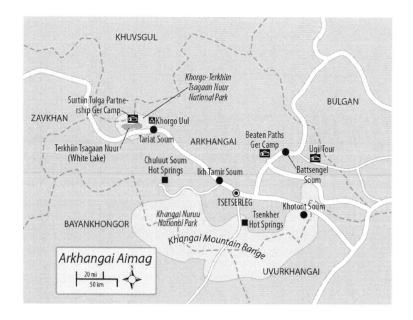

its borders with Bulgan, Uvurkhangai, Bayankhongor, Zavkhan, and Khuvsgul aimags, all of which can be reached by shared transport.

## TSETSERLEG (ЦЭЦЭРЛЭГ)

The *aimag* capital, whose name means "garden," lies on the northeastern slopes of the Khangai Mountains and is one of the more charming *aimag* centers in Mongolia. As with Khovsgul to the north, many have referred to it as "the Switzerland of Mongolia" because of its quaint, mountain village feel. Geographically it is located within Erdenbulgan Soum and shares its name with Tsetserleg Soum in the north. For this reason most people refer to it simply as "the *aimag*," though you will come across the same thing in most *aimags*, just as most countryside residents refer to UB as "the city."

Tsetserleg was an ancient cultural and commercial center of Mongolia. It was established at the site of Zaya Khuree Monastery which was built by the first Khalkh Zaya Pandita, Luvsanperenlei. The monastery still stands today as one of the main points of interest in Tsetserleg, along with the large Buddha statue that watches peacefully over the town.

The center of Tsetserleg consists of one main street that runs through the town. At one end of the street lies the market and at the other is the monastery. There are some residential apartments in the center of town, but most residents of Tsetserleg live in the areas surrounding the center in houses with brightly colored roofs that beautifully speckle the surrounding hills.

Walking in Tsetserleg is easy enough, but if you should need one, taxis and *mikrs* are available near the food market, across from the Arvan Hoyer (Арван Хоёр) store or parked by Hotel Od (Од).

### Tsetserleg or Tsetserleg?
The word *tsetserleg* means "garden," but it also refers to the place where the smallest children go to school (as in kindergarten). In Mongolian, it can sometimes be confusing for foreign volunteer teachers to explain that their planned visit to Tsetserleg next week does not mean they will go visit children down the street at the *tsetserleg*, but rather grownups in a different town.

## GETTING THERE

### By Bus
The bus travels daily to Tsetserleg through Kharkhorin, leaving from the Dragon Center in UB at 8:00 a.m. Purchase your ticket a day in advance in the morning, especially if you are traveling during the summer or *Tsagaan Sar*. It is not possible to

buy tickets on the bus from Kharkhorin to Tsetserleg, but you can easily find shared transport from there.

To return directly to UB from Tsetserleg purchase a ticket the day before at the ticketing counter inside the building right by the bus stop, across the street from Fairfield Guesthouse. Alternatively, for a small fee and a bit less hassle, someone from Fairfield will happily purchase the ticket for you.

### Shared Transport

*Mikrs* and *purgons* travel daily to and from Tsetserleg but are much less reliable. Look for them at the Dragon Center. For return trips to UB, find the *mikr* station by Hotel Od (Од).

## GETTING AROUND THE AIMAG

Outside the market, you can find cars going to various *soums* throughout Arkhangai as well as to nearby cities and UB. Most *soum* cars park in specific locations, which are not marked, so your best bet is to just say or point to the name of where you are trying to go. The drivers will point you in the general vicinity.

## SHOPPING

**Arvan Hoyer (Арван Хоёр)** Also known as the "12" store at the north end of town, near Bulgan Mountain. This is one of the larger grocery stores. The sign simply says "Supermarket," but locals know it by its name. It is open Sunday-Friday and has a large variety of foods, although not many vegetables.

**Ikh Delguur (Их дэлгүүр)** Has a similar selection of items to its sister store, Arvan Khoyer, but it is located further south just outside of the market.

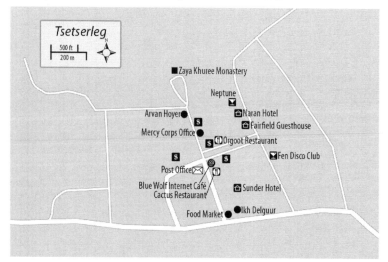

**The Market or** *zakh* **(зах)** The best place for produce. It's on the south end of town and open all year round Monday-Saturday, with the exception of *Tsagaan Sar* when it closes for an indeterminate amount of time (typically 7-14 days).

## INTERNET CAFES

**Blue Wolf (Хөх Чөнө)** Across from the post office. Has the usual telecom offerings.

## BANKS

Khan Bank (Хаан Банк) has a main branch near the government building, and there is another location across the street. There are also ATMs at the food market and in Ikh Delguur (supermarket). Xac Bank (Хас Банк) has a branch in the center as well. Exit the post office and walk east down the street parallel the tree park. The bank is half way down the south side.

## WHERE TO STAY

### Hotels

**Fairfield Guesthouse** Run by Australian expats. Though more expensive than some of the Mongolian-run hotels, Fairfield does offer some amenities favored by foreigners, and the staff speaks English. The staff is super helpful and really great with helping travelers get around Arkhangai. If for some reason you have to stay someplace else, at least swing into the café for a tasty sandwich. If you arrive by bus, just walk north towards Bulgan Mountain and you will see Fairfield on your left in a white building. *MNT17,000 per person per night (includes breakfast). Shared bathroom. Hot shower and laundry services available. 133221096; www.fairfieldmongolia.co.uk*

**Naran Hotel** Next to Fairfield Guesthouse, though not equal to Fairfield in terms of the quality of the accommodations. *MNT10,000-15,000 (depending on room). Shared bathroom. No hot shower or laundry services available. 99332900*

**Sunder Hotel** A decent place to relax and get a good night's sleep or sit in a sauna. It's the one with the pagoda on top. *MNT13,000-20,000 (depending on the room). Karaoke, bar, shower, garage, internet. 01332-22359, 99096948, 99801629*

### Ger Camps

While there are over 20 *ger* camps popping up and folding in this area each year, we can recommend a couple to look up.

**Ugii Tour** Located 20 kilometers (12.5 miles) east of the Ugii Nuur Soum center on the north coast of Ugii Nuur, it is at the most beautiful spot, and there is a small peninsula reaching out from the camp. It's a great place for fishing and watching the nearly 150 species of rare birds around the lake. There are 20 *gers* with 60 beds at a mid-range price of MNT25,000-35,000 per day. They also have Jeeps for private transport. *Contact: Dashpurev or Lkhagvajav. 99110506; dashka@ugii-tour.com*

**Surtiin Tulga Partnership** Run by a family since 2003 when they only had one *ger*. They now have eight *gers* to host up to 40 people for MNT5,000-10,000 per day. The camp has special toilets and a shower. It is located on the north side of White Lake, only 20 meters away from the edge of the water. They prepare meals using fresh fish from the lake, and if you're interested, you can arrange a fishing trip. The oldest son speaks English. If you stay here, you can also participate in the everyday life of Mongolian herder families as well. *Contact Tumee (99248651) or Batbold (99817553). surtiintulga_gercamp@yahoo.com*

**Duut Resort** Luxuriously located in Tsenkher Soum at the hot springs. It has an indoor naturally heated pool and massage rooms, laundry area, and modern men's & women's hot showers and toilets. From the hot showers you can go directly to the open air hot men's and women's swimming pools. Just next to the outside pools on the back side of the lodge, there is an open air terrace where you can sit and enjoy the clear mountain air. Internet access and a brand new gaming center. are available. The main lodge has five bedrooms on the 2nd floor with comfortable twin and queen sized beds and modern toilet facilities, and there's room for 90 guests in *gers* (MNT35,000-120,000 per day). The downstairs is a restaurant with some Western-style and Mongolian food. The resort also has a library and a video rental section, and if you are in need of anything, the manager, Munkhjargal, is fluent in English. *99291388; duutresort@yahoo.com*

**Beaten Paths Ger Camp** Located 3 kilometers (1.5 miles) outside of Battsengel Soum. Transportation to and from the *soum* center is included in the price per person. One person for one night is MNT20,000 (this includes three meals). Tourists can also ride horses, camels, or go fishing for an additional fee. The *ger* camp serves traditional Mongolian food, some Western dishes, and caters to vegetarians. The camp's owner, Baigalmaa, also speaks a fair bit of English as well as some basic French. *88176542*

# WHERE TO EAT

## Restaurants

**Fairfield Café & Bakery** Run by Australian expats, it has Western-style food and is connected to a guesthouse. Their food is probably most favored by foreigners in town and while it is a bit expensive for a local person's budget, is not considered too expensive by most tourist's standards. Also, the menu is in English, and many of the employees speak English. ₮₮

**Cactus Restaurant** May be the best Mongolian restaurant in town. The prices are reasonable, especially for tourists, and it has more variety than most Mongolian restaurants. Like most other restaurants in town though, be sure to ask what they have available that day. ₮

**Orgoot Restaurant** Features Mongolian dishes that are prepared quite well and are moderately priced. Nothing flashy about it, but it's not a bad place to get a cheap meal. ₮

## Guanzes

There is one fully vegetarian *guanz* located in the market. If you enter the market to the right side of Ikh Delguur, make your first left and then a right and it is straight ahead. It is not marked as a vegetarian *guanz*, but most menu items are vegan and quite delicious. ☰

## NIGHTLIFE

Since Arkhangai is a popular tourist destination, it does have a bit more to offer in terms of nightlife. However, one should always remember to exercise good judgment when deciding to have a night on the town. Remember that bars close at midnight, and midnight is never the safest time to be out on the street for either men or women.

**Neptune** is a newly remodeled club and the nicest place to get jiggy in Tsetserleg. It has large comfortable seating and a sizable dance floor with a DJ, lights, and a good sound system. You're likely to run into some other tourists cutting loose.

**Fen Disco Club** It calls itself a disco but primarily focuses on clients looking to sing a bit of karaoke. There is, however, a dance floor featuring many of the same dance songs you'll hear in clubs all over Mongolia. Frequented by a slightly older crowd than its larger counterpart Neptune, this club has become the popular place for after-work dance parties. It is about 150 meters south of the bus stop.

## WHAT TO DO AROUND ARKHANGAI

Arkhangai is awash with hot springs and other natural wonders. The *ger* camps are somewhat expensive for the budget traveler, so you may choose to camp nearby and visit the *ger* camp and resort facilities for the pools. Transportation to any can be arranged at the market.

The freshwater **Terkhiin Tsagaan Nuur**, or White Lake, is nestled among hills and ancient volcanic terrain in western Arkhangai near **Tariat Soum**. Smaller than the more famous Lake Khuvsgul to the north, it is also less developed overall, with the tourism industry limited to a few small *ger* camps. The lake is a fine spot for fishing and swimming, although the water is usually pretty cold. It is also a prime area for hiking and horseback-riding. According to a legend, it was created when a giant picked up a large rock and threw it away. He exclaimed upon seeing the white surface that was left, "Look, a white lake!" His exclamation became the name of the lake. In another legend the same giant used this rock to vanquish a giant snake that was plaguing the lands. The rock, known as **Taikhar Chuluu**, ended up in **Ikh Tamir Soum**.

The most popular destination among tourists and locals alike are the **Tsenkher Hot Springs**, which has a tourist resort and four *ger* camps that pump the hot spring water into showers and pools. The **Chuluut Soum Hot Springs** hits 50° C (122° F) and has 4-5 active springs.

The Guide

If you are willing to travel off the beaten path a bit, **Battsengel Soum** is a lovely destination. Nestled quietly in the Khangai Mountains, Battsengel is 68 kilometers (42.25 miles) northeast of Tsetserleg. Transportation to and from is available every day but Sunday for MNT5,000. This quaint *soum* boasts excellent fishing, hiking, and a working 16th century monastery in the center of town.

While there may not be much to the *soum* itself, you will find plenty of shops, a few small *guanzes* (open during the summer months), and a one room hotel located across the way from the post office. If you would rather not brave the one-room hotel (even though it has a bar with, wait for it . . . *two* disco balls), you can choose to camp along the river or stay at Beaten Paths Ger Camp.

## Byambaagiin Sarangerel

Twenty seven-year-old Byambaagiin Sarangerel (Sara) was born and raised in Arkhangai's *aimag* center, Tsetserleg. After graduating from high school she moved to Ulaanbaatar to study business management at the Institute of Business and Commerce. During her second year of university, she chose to take on a double major and study bank economics in the hopes of becoming a banker.

When Sara, whose name means "moonlight," returned to Tsetserleg after her second year, she was hired for the summer at Fairfield Café and Guesthouse and given the opportunity to work as a banker and receptionist. During her final year at university the owners of Fairfield, Mark and Gill Newham, visited Sara in Ulaanbaatar and spoke to her about her thoughts regarding her future career prospects. They invited her to return to Tsetserleg to work at Fairfield full time. She accepted and has been working there as the business manager since 2006.

As the business manager, Sara is responsible for many aspects of the café and guesthouse, though her main focus is making sure that the other employees work well together and provide the best possible service for the guests and patrons of Fairfield. Sara and her team of dedicated and wonderful employees seek to help tourists discover the beauties of Arkhangai as well as giving them a comfortable place to stay along the way.

Sara shares her thoughts on her job: "When you see your co-workers are happy working together and serving our customers from their hearts, then you know that you are in the right place. When people from all over the world come and share their adventures with you, both their joys and their sorrows, then you feel, yes, I'm in the right place. My favorite part of the job is when you have done your best to help someone who came to you for help or in distress and finally they thank you with their warm smiles and deep gratitude."

In addition to her work at Fairfield, Sara works with an international relief organization called Samaritan's Purse. Samaritan's Purse is an organization based out of the United States that works to bring Mongolian children who need heart surgery to American or Canadian hospitals. Sara has accompanied children and their mothers to America twice as a translator.

In the next couple years Sara plans to pursue a master's degree abroad in Business Management in the hopes of one day starting her own tourism business in Arkhangai. Through tourism she hopes to further expose Arkhangai's beauty and culture to the world. If you're in Tsetserleg, stop in Fairfield and say hello.

## Mercy Corps Tourism Project

Like many places in Mongolia, Arkhangai is struggling to pull human and financial resources out of UB toward the countryside. Tourism is one way to do so, so along with its other small business development initiatives, the international aid organization Mercy Corps has partnered with a local NGO called Knowledge Network. Together they created a website, which launched in January 2011, to help connect rural tourism resources directly to customers—like you! This site features many of the current *ger* camps in Arkhangai as well as guesthouses, activities, and guides' and drivers' contact information. Bring your tourism money directly to them by planning your trip to Arkhangai using www.travelarkhangai.com.

# Bayankhongor Aimag (Баянхонгор аймаг)

Not only does beautiful Bayankhongor Aimag (pronounced like "buy-in-hunger") have a **dinosaur park** in the capital, but it also has some of the most interesting natural wonders of Mongolia among its three climate zones. Evergreen forest covers about 12,500 hectares (30,800 acres) in the north and are capped by the southern part of the **Khangai Mountain Range**. The central section of the *aimag* includes valleys and steppe with a natural hot spring as well as the birds of **Buun Tsagaan Nuur**. Saxaul desert brush covers about 477,000 hectares (1,179,000 acres) in the south. The southern part of the *aimag* is also host to the Altai Mountain Range's **Ikh Bogd Uul**, which sits above the **Gobi Desert** where the convergence of ecosystems is indescribably fascinating.

Because of its distance from UB (620 kilometers, 282 miles), Bayankhongor doesn't have much of a formal tourism sector, although there is some regional domestic and bicycle tourism to **Shargaljuut Rashaan** and the **"Strange Monk Monastery" in Erdenetsogt**. It is a perfect place for adventurous travelers seeking nearly untouched wonders and willing to work for their rewards. Many of the attractions are spread out, requiring difficult-to-book private transportation, and they take some time to reach. In the south, dinosaur fossil sites are otherworldly to witness but have been picked through fairly thoroughly. If you want to see the bones, visit the *aimag* museum. If you want to see the **Tsagaan Agui** and **Bichigt Khad petroglyphs** that depict life back as far as 5,000 years ago, the tour company Mongol Khan Expeditions is your best bet. The owner, Bodi, speaks English well and is from Bayankhongor, though the company is based in UB.

Some Bayankhongor Soum English teachers can double as tour guides and drivers in the summer if they are available and you're in a pinch. Go to the Provincial Government Palace (Төр захилганий ордон) on the main square and ask for the **American Culture Center**, "Amerik Soyl-EEN Tuw" (Америк Соёлын Төв). If you can't find anyone there, try the nature and tourism office in the green building just off the southwest tip of the main square0.

The Guide

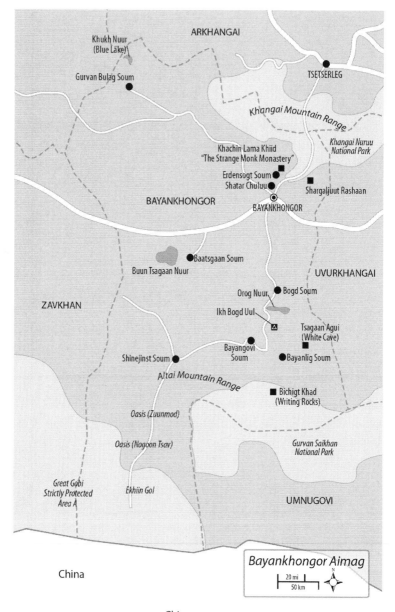

# GETTING THERE

## By Air

EZnis Airways planes usually arrive two days a week for around $330 round-trip from Ulaanbaatar. You must arrange private transportation from there by taxi or walk a few kilometers north into to town. It is usually possible to hitch a ride with fellow passengers.

## By Bus

Daily buses leave at 8:00 a.m. from the Dragon Center in UB for MNT21,000. Book tickets up to two days in advance at the Bayankhongor window at the Dragon Center and be on time for the bus. Tickets from Bayankhongor can be purchased from the bus station near the market. The trip takes anywhere from 10 to 15 hours.

## By Shared Transportation

If the bus is sold out, you can book a *purgon* from the bus company or try hiring one of the private drivers milling around the station for MNT25,000. Private drivers often leave in the evenings and drive overnight, which is extremely exhausting and best avoided.

# GETTING AROUND THE AIMAG

Buses and *purgons* can be booked from the bus station and from the market's east side by the outdoor billiards tables. Drivers sometimes hang around the north side as well. Taxis all over town queue at the northern entrance, though it's doubtful you'll need one unless you're in a pinch trying to find a ride to Erdensogt or the Shatar Chuluu.

# BAYANKHONGOR SOUM (БАЯНХОНГОР СУМ)

The capital of the *aimag* is known as "The Rich Darling." The town is laid out in a small grid with one main boulevard running from the airport in the south past the Government Palace (Тор захилганийн ордон) and the town square, with its colorful globed lights and *soyombo*-topped statue, to the north. The boulevard is connected at regular intervals to a parallel second paved road to the west that leads to the foot of **Erdene Mandal Stupa Hill**. This hill is technically in the center of town, and it is fun to hike up it and see the view. But most of the action is just east and south. Most shopping, eating, and administration happens in the long, gridded rectangle with the market as the southern border and the *aimag* government square at the north. Between them is the **Dinosaur Park**, middle market, and most of the hotels.

Bayankhongor Soum sits in a valley surrounded by mountains that have the undesirable effect of trapping coal and other smoke over the town during the long winters. Unless you want to see what the London fog looked like during the days of the industrial revolution, Bayankhongor is a better place to visit in the summertime.

For a bit of a challenging climb and the best view of the town and surrounding valley, walk up **Ikh Nomgon Uul**. This beast stands tall on the east of the city next to the **Tuin Gol**, where you should certainly plan an afternoon picnic in the summer or a game of makeshift curling in winter. Give yourself about two hours to get up and back to town for a trip to the **Natural History and Ethnographic museums,** which sit across the **Children's Park** from each other.

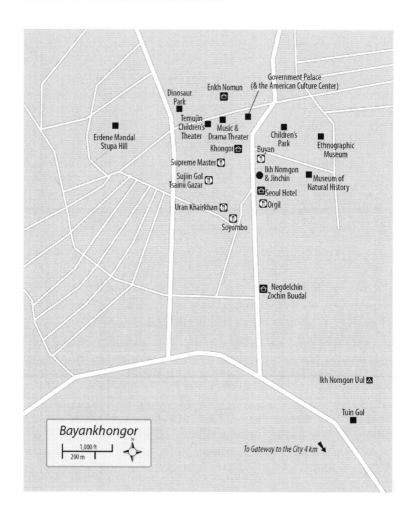

# WHERE TO STAY

## Hotels

**Seoul Hotel** Decent beds, hot water, and a great location. They have some luxury rooms with hot shower, toilet, and mini-bar. Regular rooms have a toilet in the room or shared toilet and shower (MNT20,000 for one person, MNT30,000 for two people). *Free parking. No laundry or kitchen. Bar, club, and restaurant attached.*

**Negdelchin Zochin Buudal (Нэгдэлчин зочин буудал)** At 30 rooms, it is the biggest hotel here, but it has seen better days. Lux rooms have a bathroom en suite with a shower and a sofa. All other rooms have shared shower and toilet downstairs (from MNT6,000-10,000 per person). *Laundry available (8am-10pm). Kitchen available. Restaurant attached. 99252560, 99442266, 01442-22061*

**Khongor (Хонгор)** Small and quaint and on the main avenue. Khongor has four rooms, each MNT20,000 per night. The rooms feature differing combinations of accommodations. One room has one bed, another has two beds, and two rooms have four beds. All have toilets in the room. *No shower, kitchen, or laundry. Restaurant attached. 99447337, 99447788, 01442-23300*

**Enkh Nomun (Энх Номун)** Locals and countryside residents rent rooms in the evenings and weekends to party late into the night. The rooms are nice. Lux and half lux rooms have a toilet with a shared shower. *Laundry (MNT500 per item, MNT1,300 for a coat; 9am-6pm. Shared hot shower. Shared kitchen. Small shop downstairs. 99448174, 99448361, 01442-22255*

## Ger Camps

**Mandukhai Ger Camp** A seasonal camp only a few kilometers down the Tuin Gol from the Bayankhongor Soum center. On one side, the Nomgon Uul provides a few extra hours of shade in the morning, and the other side is open to the flat, expansive steppe. There are usually around 10 *gers*, each for MNT25,000, though some have three beds and some have five beds. The camp also has volleyball, basketball, and other sport activities including horseback riding. English language is minimal at best. *99442009, 99442808, 99052577, 88118680*

# WHERE TO EAT

## Restaurants

**Seoul** One of the nicer restaurants in town. Located within Seoul Hotel on the main avenue across from the post office, this restaurant offers traditional Mongolian dishes and some Korean fair, including larger dishes meant to be shared. Fried chicken is listed on the menu and often available. The bar has a few harder offerings but no cocktails, and the beer is reasonably priced. ₮₮

**Soyombo (Соёмбо)** Has lovely table settings, a large menu, and concern for presentation, though the food is not always as tasty as it looks. Menu items vary by day and season. It is a colorful yellow building on the main road near the post office. ₮₮

**Buyan (Буян)** Used to be the only restaurant in town and is usually the only place open on Sundays. Well-known and well-liked by the locals, it has some variety on

The Guide

the menu, including the exotic Taiwan Soup (Тайван шөл) with mushrooms, tofu, meat, and vegetables for 4-6 people. The *huurga* (hot plates) are fattier and oilier than any other place in town. Look for it on the main road to the left of Их Номгон supermarket tucked in the corner. ₮₮

**Uran Khairkhan (Уран Хайрхан)** Offers regular Mongolian food, but also carries dried tofu (шар бууруцгний мах) and vegetarian meals. Occasionally, you can find desserts in the refrigerated display case as well as a Mongolian version of kimbap. It sometimes has had gourmet Korean teas too. Dance club upstairs after 9:00 p.m. ₮-₮₮

**Orgil (Оргил)** On the main street, just south of Seoul in the dark brown building. It is fairly new with a good menu and good cook who can churn out a Greek salad and other non-typical fair. The Mongolian food is also pretty good and high quality, and the atmosphere is nice. Beer prices are good, but the flashy bar usually only has vodka by the bottle. Dance club after 9:00 p.m. ₮₮

### Guanzes

**Supreme Master (Их багш цагаан хоол)** Our choice for the best *guanz* in town, though it may or may not be open when you try to visit. It's a block behind the post office near the north entrance of the middle market. They have vegetarian versions of traditional Mongolian food using beans and tofu. The staff is kind but speaks no English. ₮

**Sujiin Gol Tsainii Gazar (Сужийн гол цайны газар)** Around the corner from the Supreme Master but inside the grounds of the middle market tucked in the corner. It's a small place with friendly staff, though there's not much on the menu. It's worth a stop for the best *peroshki* (not available in summer) and best *khuushuur* in town for the price. Great deal. ₮

## GROCERY STORES

**Ikh Nomgon (Их Номгон)** On the main avenue, across from the post office. It is the largest and most convenient store in town. You can find all the basic toiletries and groceries at good prices. It often carries wet tofu and cheese.

**Jinchin (Жинчин)** A small and understated shop next to Ikh Nomgon with a friendly staff. They regularly have canned vegetables, beans, and sauces.

## WHAT TO DO IN BAYANKHONGOR SOUM

**Erdene Mandal Stupa** lies next to communications antennae and a satellite dish atop the main hill in the center of town. Take the ten-minute walk to the top to see some stunning views of the expanding town. On the north side, there is a road that goes past the monastery and up to the top. The south side has a little rocky trail that dumps you into a neighborhood with a row of neat and ornate doors on the fences. Most prominent at the top are the cell phone towers, but among them stands the Buddhist stupa where residents meet to welcome the first sun of the new year during the Lunar New Year (*Tsagaan Sar*) festivities. If you're in town for the holiday, it's a really fun tradition to take part in. People softly chant "*khuree*" and throw candy to the rising sun. Supposedly women are not allowed to take part in the ceremony, but tell that to the hundreds who show up every year anyway. Directly to the east from the top is the Ikh Nomgon Uul.

The **Music and Drama Theater** (Хөгжмийн драмын театр) is a typical Mongolian theater with close to 400 seats and a decent-sized stage. Look for traveling and local performances posted along the façade. Shows typically cost around MNT3,000. During the theater events, the whole town turns up, so get there early—that is, get there right on time, as shows tend to start quite a bit later than posted. If you're lucky, you might be able to catch a commemorative celebration out on the square itself with *morin khuur*, dance, and contortion led by the **Temujin Children's Theater**. They are known for their Temujin Opera about the origins of Chinggis Khan. It was created in Bayankhongor and turned into a movie in the 1980s starring Bayankhongor youth, some of whom now teach at the children's theater in Bayankhongor. They still perform the show each year. The Children's Theater is housed in the bright red and yellow building near the dinosaur park.

The **Ethnographic Museum** is a virtual gold mine of handicrafts unique to the area. You can view many unique artifacts including the Green and White Tara created by the famous Bayankhongor craftsman E. Sambuu. This museum includes information on nomadic life like the construction of *gers* and wedding ceremonies. Most stunning is the unique metalwork produced by artisans who never took apprentices during Communism, making theirs a virtually lost art form.

There is also information about Bayankhongor during Manchurian rule and more on the communist times. The museum often shows exhibitions of contemporary local folk artists, including Mongolian script contests where local teachers compete for the best handwriting in the nation. The guide, Otgoo, can lead English-speaking guests through this and the **Museum of Natural History** across the Children's park.

Among its typical taxidermy, the Natural History Museum also has geological exhibits with marble and volcanic rocks. The highlight of the museum is the complete skeleton of a Tarbosaurus on the second floor, which was found in Bugiin Ravine in the Gobi. Ask for Otgoo (pronounced "Aught–go") who speaks English and can lead you through both museums for MNT2,000 (plus extra for camera or video).

The **Children's Park** sits just east and south of the government square and shows the scars of countless attempts to cultivate donated trees. It also contains interesting and aging odes to communist times and statues of the animals found in the *aimag*. Near the sport hall on the north side, children hang out in and around an old, dry fountain, but it's not the kind of park for playing games and running around. It's more of a statue park.

**The Bayankhongor American Culture Center (Америк соёлын төв)** or "BACC" was the brainchild of Oyuntugs, an English teacher at a local community college. She wanted to meet the need for a public English education center and adequate English resources after community members requested several English-based classes. The curriculum she proposed would include advanced speaking and incorporate music, film, computers, and other pop culture, which did not exist for Bayankhongor youth who have few after-school activities. Indeed, teachers would have had to go all the way to UB for such resources. She wrote a proposal to the government seeking their help.

To accommodate the petition, the *aimag* government gave rooms in the main government building, including electricity and heat. Additionally, the *aimag's* head foreign language methodologist has made her office in part of the space to ensure that it remains accessible as a resource and teaching room.

Now, the BACC serves as an English education center with subscription language classes including TOEFL (a required language test for American universities), eleventh grade Concourse Exam preparation, advanced conversation, and elementary English. BACC volunteers also occasionally work on television, facilitate a weekly movie night for children, and hold other events such as trivia competitions that pit local businesses and government agencies against each other. It's a good gathering place for the motivated English-speakers in town, so if you're in need of someone who speaks English, you should look here first.

**Ikh Nomgon Mountain (Их номгон уул)** guards over the eastern part of the valley. You can see this so-called sleeping giant tiger curled up and watching over the town. For the best view, see it from the Erdene Mandal Stupa. You can walk to the foot of the mountain from the center of town in 15 minutes and to the top in an hour or so. Views stretch impressively into the expansive and undeveloped valleys over mostly bald mountain-tops.

**The Gateway to the City** is on the main road connecting Bayankhongor with UB through Uvurkhangai from the south. If you come to the *aimag* by bus or *purgon* you'll come in by this route. About 11 kilometers (5 miles) outside of town is the city gate, which makes for a nice day hike destination. Climb up the small cliff next to the road to see the Tuin Gol cut its deltas into the wide valley. Watch the animals graze peacefully in the pasture, and you can see town from an interesting perspective. In the distance to the south is Ulziit Soum. Between this village and the gate is the road that leads to Shargaljuut Rashaan. If you're feeling particularly adventurous, hitch a ride there for the evening.

# WHAT TO DO IN BAYANKHONGOR AIMAG

**Shargaljuut Rashaan (Шаргалжуутын рашаан)** is Bayankhongor Aimag's premiere domestic tourist attraction. The spas attract mostly Mongolians and other Asian tourists seeking a resort-like respite and the healing properties of the bubbling waters, springs, and baths. Cars must be contracted but leave daily from the market at negotiated rates. The roads are not well maintained, but the trip is not too long.

The 300 hot and cold springs are located in a valley just outside the village and are lined with *ger* camps and bathhouses where the water can reach up to 50° C (122° F). It is considered to exist in a unique location and is thought by some to be one of the best treatment spas in the world. Look for different rocks with symbols on them telling which ailment they can improve. Especially look for the gender-specific rocks to bring general good health to you, whether miss or mister.

## Erdensogt Soum (Эрдэнэсогт сум)
**Khachin Lama Khiid (Хачин ламаын хийд)** "The Strange Monk Monastery" is about an hour away by bus in Erdenetsogt, a quaint little village whose town center has hosted the monastery since 1905. This is a popular tourist attraction for domestic tourists, and foreigners on motorcycles and bicycles often wander by as well. The old monastery is basically a museum; ask the nearby caretaker to open it.

Plan to camp because the *guanz* and hotel are often not operational. There are some small shops with basic food stuffs, though. To get there, you can find daily *mikre*s and a small bus at the Bayankhongor market on the east side by the outdoor billiard tables. They only leave in the evening around 6:00 p.m. and return the next afternoon around 1:00 p.m. from the center of the *soum*. They cost about MNT2,500 each way. Better yet, you can walk back to Bayankhongor in about 6 hours through the valley and see the Chess Stones.

**Shatar Chuluu (Шатар Чулуу or "Chess Stones")** are also near Erdenetsogt *soum* center. It is a historically and culturally significant relic from perhaps as far back as 5,000 years ago, though no one is quite sure. Stones in the shapes of animals and people mark the grave of a presumed former Turkic king, perhaps during the Goturk Empire of roughly 552–747 C.E. Most spectacularly, this site, like many around the country, has not been preserved in any way and is not marked, covered, or fenced off. Look for wandering yaks and goats foraging. You can hire a driver to

The Guide

get to it, but you might need some Mongolian help, especially to bargain. If you want to go it alone, just write "Шатар Чулуу" (*Shatar Chuluu*) on a piece of paper and show it to the drivers hanging out in the market by the billiard tables. Look for it to cost around MNT20,000. You could walk there in a day or fold it into a walk to Erdenetsogt to see the monastery and come back the next day by *purgon* for MNT1,500.

## Gurvan Bulag Soum (Гурван булаг сум)

**Khukh Nuur (Хөх нуур or "Blue Lake")** is a pristine lake in Gurvan Bulag Soum on the road to Zavkhan Aimag, about 30 kilometers (18.5 miles) north of the *soum* center. It's an easy hike from the *soum* center following the road and then the river north. It is also possible to find local drivers in the *soum* center. It is a very clean and fresh lake with many kinds of fish and waterfowl, but it is way off the beaten path for foreign tourists. The town has food and hotels, but plan to camp by the lake because it is beautiful. The evenings get chilly even in the height of summer, so bundle up. If you're looking to bird watch here and at Buun Tsagaan Lake, you can try booking a driver ($55 per day plus gas) or a tour company that will show you both in the same trip.

## Baatsgaan Soum (Баацагаан сум)

**Buun Tsagaan Nuur (Бөөн цагаан нүүр)** is a popular destination among dedicated birders for its relative accessibility and variety of species. The surrounding area is also host to volcanic rock formations, streams, and cave paintings.

Bayankhongor Soum will be your jumping-off point for reaching the lake region. The lake itself is about 150 kilometers (93 miles) southwest of Bayankhongor Soum, but only 10 kilometers (6 miles) outside the Baatsgaan Soum center. It is possible to book transportation to Baatsagaan from Bayankhongor Soum, but accommodations are a little harder to come by. Sometimes there are *ger* camps down on the lake, but this is also a great place to put your personal tent to good use. If you want something a little more reliable, contract drivers in UB from tour companies like Mongol Khan or Offroad Expeditions.

There are many birding prizes here, where the Baidrag Gol terminates into the saltwater lake. Among them are the vulnerable Dalmatian Pelican and Relict Gull. Birders visit this area for the high quality and diversity of northern Asian water fowl, marsh birds, and shorebirds found on the lake and neighboring wetlands. The most popular finds include the Whooper Swan, Red-crested Pochard, Stejneger's Scoter, Palla's Gull, White-winged Tern, Palla's Fish Eagle, Pied Avocet, Asian Dowitcher, Mongolian Sand Plover, Temminck's, Little and Long-toed Stint, and Paddyfield Warbler. For more birding in the **Altai Mountain Range** in Bayankhongor's southern region, you can seek out the vulnerable Hodgson's Bushchat, and you will be happy to find Altai Snowcock and Daurian Partridge in the upper reaches as well.

## Bogd Soum (Богд сум)

**Ikh Bogd Uul (Их богд уул or "Great Holy Mountain")** is a place you have to see to believe, as one of the most impressive convergences of ecosystems exists right at its feet. A four hour, 110-kilometer (68-mile) drive from Bayankhongor Soum, and just 15 kilometers (9 miles) from Bogd Soum center, the mountain stands tall at 3957 meters (12,982 feet). From Bogd to the foot of the mountain you'll wind through thick, tall prairies full of camels, goats, sheep, cows, and yaks grazing until you reach the saltwater **Orog Nuur (Орог нуур)**, a shrinking lake beside a large sand dune. The dune is made up of sand that has blown up and over the Ikh Bogd Uul, which is a northern peak in the Altai Mountain Range. Your goal should be to book a driver, either in Bayankhongor Soum or through a tour company, who will drive you to the top of the often snow capped Ikh Bogd for a swim in the pristine alpine lakes. But you can also take a post bus or *purgon* to Bogd and walk to the mountain from there. If you're up for an extreme adventure, it's a strenuous yet rewarding 20-kilometer (12.5-mile) hike to a site where *ger* camps sometimes pop up. It's another less demanding 25 kilometers (15.5 miles) down the south side to Bayangovi Soum (N44°44'3.73", E100°23'31.53") where you can find transportation either toward Bayankhongor or Shinejinst another 100 kilometers southwest. It can snow even during the summer, so dress in layers.

## Bayanlig Soum (Баянлиг сум)

Among the southern districts of Bayankhongor, Bayanlig is a somewhat popular site on some of the longer Gobi tours that run through Umnugovi Aimag because of its unique geology and prehistoric remains. It is home to the Tsagaan Agui and Bichigt Khad, and it is possible to get there by coming to Bayankhongor Soum via bus and arranging a ride via *purgon* at the bus station. The station is not open for ticketing in the evening when the buses arrive, so you'll have to purchase a ticket the next morning.

Once you get to the *soum* center, there are many businesses, including a two-story orange hotel in the center of town near the government building. There is no shower or toilet in the hotel, but there is a shower house about 100 meters away. The hotel offers Mongolian breakfast, lunch, and dinner and felt products. There is also a shop that sells basic foods and refreshments. It is also possible to book a driver to the sites here, though the drivers don't speak English.

**Tsagaan Agui (Цагаан агуй or "White Cave")** is 40 meters long and crystalline with three major chambers. According to some scientists, the first ancient Asians

The Guide

lived here about 750,000 years ago, but it was only discovered by archeologists in the late 1980s. In the 1990s, excavations revealed evidence of rhinos and hyenas that were up to 35,000 years old. There are cave paintings showing various animals. The site is reachable from Bayankhongor Soum in one day by private transport, but it takes all day at a cost of around MNT200,000.

**Bichigt Khad (Бичигт хад or "Writing Rocks")** petroglyphs, located near the Tsagaan Agui, are coveted by Mongolians and anthropologists. Thought to have been inscribed around 3000 B.C.E., they depict nomadic life at the time and indicate a few similarities with today. Most impressively, though, ox carts and plows are depicted, revealing some agricultural activity uncommon now and previously thought not to exist in the region. The symbols relate mostly to animals and resemble the cave drawings in Khovd, which are some of the oldest found in the region.

**Oases (баян бүрд)** Known to Mongolians as *bayan burd* or "rich spring," these random areas in southern Bayankhongor are mysteriously spectacular set against the bone dry surroundings. As the story goes, traders stopped at these oases while traveling on the old caravan routes between China and the West. It is also thought that the thirteenth Dalai Lama refreshed himself here as he fled from Tibet in 1904 toward present-day Ulaanbaatar.

Here, you can see how life is nurtured by small amounts of water even in the most inhospitable of environments. They are welcome zones of respite in the desolate, empty Gobi. Note that traveling alone through this region is not recommended because these oases really are in the middle of nowhere. You will not wander upon these desert oases alone. Rather, you must hire a driver and guide who know the area well. The oases have names such as Zuunmod, "Hundred Trees" (Зуунмод), which sounds reassuring, and Shar Us, "Yellow Water" (Шар Ус), which sounds a little scary. But don't worry, it's named that because in Buddhism, yellow is a regal color. Previously worn by criminals, yellow was chosen by Gautama Buddha (regarded as "the Buddha") to symbolize humility and detachment from materialism.

### Shinejinst Soum (Шинэжинст сум)

This district is home to the Great Gobi Strictly Protected Area A and the fertile oases within, but it is virtually impossible to see without private transportation. Because of its remote location, it will cost you about MNT300,000 round trip, and you should probably contract a driver in UB to meet you in Bayankhongor.

**Ekhiin Gol (Эхийн гол)** is the biggest and most well known oasis not only because it is one of the hottest spots in Mongolia but also because it is one of the most fertile parts of the *aimag*. It is about 17 kilometers (10.5 miles) long and 5 kilometers

(3 miles) wide and sits in the lowest point of Bayankhongor Aimag. It is in the Great Gobi Strictly Protected Area A and is the southernmost inhabited part of the *aimag*. Because there are seven natural springs in the area, the *oasis* supports some of the *aimag's* best fruit and vegetables, including melons and tomatoes. Also in Shinejinst Soum is the fossil site known as Green Gap (Ногоон цав). Fossils from here can be seen in the *aimag* museum and in UB.

**The Great Gobi Strictly Protected Area A** has been designated a United Nations International Biosphere Reserve, the largest of its kind in Asia. The Mongolian *Khural* included it in the Special Protected Area (SPA) network in 1995, though it had been protected by the government since 1975. It encompasses 45,000 square kilometers (28,000 square miles), although most of it is in Govi-Altai Aimag.

## Sumiyagiin Oyuntugs

Oyuntugs (pronounced "Oiyun-toogs") is a married mother of two in her mid twenties. She has a tourism degree from the National University in Ulaanbaatar, and her husband "Shawn" works at a local Xac Bank and sometimes moonlights as a taxi driver. The couple lived near Ulaanbaatar for a few years while she was the tourism director for one of the most elegant *ger* camps. They returned to Bayankhongor to live in her family's compound because as the youngest child, it is her duty to look after her aging parents, despite other siblings who also live nearby. She takes her responsibility to her family seriously, and though this altered her career path, Oyuntugs feels she has plenty of time in the future to realize her professional goals.

The Bayankhongor American Culture Center (BACC) was a project she conceived while working as an English teacher at a local business school with underperforming and unmotivated students. She was constantly being asked by community members for English courses, and since none existed outside the schools, she went about finding a way to get them started.

Oyuntugs approached the *aimag* government in January 2009 about acquiring a space for the BACC. The local government gave two rooms in the *aimag* government building and has promised to provide rooms in the future education center, which is currently being built near by the Children's Palace. Through a grant, she and local volunteers were able to paint the walls and have desks and shelves made from local materials. They also set up new computers, a TV, and other equipment needed to make the empty room into a nice learning space ready for their September 2009 opening.

Like many Mongolians, Oyuntugs' dream is to attend school in the United States or another English-speaking area where she can enhance her tourism experience and English competency. Also, like many Mongolian women her age, she has small children and a household budget that requires her to contribute financially, which prevents her from being able to take the time for such pursuits. She continues to look toward tourism jobs in UB and toward living abroad.

Because of her tourism background and English skills, she is a good person to get a hold of in Bayankhongor if you can. She has worked some with the local government to promote tourism and could help you find local resources like drivers and accommodations if she is available. *oogiituugii@yahoo.com*

The Guide

The park is part of the last remaining habitat of the Gobi Bear (*mazaalai*), of which there are only 25 known individuals remaining. You're not likely to see them or the ibex that roam these grounds, but you probably will stumble upon wild Bactrian camels and some of the 410 plant species. There are also more than 150 bird species and 15 kinds of reptiles and amphibians found here. With the more severe weather and increased desertification brought by climate change, the biodiversity of the region is in great danger.

Even though it is "strictly protected," you can enter the reserve. You will need to purchase a MNT2,000 pass from park rangers.

# Bayan-Ulgii Aimag (Баян-Өлгий аймаг)

The high plateau of Bayan-Ulgii is one of Mongolia's most dynamic places. Here, the expanse of the Gobi culminates in the rugged, stalwart peaks of the **Altai Mountain Range**. Rising from **Tavan Bogd** ("Five Saints"), Mongolia's highest peak, **Khuiten Uul** (4,374 meters, 14,350 ft.), serves as an impressive gatekeeper at the point where the Mongolian, Russian, and Chinese borders meet.

Bayan-Ulgii is politically Mongolian, but culturally it belongs to Central Asia. About 90 percent of the population is Kazakh, the largest minority group in the nation. Although they are nomadic herders like Mongolians, the Kazakhs are distinct from their neighbors, with their own traditional clothes, language, and homes. Kazakh *gers* tend to be larger and more exquisitely decorated than Mongolian ones, and unlike Mongolians, Kazakhs generally use their airy *gers* in summer and move into mud-plaster homes for winter.

Carved out of the larger western Mongolian province as a Kazakh homeland in the 1930s, Bayan-Ulgii and the people here have retained their language, customs, and culture to a greater extent than their brothers and sisters in Kazakhstan. It is still possible to see men hunting with golden eagles and women embroidering incredibly detailed tapestries in Bayan-Ulgii.

Still, many Kazakhs were enticed by a Kazakhstani government "repatriation" program and left Bayan-Ulgii in search for new opportunities in the 1990s. Many found that the promised opportunities and satisfaction of returning to their spiritual homeland did not meet their expectations and have returned to Mongolia, but the overall population of Bayan-Ulgii is less than it was during socialist times. At present there is a great deal of coming and going between Bayan-Ulgii and Kazakhstan as young people go to study in Almata or Astana, and older folks head off in search of often temporary work in Kazakhstan.

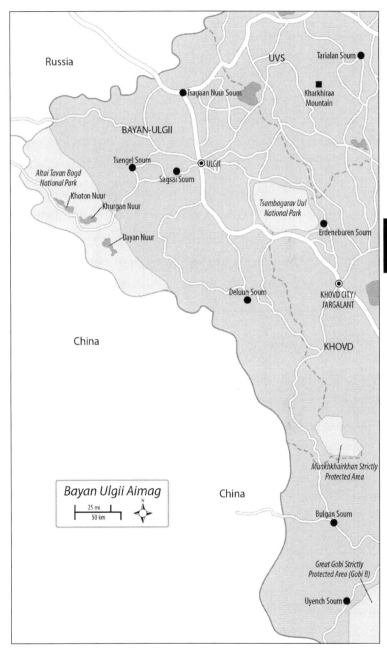

Russia

UVS

Tarialan Soum

Tsagaan Nuur Soum

Kharkhiraa
Mountain

BAYAN-ULGII

Tsengel Soum

Altai Tavan Bogd
National Park

ULGII

Sagsai Soum

Khoton Nuur

Khurgan Nuur

Tsambagarav Uul
National Park

Dayan Nuur

Erdeneburen Soum

Deluun Soum

KHOVD CITY/
JARGALANT

China

KHOVD

Munkhkhairkhan Strictly
Protected Area

*Bayan Ulgii Aimag*

25 mi
50 km
N

China

Bulgan Soum

Great Gobi Strictly
Protected Area (Gobi B)

Uyench Soum

The Guide

While ground transport is regular and, in recent years, increasingly comfortable and reliable, the 50- to 60-hour (1,698-kilometer; 1,055-mile) journey from Ulaanbaatar to **Ulgii**, the *aimag* center, can be particularly arduous.

# ULGII (ӨЛГИЙ)

Ulgii residents often refer to the area as if it were a separate country from the rest of Mongolia and with good reason. The city is surrounded by rocky mountains, and only the Khovd Gol passing through the town gives a sense that a larger world exists beyond the ring of dry peaks. The city center is small, and fences built of dried mud bricks dominate the residential districts where the majority of population lives. The houses are also mostly built with wooden frames plastered over by mud. All the shades of brown and grey recall the remotest corners of Central Asia more than the mild green grasslands of Mongolia. China's Xinjiang Autonomous region, home of the Uighurs, and Kazakhstan lie just on the other side of the Altai Mountains. Ulgii is a friendly town, and it's worth sticking around for a few days to wander around the bazaar, take a look at the mosque, and get to know a Kazakh family or two.

Many Kazakhs seem to have an affinity for languages. It is possible to find some people in Ulgii who speak Kazakh, Mongolian, English, Russian, and even Tuvan. Ulgii also has the most developed tourism sector in western Mongolia, with several homegrown tour agencies, art shops, and a handful of freelance tour guides. All of this contributes to making Bayan-Ulgii's treasures surprisingly accessible despite the *aimag's* isolation.

# GETTING THERE

## By Air
From Ulaanbaatar, there are two Aeromongolia flights per week and three per week on EZnis airways during the summer. EZnis also now offers flights from Khovd and Ulaangom to Ulgii (twice and once a week, respectively, during summer months). Like all of the destinations in western Mongolia, the cost is significant for foreign tourists. Expect to pay over $300 for a round trip. Ulgii's airport is several kilometers to the northwest from town center. There will probably be some taxis waiting around when the plane lands. If not, you can ask the airport personnel to call one for you by simply saying, "taxi?"

## By Bus
Buses go to and from Ulaanbaatar three times a week, generally Monday, Wednesday, and Friday, with an extra Saturday service during summer. Buses arrive at and depart from the Dragon Center in Ulaanbaatar. The buses arrive at and depart from is the theater in Ulgii, conveniently in the center of town.

You can purchase tickets (MNT68,000) a day or two in advance in Ulgii from an office in the wing of the theater on the right.

The bus is likely to arrive in Ulgii (or Ulaanbaatar) in the middle of the night; fortunately, most of Ulgii's hotels are very close to the theater.

### By Shared Transportation

UB-bound *purgons* also leave from the theater, at a quoted price of MNT68,500 one way. From UB, *purgons* leave from Narantuul.

## GETTING AROUND THE AIMAG

In a tourist-friendly turn of events, many drivers from Ulgii's *soums* have begun putting signs stating (in Cyrillic) their destination in the window, although you may have to ask around to find cars headed for the closer villages. Shared *purgons* and Russian jeeps also travel between Khovd and Ulgii on a daily basis. In both cities, look for vehicles with Bayan-Ulgii/Khovd signs in the window in front of the main market entrance. Shared vehicles generally leave after 3:00 p.m., but it's a good idea to talk to a driver in the morning to secure your spot in the car. Leave a phone number if you have one, and either come back in the afternoon or ask the driver to pick you up at your hotel when he is ready to leave. Travel between Ulgii and Khovd can take anywhere from 6 to 12 hours, depending on the speed of the driver and the number of repairs that need to be made.

If you are lucky enough to leave with a few hours of daylight left, the Bayan-Ulgii to Khovd run is one of the prettiest drives you can make in a public vehicle. You will pass the large Tolbo Nuur outside of Ulgii and a few more high-altitude lakes along the way and see a view of snow-capped Tsambagarov Uul as you enter Khovd Aimag.

## LOCAL TOUR GUIDES

Bayan-Ulgii's tourism sector is more developed than the rest of the remote western *aimags*. In addition to a couple of homegrown travel agencies, there are a number of good freelance tour guides in the area. We like the idea of hiring locally when possible as it ensures that more money goes directly to the communities you visit.

> **Blue Wolf Travel Company** Blue Wolf is Ulgii's most prominent local travel company. They specialize in small group tours around Bayan-Ulgii and western Mongolia. Blue Wolf also organizes an annual Eagle Festival, held the last weekend of September in Sagsai Soum, about an hour's drive from the *aimag* center. They also operate a *ger* camp in Sagsai and a small *ger* guesthouse in Ulgii. *50420303, 99110303; info@bluewolftravel.com, mongol_altai@yahoo.com; www.bluewolftravel.com*

The Guide

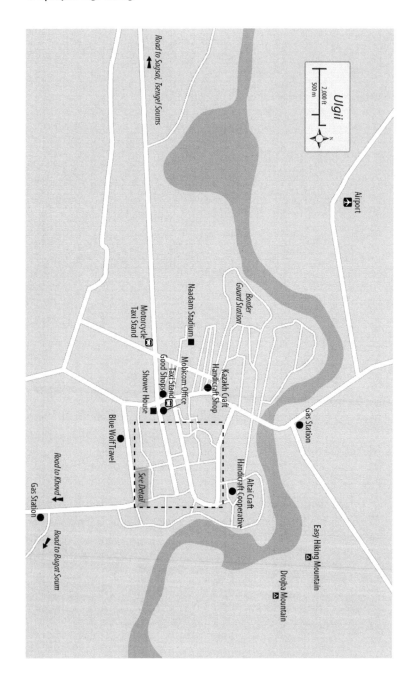

Ulgii

2,000 ft
500 m

N

Road to Sagsai, Tsengel Soums

Airport

Naadam Stadium

Border Guard Station

Motorcycle Taxi Stand

Good Shops

Mobicom Office

Taxi Stand

Shower House

Kazakh Craft Handicraft Shop

Gas Station

Blue Wolf Travel

Road to Khovd

Gas Station

Road to Bugat Soum

See Detail

Altai Craft Handicraft Cooperative

Easy Hiking Mountain

Drojba Mountain

## Independent Guides

The following guides speak English excellently and have experience working with tourists. They are reliable, knowledgeable, and friendly.

**Sabit** An English teacher at Ulgii's 5th school, Sabit has worked closely with Peace Corps Volunteers in town. He has his own Russian Jeep and can be your guide, translator, and driver all in one. *99429910, 93057710; sakok_nur@yahoo.com*

**Erlan** A primary school teacher, Erlan speaks English and Russian. He has worked with tourists, journalists, and researchers studying eagle hunting. *99425394; erka_erlan@yahoo.com*

**Nurbol** Speaks Kazakh (helpful for remote villages of Bayan-Ulgii where little to no Mongolian is spoken), Mongolian, Russian, English, and a few words of almost any other language you can think of! He's one of the nicest guys around and has plenty of experience going to Tavan Bogd Park, as well as taking tourists to visit his family in remote areas of Bayan-Ulgii province. *99426878; nucnai@yahoo.com*

**Agii** An English teacher at local School #4, Agii's English is amazing by comparison. He also speaks Mongolian, Kazakh, and Russian. He has been guiding tourists for over five years, including large groups. Agii is able to supply tourists with everything they might need from tents and camping equipment to kayaks(!). *99107676; maksum_agii@yahoo.com; www.kobeshtravel.com/*

The Guide

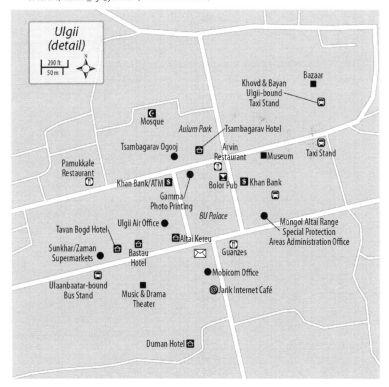

**Aynabek** Aynabek runs an English institute in Ulgii city and speaks French alongside Mongolian, Kazakh, Russian, and Turkish. He's up for anything and can help you get anywhere you want to go. *99096385; aynabek@yahoo.com; www.backtobektravel.com*

## WHERE TO STAY

**Tsambagarav Hotel** This new hotel, opened in 2010, has become the lodging of choice for government officials and other big wigs in Ulgii on business. The quality of the rooms and the fact that each has its own bathroom, hot water, and television help to explain the hotel's popularity. Naturally, the room rates reflect this, too. A single with two twin beds is $30, the double with one large bed is $23, and the lux is $40. Tsambagarav is a tad pricier than anywhere else in town, and they list prices in dollars, although they surely accept tugriks.

**Tavan Bogd Hotel (Таван богд)** Tavan Bogd's rooms are serviceable, and the lux rooms have nice sitting areas. All rooms have their own toilets; lux rooms have a bathtub. Singles start at MNT18,000, doubles are MNT30,000, and the lux is MNT25,000 per person. Don't count on the posted room rates to be the same as what they charge you. The hotel implements a strange fixed-rate system for some rooms, which ensures that unless you have a very large group that doesn't mind cuddling, each person pays almost as much as they would for a single. *99429556, 99428899 (Ask for Rosa.)*

**Blue Wolf Travel** Has some nice guest *gers* with bathrooms and shower facilities for $10 per person behind their offices. *50420303, 99110303*

**Bastau Hotel** While their Spartan rooms are probably the least inviting in town, their prices make Bastau the most attractive option for ultra-low budget travelers. Singles are MNT7,000, doubles MNT10,000, triples MNT15,000, and the lux is MNT20,000-25,000. The simple rooms share a bathroom, while the lux rooms claim to have hot water. We're pretty sure they mean in winter, when the city's heating plant is working and all major buildings get hot water. *113629*

**Duman (Думан)** Prices of rooms here vary widely, even for the same number of beds, depending largely on the size of the room. This is a definite case of the more you pay, the more you get. The most expensive rooms (MNT90,000) tend to have hot water. Annoyingly, foreigners pay about a third more than Mongolians here (singles start at MNT18,000-35,000). Despite the very popular disco bar in the building, Duman was the hotel of choice for the Mongolian President and other visiting dignitaries for many years. *95416998, 9542 6466*

## WHERE TO EAT

Ulgii doesn't have a vast number of eateries, but what it lacks in quantity, it makes up for in quality.

**Pamukkale Restaurant** If you've made it all the way to Ulgii, you probably deserve a break from boiled mutton. This Turkish restaurant is hands-down the best food in western Mongolia. No trip to Ulgii is complete without a plate of tender, exquisitely spiced kebab from Pamukkale. Nothing on the menu is bad, but the sis (shish) kebab and chicken grill are highly recommended, as are the honey-soaked desserts: *revani* and *shekerpare*. It is a halal restaurant though, so don't plan on having a beer with your meal. ₮₮

**Bolor Pub (Болор)** Serves the Mongol standards, done well. The interior looks like that of a more expensive restaurant. Their *Tsoivan* is always a good bet. ₮

**Arvin Restaurant (Арвин Ресторан)** Known around town as "the Mongolian restaurant," Arvin's menu does feature a Kazakh dish or two. The schnitzel is good, as is the *sirne* (сирне), but we like their attempt at Mongolian-tropical fusion best: *beefschtteiks* with cheese and pineapple. The menu is in English and Mongolian. Arvin is just a tad more expensive than the average straightforward Mongolian restaurant. ₮₮

**Tsambagarav** Another decent Mongolian restaurant, the hotel's food is cheaper than Pamukkale and offers some nice-sized portions. Stir-fries and chicken dishes are available, alongside a very tasty, spicy vegetable salad. Nice décor. ₮₮

### Guanzes

There are several decent, cheap *guanzes* across the street from the southeast corner of the square, near the Tavan Bogd National Park office.

# WHAT TO DO IN ULGII

Ulgii's **Music and Drama Theater (Аймактык Музыкалы Драма Театры)** holds concerts frequently; look for signs advertising that day's performance in front of the theater. The predominant instrument of Kazakh folk music is the *dombra*. It looks simple, but the best *dombra* players use an amazingly wide repertoire of picking techniques to create soulful, spirited, and often very fast-paced songs.

> ## Kazakh Food: Hungry Enough to Eat a Horse?
>
> Much of Kazakh food is similar to Mongolian food: the same 5 ingredients, boiled, steamed, or fried. Some dishes look slightly different but are close relatives. Kazakh *bes barmak*, for instance, is almost identical to Mongolian *tsoivan*, except that the noodles are cut wide, the size of lasagna, rather than the linguine-type noodles used in the Mongol dish.
>
> One dish that is entirely Kazakh, however, is *kaz* (horsemeat sausage), made by packing meat, fat, and whole rib bones into a sleeve of intestine. When finished, *kaz* looks a little like a party balloon, just waiting to be twisted into a dog or hat for a five year-old's birthday party. Many Westerners, and Americans in particular, are unsympathetic to the idea of eating horses, but for those willing to risk the disgusted stares and angry berating of friends back home, a bite of *kaz* is the single best culinary moment you will ever hope to enjoy in the Mongolian *hudoo*. The meat is salty and oh-so delicious, and even the yellow fat seems to melt right in your mouth. (And we'll even let it slip that the author of this section is a very happy vegetarian back home in America.)
>
> Kazakhs often eat together from a common platter, more like their brethren in the Middle East or Central Asia than their Mongolian neighbors, who generally eat from individual bowls. If dinnertime comes while you're visiting a Kazakh family, you'll probably be invited to join in just like an itinerant relative, so wash your hands, grab a fork, and dig in!

You might wander by the **mosque** to get a look at the home of the Mongolian Kazakh community's brand of central-Asian-influenced Islam.

Duman and the **BU Palace** just off the square offer beers and evening disco dancing, set to a soundtrack of upbeat Kazakh, Turkish, and Indian pop music.

There is good hiking to be done in the mountains that ring Ulgii. For a short walk, head to **Drojba Mountain**, visible on the east side of town and identifiable by the star that graces its face. To get there, cross the bridge to the far side of the river from the city center, than head east for 1.5 kilometers (1 mile). You can reach the mountain, climb it, and be back in town in about 3 hours. The far side of Drojba is a giant drift of sand, not quite a dune, but still fun to jump around on. The smaller mountain just before Drojba is even easier to hike and will also give a good view of the city.

For a longer hike, follow the river upstream (west) towards Sagsai Soum. It enters a gorgeous canyon pass about 6 kilometers (3.75 miles) from the bridge. There is also good day hiking in the more gradual mountains to the south of town. Just choose a peak and head towards it.

## SHOPPING

Kazakh embroidery makes for some of the most beautiful, useful souvenirs you could hope to find. There are a number of art shops around Ulgii, including **Altai Kereu** next to Bastau Hotel, and shops just outside the museum as well as in its lobby. However, two of the best shops are **Altai Craft** and **Kazakh Craft**. Both offer a wide range of products, including bags, purses, pillow cases, Kazakh hats, and the large tapestries that hang in Kazakh *gers*. Each company has its respective sewing workshop and store at the same location, allowing you to see how the products are made before you pick out something to take home. Both of these stores are somewhat poorly marked and difficult to find, but that just adds to the adventure.

**Altai Craft** Altai Craft was started by an American woman as a means of employing women from families with no other source of income, and is now run entirely by local staff. Their large workshop and showroom is located behind the market in a long building with a brown metal roof. The staff is very friendly and happy to show you what they are working on. In addition to purses and tapestries, they also make some delightful *ger*-shaped Christmas tree ornaments. *91422279 (Speak to Amaka); www.altaicraft.com*

**Kazakh Craft** This shop makes updated versions of classic Kazakh designs on purses, vests, and pillows, among other items. Like at Altai Craft, many of the women working here are without other means of making a living. The owner, Narbek, who speaks English, is passionate about preserving Kazakh culture, and if he's not too busy running the business, he's a fascinating guy to talk to. Kazakh Craft goods can also be found in a number of Ulaanbaatar gift shops, including those at the State Department Store, the National History Museum, and the Choijinlama Monastery. *99429906; kazakhcraft@yahoo.com; www.kazkahcraft.com*

The market, known in Ulgii as the ***bazaar***, is also a good place to search for Kazakh treasures. On top of the usual foodstuffs and household goods, the bazaar's narrow, labyrinthine lanes contain vendors selling the odd wall hanging, *kapesh* (Kazakh hat) and brightly colored headscarves. There is usually someone with a few *dombra*s set up near the main entrance; the musical instruments are attractive and not very expensive, and are surprisingly light, which is good if you're headed back to UB by plane. Unfortunately, the long trip by land may be more than a *dombra* can take if it's not packed carefully.

## AROUND BAYAN-ULGII

**Altai Tavan Bogd National Park (Алтай таван богд)** is a breathtaking national park on the western border with China and Russia and Mongolia's largest park. **Khuiten Uul**, the country's tallest mountain at 4,374 meters (14,350 feet), is flanked by four other peaks (Naran, Ulgii, Burged, and Nairamdal); together they make up

The Guide

### Khasim Narbek, Kazakh Craft Founder

Khasim Narbek is both a savvy businessman and a cultural preservationist. Born in 1974, Narbek grew up in Bayan-Ulgii and studied art in Almata, Kazakhstan. He started Kazakh Craft after returning to Ulgii in 2001, originally producing specialized leather equipment such as hoods and gloves for the prized local hunting eagles. In 2005, he noticed that tourists passing through Ulgii had taken significant interest in Kazakh embroidery, paying good money for the brightly colored, antique, hand-made tapestries that most Kazakh families decorate the walls of their *gers* with.

"The old wall hangings were becoming rarer," he says. "They had all been sold to tourists!"

With just three employees, Narbek set about expanding his product line to include wall hangings and other items featuring Kazakh embroidery, which revolves around distinct symmetrical and floral patterns. Today, Kazakh Craft employs more than forty women and sells its goods in Ulgii, Kazakhstan, and Ulaanbaatar and via their website.

While building his successful company, though, Narbek has taken a personal interest in seeing that the traditional crafts of his people continue. He has amassed a large collection of antique wall hangings, and uses their designs to inspire his company's new products. While he tweaks their patterns and colors to appeal to the contemporary Western tourist, he hopes to exhibit his collection one day. Similar wall hangings, he says, were made throughout central Asia from Turkey to Kyrgyzstan to Kazakhstan. "They are related to the nomadic life," he says. "They decorated every *ger*! Our company was founded by women who still carry knowledge of the trade and has brought them together with a passion to help keep this art form alive."

the Tavan Bogd ("Five Saints"). The park offers nearly endless hiking among mountain streams and lakes, snow melt bogs, and Altai foothills, along with serious mountaineering opportunities.

Tavan Bogd is snow-capped all year round, and any of the peaks make for a challenging climb. Especially on Khuiten, you will need climbing equipment including ropes, cramp-ons, and ice axes to make an ascent. For any of the peaks an experienced guide is recommended. Neighboring **Malchin Peak (Малчин уул)** is and easier climb that doesn't require all the gear and can be done in a few hours. It still rewards you with great views of the surrounding area. It is also possible to hike on the **Potanii Glacier**, the largest in the area. As with all glaciers, hike with caution since Potanii is not without crevasses.

About 90 kilometers (56 miles) south of Tavan Bogd, you'll find a pair of striking lakes, **Khoton Nuur (Хотон нуур)** and **Khurgan Nuur (Хурган нуур)**, as well as the somewhat less majestic **Dayan Nuur (Даян нуур)**. The lakes region also provides great hiking with a little less permanent snow.

There is nothing to speak of in the way of accommodations or *guanzes* in the national park, and there aren't even many herding families in the area. You should plan on camping throughout your trip, and bring all the food and water you'll need. The Altai are cool even in summer, and it can be downright cold at night. Snow falls sporadically throughout what is considered summer in other parts of the country, especially in the immediate vicinity of Tavan Bogd. Bring a warm sleeping bag and clothes and pack a pair of long johns just in case.

Entrance into the park requires paying a MNT3,000 fee, which you can do at the **Mongol Altai Range Special Protection Areas Administration Office (Монгол Алтайн Нурууны Улсын Тусгай Хамгаалалтай Газруудын Хамгалалтын Захиргаа or MARSPAA**—try saying that three times fast) in Ulgii. You can also pay upon meeting a ranger in the park itself. The MARSPAA office may also be able to help you find a reliable driver. You will also need to get a border permit to enter the park, and where you obtain this document depends on where in the park you plan to go. For Khoton Nuur and Khurgan Nuur, you can get the permit at the **Border Guard Department (Хилийн цэрэгийн газар)** near the Naadam Stadium in Ulgii. For the Tavan Bogd region you may be able to get the permit in Ulgii, but you may also be told you have to go to the border guard garrison in **Tsagaan Nuur Soum (Цагаан нуур сум)**, the border town with Russia. In this case, you may want to leave in the afternoon, camp out next to the lake just outside the Tsagaan Nuur Soum center for the night, get your permit in the morning, and spend the day driving parallel to the Russian border until you reach Tavan Bogd. No one ever said traveling in Mongolia was easy, but then the most worthwhile adventures never are. Fortunately, on the way back to Ulgii you can take the more direct route through Ulaankhus Soum. Border permits cost MNT5,000, and you will need to go with your guide and your original passport (no photocopies) to receive it.

### Tsengel Soum (Цэнгэл сум)

Chances are you'll pass through Tsengel on your way to the lakes region of Altai Tavan Bogd National Park. Even if you're not headed for the park, Tsengel is a worthwhile destination on its own. The *soum* has a couple claims to fame: it is the westernmost settlement in Mongolia, and Louisa Waugh's 2003 memoir *Hearing Birds Fly* details life in the village in the late 1990s. Tsengel also one-ups the rest of Bayan-Ulgii in the cultural and ethnic diversity department; alongside the Kazakhs and Mongolians there is a large Tuvan population.

Tsengel sits along a verdant swath of green beside the Khovd River. The river is quite deep and is one of the best swimming spots in western Mongolia. Local children practically live there during summer, and even the yaks join the fun, swimming home from the pastures on the far side each night with just their noses and eyes visible until they slosh out on the other side. Follow the river upstream on the path that hugs the mountains south of the town for about an hour, and you'll find a fresh water spring revered by the locals set in a grove of pine trees.

The mountains on the southern edge of town offer easy climbing with good views of the valley and a couple *ovoos*, but be respectful around the cemetery that sits on the ridge in between the town and the mountains.

### Deluun Soum (Дэлүүн сум)

Deluun Soum has one of the strongest communities of genuine eagle hunters in Bayan-Ulgii. There are only about a dozen eagle hunters here, so the hunting is still good, and virtually all of the hunters work with eagles trapped from the wild, in the traditional way, rather than taken from the nest as chicks. Khuatkhan, an eagle hunter with over 30 years of experience, has been helpful to those interested in learning more about this centuries old Kazakh art. Ask around the *soum* center, which is about a four-hour drive from Ulgii, to find someone who knows where to find his camp.

Eagle hunting is a winter activity, generally practiced between November and February, but if you're in Deluun during the summer and looking for a good countryside experience, many of the *soum's* residents can be found in the **Tungirik Valley**. This forested valley, 60 kilometers (37 miles) south of the *soum* center, also has great fishing. The mountains around Deluun are stocked with ibex and argali sheep.

Ask around and you might find a local who can lead you to a valley where you'll find many petroglyphs spread out over ten or fifteen kilometers.

---

### *Life at the Mongolian Muslim Frontier*

Kazakh culture is rooted in two major forces: nomadism and Islam. Like all nomads, the Kazakhs are pragmatic, and because the mobile lifestyle makes it difficult for people to amass libraries of religious texts or worship in a mosque regularly, Bayan-Ulgii may not seem like a particularly religious Muslim area. In truth, Mongolia's Kazakhs are not as strict practitioners of the religion as many other regions of the Muslim world; few Kazakhs break for daily prayer, many men drink alcohol, and modern women wear simple headscarves rather than burkas or veils. But Kazakh culture is still deeply influenced by Islam, and the discerning traveler will notice that Kazakhs are generally more conservative than their Mongolian neighbors in dress, thinking, and behavior, especially when it comes to dating. Their conservatism shouldn't be intimidating, however. The Kazakhs of Bayan-Ulgii are among the most hospitable and welcoming people in the country.

---

#### Sagsai Soum (Сагсай сум)

Sagsai is just an hour's drive through a tight mountain pass from Ulgii. It is notable mainly for its role in hosting the Blue Wolf Travel company's annual Eagle Festival in the final week of September. The company also operates a *ger* camp in the *soum*, near the banks of the Khovd Gol. Another thirty kilometers or so down the road is the **Zoct Summer Camp** (Зост лагэрь), a Soviet-style collection of wooden cabins along the river where children and work groups come to relax during the summer. There's plenty of good hiking in the hills between the *soum* and the camp.

# Bulgan Aimag (Булган аймаг)

With a population of around 67,000, Bulgan, located 330 kilometers (205 miles) from Ulaanbaatar, is rich in coniferous trees, rivers, and volcanic mountains. Book a car from Erdenet, the mining enclave and city-province on the train route, and head to Bulgan for some serene scenery.

Though cold and snowy in the winter, Bulgan's summers are warm and tranquil. The shallow and plush Burengiin Mountain Range cuts across the *aimag* and the **Khugnu Khaan Uul** peaks into southern Bulgan Aimag. The north supports a small timber industry (both legitimate and not) in its coniferous forest while the south is covered by grasslands. Spread between are wheat and vegetable crops making Bulgan part of Mongolia's agricultural heartland. The Selenge River traverses the *aimag's* north while the Orkhon and Tuul rivers amble through the southern parts, each supporting fish, vegetation, and herds.

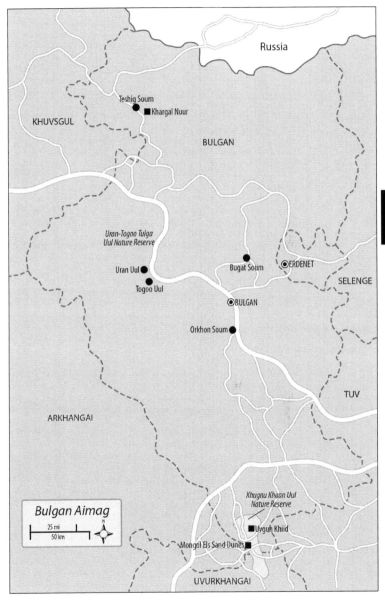

Bulgan Aimag

25 mi
50 km

The Guide

The **Uran-Togoo Tulga Uul Natural Reserve** is on the way to Khuvsgul Aimag. Find a driver going that way, or hitch or hike westward. Otherwise, it makes a nice day trip from the *aimag* center. The northern district bordering Russia, Teshig is host to the peaceful **Khargal Nuur**, a lake in the northeastern portion of the *aimag*.

## BULGAN SOUM (БУЛГАН СУМ)

Bulgan is a nice place to spend a couple days if you are in between trips, or simply want to enjoy some peace and quiet after the bustle of Erdenet. The *aimag* center is the only modern part of the whole province. It has larger buildings, accommodations, a variety of food options, transportation, and internet. The rest is rugged and rural. Relax and quench your summer thirst with a nice bowl of *airag*—regarded as among the country's best—outside a *guanz* while watching horse carts and Land Cruisers battle for road space.

The *aimag* center isn't very big, but it has plenty of friendly people, a wide variety of Mongolian foods and drinks, and a lovely little park worth visiting. With a short walk around the town to visit the **Dashchoinkhorlon Khiid** or the **Ethnography Museum** next door, you will inevitably encounter a barrage of "hi bombs" wherever you go as curious folks notice you're not from around there. There are a couple schools around, but expect this city to be empty during the summer, as most children go to the countryside during their break. If you feel like volunteering or having a chat, the staff at World Vision in Bulgan is always up for some impromptu English classes and eager to meet travelers.

Attractions around the city are the **Bulgan Uul** (Bulgan Mountains) and a quaint little park with statues of the famous cosmonaut and 2000-2004 defense minister **Jügderdemidiin Gürragchaa** as well as various famous wrestlers. Also, be sure to walk down to the river to cool off. Cross to the other side for a peek at the **Mausoleum** of revolutionary hero Magsarjaviin Khatanbaatar.

## GETTING THERE

There are no direct routes to Bulgan save for a weekly *mikr* that leaves UB and Bulgan on Tuesdays or Thursdays, but this is not recommended as it is cramped and filled with goods. Otherwise, getting to Bulgan requires a combination of train and public automotive transport via nearby Erdenet.

### By Bus
The only direct bus from the Dragon Center in UB to Bulgan is not very comfortable and runs only on Tuesdays and Thursdays (MNT12,300).

A bus leaves the Dragon Centre for Erdenet (MNT11,000) four times a day (8:00 a.m., 10:00 a.m., 2:00 p.m., 4:00 p.m.). From there you can take a taxi to Erdenet's *dumug* to find Bulgan-bound drivers. The cars to Bulgan gather on the opposite side of the road from the taxi stand 20 meters away.

## By Train

Bulgan is not directly accessible by train, but it can be reached from Erdenet by automobile. From UB, take the train overnight to Erdenet (MNT12,500). From the train station, you can either get on a blue and white bus that has "ET – Bulgan – ET" on the front (MNT3,000; Monday-Friday) or take a *mikr* (MNT700) to the "dummok," where a taxi driver will adopt you if you simply mention the word Bulgan (MNT4,000). A little less than an hour of driving will find you in the capital of the province.

## By Private Transportation

Private cars from Erdenet will set you back at least MNT50,000, and though you might have a little flexibility to stop at an *ovoo* or two along the route, it's not worth

The Guide

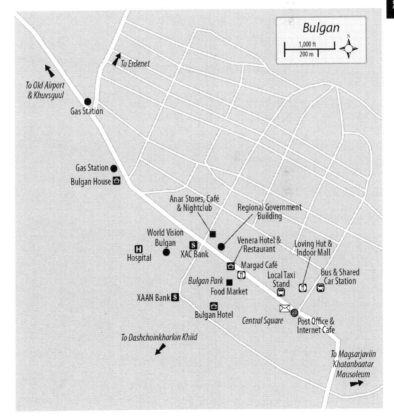

the money when the other routes are so easy and affordable.

### Hitchhiking

Hitchhiking is possible. If you are out hiking, biking, or your horse has died, you can hang out your arm. Otherwise, there are easy and accessible ways to reach Bulgan without hitchhiking. Nevertheless, cars from Bulgan to Khuvsgul are hard to come by, so you might consider hitchhiking if you want to continue west.

## GETTING AROUND THE AIMAG

Post office buses run to *soums* about twice a week. For most *soum* centers, you can find a driver at the car station opposite the Bulgan government building. Prices and availability vary greatly.

## WHERE TO STAY

**Venera (Вэнэра)** The best place to stay in town. Look for it close to the main government building. Venera has six rooms that run between $18 and $23. In addition, Venera is by far the best restaurant/bar/disco club/karaoke club in town. Laundry service is available, and you will pay by the kilo. *01342-22090, 99080944, 99604099*

**Bulgan Hotel** Has a good location in town, close to the Khan Bank. It has 10-15 closet-sized single, double, and triple rooms for $5-15 per person. Two rooms have toilets, and all share showers. Internet is available. There is sometimes laundry service available. No kitchen for guests, though there is a *guanz* downstairs. *01342-22811, 91717856, 99349243*

**Bulgan House** Close to a gas station just outside Bulgan on the main road. It has four rooms with toilets in the house and an outhouse. Rates are $10-12. It's a decent place, but Venera has siphoned off some of its business since it opened. Bulgan House also has a restaurant and bar and supposedly a sauna. Laundry service is available overnight, and if you need it, the staff can arrange automobile repairs. *96345555, 96346666*

## WHERE TO EAT

**Margad (Маргад)** The best place to eat in Bulgan. Good food, cheap, and generally quick, although Margad's times of opening and closing seem to shift around somewhat. A one-minute walk down the right side of the main street from Venera, Margad has the best *tsuivan* in town. With one of these and a "tom" (big) Borgio beer, your day will be complete! But be warned, the oil can be a bit much to handle and can bring an end to your day. There aren't really any standard vegetarian options but you can order the *khurag* "makhgui" without meat, making it a sweet pepper hot plate, which is pretty good. The *bainshtai shul* (байиштай шөл or "little dumpling soup") is also good. The staff is young and friendly, but they do not speak English very well. ₮₮

**Venera (Вэнэра)** Situated down the main road in Bulgan on the right side, Venera doubles as a hotel. The seats are not the greatest things nor are the "sofas" that sink in. Unless you have short, short legs, you are better off going for the regular tables in the back of the place. The food is pricey by Mongolian standards, but it can be worth it for the fried chicken or mutton *khurag*. The *tsuivan* is rubbish, so go to Margad for cheaper and tastier food. No one there speaks English, but foreign tourists frequent it, so you won't stand out too much. ₮₮₮

**The Loving Hut** The only real vegetarian option. To find it, go down the main street, and take a right at the first road. The Loving Hut is in the same building as the Bulgan Ikh Delguur close to the bus station. It is small but wonderfully staffed with friendly albeit non-English speaking people. However, be warned; stomach "issues" due to what we assume to be unwashed vegetables have been reported. *Mantuu buuz* and regular veggie *buuz* are filling and cost next to nothing. MNT1,050 gets you three *buuz* and a milk tea—what a deal! Just steer clear of the *sharbuurtsgiin khurag* (tofu hot plate). ₮

**Anar (Анар)** The newest place in town but also a good place to eat. It's just off the main street when you drive into town, right before the government building. There is a huge sign advertising the bar, nightclub, and café. The food is good, and the great people who also run the shop downstairs run the restaurant. The place is smoky and fun, but it's best to leave by 11:00 p.m. when the local party scene gets drunk and starts swinging at each other. Food is mid-range and beer is cheap for a nightclub. Look for Otgonbayar on Friday nights. He's an English teacher, Friday night regular, and a sure bet to chat your ear off! ₮₮

# WHAT TO DO IN BULGAN SOUM

**Dashchoinkhorlon Khiid (Дашойнхорлон хийд)** is a small monastery worth a quick peek inside. The modern monastery replaces the Bangiin Khuree Khiid where 1,000 monks and several stupas did not make it through the purges of the late 1930s unscathed. The replacement Dashchoinkhorlon Khiid houses statues, paintings, and about 30 monks.

If you're up for a little walk, you can see the ruins of the Bangiin Khuree 2.5 kilometers (1.5 miles) southwest of the city. There is a ruined pavilion and temple built toward the end of nineteenth century and other remnants of a hasty retreat.

**The Ethnographic Museum** (MNT1,000) next door to the modern monastery in town is similar to other *aimag* museums in that the exhibits are not well preserved and a bit tacky, but there are some unique finds such as the surgical tools and herding accoutrement that make it interesting enough for a visit.

**Magsarjaviin Khatanbaatar Mausoleum** is something to keep your eye out for if you're walking along the river. It is the final resting place of Revolutionary hero Magsarjaviin Khatanbaatar. He was an important leader in ousting the ruling Manchurians of the crumbling Qing Dynasty in 1911, and his remains are inside the blue concrete *ger*. Murals depicting the battles line the walls, but the building is locked. The Ethnographic Museum staff should be able to help you get in.

The Guide

# WHAT TO DO IN BULGAN AIMAG

**Uran-Togoo Tulga Uul Nature Reserve** (Уран-Тогоо тулга уулын дурсгалт газар) contains a number of extinct volcanoes named for their shapes. The park is 60-90 kilometers (37-56 miles) west of the provincial capital on the road to Khuvgsul. Though this area is worth seeing, especially if you're in the area and on your way to Khuvsgul, it is perhaps a little overhyped. So with your expectations lowered a little, you can relax and enjoy the hike up the west side.

The biggest sight at this "Hearth Park" is **Uran Uul (Уран уул or "Maestro Mountain")**. It has a crater 500 to 600 meters (1640-1970 feet) wide and 50 meters (164 feet) deep, and inside, there is a pond and a few trees atop the high ground. The nearby **Togoo Uul (Тороо уул or "Cauldron Mountain")** and the smaller **Jalavch Uul (Жалавч уул or "Small Pot Mountain")** round out the dead volcanic features. If you have your own tent, this park makes for a memorable sunset and cheap overnight on your way westward. Do watch out for flies in the summertime, though, because they are thick and motivated.

**Khugnu Khaan Uul Nature Reserve** (Хөгнө хаан уул) occupies the southern tip of Bulgan Aimag just north off the road 250 kilometers (155 miles) from Ulaanbaatar and 75 kilometers (46 miles) from Kharkhorin, but it's not directly accessible from the Bulgan *aimag* center. The reserve, which was set aside in 1997, is not well known or often visited. Despite this, it is a great place to explore with a backpack and a tent because of the interesting convergence of taiga and steppe landscapes all the way up to its approachable 1,976-meter (6,483-foot) peak. You have a shot at seeing ibex, wolves, and several varieties of hawk. Since the main road to and from UB is so close, you could easily find a ride if you want to stay a few days and then hitchhike on toward Arvaikheer or Kharkhorin.

Inside the park along the southern approach are the ruins of a mid-seventeenth century Zanabazar monastery, the **Uvgun Khiid (Өвгөн хийд)**. The monastery, which housed up to 1,000 monks, was built by Zanabazar, but it became part of the front lines in a religious-political conflict. During this time, Tibetan Buddhist religious leaders doubled as the political elite and controlled armies. A rivalry then existed between Zanabazar, whose domain was central Mongolia, and Galdan Bochigtu, who held lands in western Mongolia. Galdan Bochigtu disagreed with Zanabazar's intent to cede power to the Manchurians who were encroaching into Mongolia through a series of alliances and payoffs in an effort to undercut the waning Ming Dynasty. The conflict came to a head at the monastery, which was burned to the ground by Galdan Bochigtu's forces.

The current monastery by the same name houses a small group of about 10 monks and sits at the bottom of the approach to the mountain (N47°25'33.49", E103°41'36.73"). Entrance is MNT1,000. The felled monastery is up the hill about 2 kilometers (1 mile).

### Teshig Soum (Тэшиг сум)
On the Russian border, Teshig Soum is in the northeast part of Bulgan Aimag. The *soum* center is accessible by a post bus leaving from the *aimag* center every Thursday at 9:00 a.m. when it does the mail run throughout the major villages in Bulgan, ending in Teshig. For MNT12,000, you can get to the *soum* center and find your way east to the vast Khargal Lake (Харгал нуур) and its surrounding romantic, rolling terrain. It's a wonder someone hasn't invested in a yoga or spa retreat there, but since they haven't you'll practically have the place to yourself. You can sometimes find *ger* camps in the area, but bring your own tent.

### Bugat Soum (Бугат сум)
If you're in a taxi or have hired private transportation from Erdenet, you'll likely get there by going through Bugat Soum on the northern route because it is about

The Guide

---

## Mongolians in Space

**Jugderdemidiin Gurragchaa (Жүгдэрдэмидийн гүррагчаа)** (born 1947) was the second Asian in space (behind Pham Tuan of Vietnam in 1980) and the first Mongolian. As a member of the Soyuz 39 mission along with Soviet cosmonaut Vladimir Dzhanibekov, he departed from earth on March 22, 1981 to dock with Vladimir Kovalyonok and Viktor Savinykh, who had been left aboard Salyut 6, the second-generation soviet orbital space station. While in orbit, the four carried out experiments on earth science for nearly six days and spent two days concentrating almost exclusively on studying Mongolia from space.

Hailing from Bulgan Aimag's rural Gurvanbulag Soum, Gurragchaa attended the Ulaanbaatar Agricultural Institute before being drafted into the Mongolian army in the late 1960s. In 1973, he attended the Zhukovskiy Air Force Academy in Moscow and rose to the Rank of Major General. Eventually, he found his way into the Cosmonaut Training Center in Moscow by 1978 where he spent the following three years preparing for the Soyuz mission.

Upon returning home from the eight-day space mission on March 30, 1981, he was awarded the title of "Hero of the Soviet Union," the highest honor in the nation. The Zaisan Memorial south of Ulaanbaatar is dedicated to Russian-Mongolian friendship, and it includes a mosaic mural depiction of Gurragchaa's 1981 flight among its scenes.

Gurragchaa's renown brought him to parliament in 1982 where he became a deputy in The People's Great Khural until the government collapsed in 1990. After overseeing elections and holding down other bureaucratic functions following the democratic changeover, he was appointed as Mongolia's defense minister from 2000 to 2004.

halfway between Erdenet and Bulgan. The road is not very good, but the view is great as you wind down and through the valley. Keep your fingers crossed tightly and maybe you'll see wild deer or *"buga"* for which the area is named. Hikers making the trek from Erdenet to Bulgan can stop in Bugat along the way to resupply.

**Stone Statues** dot the countryside in proximity to Bulgan. For a touch of history, check out Orkhon Soum's seven Stone Age **Deer Stones (Орхон сумын Буган хөшөө)** located about 20 kilometers (12 miles) southeast of Bulgan just east of Orkhon Soum center. Or you can head north from Bulgan City instead for a look at the man stones of Zuun Turuunii Khun Chuluu (Зүүн түрүүний хүн чулуу) from the Turkic period. These stones are also sometimes referred to as *"balbal,"* which is supposedly an ancient Turkic word for ancestor. These stones are said to mark the graves of chiefs and clan leaders or their fallen enemies.

# Darkhan-Uul Aimag (Дархан-уул аймаг)

With plush green countryside surrounding the city, Darkhan (pronounced "Darhn," with rolled "r" and wet "h") offers a combination of UB convenience and amenities with Mongolian herder hospitality and charm. The *aimag* is essentially the city itself; the three other residential districts outside the capital are not of much interest for tourists. Although Darkhan is also not necessarily a tourist destination in and of itself, it is definitely worth a look, especially for travelers arranging a trip to **Amarbaysgalant Monastery** in Selenge or **Cold River** camp or as a stopover on the rail line heading to or from Russia or Erdenet.

Darkhan City has a population of 92,400 and lies 219 kilometers (136 miles) north of Ulaanbaatar along the main north-south highway. It is the administrative and cultural center of Darkhan-Uul Aimag, which is wholly surrounded by Selenge Aimag. It is generally listed as the third largest city in Mongolia behind UB and Erdenet, but many locals insist that it is in fact the second largest, especially as the suburbs swell with job-seekers who have abandoned herding after recent devastating winters.

The city was founded in 1961 to relieve migration toward UB with the intention of developing it into the northern industrial and manufacturing center of Mongolia, as revealed by the name itself, which means "blacksmith" or "tradesman." While a small industrial sector remains today, primarily metal, cement, and leather processing, the city has also become one of the largest agricultural centers in the region and the country.

Planned and built according to Soviet aesthetics, apartment blocks dominate the landscape, including the famed 16-story building near the theater that was once Mongolia's tallest building. The city is divided into two sections, old and new. **Old Darkhan (*Khuuchin Darkhan*, pronounced "HOE-chin Darhn")** is part of the original wave of development dating to the 1960s and is filled with aging soviet infrastructure. **New Darkhan (Shine Darkhan, pronounced "shin Darhn")** is, of course part, of a more modern development and has most of the city's amenities and points of interest.

Darkhan is spread out, and although you can walk between destinations in the old and new sections in about an hour, local taxis (MNT350 per person) and *mikr*es (MNT250 per person) can be hailed almost anywhere in town. In fact, they may hail you as they drive by, honking their horns and hanging halfway out the *mikr* windows while shouting their route. *Mikrs* generally follow one path through the city and will drop you at any point along the way.

The name of the market in Darkhan comes from the Russian word *birja*. In Mongolian, they drop the last vowel, so if you're near the train station or trying to find the market, you'll be looking for the *birj* or бирж (pronounced "Beerj").

# GETTING THERE

Darkhan lies along both the major north-south highway and rail line in Mongolia, connecting it with Ulaanbaatar to the south and the Russian border to the north. Much of the transportation conveniently comes to and from the ***Olon ulsin khudaldani tuv* (Олон улсын худалданы төв or "International Trade Center")**.

## By Bus

Buses traveling between UB and Darkhan depart hourly from both cities starting at 9:00 a.m. (MNT6,000 one way). Buses leave from and arrive at the Dragon Center in UB; the station in Darkhan is the International Trade Center in Old Darkhan. Buy tickets the day of your travel and expect the trip to take around 3.5 hours.

You can purchase tickets back to UB or to some other destinations from the cashier located in the small office adjacent to the parking lot of the International Trade Center.

## By Shared Transportation

A crackdown by the local police on vehicle overcrowding has made transportation by *mikr* a much more comfortable travel option to UB and Erdenet.

*Mikrs* regularly arrive at and depart from the International Trade Center heading towards both Ulaanbaatar (MNT6,000) and Erdenet (MNT5,000-7,000; 6 hours). You can sometimes catch one to Khuvsgul from here as well (MNT25,000-30,000; 16 hours).

## By Taxi

Private taxis also depart regularly from the International Trade Center to Ulaanbaatar (MNT12,000 per person; 2.5-3 hours) and Erdenet (MNT10,000 per person; 2-2.5 hours). Make sure to take the licensed taxis (marked with a sticker on the front or side of the car) directly in front of the entrance to the trade center as opposed to the unlicensed drivers who will try to grab as you approach. Unlicensed drivers are unreliable, may shake you down for more money, and take longer to fill up.

Private taxis depart regularly from the market in Old Darkhan to Darkhan-Uul *soums* (Sharin-gol, Khongor, and Orkhon), Zulzeg tourist camp area as well as several *soums* in surrounding Selenge Aimag (Sukhbaatar, Khutul, etc.). Prices range from MNT7,000-12,000 depending on the distance.

## By Train

Trains arrive and depart daily from UB and Erdenet. From UB it takes seven hours (third Class MNT5,000, half coupe MNT10,000, coupe MNT15,300). Trains depart at 8:50 a.m. and 11:00 p.m. Darkhan to Erdenet is about 5.5 hours (third class MNT4,100, half coupe 7,700, coupe 12,000). This train departs at 3:00 a.m. Trains are a great way to see the countryside; however, most run at night and are painfully slow. Locals can sometimes purchase tickets to Beijing and Moscow in Darkhan, but foreigners should purchase those in Ulaanbaatar.

# GETTING AROUND THE AIMAG

*Mikrs* depart regularly from the market in Old Darkhan to Darkhan-Uul Soums (Sharin-gol and Orkhon) and the Zulzeg tourist camp area as well as *soums* in surrounding Selenge Aimag (Sukhbaatar, Khutul, etc). Prices range from (MNT5,000-7,000), depending on the distance.

# WHERE TO EAT

### Restaurants

**Bulgogi Family** The only true Korean Restaurant in town. Bring an appetite and a friend because the best dishes are large portions and meant to be shared. Open every day for lunch and dinner. ₮₮

**Modern Nomads** The most Western friendly place to eat in Old Darkhan, especially if you're looking for a cocktail or cold draft beer. They have interesting versions of American dishes, and though the Mongolian dishes are overpriced, they are well prepared. This is the place to go if you are looking for a burger or a club sandwich. The cement patio with tables serves as a beer garden in the summer and is the perfect backdrop for enjoying an "Island Tea." ₮₮

**Nice Café** On the main road between the Russian consulate and the Darkhan Hotel. It is a decent place to grab a variety of Mongolian and Chinese dishes. The prices are good, especially since some of the dishes feature the holy grail of *dining*: vegetables and chicken. Ask for rice per person if you share a dish. ₮₮

**Saintain** Located between Nice Café and the Bulgogi Family restaurant, Saintain serves tasty Mongolian dishes. It is well known around town for its delicious roasted chicken dish. It is a reliable place for a good meal, and the price is just about right. ₮₮

**Texas Pub** Also on the main road, Texas Pub has a nice comfortable atmosphere to kick back and enjoy a drink with friends, and you won't have to worry about rowdy Mongolians looking to fight like you can in the night clubs. This is the place to go if you are looking for an actual steak, not just bits of meat with your noodles or rice. Though the steak is not the best you'll ever have, it's a nice change from mutton and goulash. The Mongolian food is average and so are the beer prices. ₮₮

**BBQ Chicken** An international chain franchise from Korea that you might (or might not) recognize. It serves a variety of tasty chicken dishes and sandwiches. It's located in the International Trade Center, so stop in for some soft-serve ice cream—it's the only place in town to get it—before you board your bus. ₮₮

The Guide

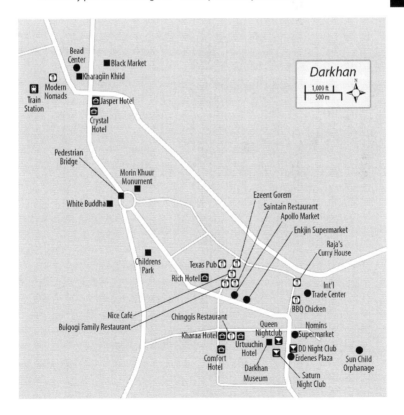

**Ezeent Gorem (Эзээнт горэмь)** "The Empire" is the place to go if you want pizza and a flair for the West with a Mongolian twist. It's a restaurant and pub with a variety of Mongolian and Western dishes to pair with wine, cocktails, draft beer, and coffee. Look for live music on most weekends and an outdoor beer garden in the summer. ₮₮

**Chinggis Pub & Restaurant** Sandwiched between the Kharaa (Хараа) and Urtuuchin (Өртөөчин) hotels. It's the closest thing to an actual pub in Darkhan. It has the nice, laid back atmosphere you want after a long bumpy trek in a Jeep. Just sit back here and enjoy an ice cold draft beer and standard Mongolian dishes. Some staff members speak a little English. ₮₮

**Raja's Curry House** In the International Trade Center, Raja's is operated by a Malaysian man and his Mongolian wife. With some of the most flavor you'll find in town and very reasonable prices, it is a great place to enjoy if you're looking to break out of a food funk. They serve a variety of delicious Indian-Malaysian dishes and curries. ₮/₮₮

## Guanzes

**The International Trade Center Food Court** Has a large variety of food stalls including Mongolian, Russian, Korean, kebabs, and vegetarian stalls. Cleaner and tastier than the cafés at the Bead Center and market. ₮

**Bead Center** Directly across the street from the *birj* in Old Darkhan. It has Mongolian and Russian food and might be better than the food stalls in the market itself. ₮

# GROCERY STORES & SHOPPING

**Apollo & Enkhjin Supermarkets** Small shops in New Darkhan near the post office. They have a variety of imported American, Korean, and German food products. Meat, fruit, and vegetable selection is limited, though.

**Nomin** The closest thing to a mall in Darkhan, though it does have a hint of Costco-style bulk shopping centers, too. It has a variety of shops and stalls inside, selling everything from clothes to cell phones. This is a good place to pick up camping or fishing supplies. It also has a large supermarket inside, the same as the one in the State Department Store in Ulaanbaatar. Look for the famous Darkhan Neekhii Company leather products (summer and winter coats), cashmere, and camel clothing.

**International Trade Center** Has two floors of market shopping. Food and souvenirs (best place in town) are on the first floor while clothes and other supplies are on the second floor. It's the place to get fresh meat and vegetables if you are staying in New Darkhan.

**The Birj (Black Market)** A large indoor/outdoor market in Old Darkhan where you can find most things for cheap. Good deals on clothes and boots.

**Erdenes Plaza** One of Darkhan's newer additions complete with upscale clothing shops, a two-screen movie theatre, night club, and arcade.

# Darkhan's Mediasmith Javkhaa Ara Ragchaasuren

Javkhaa Ara Ragchaaasuren is a small, smiley guy who drives a colorful later model four- wheel drive hatchback. He wears dark jeans with designer white streaks in the deep creases on the front and tops off his everyday look with stylish dark sunglasses. His accented English is a little broken at times but remarkably well rounded, especially considering his limited formal English classes or tutors. Javkhaa, by anyone's measure, is pretty put together.

Since 2002, Javkhaa has made nine serial radio dramas, each with 10 to 60 episodes, many of which played nationwide. He's made four video documentaries in Mongolian with Orkhon Productions, his own media company. He also owns and runs Orkhon Radio FM 106, playing foreign and local music with dance beats and catchy hooks that he mindlessly sings along to, bobbing his head as he works. Javkhaa is Darkhan's homegrown media mogul and entrepreneur, and he's only in his early 30s.

On any given day you can find Javkhaa hunched intensely in front of a computer with his ears cupped by huge black earphones. His small studio, complete with sound booths and cloth walls is usually crowded and buzzing with action. The computer in the broadcast studio plays the day's lineup—all hits, all the time—and lights up the room with the zigging and zagging lines of the digital equalizer displayed on the computer monitor. He is constantly on and off his phone effortlessly switching from English to Mongolian and back as needed. You might also catch him working his thumbs in tandem on tiny phone buttons as he sends a text message, though he prefers to just talk and get it over with.

Not surprising considering his friendly, warm disposition and his tractor beam-like charisma, Javkhaa is frequently out of his studio ferrying his kids, wife, or friends where they need to be like a do-it-all suburban dad. In fact, he often travels around with a small entourage, usually part of his 5-10 member production team carrying cameras and other equipment depending on the project he's working on—and he's always working on something.

Javkhaa's projects often revolve around Mongolian life. He is intensely proud of his heritage, and he has tackled many subjects in Mongolian. His first English radio drama, "The Secret History of the Mongols," an adaptation of a Mongolian version he did a few years prior, dropped in the summer of 2010. He and his English teacher friend, Nargi (who does an awesome Elvis impersonation and sounds like he might be from California, dude), wrote, directed, and produced the drama. It features Javkhaa's voice and many of his foreign friends play the parts of the fabled founders of Mongolia including Chinggis Khan, his frenemy Jamukha, his mother O'luen, and many other characters from the well known origin story. You can pick up a CD in UB book stores or stop by Javkhaa's for some tea and walk away with your copy.

Though Javkhaa has built a self-sustaining media company from the ground up, he has his sights on more. Now, this married father of one daughter and two sons is getting into the tourism business because he wants to share Darkhan's fresh air, friendly people, and beautiful natural nomadic lifestyle. He and his group have *ger* camps next to the Kharaa River meant to showcase the Mongolian nomadic lifestyle. They will organize tour trips to Khuvsgul Lake and Lake Baikal from Darkhan, a rare convenience for Mongolians and foreign travelers. He thinks Darkhan is the best place to start a journey for these two lakes because they are very close. If you feel the same way, look him up. If he's available, you're guaranteed to have a great time with him. Contact Javkhaa at 99093126 or javkha_ara@yahoo.com.

The Guide

# WHERE TO STAY

There are a couple of hotels located in the apartment buildings adjacent to the train station. Some trains arrive late at night, and these hotels offer the closest location for lodging. However, they can be unreliable, and it is not the best area of town to stay in. We recommend catching a taxi to the New Darkhan hotels or, if no taxis are available, making the 15-minute walk to the Jasper or Crystal Hotels.

**Kharaa Hotel (Хараа)** A quite nice hotel on the inside, so don't judge a book by its cover. All rooms have en suite bathrooms, hot-water, and TV. Laundry service and parking garages are available. Breakfast is included. The restaurant is on the first floor. *Standard double MNT20,000, deluxe double MNT27,000, triple rooms MNT35,000. 976-99372828, 99093502, 99379985, 99379165; kharaa_hotel@yahoo.com*

**Urtuuchin Hotel (Өртөөчин)** A comfortable hotel in New Darkhan. Amenities include a fifth-floor restaurant, café, meeting rooms, business center, ATM, internet, garage parking, hot water, and laundry services. Breakfast included. *Standard single MNT15,000, double MNT18,000 triple MNT20,000, half deluxe double MNT20,000-30,000,half deluxe triple 35,000-60,000. Visa and MasterCard accepted. 0137228195; marketing@darkhan-urtuuchinhotel.mn; www.darkhan-urtuuchinhotel.mn*

**Comfort Hotel** Directly beside the Urtuuchin. It's a newer hotel that offers the nicest accommodations in Darkhan. Amenities include a bar, restaurant, internet, and TV in rooms. Hot water, karaoke, and laundry services available. *Visa and MasterCard accepted. Standard single MNT30,000, double MNT35,000, half deluxe queen MNT42,000, deluxe queen MNT68,000-72,000 (includes hot-tub and mini-fridge), family MNT70,000 (includes king bed and kitchen). 0137229091; tsetsegee_8101@yahoo.com*

**Rich Hotel** Has newly renovated rooms and the friendliest staff in Darkhan, so don't be fooled by the apartment building exterior. All rooms have en suite bathrooms with hot water and TV. Laundry service available. Breakfast included. *Visa and MasterCard accepted. Standard single MNT10,000, double MNT25,000, triple MNT30,000, deluxe single MNT25,000, deluxe double MNT40,000, family MNT40,000. 0137227205*

**Jasper Hotel** The best option in Old Darkhan. It offers clean, renovated rooms, all with hot water and bathrooms. They have pictures and booking on their website, but it's only in Mongolian. Lux rooms have a large bed, TV, mini-fridge, and large bathtub, and include breakfast. Amenities for the hotel include a decent restaurant, billiards, karaoke, and laundry service. *Visa and MasterCard accepted. Standard single MNT15,000, double MNT20,000, triple MNT30,000, triple lux MNT35,000. 99407171, 99379202, 01372-36964; http://darkhan-jasperhotel.com*

**Crystal Hotel** Right next door to the Jasper Hotel but not quite as nice as its neighbor. Amenities include a restaurant and laundry service. TVs, bathroom, and hot water can be found in all rooms. Breakfast included for deluxe room. *Standard with one, two, or three beds MNT15,000-20,000, deluxe MNT25,000. 99372211, 99372237, 99407171, 01372-36966*

# WHAT TO DO IN DARKHAN

To fill your day in Darkhan before the evening mosquitoes try their best to eat you alive, set out on a walking tour of town. Start out behind the theatre in New Darkhan at the south entrance to the **Children's Park**, one of one of Mongolia's largest. Take a relaxing stroll among the many singing (and sometimes scary) animal sculptures, then wander across the huge Mongolian map. At the north end of the Children's Park, stroll up to the **White Buddha** statue on the hill. Observe the ritual of walking around it three times clockwise and take some pictures of it standing proudly above you.

From there, stroll over to the **pedestrian bridge**, Mongolia's only suspension bridge. It lights up at night, bringing some rare Vegas flair to the old industrial town. From there, walk towards the **Morin Khuur Monument ("The Horse-head Fiddle")**. This whole tour should take about an hour. You can reach the black market and train station in about a half an hour or turn back toward the theater and reach the International Trade Center in the same time by foot.

If you're up for more of an adventure, head out of town in any direction toward the mountains, or head west toward the **Kharaa River** for some swimming or fishing. Along the way you might recognize some of the vegetation. One plant found here is the light blue-grey herb sage that is edible and makes a nice aromatic addition to a meal. Another is a plant used for making hemp and which is illegal to smoke in Mongolia.

**Darkhan Museum**, also called the "Museum of Folk Art," may not really be worth the price of admission (MNT3,000) if you have been to another Mongolian

The Guide

## Volunteer Opportunity at the Orphanage

**The Sun Child Orphanage** in New Darkhan near the Nomin Supermarket is a Japanese-funded center for children displaced by poverty, abuse, or lack of family. It is home to 41 children living at the main orphanage center and 14 university students who return during the holidays and summers. Some are full orphans with no family to claim them, but many are "half orphans" who have family that cannot provide for them. These children will often visit family members, but they live at the orphanage center full-time. Unlike many other orphanages, they feel it's more like a big family where the older brothers and sisters are constantly helping out with the little ones.

All the children are required to participate in at least two classes offered in the arts, including music, contortion, dance, and handicrafts. They often hold small concerts for various groups and are usually invited to perform in Japan at least once a year. Some of the little artists also create crafts like shagai and slippers, which you can buy at the orphanage.

The 13 full-time employees at Sun Child include arts teachers, English and Japanese language teachers, and five housemothers. If you would like to stop by to meet with the children, buy some handicrafts, or volunteer your time, summer is best because there is plenty of free time. Contact sunschild.happychild@gmail.com.

museum already. General Mongolian exhibits include taxidermy, though this one displays some creepily noteworthy decomposing snakes and frogs in a small tank, and you can get your picture beside the scale model of the Darkhan power plant. The information is almost all in Mongolian.

**Kharagiin Khiid** is one of the most remarkable points of interest on your walk. Situated in a log cabin in Old Darkhan near the *birj*, it is a very active monastery with the feeling of a pilgrimage center. There are a multitude of protective deities on the grounds and a tree covered with blue silk scarves or *khadags*.

**Darkhan Nekhii (Дархан Нэхий)** is a famous two-part factory for animal skin tanning and garment sewing that uses raw materials from contracted herders in eight Mongolian provinces.

The tannery was established in 1972 with technical and financial assistance from Bulgaria. It is now equipped with European machines added in 2002-2006 that annually process around 1.5 million semi and finished double-face skins through chemical and mechanical processing. The sewing factory has German and Japanese equipment that roll out finished coats and other garments in 120 designs.

They don't offer tours of the factory, but the semi and full sheep, goat, lamb, kid, and marmot fur products can be found in Erdenet and Murun in Mongolia as well as in Kirov, Moscow, Irkutsk, and Ulan-Ude in Russia. In Darkhan, you can find these products in Nomin and in some of the boutiques.

### Nightlife

All three of Darkhan's safest and most worthwhile clubs are located in the same area of New Darkhan.

**DD Club** In the basement of Erdenes Plaza. This is one of Darkhan's newest grooves. It is the closest thing you'll get to a big city club, including the ear-splitting beats and pricy drinks. Bust a move on the elevated see-through dance floor. *Cover MNT5,000.*

**Queen** An older club that's starting to show its age but is still popular among the many college students in Darkhan. There's a 100 percent guarantee of getting groped after 11:00 p.m.—men and women both. *Cover MNT2,000.*

**Saturn** Was renovated a few years back. Like Queen, it is also popular with the local college students. Fortunately, entrance does not come with any grope guarantee. *Cover MNT2,000.*

## BANKING & INTERNET

**ATMs** can be found throughout Darkhan. The most convenient are the Khan Bank ATMs located at the train station, at the bank's main branch across from the black market in Old Darkhan, at the branch across from the theatre in New Darkhan, and at the woman's center behind Erdenes Plaza.

Darkhan has several branch offices for all of Mongolia's major telecom companies. You can purchase new phones, SIM cards, and phone cards at any of these stores. For used phones and phone repair, go to the International Trade Center or find stalls in the market.

**Internet Cafés** are aplenty in Darkhan, so just look for the "Интернет кафе" signs. There is a nice one in the first floor of the post office with the telecom office. There is also one next to the Saintain Restaurant called **Parmida** that has relatively fast wireless internet if you happen to have your own computer.

## WHAT DO AROUND DARKHAN-UUL AIMAG

**Amarbayasgalant Monastery** is 100 kilometers (62 miles) from Darkhan in Selenge Aimag. You can sometimes find cars to the monastery from the Darkhan market or call the monastery directly to arrange a ride. Call 11322529, 99124006, or 99011818. See page 293 for more information.

**Cold River (Хүйтний гол or *Khuitnii gol*)** tourist area lies about 30 kilometers (18.5 miles) east of Darkhan. There are several tourist camps and many opportunities for outdoor activities. One camp built by the Russians, **Zulzaga Camp** (Зулзага), which means "youngster," is a children's camp. Perhaps due to budget shortfalls after the government changeover in the 1990s, adults also retreat there as well. Cars leave from the market, but you may want to contact Javkha Ara to arrange something more comprehensive.

# Dornod Aimag (Дорнод)

Delightful Dornod Aimag is the easternmost province in Mongolia; from its farthest corner, you can see Russia, China, and Mongolia all at the same time. The *aimag*, which means "far eastern," used to bear the name of the Stalinist leader of Mongolia whose complicated legacy is still debated in Mongolia and for whom the *aimag* center, **Choibalsan**, is still named.

The climate of Dornod is generally warmer and dryer than in much of Mongolia, and there tend to be far fewer and less severe winter storms. The *aimag* boasts plenty of forests and rivers in the north and is replete with wetlands and lakes including **Buir Nuur** and **Khukh Nuur**, the lowest point in Mongolia. In the far east, the **Numrug Strictly Protected Area** contains Manchurian flora and fauna that can only be found in this part of the country along the **Khyangan Mountain Range**, which runs into Mongolia from Manchuria, China.

Despite some mountains, the *aimag* consists mostly of grassy steppe. Dornod is a favorite of birdwatchers because the eastern grasslands are located along three major migratory flyways, and while the region lacks a lot of habitat diversity, spring and fall migration offer great treasure hunts for birders. Climate change and over-grazing are accelerating the pace of desertification, and wetland habitats are decreasing. But although they are under intense threat, there are still some places for the cranes to drop in on passage or to breed.

Internationally, the region is most renowned for its teeming herds of wild white gazelles numbering in the tens of thousands as seen on the groundbreaking BBC series, "Planet Earth," which originally aired in 2006 and which also features the Bactrian camels of the Gobi. You should get a chance to see them prancing in the distance on the bus ride to Choilbalsan, but if you don't, you should try to make it to **Dornod Mongol** protected area.

Along with the majority Khalkh Mongols, Dornod also contains large ethnic minorities. Serglen, Bayantumen, and Choibalsan soums have large populations of Uzemchin, who left Inner Mongolia as the Japanese withdrew in defeat at the close of World War II. There are also Buriat, Barga, Uriankhai, Ould, and Kazakh minorities in Choibalsan and across the *aimag*.

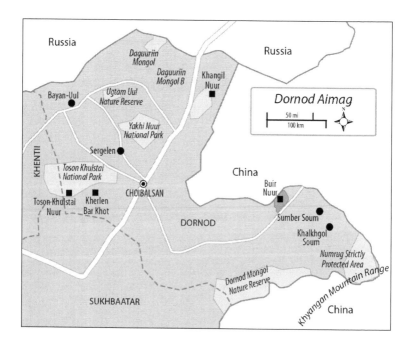

# GETTING THERE

### By Bus

Buses leave daily at 8:00 a.m. from Ulaanbaatar's eastern transportation center, Bayanzurkh Tovchoo, to Choibalsan (MNT28,000; 12-13 hours). Buy the ticket the day before to ensure a seat, especially if you're traveling with companions. Seats are sometimes available the morning of departure, but they go fast. The bus will leave at sometime between 8:00 and 9:00 a.m., but it's a good idea to be there by 7:30 a.m. to ensure you get your luggage under the bus and to protect your seat.

Tickets back to Ulaanbaatar can be purchased from the bus station in Choibalsan.

### By Shared Transportation

*Mikrs* from UB also depart from Bayanzurkh Tovchoo. You can book tickets (MNT30,000) with the bus company the day before or hire one of the drivers hanging around looking to pick up the overflow, which may cost you more. Get there early, but expect to wait. Departure is usually not until 9:00 or 9:30 a.m. for seats booked the day before and may extend into the afternoon, depending on how long it takes the vehicle to fill.

### By Private Transportation

The road can be quite rough, so small vehicles like taxis don't often make the trip. You can always hire private vehicles from guesthouses or driver services. However, Dornod is not a high traffic area, so you might have a problem finding a seasoned driver. Local drivers can be booked for some excursions from Choibalsan, especially from the hotels, but Jeeps are available at the black market. Prices are usually about MNT50,000 per day plus fuel.

### Hitchhiking

You should be able to stand on the road at any point in the countryside if you happen to be there already, but it would be difficult to hitch a ride all the way to or from UB.

# GETTING AROUND THE AIMAG

Choilbalsan is the hub to all intra-*aimag* destinations. All vehicles going to *soums* are parked outside of Choibalsan's black market with dashboard signs displaying their destination. Prices vary by *soum* and are sometimes negotiable.

# CHOIBALSAN SOUM (ЧОЙБАЛСАН СУМ)

During an administrative reorganization in 1941, the *aimag* and *aimag* center were named Choibalsan by the then-sitting dictator, Khorloogiin Choibalsan. In 1963, the *aimag* was given the current name, Dornod, but the name of the *aimag* center remains.

Choibalsan was leader of the Mongolian People's Revolutionary Party from 1936 until his death in 1952. He was renowned for his personality cult but his violent Stalinist purges gutted the country's population of religious figures, political dissenters, and intellectuals. Despite all this, literacy skyrocketed, the country's first infrastructure was laid, and Mongolia enjoyed relative prosperity during his regime, which accounts for his mixed legacy among the Mongolian people.

## The Battle of Khalkhin Gol

The skirmish of Khalkhin Gol is not well known in the West, but it may have been one of the most important engagements on the eastern flank of World War II. It is significant to the war as a whole because it guaranteed that the Axis Powers (Germany and Japan) would not connect their forces through the USSR. Instead, a new water-based route through Southeast Asia was chosen, which eventually led to the attack on Pearl Harbor two and a half years later. That strike on the American base in Hawaii was meant to disable the American fleet and prevent it from interfering with the Japanese attacks on Dutch and British colonies in Southeast Asia that were sought for petroleum and other strategic benefits. The events at Pearl Harbor, including the loss and injury of 3,684 American soldiers, precipitated the American involvement in the global war in the European and Pacific theaters.

The Battle of the Khalkhin Gol was also the first victory for Georgy Jukov, a famed Soviet general who led the first successful Soviet counteroffensive on their western front at Stalingrad against the invading Germans two years later.

The incident itself began in May of 1939 when a Mongolian cavalry grazed their horses on disputed pasture on the eastern banks of the Khalkhin Gol. After skirmishes back and forth, the Red Army brought tanks and nearly double the Japanese troops who had been perched on the border in the puppet state of Manchukoku, the renamed Manchuria. The battle was reported at the time as an overwhelmingly decisive victory for the Russian and Mongolian forces, though records released after the collapse of the Soviet Union show that they sustained significant casualties that were not reported at the time. Regardless, the battle was a decisive turning point in the war and is remembered with pride in Mongolia as a triumph against the Japanese.

Manchukoku was taken by the Japanese Kwantung Army in 1931 and set up as a puppet state, receiving total cooperation from the Manchurians. The encroachment into this area was seen as an act of aggression that soured relations in the region throughout World War II and remains a bone of contention for the Chinese and the Mongolians even today.

Now, on the banks of the Khalkhin Gol in Khalkhgol Soum there are endless Soviet-style memorials honoring Russian and Mongolian soldiers who fought and died there. In Choibalsan, history of the battle is also preserved in the G. K. Jukov Museum.

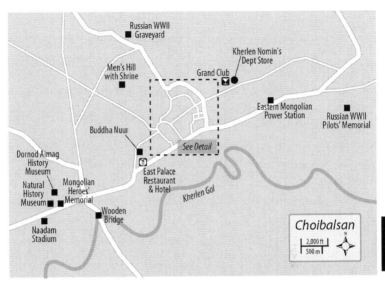

Russian WWII Graveyard

Men's Hill with Shrine

Kherlen Nomin's Dept Store

Grand Club

Eastern Mongolian Power Station

Russian WWII Pilots' Memorial

Buddha Nuur

*See Detail*

Dornod Aimag History Museum

East Palace Restaurant & Hotel

Natural History Museum

Mongolian Heroes' Memorial

Kherlen Gol

Wooden Bridge

Naadam Stadium

*Choibalsan*

2,000 ft
500 m

The Guide

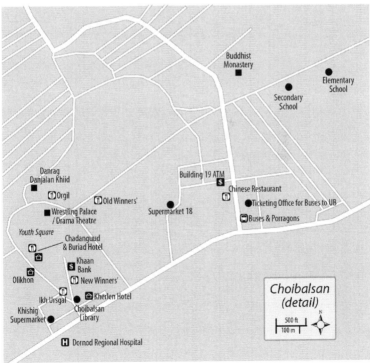

Buddhist Monastery

Elementary School

Secondary School

Danrag Danjalan Khiid

Building 19 ATM

Chinese Restaurant

Orgil

Old Winners'

Supermarket 18

Ticketing Office for Buses to UB

Wrestling Palace / Drama Theatre

Buses & Porragons

Youth Square

Chadanguud & Buriad Hotel

Khaan Bank

Olikhon

New Winners'

Ikh Ursgal

Kherlen Hotel

Khishig Supermarket

Choibalsan Library

*Choibalsan (detail)*

500 ft
100 m

Dornod Regional Hospital

The town also boasts a hospital that is by far the largest in the region and features an oncology ward as well as a suite of new Belgian diagnostic equipment.

The area is fairly rich in coal, which is mined nearby and burned in Choibalsan's **Eastern Power Systems** to supply electricity to all of eastern Mongolia. (With some wrangling and a Mongolian guide with you, you can probably get a tour if you're interested.) Dornod also contains the site of a former Russian open-pit uranium mine located 120 kilometers (75 miles) north of Choibalsan. The area is now explored and managed by the Canadian-owned Khan Resources. There used to be as many as 100,000 Russians in Choibalsan, but almost all left in the early 1990s. Their legacy remains as can be seen in a stand of trees that line the main boulevard east past the power plant to a spire commemorating Russian pilots killed at the Battle of the Khalkhin Gol. The other bequest from the mass Russian exodus is a group of crumbling buildings whose building materials have been reclaimed and reused by Mongolians.

Many foreign volunteers work in the schools and government institutions of Choibalsan. They can be found gathering in local watering holes on any given Friday evening or at one of the many Chinese restaurants. Like Erdenet, another Russian mining town in northern Mongolia, white people wandering the streets are still often assumed to be Russian, especially among the older generation.

## WHERE TO STAY

**Buriad Hotel (Буриад)** The nicest and most helpful staff out of all hotels visited. All rooms come with free internet, a free hour of pool (the game, not the swimming kind), and breakfast in the restaurant. All rooms also have a toilet and a shower with hot water and range in price from MNT24,000 to MNT40,000. There is a sauna and hair salon in the hotel, too. Laundry costs MNT1,500 per kilogram. *99577427*

**Kherlen Hotel (Хэрлэн)** Has a friendly and helpful staff. The one-bed room is MNT15,000, the two-bed room is MNT20,000, the three-bed room is MNT27,000, the four-bed room is MNT32,000, and the lux room is MNT36,000 for one person and MNT60,000 for two. It includes free breakfast. All rooms have a toilet and shower with hot water. There is a restaurant and a cashmere store in the hotel as well. Laundry prices range from MNT500-5,000 per piece. *50581250*

**East Palace** It is the swankiest of all hotels in town, and also the most expensive. Their rooms come with single, twin, or double beds ranging from MNT50,000-120,000. The superior room is MNT150,000. Though there are four "levels" of room choices that differ in price, we don't really see a difference in room quality. If you've been in the countryside for a few long days, then a room here will seem luxurious no matter what room you choose. Breakfast and use of the fitness club are free for hotel guests. Don't expect the fanciest fitness club you've ever seen, but it is one of the only fitness clubs you'll see outside of Ulaanbaatar. There is a sauna, a restaurant, and a shop located within the hotel. Laundry and ironing ranges from MNT3,000-5,000.

**Olikhon Hotel (Олихон)** All rooms all have two beds, a toilet, and a shower with hot water. The prices are MNT30,000-80,000. There are two saunas: one ranges in prices from MNT3,500 (for one person) to 10,000 (for four people). The other sauna ranges in prices from MNT5,000 (for 1 person) to MNT12,000 (for four people). There is a restaurant and a supermarket next door. Laundry and ironing available.

**Orgil (Олгил)** If you're in a pinch, there is a super cheap hotel behind the library with a good Chinese restaurant in it. All rooms have two beds and a toilet in them. Orgil does not provide a laundry service nor are there showers. Check out is at 12 noon. The Chinese restaurant located at the bottom of the hotel is the best in town. Rooms here are MNT12,000 to MNT18,000.

# WHERE TO EAT

## Restaurants

**Chadanguud (Чадангууд):** Inside the Buriad Hotel, Chadanguud has fancy Mongolian food. This place also has an extensive vegetarian menu including lasagna, soups, *buuz*, *khuushuur*, and *tsuivan*. The food is very good, but it takes a long time to be served. The food is worth the wait, but you might get there and order before you are terribly hungry. ₮/₮₮

**Ikh Ursgal (Их Урсгал)** Has three huge benefits. The service is excellent, the staff is happy to see foreigners, and it's the best Chinese restaurant in town. We especially recommend #26 on the menu (beef, fried potatoes, peppers, onions, corn, peas, sometimes tomatoes, bread, eggs—it's to die for). The chilled cucumber and cold beef salad (*seruun salat*, сэрүүн салат) is good. Try the *sharsen mantuu* (steamed or fried dumplings with no filling). You won't be disappointed. ₮₮

**Chinese Restaurant** By the wrestling palace and monastery. This place has perhaps the biggest lazy Susan (rotating tabletop) in Mongolia. You can get the usual vegetable and meat platters to share as well as good, spicy Sichuan-style food. There is nice Mongolian artwork on the wall in the main dining area and private rooms are available for larger parties at no cost. ₮₮

**Old Winner's** A quiet, little restaurant. We recommend the Winner's Special because it has meat with an egg on top and a bunch of salads on the side making it a great and tasty deal. This place does not really have vegetarian options (outside of eggs and rice). Service can be slow, so bring some cards or a book. ₮₮

**Olikhon Restaurant (Олхон)** Above the main grocery of the same name. Olikhon is a place to sit outside and take in the summer evening. Relax on the deck underneath the umbrellas and enjoy it in peace, as the place is usually empty. The *khonini shorlog* (sheep kebab) is good, and there are numerous chicken dishes that are tasty albeit sometimes unavailable. There are a few vegetarian options such as an omelet (MNT1,600) that comes with a portion of rice. ₮/₮₮

## Guanzes

For good *khuushuur* (MNT400) and *peroshki* (MNT350), there is a good little *guanz* in the south corner of Building One on the southeast side of downtown. Great *kimchitei khuushuur* (MNT450) as well as average *khuushuur* and other typical salads in the two-story building just east of the Health Department and north of School One for MNT450.

## Grocery Stores

**Olikhon (Олихон)** Part of the hotel and restaurant of the same name a few minutes' walk north of the post office, across from the Chadanguud hotel in a green two-story building. It is your best bet for fruit, and it sometimes carries watermelon, pineapple, and grapes as well as the usual apples and oranges! Other products that you can't often find in the countryside but can find here are cheese, bacon, fresh tofu, a variety of spices, lentils, dried beans, yogurt, brown sugar, lemon juice, hot sauce, balsamic vinegar, good ice cream, and a good juice selection. If you are staying in a location where you can cook, this is a great place to shop for your meals. A second Olikhon by the black market is where you can sometimes find cheap tuna fish and good toiletries. If you are with a large group this is a good place to buy food in bulk.

**Khishig (Хишиг)** A great store where you can buy oatmeal, cheese, chicken, and sometimes bacon. There is usually yogurt, wheat bread, fresh tofu, brown sugar, and vegetables (lettuce, eggplant, broccoli, and red cabbage) that you can't get other places. Its located next to the post office and telecom building.

**Supermarket 18** Just east of the center of town in a long two-story gray building. If you are looking for the best beer selection, you've come to the right place. Sometimes they also have American foods, and you may be able to find cheap tuna fish, if you're getting fed up with *buuz* and *khuushuur*. They also have toiletries and other necessities.

**Kherlen Nomin (Хэрлэн Номин)** The national supermarket chain has a wide variety of goods, often at very low prices. It's located in the massive former carpet factory complex on the northeast side of town that shares the Nomin shopping center.

# WHAT TO DO IN CHOIBALSAN

## Museums

Choibalsan is filled with museums and memorials. The **Dornod Aimag Museum** (admission MNT1,000; 10:00 a.m.-5:00 p.m.) is in the former government house. It is more compelling than most other *aimag* museums. It contains some historic Choibalsan treasures and a colossal *togoo* (curved bowl-like pan) capable of boiling mutton for 500 people, which dates back to the mid-nineteenth century during the heyday of the Qing Dynasty. It must have made for an amazing feast. The museum also acts as an art museum for spectacular paintings and historical photos.

On the west side of the square you'll find the **Natural History Museum** with the usual taxidermied animals and displays of plants and animals from the region. While you're out and about museum hopping, don't forget to check out the **Mongolian Heroes' Memorial**, a tall arch with a soldier on horseback charging towards the enemy. It is on the south side of the main road west from downtown by about 5 kilometers (3 miles).

If you want to learn about the 1939 Battle of the Khalkhin Gol, take a little walk to the **G. K. Jukov Museum**, about 1.25 kilometers (1 mile) northeast of the drama theatre and 200 meters north of the main road. If it's locked, the caretaker lives next door.

**Danrag Danjalan Khiid (Данраг данжалан хийд)** was a monastery complex built around 1840. As in almost every other monastery, in 1937 the hundreds of monks who practiced there were rounded up and dispatched as you might expect from the Stalinist regime. The monastery partially reopened in June of 1990.

One of the biggest rivers in eastern Mongolia is the **Kherlen Gol (Хэлэн гол)**, which runs through Choibalsan. It may have lots of mosquitoes in the summer evenings, but don't let that stop you from enjoying it during the day. It originates in the western part of the *aimag* and flows all the way to Inner Mongolia's Hulun Dalai, China's fifth largest freshwater lake. If you are interested in birding, the Kherlen Gol area is a great place to find migratory cranes and other birds. There is also great fishing to be done. Taiman up to 2 meters (6.5 feet) long and 37 other varieties fill the waterway. If you didn't bring your own equipment, you can find some basic fishing gear in the black market.

On the west end of Choilbalsan is lovely **Buddha Nuur**, so named because of the large Buddha statue in the center. It is tons of fun, particularly in the summer when paddle rafts are available or in the winter when kids and adults skate on the ice.

And a little farther out, is the **Yakhi Nuur National Park (Яхь нуур)** near the borders of Choibalsan, Sergelen, and Gurvanzagal soums. This is a great place to view numerous species of animals such as white antelopes, wolves, marmots, and steppe foxes as well as migratory and sedentary birds and spectacular landscapes featuring rocky hills, valleys, and mountains.

## NIGHTLIFE

**The Grand Club** is a great choice for dancing and has a live local DJ! There aren't many foreigners in town most of the time, but you'll easily be able to cut a rug with the young folks of Choibalsan. It's located next to the Nomin on the northeast side of town.

# WHAT TO DO IN DORNOD AIMAG

Dornod Aimag is teeming with protected regions and national parks. If you are interested in bird or animal watching or just nature walks, this is a great region to visit.

For birdwatchers, Choibalsan Soum, located along three major migratory flyways, is a good place to start your excursions into Mongolia's grasslands. There is generally wonderful birding in the steppe with its prolific grassland species, but birdwatchers often seek out the cranes. Demoiselle cranes are succeeding throughout the country. Other targets include the swan and bean goose, spot-billed duck, Baikal teal, relict gull, lesser kestrel, Amur falcon, oriental scops-owl, great bustard, Chinese pond heron, oriental plover, scaly, dusky and eyebrowed thrush, Siberian blue robin, white-cheeked starling, two-barred and Radde's warbler, Siberian accentor, and Baikal wagtail.

**Dornod Mongol (Дорнод монгол)** has been protecting the **Khyalganat** ecosystem and the habitat of white antelopes since 1992. If you've seen the television series Planet Earth, you have seen the spectacular views of these herds running through the countryside. This area covers 570,300 hectares (5,703 square kilometers, 2201 square miles) of land, including Matad, Khalkh-Gol, and Erdenetsagaan Soums. There are sand hills and beautiful legendary mountains in the area, as well as 153 species of flora and 26 kinds of mammals. Some rare birds, like falcons, fly through this area.

**Numrug (Нөмрөг)** is a strictly protected bit of land in the wooded and steppe regions of the **Khyangan Mountain Range** along the border. It contains the **Gurvan Goliin Belchir**, a confluence of three rivers (N46°46'48.37", E119°29'47.56"). The area has been protected since 1992 because of its unique suitability for flora and fauna. It contains many animals that are found nowhere else in Mongolia including moles, otters, brown bears, wild ducks, cranes, and condors. It's not easy or cheap to get there because of its location on the far east portion of the *aimag* near the Chinese border, 400 kilometers (250 miles) from Choibalsan. You need a permit for the reserve, which you can get from the Nature Protection Office, a three-story green building with the gazelle mural on the side. Look for it near the Mormon church and east of the Tovan Hotel.

**Daguuriin Mongol and Daguuriin Mongol B** is 30 kilometers (18 miles) from the Russian border in the northeast part of the *aimag* (N50°3'29.18", E114°45'48.82"). The whole area, which means "Mongolian Enclosure" is dotted with pristine blue lakes and was made into a preservation area with the purpose of protecting the habitat for migrating and aquatic birds including the steppe, waterways, and swampy areas in the fragile but flourishing ecosystem. The joint Mongolia-Russia-China

Daguur preservation area is part of an international network of areas protected for the migration and breeding of northeast Asian cranes, which are symbols of long life and prosperity. Siberian, white-neped, Demoiselle and other kinds of rare northeast Asian cranes lay their eggs and gather in large numbers here as they travel from Russia to China. You can also find whooper swan, relict gull, mandarin duck, and great bustard. The southern, smaller B section (N49°42'13.54", E115°11'12.01") is in Chuluunkhoroot Soum and includes part of the Ulz Gol. The larger northern section, also in areas of Chuluunkhoroot Soum, bleeds seamlessly into Russia on the south shore of Russia's Tari Lake.

Also along the northern border is **Ugtam Uul Nature Reserve (Угтам уул)** throughout which are scattered ruins of monasteries, and Khairkhan Uul (N49°22'15.00"N, E113°32'42.67"), a pointy mound of a mountain dropped in among the trees and flat surroundings. On the border of the park is the winding Ulz Gol and is about 35 kilometers (22 miles) east of the Bayandun *soum* center.

**Toson Khulstai National Park (Тосон хулстай)** is a huge nature preserve adjoining Dornod and Khentii *aimags* along the main road to Khentii's Undurkhaan Soum. The area covers **Tsagaan Ovoo, Khulunbuir,** and **Bayantumen** soums and is a main reserve for white antelopes. You can find rare cranes, steppe bustards, and hedgehogs around these areas, and you'll also find plenty of fruit for the picking around the **Toson Khulstai Nuur** and other lakes and rolling hills.

Also on the main road to Khentii's Undurkhaan, 90 kilometers (56 miles) west of Choibalsan, is **Kherlen Bar Khot** (N48°03.287', E113°21865'). The 10-meter (33-foot) high tower was part of a twelfth century city of the Khitan, a once powerful

The Guide

## Bujen: Advancing Women and Children of Choibalsan

Bujen (Бүжэн) is the head of LEOS (Progressive Women's Thinktank), a local organization that supports women's rights in Choibalsan. In her mid-50s and full of energy and enthusiasm, she regularly coordinates conferences, seminars, and social activities like ballroom dancing to create and maintain dialogues among her members, which she hopes will affect the community as a whole.

While Bujen doesn't have children of her own, she does run the "Gerel Tuv" (Light Center) orphanage located in the northwest of the city. She and her husband Ochirsuren speak English well, especially where the technical aspects of social work are concerned. In fact, Bujen spent time in the United States for an intensive English training program. If one were to simply turn up in town looking to do some volunteering, they should be among the first people approached. Bujen and her organizations welcome your perspectives and help either at the orphanage or the thinktank. If you're in the area and want to volunteer for a few hours or a few days, she asks that you contact her at 99286761 or LEOS_Dornod@yahoo.com.

group that was eventually assimilated into Chinggis Khan's emerging empire. There are also some deer stones (*balbal*) called the "Chinggis Bed" commemorating an apparent overnight camp by the (in)famous great khan. If you're on the way, you should stop and have a look, though you can also see a picture of the tower in Dornod Aimag Museum.

## Khalkhgol Gol Soum (Халхгол Гол сум)

This *soum* is not at all close to Choibalsan. It's it tucked up underneath the Chinese border 155 kilometers (96 miles) from Choibalsan across the Menengiin Tal, the largest uninterrupted steppe in all of Mongolia, which is more or less connected all the way into Sukhbaatar Aimag. It is beautiful and interesting place to go to because of its history. There's a military base here as well as a large Buddhist monument. The banks of the Khalkhiin Gol are of interest to war historians because of the battles against the Japanese in 1939. The dry, unpolluted air and untouched region nearly guarantees that most of the relics lying around have been well preserved. Endless war memorials are on the banks of the river. These memorials are socialist masterworks, built to honor the Russian and Mongolian soldiers who died along the river.

This *soum* also contains **Buir Nuur (Буйр нүүр)** a large and picturesque freshwater late. It has excellent fishing. The best way to get there is from Khalkhiin Gol's *soum* center with a private driver or a 20-kilometer (12-mile) hike following the river.

## Sumber Soum (Сүмбэр сум)

About 35 kilometers (22 miles) from the *soum* center on the banks of the Khalkiin Gol is **Ikh Burkhant (Их Бурхант)**, where there is a massive 30-meter (100-foot) tall likeness of the Janraisig carved into the hillside by over 100 artists. The carving, the name of which means "Great Talisman" or "Great Sacred Protector," was commissioned in 1864 and reconstructed between 1995 and 1997. It became a place of reverence because the Janraisig is a protector from the eight Buddhist sins.

# Dornogovi Aimag (Дорноговь аймаг)

Dornogovi, the "Eastern Gobi" *aimag,* is most seen by travelers entering Mongolia from China on the **Trans-Mongolian Railway**, the offshoot of the Trans-Siberian Railway that connects Russia's Ulan Ude to Beijing through the Chinese border town of Ereen (Erlian). **Zamiin-Uud**, on the Mongolian side of the southern border, is the last stop as the train leaves Mongolia. The railroad traverses about 500 kilometers (311 miles) of Dornogovi desert through seven *soums,* including the *aimag* center, **Sainshand**.

Though Dornogovi is not considered the main Gobi Desert tourist area, there are still some sights to take in, especially if you're just looking for a sample of what much of the semi-arid Gobi itself looks like. Dornogovi is most well known for the legendary poet, writer, artist, composer, and monk **Danzanravjaa**, who was born there. His **Khamariin Khiid** and nearby **Shambala Energy Center** have become major pilgrimage sites and are easily accessible by *purgon,* either from the train station in Sanshaind or through your hotel (for more information, see page 42). Then there's **Ikh Nart Nature Reserve**, a remote park with unique wildlife and natural springs that is neither well known nor well traveled and hence prime for adventure seekers.

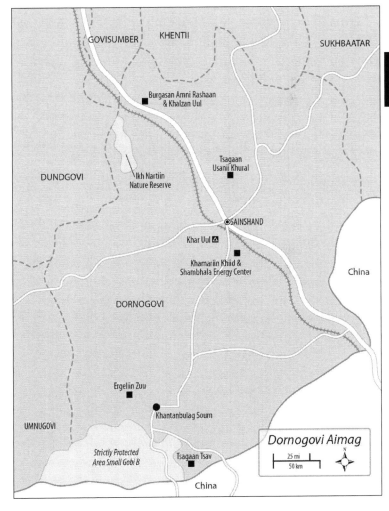

The Guide

Dornogovi Aimag

25 mi
50 km
N

If you are coming from China looking to get the quintessential "Gobi experience," you might be more satisfied planning a trip to and through Umnugovi Aimag, west of Dornogovi. Though it is possible to book a driver for the 340-kilometer (211-mile) drive across the desert from Sainshand to Dalanzadgad in Umnugovi (MNT50,000 plus fuel), you may do better to contact a tour company in UB that will contract a driver for you, especially if you're short on time. If you do try on your own, it may take a few days to find the right driver, and you will probably have to pay for his return trip to Sainshand, with or without you. A good strategy for the trip is to make a loop from Sainshand to Dalanzadgad (and Gobi attractions) to Ulaanbaatar in 5-7 days. From UB, you can easily continue on your way toward Moscow on the Trans-Siberian or back toward China. To book shared tours of the Gobi with other travelers, you'll need to get to a guesthouse in UB not Sainshand.

# SAINSHAND (САЙНШАНД)

The provincial capital of Dornogobi, **Sainshand**, is 470 kilometers (292 miles) from Ulaanbaatar and one of the main stops on the rail toward the Chinese border. Because of that, there are some nice shops, restaurants, and hotels

Sainshand, which translates as "good little spring," is divided into two parts: **Ar shand (Upper Sainshand)**, where the train station is located, and **"Umnu shand" (Lower Sainshand)**, two kilometers (1 mile) away in the central part of town.

Many people stop to enjoy the sand dunes and camels on the way to or from Khamariin Khiid.

## GETTING THERE

### By Bus
There is no direct bus to Saishand. Local residents generally prefer to use the twice-daily train between Ulaanbaatar because it's safe and reliable. There is a bus from Ulaanbaatar to Zamiin-Uud, which you probably want to avoid.

### By Train
The train from Ulaanbaatar to Sainshand leaves twice a day at 9:30 a.m. and 4:30 p.m. The train from Sainshand to Ulaanbaatar leaves daily at 9:00 p.m. and arrives in UB around 8:00 a.m. The train traveling from Beijing arrives in Sainshand at around 10:00 a.m. daily. This train also takes passengers from Sainshand to Ulaanbaatar.

Tickets from Ulaanbaatar to Sainshand or vice versa are MNT7,400, half coupe is MNT13,200, and full coupe is MNT23,000. If you're in UB and want to take the earliest train down to Sainshand, then it is best to buy a ticket one day in advance, but it will come with a MNT1,000 charge.

It's important to note that you will only be able to book international Trans-Mongolian Railway tickets from Ulaanbaatar, so if you plan to stop in Sainshand on your way toward China or Russia, you will need to cross those borders by exiting the train and finding your way across. You can, however, buy tickets to Sukhbaatar on the northern border and Zamiin-Uud on the southern border at Sainshand's station.

## GETTING AROUND THE AIMAG

You can hire private drivers to some attractions in the desert from around the main square, the train station, and sometimes the market, but the options aren't numerous unless you plan to go to the Khamariin Khiid.

## WHERE TO STAY

**Dornogobi Hotel** This brand new huge hotel finally opened after years of construction and anticipation. Rooms are very nice and clean. Dorm beds with bunks are MNT15,000, and twin rooms are MNT35,000. The lux rooms (MNT55,000 for one person, MNT59,000 for two people) feature king-sized beds with en suite shower and a television. There is a fitness/aerobics room, sauna, photo processing, hairdresser, and shower rooms on ground floor. Laundry service is by piece, ranging from MNT500 for socks to MNT12,000 for a jacket. *0152223657, 0152223656.*

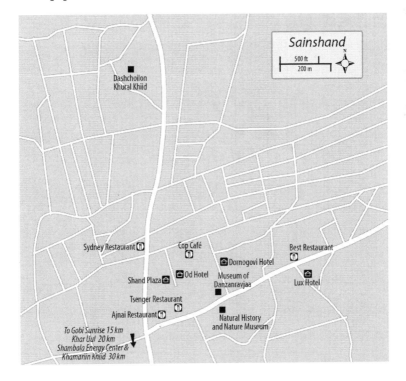

**Od Hotel** Located inside the government building, accessible from the north side. Dorm beds start at MNT5,000 per bed while a lux room with two beds is MNT30,000. There is a *guanz*, fitness club, and transportation booking. An English-speaker is available to assist travelers. *0152223245, 99281858*

**Shand Plaza Hotel** An older hotel near the government building, rooms here are worn but the place is well established and reliable. And it has hot showers. It's the green building northwest of the square next to the Khan Bank; taxi drivers know it well. One room is in the style of a *ger* with four twin beds for MNT20,000 per night. It provides travelers with a hint of the *ger* experience, without the inconvenience of an actual *ger*. There is a room with two twin beds (MNT30,000) and a room with five twin beds (MNT50,000). The lux room has one big bed and hot shower for MNT65,000. Restaurant and bar are on the first floor. Massages available for MNT15,000 and laundry service is per item from MNT500 for socks and up to MNT4,000 for a coat. They also operate a *ger* camp about 15 kilometers (9 miles) outside Sainshand. *0152223509, 99148352*

**Gobi Sunrise** Is a *ger* camp with toilets and hot showers about 15 kilometers (9 miles) outside of the city center. Prices range from $10 for lodging to $25 with full board. Many people like to leave from the city center early in order to watch the sunrise out near the sites, especially on Bayanzurkh Uul or at the energy center, so staying here would get you a head start. It's connected (professionally, not physically) to the Khamariin Khiid, and you can book tours, guides, and services all around the area. *99113829, 99090151; gobisunrise@yahoo.com (N44°45'25.44", E110°11'14.20")*

# WHERE TO EAT

**Sydney Restaurant** By far the most high-end restaurant in Sainshand. Though the prices are still reasonable, it is more expensive than others—and well worth it. The restaurant opened in summer 2010 and is owned by a friendly young Mongolian couple that lived in Sydney, Australia for many years. They came back to Mongolia to open a restaurant and share some great Australian, European, and American dishes alongside their more familiar Mongolian dishes. Their eclectic menu (in English) ranges from Sydney salad to apple pie to Hawaiian pizza. The interior is gorgeous with hand painted walls, Australian-themed art by the talented owner, and a wonderful bar. And on top of it all there's free wireless! ₮₮/₮₮₮

**Ajnai Restaurant** On the second floor of its building. Ajnai serves Mongolian and Chinese food dishes, but the Chinese selections are limited. Another pleasant *ger*-themed interior design at this restaurant. ₮

**Cop Café** It is very clean, bright, and has nice spaces with nice plants. They serve foods like pizza, cheeseburgers, spaghetti, and fries, along with Mongolian dishes. It has a pleasant atmosphere with music and lots of sunlight. ₮₮

**Tsenger Restaurant** On the second floor of the big blue building in the southwest corner of the square, next to the Eiffel Tower. There are two entrances. Sometimes one is locked at night; if so, go to the east side of the building to enter. The entrance on the front of the building opens into a shop that has stairs up to the restaurant. Tsenger has Mongolian and Chinese dishes you can enjoy in the dining area while watching fish swim in their tank. The menu is illustrated, so if you really aren't sure what you are ordering, that should help. ₮₮

# WHAT TO DO IN SAINSHAND

Though there are museums, mountains, and Gobi desert to see in and around Sainshand, be sure to take a walk near the park in the evening to take in the miniature Eiffel clock tower and the interesting lights and water fountain on the main square. If you're up for a little more of an evening walk, check out the **tank monument** about a kilometer up the road toward the train station (N44°54'10.59", E110° 8'5.66").

**Museum of Danzanravjaa** (entrance MNT2,000), located on the south side of the park, honors the famous local lama, writer, poet, composer, singer, and artist Noyon Khutagt Danzanravjaa. The museum houses his paintings, costumes, medicinal herbs, and gifts he received from Chinese and Tibetan leaders, including Buddhist statues presented to him by the tenth Dalai Lama. In front of the statue is a jar containing some of Danzanravjaa's preserved remains, while the rest of the mummified body was lost with the Khamariin Khiid in 1938.

On the main street across from the Danzanravjaa museum is the **Natural History and Nature Museum** (entrance MNT1,000). It has the usual stuffed Gobi animals, but there are a few interesting extras. Since this region used to be under the ocean, the museum has a small collection of seashells and marine fossils from the area as well as some dinosaur fossils. The history section includes some information on local hero Manzav, who fought for Mongolian independence in the 1921 revolution. The *pièce de résistance* is the *morin khuur* (horse-head fiddle) from 1940 with images of Lenin and Sukhbaatar carved into it. Mongolophiles will also appreciate the thirteenth century wooden breastplate worn by a Mongol soldier in Korea.

**Dashchoilon Khural Khiid** is a large, active monastery complex surrounded by a thick wall. Opened in 1991, it currently houses 25 friendly monks. Visitors are welcome any time, but there is no photography allowed.

**Khar Uul ("Black Mountain")** is about 20 kilometers (12 miles) southwest of Sainshand, about a 3-hour walk across the open land. Another 10 kilometers or so up and over on the southern pinnacle of the ridge is **Bayanzurkh Uul ("Rich Heart Mountain")**. There are a few heavily decorated *ovoos* along the ridgeline. The stone cairns set up ridiculously fantastic views out over the countryside. A path leads down the south side below the summit to a white Buddha statue (N44°41'24.19", E110° 2'35.77"). It's also about 20 kilometers (12 miles) from the Gobi Sunrise *ger* camp.

**Tsagaan Usanii Khural (Цагаан усаны хурал)** (N45°14'18.79", E110°10'49.27") is a wetland dominated by vegetation about 40 kilometers (25 miles) north of

Sainshand. It's an important wetland that has been studied and protected to ensure the health status of its unique wildlife.

# ZAMIIN-UUD (ЗАМЫН-ҮҮД)

Zamiin-Uud or "The Road's Gateway" is 780 kilometers (485 miles) from UB and the international entry point connecting Mongolia to China at Erlian (Ereen). While China's tracks are standard gauge (used by 60 percent of the world's existing railway lines), Mongolian lines are the wider Russian gauge used in the former Soviet Union and Finland. Consequently, international trains must have their bogies (wheels) changed in Erlian. The train usually arrives in the middle of the night or very early in the morning, and it takes about two hours to switch over. During the peak summer season, there are over 250 train cars that undergo this procedure daily. Since the number of passengers has grown in recent years by as much as 40 percent (as in 2010), efforts are being made to grow that border crossing capacity by adding more cars to each train during the peak times, which will add a little time at the border while passports are checked and the trucks are changed.

Nearly half of Mongolia's yearly passengers in buses and trains come from China. Imports from China are increasing rapidly as well (50 percent increase from 2009 to 2010 alone), and much of the increase is from small-time traders and small-time wholesalers. With Zamiin-Uud's position as a major gateway, traders use this route to import food, construction materials, and consumer goods while exporting livestock products. The town has quickly grown into a booming trade center of nearly 13,000 people, up from the meager population of 1,000 in the early 1990s.

## Where to Stay in the Zamiin-Uud

**Jinchin** It's about 50 meters from the train station. Their 23 rooms range from MNT5,000-25,000. It's a good, convenient place to crash if you find yourself exhausted on the Mongolian side of the border. They have a *guanz* and luggage storage. *02524553289, 99179983*

# WHAT TO DO IN DORNOGOVI AIMAG

## Khamariin Khiid & Shambhala Energy Center

When you get off the train, there will be drivers asking to take you to the monastery in a *purgon* or *mikr* (MNT10,000-15,000). Though they generally don't speak much English, you can set a time with them, and the driver will pick you up from your hotel, usually very early in the next morning. If you rent a private car for the day, it's MNT30,000-50,000 depending on the driver and the car. If you have a group of five or more, this can be a pretty good deal.

**Khamariin Khiid (Хамарын хийд)** (N44°35'50.02", E110°16'25.44") is usually open every day before noon, but the schedule can change, particularly on auspicious days. During *Tsagaan Sar*, it's open all day. The grounds, whose name translates as "Nose Monastery," were founded by **Noyon Khutagt Dulduitiin Danzanravjaa**, a Mongolian intellectual and leader of the Red Hat sect of Buddhism during the nineteenth century. It is 50 kilometers (31 miles) and an hour's drive south of Sainshand. At its height, the monastery held over eighty temples, four main court-yards, four colleges, a children's school, and over five hundred lamas. It was destroyed in 1938, but since 1990, two small temples and several monuments have been reconstructed, and it has more than ten lamas in residence.

Off the side of the path leading up to the Shambhala Energy Center, there are caves that were used by Danzanravjaa and other monks for meditation. On the top of the cliffs above the caves is a small hole that opens into a network of more caves, which supposedly allows certain auspicious desert energies to enter the area.

**Shambhala Energy Center**, also known as the "Energy Center" (Энерги төв), is two kilometers (1.24 miles) north of Khamariin Khiid (N44°37'3.56", E110°16'29.79"). It is Danzanrajvaa's three dimensional interpretation of Shambhala, a mythical, mystical Buddhist city inhabited by the enlightened and symbolizing the fundamentally good, warm, intelligent nature of mankind. This ideal state can be cultivated through meditation, and when practiced in daily life, it can radiate throughout society by way of family, friends, and encounters with strangers. Coming to the site is supposed to help people reconnect with their inner good and shrug off their ego, self-doubt, and other destructive attitudes.

Danzanravjaa's Shambhala is a huge square encircled by a wall of 108 stupas in addition to other larger stupas, *ovoos*, and other structures. It has four gateways used appropriately based on the social status of those entering and exiting the Shambhala. Tradition dictates that visitors enter using the central gate (where the path leads to the large brick structure) with two doorways: the Golden Doorstep, where pilgrims and worshippers entered leaving all harmful thoughts behind, and the Silver Doorstep, where they exited having only enjoyed auspicious thoughts during their time in the Shambhala. Noblemen entered through the right gate while lamas and teachers enter through the left gate, practicing the same regard for positive energy.

The large *ovoo* on the small hill is the "Brain Ovoo," where some people report feeling a radiating heat. It is the central point of energy on the grounds and is supposedly calm even during dust storms. Among the other key structures of interest inside is the small Zodiac, a circle with 12 equal parts, in front of three *ovoos* sequentially representing the past, present, and future. To ensure a quick reincarnation, tradition holds that you should put a white stone on the future *ovoo* while saying your name (last name first, first name last).

Much of the original Shambhala was destroyed during the late 1938 raids, but all 108 *ovoos* have been rebuilt, along with four gateways and eight larger stupas. Though most of the money was raised from Mongolian sources, actor Steven Seagal reportedly made a contribution that paid for one of the stupas.

**Ikh Nartiin Nature Reserve** (Их нартын байгалын нөөц гадар) (N45°43'22.84", E108°38'41.57") in the grassland and semi-desert steppe across Dalanjargal and Airag soums in northern Dornogovi is home to one of the last remaining populations of argali sheep. The reserve is only about 4 hours from Ulaanbaatar by paved road. It's open all year with no entrance fee. If you have your own tent, you can camp in the park. Nomadic Journeys also has a *ger* camp in northwest part of the park with basic accommodations. The GPS coordinates included here are those of a research facility within the park.

## Other Points of Interest

**Khalzan Uul** (Халзан уул) and **Burgasan Amni Rashaan** (Бурнгасан амны рашаан) are near the road from Choir to Sainshand. If you take the overland route, especially with a tour, it's likely you will stop here to drink some cold water from the curative natural springs. The springs have several mouths each, and the various mouths are thought to have healing qualities corresponding with different body parts, as is a common belief for most *rashaan* around the country. At the very least, the water is clean, drinkable, and refreshing, especially on a hot summer day.

## Khantanbulag Soum (Хантанбулаг сум)

This district is filled with petrified forests and the **Strictly Protected Area Small Gobi B** (Говийн бага Б). The area is also home to the Asiatic wild ass or *khulan* whose habitat is being interrupted by the various mining explorations and access roads. You will have to hire a private driver to these from the *soum* center, though there aren't many to choose from.

**Tsagaan Tsav** (Цагаан цав) is a petrified forest about 140 kilometers southwest of Sainshand, near the Chinese border just outside the Small Gobi B. Rare petrified trees lay littered on the Gobi surface. Nearby **Ergeliin Zuu** (Эргэлийн зуу), also called Altan Uul, is a small protected area 30 kilometers (18.5 miles) northwest of the Khantanbulag *soum* center. There are various interesting rock formations, especially on the sheer northern face, but it is most known for dinosaur fossils found here by American, Russian, German, Polish, and Bulgarian paleontologists since 1923.

# Danzanravjaa

**Noyon Khutagt Dulduitiin Danzanravjaa (Ноён хутагт Дулдуйтын данзанравжаа)**
(1803-1856) was born into a very poor family in present-day Dornogovi Aimag. His mother died during his birth or shortly after, and the infant Danzanravjaa was raised by his father Dulduit, who was a beggar. In 1809 Danzanravjaa began studying with a Buddhist teacher and quickly gained acclaim and respect for his writings. In 1811 he was declared the fifth reincarnation of the Gobi Noyon Khutagt or "wrathful noble saint" and given that title. Soon after he completed his training in the 1820s, he founded three monasteries , including Khamariin Khiid, where he formed a professional theatre company and school where students learned many subjects regardless of social class and gender, something very unusual at the time.

It was here in 1830 that he first shared his famous adaptation of the play, *Saran Khukhuu, The Moon Cuckoo*, a ten-volume operetta that satirizes corruption. The musical is about a moon cuckoo who sings in a forest about dishonest and deceitful humans like the evil friend that magically turned him from a prince into a bird. His songs encourage people to forgo betrayal and evil thoughts and instead to understand the real meaning of life. He finds the life of the cuckoo perfect for him because he is able to use his new incarnation to enlighten people with his beautiful voice, and he doesn't want to be released from his spell.

The play is originally from India and dates back many centuries. After a trip to Tibet in 1832, Danzanravjaa brought it to Mongolia and recomposed it for a Mongolian audience. At the time, Tsam was one of the only performing arts Mongolians had been introduced to. Despite this limitation, he was able to hire costumers and set builders and cast actors, using both male and female players at a time when men played all the roles in China and Tibet. Then, as now, the *Saran Khukhuu* was performed in 30-day blocks and included over 100 actors and 60 musicians.

In addition to his adaptation of the *Saran Khukhuu*, Danzanravjaa also wrote more than 300 poems and over 100 songs. Perhaps because of his impoverished upbringing, he was especially disdainful of greed and dishonesty, and many of his own writings covered this subject. He was skilled in traditional medicine, tantras, and martial arts. He traveled throughout Mongolia and Asia extensively.

Still, the beloved Danzanravjaa was not without critics or his own glaring flaws. He was well known for having a short temper, especially when he drank heavily, which was apparently often. He was considered a strong nationalist leader, which made him an enemy of the more prominent Yellow Hat Buddhists and the Manchurian-ruled Qing Dynasty, both of which are suspected of poisoning him to death to silence him.

Upon his death, a disciple of Danzanravjaa became the keeper of his possessions, legacy, and monastery. The artifacts, monastery grounds, and stories remained in that family for five subsequent generations until the monastery was destroyed in the 1938. The curator at the time moved ahead of Stalinist raids by secretly sneaking out 1,500 books, costumes, and memorabilia and buried the 64 crates of artifacts in various locations near the monastery. The hidden locations were passed down to the final curator's grandson, who dug them up in 1990 and established the Danzanravjaa Museum in Sainshand.

Danzanravjaa remains an important figure in Mongolian history through his poems and songs and as the father of Mongolian theater. His *Saran Khukhuu* was performed in 2004 for the first time since 1920. The cast of over 100, accompanied by 60 musicians, put on the show for 30 days at the State Drama Theater in Ulaanbaatar.

The Guide

# Dundgovi Aimag (Дундговь аймаг)

A lot of tourists pass up this "middle Gobi" *aimag* for the perhaps more dramatic sights of Umnugovi, but Dundgovi has all the key ingredients of a good desert adventure: the towering **Uush sand dunes**, camels, mazes of scrub brush in the **Zagiin Us Nature Reserve**, eerie ruined monasteries like **Sum Khukh Burd**, the surreally shaped rock formations of **Baga Gazriin Chuluu**, and the like. Its northern *soums* boast wide grasslands, but the southern reaches are pure Gobi.

Dundgovi has historically been connected to the development of *urtiin duu*, the long song. The genre is unique to Mongolia, and it evokes the expanse of the desert steppe that defines Dundgovi. There is even a long song school in rural **Deren Soum**, just north of **Mandalgovi**, the *aimag* center.

The *aimag* is also dotted with the graves of pre-Chinggis warriors, marked off from the surrounding Gobi wilderness by the small ritual mounds and stones piled on top. Thanks to Mongolians' deep respect for their ancestors, these burial sites have been around for centuries and will most likely last several more.

Dundgovi is primarily an agricultural province, and it survives on the threads of camel and cashmere wool production. Aside from raw textiles, Dundgovi is known

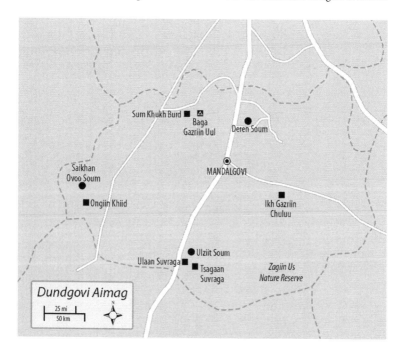

throughout Mongolia for its fine *airag*. Here, the slightly sour-tasting, fermented vodka is usually made from the milk of the hardy, dual-humped Bactrian camels that traverse the desert.

The *aimag* hasn't yet benefited significantly from the mining boom to its south, and Dundgovi's development is driven more by its proximity to Ulaanbaatar. This makes it an appealing destination for travelers who want to do the Gobi but don't want to spend the entirety of their trip in the desert. Mandalgovi is a mere six hour bus ride from UB, on a mostly paved road.

## MANDALGOVI (МАНДАЛГОВЬ)

During the communist era, Mandalgovi played host to a garrison of Russian army troops, and the remains of a base are still on the western outskirts of town. Mandalgovi's economy was hurt when the Russians pulled out and was further traumatized by the *dzud* of 2000 and 2001. Now its downtown area is starting to come together. The main stretch features a well-kept decorative garden area and a new monument to a former Parliament Member from Dundgovi who died in a tragic car wreck. From the rare elevation of **Khar Ovoo**, a popular park just north of the town center, you can view the town and the desert that surrounds it.

Mandalgovi is one of the smaller *aimag* centers by population, and there isn't always a lot going on there. But the people can be phenomenally friendly, especially if you go out of your way to engage them, or speak a bit of Mongolian. The city is as good a place as any to find a real conversation or a genuine interaction with the local community.

## GETTING THERE

### By Bus
Ulaanbaatar to Mandalgovi (MNT12,000; 6 hours) buses leave twice daily at 8:00 a.m. and 2:00 p.m. Buy your tickets from the Dragon Center one day before travel. From Mandalgovi to UB, tickets should also be purchased a day in advance from the bus station, and if you need it, the Tourist Information Center can help.

### By Shared Transportation
*Mikrs* to Mandalgovi from UB (MNT15-20,000; 6 hours) can be found in front of the Dragon Center and Narantuul. From Mandalgovi to UB, vehicles can be found in front of the post office taxi stand.

The Guide

## LOCAL GUIDES & TOURIST INFORMATION

The Tourist Information Center in Mandalgovi is located next to the Khan Bank in the center of town. From there, you can hire local guides and drivers and get details on the best trips to fit your budget and interests, including **Ger-to-Ger** participants looking to host travelers. The guides are mostly English teachers and students supplementing income during their summers. Contact Narangarav, the facilitator of the center, at 0159222612, 98994237, or 99844333 or via email at nangaa_j999@yahoo.com or narangarav.j@gmail.com

Other drivers to contact are Jambaltseren, who has 34 years of driving experience (99596969, 98256969, 91596969), Osorjamaa (95229376), and Shatarbaatar (99089509). You'll need a translator to help arrange your travel plans.

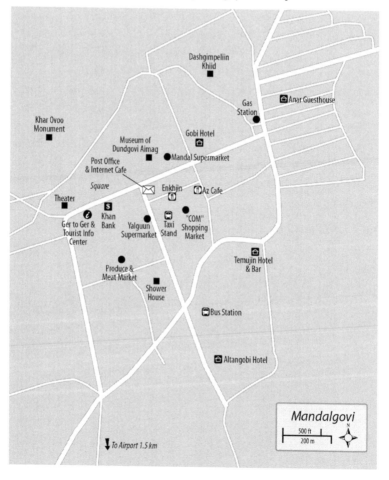

# WHERE TO STAY

**Anar Guesthouse** A *ger* guesthouse and our pick because the price is right and the experience is better than a hotel. The owner-operator, Ganbaatar, can make food for you, but you also have use of the kitchen. The guesthouse has a shower and the *gers* have four beds at MNT6,000 per person. *99697456, 99009428; zaanaa_d999@yahoo.com*

**Temujin Hotel** Though it is the cheapest hotel, we recommend visiting it for a drink but not necessarily staying overnight unless you are really trying to save money. About 15 rooms are available. The suites that are big and bright while cheaper rooms are very small. Standard rooms start at MNT8,000, and larger shared rooms are MNT10,000 per person. The half lux is MNT22,000 per person, and the lux is MNT25,000 per person. Temujin has karaoke, a bar, a pub, a dance hall, and a shower. *99039050*

**Altangobi Hotel** The biggest and most expensive hotel in Mandalgovi. They have large, clean rooms on four floors. All prices are per room. Standard double and triple rooms are MNT24,000-30,000 while the lux is MNT140,000 per night. The second floor has a restaurant and the first floor has a karaoke bar with an English song (only one). They also have private karaoke rooms on both the first and second floors. *0159222267, 99000079, 98213891*

**Gobi Hotel** Gobi hotel has been operating since 2000. This hotel is smaller than others, but the rooms are clean, big, and bright. The staff is good, and the manager speaks English. During the summer they usually book up, so reservations made two days in advance are usually required. The dorm room fits up to nine people at MNT9,000 per bed. A standard triple is MNT10,000 per person, and a standard double is MNT12,000. The half lux, which accommodates two guests, is MNT13,000 per person while the lux, also double occupancy, is MNT15,000 per person. Laundry, restaurant, and shower available. *0159222733, 99594959, 99686847; Bago_zorig@yahoo.com*

# WHERE TO EAT

**Az Café** Newer than most restaurants and has Korean food. It's big and clean and has good service. The Mongolian food is a little cheaper than the Korean food, but all prices are reasonable for the quality. ₮₮

**Enkhjin Restaurant** Has two floors. The first floor has one big room with many tables while the second floor has private karaoke rooms for parties. It is clean, but dark. The Chinese stir-fry, soup, and *khuushuur* are good, and so is the service. You can also get cold beer and a few different kinds of liquor. ₮₮

**Altangobi Hotel** The restaurant on the first floor of the hotel is very big and comfortable. Prices are on par with the rest of the places in town, so it's a good place to eat if you're already at the hotel and don't feel like venturing far. ₮₮

**Gobi Hotel** The restaurant of this hotel has decent standard Mongolian fare. While they have fewer choices than other restaurants in town, the prices are pretty good. ₮/₮₮

## SHOPPING

Most shops and markets are concentrated in the center of town, so you can be adventurous and duck in and out as you wish. Stall owners sometimes bargain for materials and goods, but don't expect to haggle at supermarkets or in small shops.

**Yalguun Supermarket** Near the post office and taxi station. It's the easiest for travelers to find and use. They have all the typical toiletries as well as packaged food and drinks. The quality of the produce varies by season.

**Mandal Supermarket** Also in the center of town with easy access to hotels and transportation.

## WHAT TO DO IN MANDALGOVI

### The Museum of Dundgovi Aimag

Established in 1949, this museum has grown to include a variety of well-apportioned exhibits with over 4,500 pieces, including bronze statues and other interesting functional artisan works. There is information on famous local heroes including the Zava Damdin lineage, approximately equivalent to the bogd khan line of lamas in Mongolia. You might also like the display of traditional Mongolian folk toys, displays of animal and mineral resources related to the era, or Bronze Age artifacts. Some of the 800 or more artifacts are from the formation of *Ikh Mongol,* the Great Mongolian Empire, dating back 800 or more years.

## WHAT TO DO IN DUNDGOVI AIMAG

On the road between Choir and Mandalgovi, about 70 kilometers (43.5 miles) from the *aimag* center, is the 30-kilometer (18.6-mile) long expanse of granite spires known as **Ikh Gazriin Chuluu (Их газрын чулуу)**. The oddly shaped stone pillars are held in high regard by locals, and they designate a place of spiritual pilgrimage for some. More than 40 caves pierce the mountains. If you're are traveling by private transport or with a tour, you will likely stop here, and some photo safaris make the trip here as well.

### Ulziit Soum (Өлзийт сум)

Dominating the southern border with Umnugovi Aimag, Ulziit contains a number of worthwhile natural sights. You'll do best to hire a driver in Mandalgovi and spend a few days in the area, driving from sight to sight and camping in between. Be sure to bring all the water and other supplies you'll need.

Ulziit's **Uush Sand Dunes (Өөш манхан)** are not the biggest dunes in the country, but they're quite large and very pretty nonetheless. They provide a break from the typical rocky flatness of the Gobi. Locals believe the dunes have medicinal properties, and there is a small active sanatorium at their feet as well as a few *gers* in the summer. One of the summer residents, Davaa, is a good guy who speaks no English but is a great mime. He might take a moment to tell you about the dunes.

At the southeastern edge of Dundgovi and extending into Umnugovi, the **Zagiin Oi Nature Reserve (Загийн ой)** is 50 kilometers (31 miles) southeast of the Uush sand dunes. The park protects and is named after the saxual scrub brush (*zag* in Mongolian) that characterizes the park's habitat. The *zag* forest provides a home to a wealth of wildlife and also serves as a key protection against soil erosion. In other parts of the country, it is threatened by people who collect the brush for fuel, but the park ensures that the plants within are safe from at least that threat. The park is home to both black and white-tailed gazelle populations. Expect to pay the MNT3,000 park fee when you see a ranger.

## Norovbanzad & the Urtiin Duu

**Namjiliin Norovbanzad** (Намжилын Норовбанзад) (1931-2002) was the premier long song or *urtiin duu* (pr. orteen-dough) singer of the twentieth century. She was awarded many state praises and prizes such as The People's Actress and Labor Hero. In 1993, she won the Fukuoka Asian Culture Prize in the arts and culture category.

As a native of Dundgovi Aimag, Norovbanzad learned to sing not in a school but in the remote countryside. Nor was she influenced by European styles. Instead, she was trained by her family of herders in the traditions of the style, which is now on the UNESCO List of the Intangible Cultural Heritage of Humanity.

The folk style of the songs – open, wide, and romantic, to represent the boundlessness of the open steppe – is still used to coax animals to move, give milk or give birth. The songs have a mystic, distant quality that musically expresses deep emotions for loved ones, the land, nature, and animals, which can be heard among Norovbanzad 's most famous titles "The Sun Over the Placid World," "The Four Seasons of the Steppe," "A Graceful Black Horse," and "Rich Mongolia."

Norovbanzad's talent was legendary. It was said that she memorized and could recite over twenty thousand verses, and that her powerful voice could fill a theater without amplification. But it wasn't until the late 1990s that her voice and the style of long song took on a new life, heard around the world as an element in the burgeoning electronic music scene. After Mongolian hip hop artists paired her music with strong beats, German artists Enigma featured her on the songs "The Child in Us" and "Carly's Song," which was featured on the soundtrack of the Sharon Stone film *Sliver*.

In a 2005 interview with Public Radio International, an American producer and distributor of arts and culture programming, she was characterized by ethnomusicologist Peter Marsh as "the Mongolian Dolly Parton because of her ability to adapt strong countryside traditions to a modern stage, to a modern life." (Dolly Parton, known as the "Queen of Country Music," enjoyed success in the 1970s as a pop singer and then as a prolific 1980s actress starring alongside Julia Roberts, Sylvester Stalone and other notable actors.) Marsh went on to explain in the interview, which took place three years after Norovbanzad's death, that she had approved of using her music in new ways and encouraged the creative expression by Mongolian and international musicians.

On the southwestern side of Ulziit, 115 kilometers (71 miles) from Mandalgovi, lie **Tsagaan Suvraga (Цагаан суврага)** and **Ulaan Suvraga (Улаан суврага)**, white and red stupa, respectively. Twenty kilometers apart, these sites are not monasteries as their name might imply but rather temples of raw natural beauty. Both feature wind-sculpted cliffs and otherwise unusual topography.

## Adaatsag Soum (Адаацаг сум)

Another impressive set of oddly shaped rock formations, canyons, and gullies, painted in a palette of oxidized red-rust tones can be found at **Baga Gazriin Chuluu (Бага газрын чулуу)**. Baga Gazriin Chuluu and its counterpart, **Baga Gazriin Uul**, a very climbable mountain just over 1,750 meters (5,741 feet) in elevation, are located 60 kilometers (37 miles) northwest of Mandalgovi. Baga Gazriin Uul is the occasional home of the influential artist-monk Zanabazar, and the ruins of a lesser monastery still sit on the southeast side of the mountain.

Another twenty kilometers or so to the west is **Sum Khukh Burd (Сүм хөх бүрд)**, a most unusual site for Mongolia. The oasis features a small lake with that wonder of wonders, an island. This isn't just any island, however, because this one is the site of an ancient temple that some sources say was built as long ago as the tenth century, before the Mongol tribes had even decided that they could get along well enough to form a unified body. Centuries later, after the original temple had been abandoned, a controversial lama with an almost mythical reputation named Danzanravjaa built a theater on top of the ruins to stage his play *Moon Cuckoo*, which is still one of the most-performed Mongolians dramas. For more on Danzanravjaa, see page 217.

## Deren Soum (Дэрэн сум)

North and slightly east of Mandalgovi, Deren Soum is home to the Dadsuren Traditional Music Project. This project, a spin-off of the Itgel Foundation that also works with Tsataan communities in Khovsgul Aimag, is the first rural school in the entire country with the express mission to preserve the long song tradition. Mongolians and foreign musicians alike have come to study with Dadsuren Garov, himself a protégé of the master long song vocalist Norovbunzad. Shared taxis traveling from Mandalgovi to Deren leave from the *aimag* center's market. The school is housed in the *soum* center's Cultural Palace; contact the Itgel foundation via www.itgel.org for more information.

## Saikhan Ovoo Soum (Сайхан овоо сум)

Nestled among the mountains above the Ongii Gol are the ruins of two monasteries destroyed during the Stalinist purges of the 1930s. Together they are known as

**Ongiin Khiid (Онгийн хийд)**, although each has its own name: Barlim Khiid is on the northern bank while Khutagt Khiid is to the south. The river valley is incredibly picturesque and worth the trip in its own right; the monasteries simply add a level of intrigue to the beauty. A small group of monks has established a new temple on the site in recent years as well.

# Govi-Altai Aimag (Говь-алтай аймаг)

Govi-Altai (pronounced "gove-alltie") is perhaps the rawest of any of the Gobi *aimags*. As Mongolia's second-largest *aimag*, there is little here but desert to the north, desert to the south, and the intimidating Altai Mountain Range straight through the middle. No world-famous dinosaur fossil deposits. No enormous mine sites. No train lines and only a few paved roads. *Soums* with population densities below half a person per square kilometer. The southern portion of the *aimag* is made up of only four *soums*, housing just 10,000 people. The *aimag* is otherwise dominated by the **Great Gobi Strictly Protected Area**. All of this adds up to make Govi-Altai a great destination for the truly intrepid traveler.

The *aimag* doesn't see many tourists visit or stay long when they do, and you'll surely need a good sense of adventure with a healthy dose of patience if you come here. But if wide-open spaces and remote desert ecosystems are your thing, Govi-Altai is the perfect place.

There are certainly some overlooked attractions in the area, including a trio of peaks over 3,700 meters (12,200 feet). The tallest is **Suutai Uul (Сүүтай уул)**, just over 4,000 meters (13,123 feet). It is graced with an ever present skull cap of snow. While *govi* comes first in the name, the *aimag's* climate tends to skew towards the *altai*, remaining somewhat chilly even in summer. Come prepared.

Like all of the remote regions of Mongolia, if you plan on traveling to several other destinations besides Govi-Altai, we suggest you start by traveling to the one furthest from Ulaanbaatar. It is a good deal easier to get to Govi-Altai from Khovd than vice versa. Likewise, it is quite easy to backtrack towards Bayanhongor or Uvurkhangai *aimags* from the *aimag* capital, **Altai**, but probably next to impossible to hop on westward-bound public transportation from those *aimags*.

## ALTAI (АЛТАЙ)

Altai, the *aimag* center, is a small city in the arid northeast sector of the province, but it's not an unappealing one. On first look-around, the city seems larger than it really is, thanks to the fact that most of the essential components of the city, the administrative buildings, the square, the market, the sports complex, and many of the shops, are located along one road stretching through town from north to south. The people are laid back, and there are a couple of hotels and decent restaurants in a sort of entertainment district on the two streets opposite the square. While Altai doesn't quite have a metropolitan feel, the town is home to the largest medical college in western Mongolia.

Unfortunately, there's not much in the way of hiking or other outdoor activities in the immediate vicinity. However, there are a couple of great public spaces in town to sit and people watch without attracting too much attention to yourself.

## GETTING THERE

### By Air

Two EZnis flights from Ulaanbaatar service Altai each week. Non-resident foreigner ticket fees are $250-$260 each way. The EZnis office in Altai is conveniently located in the sports palace opposite the square; the desk clerk speaks enough English to make getting your ticket simple.

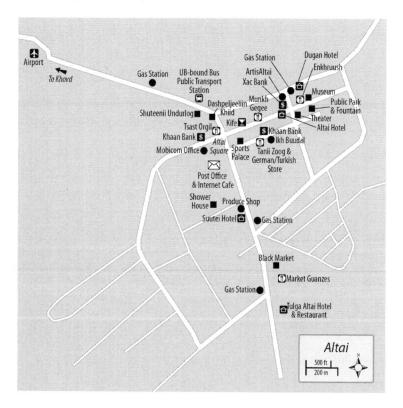

Aeromongolia now offers two flights a week as well; the Aeromongolia office is in the post office.

### By Bus
Ulaanbaatar to Altai buses leave several days a week, departing from a lot across the street from the monastery in Altai and from the Dragon Center in UB. The cost is MNT37,000, and the trip averages 30 hours or more from start to finish. In a welcome move towards convenience and traveler-friendly protocol, the bus stand in Altai has posted prices for getting off the UB bus before the big city: MNT20,000 to Bayankhongor and MNT30,000 to Uvurkhangai.

A frustrating option, though still better than a *purgon*, is to catch an Ulaanbaatar to Khovd bus. However, these buses do not stop in the center of Altai. Rather, they refuel at petrol stations on the outskirts of town and carry on. There are several stations that get business from the long distance buses, but exactly where a given bus will stop depends on the driver. The best thing to do is to go to several potential stops (ask a taxi driver where the bus might stop) and leave a mobile phone number at each location so that the driver can reach you at when he passes through. If you don't have a phone, the best you can do is hang around the petrol station until the bus comes through, which may be in the afternoon or in the middle of the night. One way between Altai and Khovd will cost around MNT25,000.

### By Shared Transportation
*Purgons* bound for Altai also leave from Naraantuul in UB daily. A seat is a slightly higher than a bus ticket.

It is possible for the determined and patient traveler to continue westward from Altai, but it is not an easy task. *Purgons* occasionally leave from the market for Khovd and even less often for Zavkhan. *Purgons* headed west and north are not guaranteed on even a weekly basis.

## GETTING AROUND THE AIMAG
The post office offers transportation to some *soums* in Govi-Altai. Check there for schedules. Vehicles to the *soums* can also be found at the market. For most of the *aimag's* attractions, namely the national parks, you'll have to hire private transportation, since they are so far beyond the *soums* and population centers.

## WHERE TO STAY
**Dugan Hotel (Дуган)** Tucked away down a dirt road near the monastery, the Dugan Hotel is an *aimag* center hotel with a *hudoo* feel. The rooms are clean and fairly large but Spartan in their furnishings; no frills here. With its basic restaurant

The Guide

and billiard tables on the first floor, Dugan seems like a long-haul trucker's kind of place. The rooms are about as cheap as they come in this town, though, and the hotel claims to have hot water. *Single MNT25,000, double MNT20,000-35,000.*

**Altai Hotel (Алтай)** This centrally located hotel and restaurant is undoubtedly the Altai accommodation for fancy folk. The hotel has recently remodeled, and even the lobby looks like the kind of room you wouldn't mind sleeping in. Annoyingly, Altai charges more for foreigners and posts their prices in dollars, although we're not entirely convinced the staff would know what to do with a stack of greenbacks if you tried to pay with them. As for the prices themselves, if Altai can convince anyone to actually pay $100 as listed for the lux room, we say, "Good for you Altai Hotel. Go get yours." But the thought of paying $100 for any hotel room in western Mongolia also makes us giggle, just a little bit. *Simple $25-30, half lux $50-60, lux $100. 24134*

**Suutei Hotel (Сүүтэй)** Hidden in plain sight, this small hotel is located on the second floor of a building with a tired-looking bare brick façade on Altai's main drag. There are only two rooms, both doubles, but they are comfortable and modern. And the hotel offers hot water. If there's no one in the office when you arrive, ask at the shops around the corner in the same building. *Double MNT25,000-35,000.*

**Tulga-Altai Hotel (Тулга-алтай)** The largest of Altai's hotels, Tulga-Altai charges more for foreign guests, but breakfast is included. There's no hot water; in fact, the hotel as a whole has a reputation for being cold, for what that's worth in a place like Mongolia. The rooms are clean enough with good light and nice common rooms in the lux and half lux rooms. Simple rooms are arranged in suites of three, sharing a bathroom among them. *Simple MNT24,000, half lux double MNT36,000, half lux triple MNT42,000, lux double MNT48,000.*

# WHERE TO EAT

## Restaurants

**Enkhruush (Энхрүүш)** Our pick. This is a popular lunch spot with locals as well. *Khuurags* of all varieties seem to be the house specialty and most commonly ordered item. The *undugtei khuurga* was more egg than meat, which is just as well, really. If your meal is good enough to make you want to sing, just move on over to the karaoke room. ₮₮

**Munkh Gegee (Мөнх Гэгээ)** A small joint across from the radio station, Munkh Gegee is another popular spot, and you will find it packed at lunchtime. The draw certainly isn't the speed of the service, however. A local says that this is the place to go for vegetarian dishes, although none were listed on the menu. Asking for meatless stir-fries (*makhgui khuurga*) is always an option. ₮

**Tsast Orgil (Цаст Оргил)** Standard Mongolian meals located conveniently in the administrative building on the corner of the square. ₮

**Tanii Zoog (Таны Зоог)** Somewhere in between a *guanz* and a restaurant, Tanii Zoog will fill you for cheap, even if it doesn't make your top ten dining experiences of the year list. ₮

### Guanzes

There is a row of *guanzes* along the far wall of the market. No major surprises here, but **Mirage (Мираж)** serves delightfully low-grease *khuushuur* and a plate of *undugtei khurag* that looks as good as any.

### Grocery Stores

The black market has all of the usual, essential items. There is a small produce shop at the road-side entrance to the Suutei Hotel building. The prize of the town is the German and Turkish store, which stocks German chocolates and other sought-after imported canned goods, like corn and beans.

## WHAT TO DO IN ALTAI

There are attractive mountains for hiking to the west of Govi-Altai. They appear deceptively close, but be prepared to walk across open fields for an hour or two at a steady pace in order to reach them. The smaller mountains to the east of the city may look less appealing from a distance, but they will take less time to reach and still offer a wide open view of the countryside.

The small and sleepy *aimag* **museum** (MNT3,000; open Monday through Friday, 9:00 a.m. to 6:00 p.m., closed for lunch from 1:00 to 2:00 p.m.) might fill an hour or so of your time. The **theater** across the street has shows almost weekly.

Across the street from the museum and in front of the equally sleepy theater, you'll find a very nice **public park**, complete with a colorfully lit fountain. Built over the summer of 2010 to commemorate Govi-Altai's 75th anniversary, the park seems to be closed during the day as well as in winter, but it is a great place to hang out and people watch in the evening when children run around splashing in the water and older Mongolians come by to make flash-photography portraits of their friends with the fountain's light show in the background.

Altai's other great public space is the **Shuteenii Undurlog (Шүтээний өндөрлөг)**, a pagoda-like temple at the top of a hill on the north side of town. Like the park, Shuteenii Undurlog is a new addition to Altai. It provides a great view of the city and the rocky desert that surrounds it. The twin tile staircases and network of fountains are about as classy an approach as might be expected for an *ovoo*, and the city should be proud of it. At the bottom of the hill you'll find the slightly older **Dashpeljeeliin Khiid (Дашпэлжээлийн хийд)**, an active monastery.

For those interested in handicrafts, **ArtisAltai** (1:30-5:00 p.m., Monday – Friday) is the best place to look in Altai. Around the corner from Khadgalamj Bank, (Хадгаламж Банк), the project aims to meld local products, contemporary ideas, and ancestral artisanship to improve the economic opportunities of low-income families. Most of their products, which include a range of jewelry made of silk, felt, nifty Mongolian del beads, and metal, are sold at handicraft shops in UB, but they keep a small stock in the Altai workshop. The craftsmen and women welcome visitors to come and watch the creative process.

If you are looking for a night of singing and a bartender that can speak English, head to **Kife**, a karaoke bar in a yellow building just off the square. The songbooks contain a plethora of English hits you can belt out for your fellow karaoke enthusiasts, and the bartender, a local English teacher, will make you feel right at home. Karaoke is MNT500 per person per hour.

## WHAT TO DO IN GOVI-ALTAI AIMAG

### Eej Khairkhan Uul (Ээж хайрхан уул) "Dearest Mother Mountain"

Perhaps Govi-Altai's premier sightseeing destination, Eej Khairkhan is a great place to explore. You can hike the 2,275-meter (7464-foot) tall peak. The mountain is virtually its own open-air museum of odd geology. The base features a series of large cauldrons carved into the rock where rain and springtime melt-water drain from one to the next to the next. Nearby are some petroglyphs, and all around are small caves and unique rock formations that take on the shapes of people and animals, sort of a stone version of the "what do you think that cloud looks like?" game.

In the 1920s, an ascetic Buddhist monk named Ravdan lived in an improved cave shelter at the base of Eej Khairkhan. His encampment became a popular pilgrimage site; the cave-house still stands today.

You'll want a guide to help you find the most interesting bits. Having traveled the 150 kilometers (93 miles) south from Altai, you may want to go ahead and continue on down to the Great Gobi Strictly Protected Area (Gobi A) or to the 3,765-meter (12,336-foot) tall Burkhan Buudai Uul, visible from Eej Khairkhan. Settlements in this region are few and far between, so bring your own supplies of food, water, and fuel.

**Great Gobi Strictly Protected Area** is 35 years old and has been recognized by the United Nations as an international biosphere reserve, the largest in Asia and fourth largest anywhere. The reserve provides an invaluable habitat to a herd of re-introduced takhi, or Przewalski's horse, and endangered species like wild ass, black-tailed gazelle, and the only desert-dwelling bear, the Gobi bear. The reserve is split into two sections, commonly referred to as **Gobi A**, located in southern Govi-Altai and Bayanhongor aimags, and **Gobi B**, located in southern Khovd and western Govi-Altai.

# Govisumber Aimag (Говь сүмбэр аймаг)

Though Govisumber is considered northern Gobi Desert, you may not find much here in terms of sweeping Gobi views or other tourists. It receives more rain than areas to the south, so Govisumber is more like what would result if the eastern steppe and the Gobi had a love child. Especially considering it is conveniently located on the train line, it can be a fun, quiet getaway to give you an overnight taste of rural Mongolia if you can't make it the more remote parts in the east or if you're en route to visit Sainshand to the south.

Govisumber Aimag, which broke off from Dorngovi Aimag in the early 1990s to declare itself a free trade zone, is the most recently established province in Mongolia. It's also one of the smallest geographically with only three *soums* (Bayantal, Shiveegovi, and Sumber) and in population, with only about 13,000 inhabitants. Its main point of interest, in fact, is that it is the smallest.

## CHOIR (ЧОЙР)

Choir is the capital of Govisumber Aimag and has a population of about 8,000 people, including the rural areas outside of the center. At an altitude of 1,269 meters (4,163 feet), Choir lies in a depression and is around 500 meters (1,640 feet) lower than the surrounding upland. It was a military base during the Soviet period until 1989 when the Soviet anti-aircraft missile units left. The Soviets took their missile units but left the runway that is 25 kilometers (15.5 miles) north of the provincial capital. It is still the longest runway in Mongolia, though it sits unused. The retreating military left behind a legacy of ecological damage here and other places during their quick getaway.

Along with Darkhan and Erdenet, Choir is one of three autonomous cities in Mongolia, although one would not be quick to find many similarities among them suggesting a clear link. There is a statue commemorating Mongolia's first Cosmonaut, **Jugderdemidiin Gurragchaa** near the railway station. While Jugderdemidiin Gurragchaa was not a native of Govisumber, he was the second Asian in space and a Soviet hero.

## GETTING THERE

### By Bus

Buses leaves once a day, at 4:00 p.m., from the Dragon Center in UB. It is a four-hour trip with one food stop.

Return buses leave at 9:30 a.m. and 12:00 noon from the kindergarten close to the Xac Bank. Consider getting your ticket the day before.

The Guide

### By Shared Transportation

Taxis from UB can be arranged in front of Borjigin sports center which is next to School #1.

Taxis leave all day from the taxi center in front of the community center and School #1. You can arrange a ride that morning by exchanging numbers with a taxi driver to coordinate a time to leave for the three-hour trip (MNT10,000).

### By Train

Choir is on the train-line, but the return timing is not convenient. Travel by train is double the time for a taxi and more than half the price. From UB, trains leave at 9:30 a.m. and arrive in Choir at 3:00 p.m. The train leaves for UB at 2:30 a.m. Hence, it's better for coming than going. The train costs MNT4,800 each way.

Taking the train to Sainshand from Choir is a good option if you want to check out more of the Gobi. The train goes south from Choir at 3:00 p.m. and arrives in Sainshand around 9:00 p.m.

## WHERE TO EAT

**Tulga Restaurant** A small Mongolian restaurant that sells all the regulars plus *peroshki*, the Russian hot pocket with meat and rice inside. There's not much fat on the meat in the *peroshki*, so it's a nice alternative. It is located off the main road that runs through Choir on the left-hand side if you are coming from UB. ₮

**Urikhan Restaurant** A good sized Mongolian joint known for their *khuushuur*. Enjoy it there or order some to go. It is located across the street from the major internet café. In the left-side entrance of a building that also has a few supermarkets and a clothing market. ₮

**Tengis Restaurant and Karaoke** Restaurant/dance club. It's a good place to go if you want to get some food before some beers and dancing. The first section is the restaurant. In the back there's a dance floor surrounded by some more tables for eating. Not a bad option for a fun evening, but just be careful of the local Mongolian guys that go there to drink. It is located left of the Mini-Market hotel and down a couple doors. ₮₮

## SHOPPING

There is a supermarket in the train station, which is one of the largest stores in Choir. For fruits and vegetables, try **Mini-market Hotel** next to the train station.

## WHERE TO STAY

The **Mini-market Hotel** host is friendly but speaks no English. Beds are comfortable, and rooms clean. There are private toilets but no hot water. MNT25,000 per person. Rooms do not need to be booked in advance.

# Khentii Aimag (Хэнтий аймаг)

Khentii, the birthplace of Chinggis Khan, is an easy 330 kilometers (205 miles), only five to six hours, from UB on a paved road. It is one of the easiest locations to visit in Mongolia and interesting due to the natural majesty of the landscape and the historical significance. Because it borders Dornod and Sukhbaatar aimags, it is in many ways the gateway to the east. If you're headed that way, you should absolutely take a few days to explore Khentii.

Khentii, particularly the northern part, is heavily forested and contains **Khan Khentii National Park** and the **Onon-Balj Basin National Park**, which cuts across portions of Dadal, Bayan-Adarga, Binder, Norovlin, and Bayan-Uul soums and into Dornod Aimag. Here you will find rivers, lakes, and mountains hosting whooper swans, spoonbills, great white egrets, and some larger birds of prey. **Galsher Soum** in

The Guide

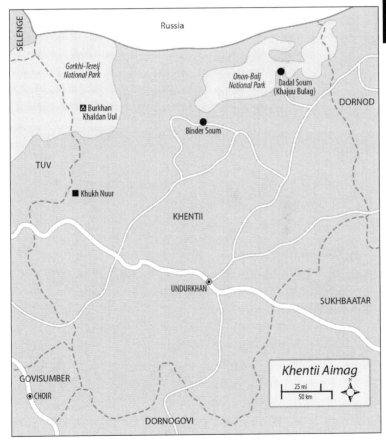

the southern part of the *aimag* is famous for its fast horses, including "Elbeg," which won the national horseracing competition 17 times.

Despite the natural attractions, the real draw for tourists tends to be the Chinggis Khan memorials that are ubiquitous across the province. Most tourists also visit his birthplace in **Dadal Soum** in the northeastern part of the *aimag* at the junction of the **Onon** and **Balj** rivers, according to *The Secret History of the Mongols*.

Something you might (or might not) notice on the drive to and from Undurkhaan and Dornod Aimag is the **Chinggis Khan Wall**. It's also known as the "Almsgivers Wall" (Өглөгчийн хэрэн) and dates back to around the eighth century. It actually has nothing to do with Chinggis and predates him by a few hundred years, though the history is a little fuzzy as to why it exists and who built it. The "wall" was mostly earthen mounds and has been reduced to ruins by now.

## UNDURKHAN (ӨНДӨРХААН)

Undurkhan is the *aimag* center of Khentii. While its name means "high king," it is flat and more plebian than you may expect it to be, almost more of a robust village than a provincial capital. Regardless, the laid back attitude and simple feel may be one of its greatest attractions. If you only have a few days in Mongolia but you are dying to see the countryside, Undurkhaan is as good a place as any to do so since getting to Undurkhaan is simple compared to many other farther flung destinations.

The surroundings are enchanting. There's enough green space that it doesn't feel as desolate as the Gobi, and during the summer you are sure to find Mongolians relaxing in the sun by the winding rivers that meander through the valleys. One of our favorite days is a cookout by the river in Undurkhaan.

While you're there, be sure to get some fish bread! It is some of the tastiest in Mongolia, and almost every *delguur* (shop) will have some in the mornings.

## GETTING THERE

### By Air

No need to travel here by air, though there is a landing strip. The *aimag* capital is a quick and comfortable five or six hour trip from UB.

### By Bus

The bus from UB to Undurkhaan (MNT10,000; 5-6 hours) leaves in the mornings from the Bayanzurkh eastern bus station. You'll have to buy your tickets a day in advance at the station, but since this bus station is much less hectic than the Dragon Center station where you get tickets for all the western *aimags*, lines are short.

Getting back to UB (MNT10,000) isn't too complicated either. The bus leaves from the Undurkhaan post office daily at 8:00 a.m., and it leaves on time. We learned from experience that if you arrive five minutes late, you might find yourself seeking out a private taxi ride, which will require waiting all day for the taxi to fill up before you can leave.

### By Shared Transportation
*Mikrs* to Undurkhaan can be booked from Bayanzurkh Tovchoo or Narantuul Market in UB for MNT15,000. They make the trip a little faster than the bus, but they're not comfortable. As always, they leave when they're full.

From Undurkhaan, *mikrs* congregate in front of the fourth school, and the price is negotiable based upon destination and number of riders. We had problems with *mikr* drivers in Undurkhaan wanting to charge us MNT100,000 or even $100 per person. Don't be fooled. A taxi is just as easy from Undurkhaan, and you might have an easier time negotiating price.

### By Taxi
You can typically get a taxi from UB to Khentii for MNT15,000 per person (MNT75,000 for the whole car) at Bayanzurkh or Naraantuul. There is not much of a need for the high powered sport utility vehicles since you will be on a paved road the whole way. On your way back to UB you can find vehicles waiting in front of the fourth school with the *mikrs*.

## GETTING AROUND THE AIMAG

Private cars and Jeeps can be hired from Undurkhaan to the *soums* and attractions from in front of either the west market or fourth school. The rate is usually negotiated based on the number of people and the destination and may or may not involve a fuel surcharge.

*The Guide*

---

### The Waiting Game
We once arrived a couple minutes late to catch the bus from Undurkhaan to UB. By 8:00 a.m., we had found a taxi to get us to UB, but we still needed to wait for the driver to fill up the car. Around noon, he drove us to the apartment he shared with his parents and his sister where he offered for us to stay until he had found enough passengers. Since he knew it would be a while, he wanted us to have company. In typical Mongolian style, his sister fed us—a lot! By 4:00 p.m. the driver finally had enough passengers, so he came back and picked us up. We had an easy trip that included singing Mongolian songs and sharing music from our MP3 players on his car radio. It was a fantastic and unique experience, but not necessarily the most efficient way to get to UB!

---

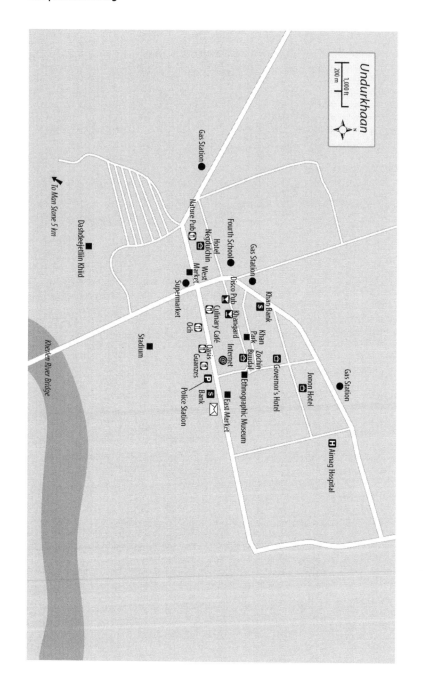

# WHERE TO STAY

**Hotel Negdulchin** The premier hotel in Undurkhaan. The prices may be a little high on the lux room end, but they have an English-speaking staff, which can come in handy. Single rooms with shared toilet are MNT15,000. Double rooms with shared toilet are MNT20,000. The lux with a private shower and toilet is MNT45,000, and the half lux with a private toilet is MNT30,000. There is a shared hot shower and also private parking. The highly recommended China Restaurant is on the first floor. It is great if you have a large group.

**Jonon Hotel (Жонон)** Has more of a relaxed style, and you may be able to negotiate the price for your room. The lux room with toilet is MNT22,000 per person, and there is one special lux room with a toilet and shower for the same price. The half lux with a toilet is MNT9,000, and a regular room with a shared toilet is MNT6,000 per person. A shared hot shower and a karaoke bar are both on first floor.

**Governor's Hotel** Has only two spacious rooms, both of which sleep two to three people at MNT20,000 per person. There is a recently renovated shared bathroom with a hot shower and toilet, and a large shared kitchen and dining area available. If you have a large group and like the idea of having the place to yourself, this is your best choice!

**Zochin Buudal (Зочид буудал)** A basic, cheap little hostel and one of the best deals in town. A private room with shower and toilet is MNT15,000 per person, a quad room with private toilet is MNT7,000 per person, and a regular room with share toilet and shared hot shower is MNT6,000 per person.

# WHERE TO EAT

## Restaurants

**Oasis** The most popular restaurant for foreigners due to the excellent food and reasonable prices. It is the only restaurant in Ondorkhaan to offer pizza (three types) and tacos. Additionally, the menu includes vegetable versions of popular Mongolian dishes, such as *khuushuur* and *buuz*. The food is made to order and may take longer than expected, so be prepared to wait. Sometimes the owner offers desserts! This is a big deal, since they aren't common in Mongolia. The owner is also one of the nicest people you could ever meet, so it's worth waiting for the food when you know someone so great owns the place. Located on the second floor of the three-story brick building beside Өгөөж. Open from 11am-6pm every day except Sundays. ₮₮

**China Restaurant** Located on the first floor of Hotel Negdulchin. It is an upscale restaurant that focuses on traditional Mongolian and Chinese platters. The food portions are large, so you may want to consider splitting, which ends up being a really great value. ₮₮

**Khangard (хангард)** The most popular upscale restaurant in town for the locals. The menu is very broad and includes many traditional dishes along with chicken and Italian fare. There is a VIP room available if you have a group and you want some privacy. ₮₮

The Guide

**Nature Pub** Next to the China Restaurant. It has a very rustic, outdoorsy feel due to the wood and stone décor. The walls display many furs and bows and arrows. The atmosphere is relaxed, and this is a good place to go for a drink and traditional Mongolian fare. ₮

**Culinary Café** The newest addition to the restaurant scene in Undurkhaan. The café is a vegetarian restaurant that also includes a bakery. The food often includes soy or tofu and some vegetable variations of traditional fare are available. Open 11am-7pm. ₮

**Och (Оч)** Specializes in large dishes of traditional Mongolian food. The décor is very modern and clean, and this restaurant stays open later than others. ₮₮

## Guanzes

There are many *guanzes* on the main street of Undurkhaan. The menus are short and include typical Mongolian *khuushuur or buuz*. The prices are essentially the same at all of them, and the service is quick. If you are in a hurry or on a tight budget, try one of these. There are multiple *guanzes* located on the first floor of the **Өргөө** building, the two-story yellow building in the center of town on the main road.

# WHAT TO DO IN UNDURKHAAN

**The Museum of Khentii**, as you would imagine, it is the premiere museum in Khentii. It is open from 9:00 a.m. to 6:00 p.m. Tuesdays through Saturdays and costs MNT1,500 per person. The museum, which is a set of small buildings from a former Buddhist temple, includes an impressive replica of Chinggis Khan's *ger*, along with an extensive collection of historical pieces from the area. Well worth a visit before you travel out to learn more about Chinggis. Khentii residents love to share about Chinggis with people that don't know he was from there.

From the Museum, take a walk over to **Khaan Park**. The centrally located city park in Undurkhaan starts at the Museum of Khentii and ends at the sports complex. It includes a monument with the image of an approaching Mongol horse and a stone statue of Chinggis Khan, but one of our favorite memories involved a photo shoot in this park posing in front of the weathered Soviet era monuments and grandiose murals and mosaics. We recommend bringing your MP3 player along and listing to some epic music while you visit to really immerse yourself in the moment.

North of the park is the **City Museum**, which has recently been renovated. This museum contains most of your typical historical artifacts and knickknacks as well as some of Chinggis Khan's armor and a massive mastodon tusk that is impressive.

**The Ethnographic Museum** is located next to the *soum* government office; this is one of the better put together museums in Mongolia. It is comprised of four buildings that were once the home of Setsen Khan, an eighteenth century Mongolian prince. The collection contains what you might expect, including religious artifacts, costumes, toys, and the like. If you find yourself in Undurkhaan, you may as well check out the cultural history here.

After (or before) visiting the Ethnographic Museum, make sure to check out the **Dashdeejetliin Khiid (Дашдээжэтлийн хийд)**, a small eighteenth century monastery right next door. This small temple was originally a part of Tsetseg Khan's palace and was converted into a monastery in the 1990s. There may or may not be lamas there at any given time; if there are lamas there, they would probably prefer not open it to the public. If you're interested in seeing inside the monastery, you would do best to try your luck on an auspicious day.

The one thing you can't miss out on is chilling by the **Kherlen Gol**, which runs about one kilometer (half a mile) south of town. It is a relaxing place to visit and enjoy the view of the mountains, and the best sunrises and sunsets in town can be viewed from the bridge. The river is also a favorite place for a *khorkhog,* so if you make some friends, invite them to the river to show you how to make this interesting Mongolian dish or ask your hotel if they can help set something up. If not, it's still a great place for a picnic or a few afternoon beers.

If you are looking for a quiet contemplative time, follow the river to check out the Buddhist monastery on the south side of town and to the west of the bridge crossing the Kherlen Gol. It has been recently renovated and is surrounded by large white walls. It is an impressive structure and one of the most beautiful places in Khentii.

Located 7 kilometers (4.3 miles) southwest of town, past the old airport, is a **Man Stone**, presumably from the Turkic era. Look for the group of blue *khadag* blowing in the wind. The intricacies of the stone carving and the age of the stone man are very impressive. Be sure to bring a small offering of food or money to leave at the *balbal.* (N47°16'43.21", E110°36'5.89")

## Nightlife

**Khangard (Хангард)** is one of the two places in Undurkhaan where you can get out and party. It is located on the second floor of the building and contains a dance club and karaoke bar. This is the most popular location in Undurkhaan for such activities. If you have spent the day getting to know some Mongolians, this is a good place to suggest for the end of the night. Karaoke is really popular with Mongolians.

**The Disco Pub** is located two buildings to the west of Khangard. The outside is dark, but there is always music playing. Maybe if the people you are with aren't interested in karaoke, you can learn take part in a fun circle dance or perhaps a festive Mongolian waltz at this disco.

The Guide

# DADAL SOUM (ДАДАЛ СУМ)

Dadal is famous for being the birthplace of the great empire-builder Chinggis Khan, and there is a Temujin statue marking the spot of his supposed birthplace (N49° 01.028, E111°37.164). But Dadal doesn't need the historical connection to make it one of Mongolia's finest travel destinations. An idyllic hamlet of log cabins and split rail fences in the taiga forest of northern Khentii near the Russian border, Dadal is imbued with an aura of peace and homeliness that is hard to resist.

Dadal is chock full of beautiful lakes, rivers, and forests. Many liken the area to Siberia which makes sense considering it is only 25 kilometers (15 miles) north of Dadal. With that said, be careful not to hike too far north, as you may find yourself in a sticky border situation. Dadal is also home to **Onon-Balj National Park**, which is a great place for fishing (both the bait and fly variety) and is home to the Taimen, Siberian White Fish, Siberian Grayling, Lenok, Umber, Baikal, Omul, and River Perch.

A sizable population of Buriats lives in Dadal. The Buriats are effectively a Mongol ethnic minority. They speak a dialect of Mongolian and share a number of cultural markers, including a tradition of nomadic pastoralism and a belief in Tibetan-influenced Buddhism. Typically a well educated people whose ethnic relatives are mostly found in eastern Siberia, the Buriats suffered mightily during the Stalinist purges of the 1930s.

There are several monuments to Chinggis Khan in the Dadal area. One is a statue commemorating his 800th birthday at **Gurvan Nuur (Гурван нуур)**, slightly northeast of the *soum* center, which also has a natural spring. This statue, built in 1962, during the communist regime, caused some heartache for the communist party officials who designed and dedicated it. They ended up exiled or imprisoned. But it was never removed, despite the official anti-Chinggis stance.

A second Chinggis monument and a neighboring *ovoo* sit on a hill at **Deluun Boldog (Дэлүүн болдог)**, several kilometers to the north. This one was built in 1990 as the communist era came to an end and marks the 750th anniversary of the *Secret History of the Mongols*. The monument makes the rather dubious claim that Chinggis was born at this exact spot, although nearly everyone agrees that he did come into the world somewhere nearby.

If you visit only one site of Chinggis-worship, make it **Khajuu Bulag (Хажуу булаг)**. Here you'll find a fresh water spring that surely quenched the great Khan's thirst at one time or another. There's no other gaudy statues or neon lights proclaiming the historic act here, but the many *khadags* tied in the thicket and the Mongolians filling their water jugs full of crisp, natural water display a deeper, more authentic respect for the man and the land he came from. The spring is about 3.5 kilometers (two miles) north of the *soum* center; follow the path around the forest from the eastern edge. From Khajuu Bulag, you can continue north on the Jeep trail for another kilometer or two to reach an excellent swimming spot. The river and the forests surrounding Dadal are the area's best attraction in the humble opinion of this author. Simply meandering around enjoying the stillness and beauty is the best reward for the long trip up. If you plan on a longer trek in the area, take a guide so you don't find yourself somewhere you don't want to be, namely Russia.

**Galtai Agui (Галтай агуй)** is an impressively deep cave 70 kilometers (43 miles) north-west of Dadal *soum* center. What's impressively deep you ask? At 80 meters (roughly 24 stories!), it's the deepest in Mongolia. Since this cave is dangerously close to the Russian border, you will need to get a permit from the border guards in Dadal before you embark on any spelunking adventure.

### Getting to Dadal

Shared Jeep or minivan taxis travel between Dadal and Ulaanbaatar directly perhaps a few times a week. Look for them around Naraantuul in UB. In Dadal, check out the shops for signs posted by drivers planning on making the trip, or just ask around to see if anyone knows a departing driver. The direct drive will usually take about 20 hours, give or take a few.

Another option is to take a bus or shared taxi to Unduurkhan. From there, a post office *purgon* shuttles people and packages through the *soums* north of the *aimag* center a couple times a week. You can find out the schedule and buy tickets at the post office. Tickets in Dadal are available at the small post office shack on the south side of town, which is where the *purgon* will drop you off when you arrive in Dadal.

### Food & Accommodations

There are several *ger* camps in the area as well as a small hotel on the main street. In the same area you'll find several *guanze*s serving all the *tsuivan* and *suutai tsai* you could want, but be warned that they close quite early, usually by 5:00 or 6:00 p.m. A few shops in town stock instant noodles, bread, processed cheese, pickles, and *hyam* in case you prefer to dine later in the evening.

## OTHER POINTS OF INTEREST IN KHENTII AIMAG

### Binder Soum (Биндэр сум)

This village also in northern Khentii has more ties to Chinggis. About two kilometers (1.2 miles) southeast of the town is a stone monument, which marks the location of the first formation of the Mongolian country by Chinggis in 1206. Binder has a guesthouse that is located to the west of the two story log cabin at the center of town. There is a *guanz* in the middle of the building and a hostel in the back. The last room on the right is the proprietor's room (MNT6,000 per person).

## Khukh Nuur (Хөх нуур)

This small lake (N48°01.150', E108°56.450') is no stranger to Chinggis lore and is believed to be where Temujin was crowned Chinggis Khan in 1206. It is located roughly 35 kilometers (22 miles) north-west of Tsenkhermandal Soum. An unassuming plaque marks the coronation spot, which is said to have been attended

## Temujin

Before he unified the Mongol tribes and before he became one of the most (in)famous rulers of all time and wreaked havoc all the way to the Volga River in Eastern Europe, Temujin was a boy called "blacksmith" who was born in the year 1162 at the intersection of the Onon and Balj rivers in northeast Khentii Aimag near the Burkhan Khaldun Uul.

*The Secret History of the Mongols*, where most information about Temujin has been derived, explains that Temujin was the third oldest son of Yesukhei, a minor Kiyad tribal chief of the relatively weak Borjigid Clan, and the first son of Oelun, his mother. As was common during the time, Yesukhei had kidnapped Oelun as she rode home from her wedding to another man. She became Yesukhei's second wife and Temujin was his second boy born within a period of a few months. As the legend goes, Temujin was born with a blood clot grasped in his fist, a traditional sign that he was destined to become a great leader.

In his early days in Khentii, Temujin was described as a weak runt of a boy who was afraid of dogs and cried often. The young Temujin spent his childhood herding animals, riding horses, and doing family chores, much in the same way as rural Mongolian boys still do these days. Things changed for the worse for him and his family when his father was poisoned by a rival tribe, leaving young Temujin as the Kiyad chief. Unfortunately, many in the tribe objected to his succession and abandoned Oelun with her three sons, a newborn daughter, and Temujin's slightly older half brother, Bekhtar. This left them in abject poverty, virtually alone on the steppe. While the family was starving, Temujin apparently noticed that his half brother seemed strong and healthy, and he discovered that Bekhtar had been spying on their former clan for the rival Tanguts. As punishment, Temujin and his brother killed Bekhtar for his betrayal.

A few years later Temujin met his future wife Borte who gave him a sable coat, a semblance of power and wealth, which he traded for a small tribal army within an established confederacy. After their marriage, Borte was abducted during a raid and held for eight months. Often cited as the turning point in his life, the rescue of Borte catapulted Temujin into long series of successful alliances, political maneuvers, and conquering battles that culminated in a ceremony near the Khukh Nuur in 1206 when Temujin became Chinggis Khan or "Ocean King."

Because the kidnapping of women had caused so much feuding among the Mongol tribes, Chinggis Khan established as part of his *Ikh Zasag* prohibited the kidnapping of women. He also declared all children legitimate, whoever the mother, and made it law that no woman would be sold into marriage, all of which were fundamental social changes.

Though he has a mixed legacy throughout the rest of the world, in Mongolia Chinggis Khan is much more than a folk hero and more like a deity. His picture hangs in most homes around the country and countless businesses and products are branded with his name and portrait. Not only is he revered throughout the country for unifying the ancient Mongol tribes and creating a storied empire, but in Khentii especially, he is revered as the hometown hero with plaques and monuments everywhere.

by 100,000 soldiers. While this is a relatively unimpressive lake in comparison to the larger and more beautiful **Khangil Nuur** located 30 kilometers (19 miles) away, it isn't a bad place to post up for a break or perhaps to have a lunch and take photographs reenacting the coronation (don't forget your ancient soldier garb!).

## Khan Khentii Protected Area

Bordering Terelj National Park to the west, this protected area contains **Asralt Khairkhan**, which at 2,800 meters (9,186 feet), is its highest peak. **Burkhan Khaldan** is a remote mountain in the range that is credited as one of the many possible burial sites of Chinggis Khan. Although no main tomb has been located, this site did have auspicious and sacred connections to the great khan. This particular hill is in the **Khan Khentii Strictly Protected Area** and fairly remote. It can be reached by traveling north along the Kherlen Gol from Mongomorit in Tuv Aimag.

**Shivertiin Agui** was formed from volcanic lava rocks. This cave is located to the South of Kherlen Ulaan Uul. The cave has an opening of two meters so this is a good cave for the novice spelunker.

# Khovd Aimag (Ховд аймаг)

Khovd is widely known as Mongolia's most diverse *aimag*. Aside from a healthy Kazakh population, about ten percent of the *aimag's* total, Khovd is home to a number of ethnic Mongolian minority groups, including the Zakhchin, Durvud, Uriankhai, Myangad, and Torguud. Many of Khovd's *soums* are historical homelands to specific ethnic groups, and as a result, traveling through the *aimag* gives you a veritable survey of Mongolian dialects and accents.

Visually, Khovd can be startling after traveling through the green taiga regions of the north or the flat expanses of the east and south; a distinctly Martian landscape dominates much of the *aimag*. The *aimag's* mountains tend to be rust colored and jagged, the red-dragon sentries at the edge of the Altai. Some resident Peace Corps volunteers once created a guessing game with photographs of Khovd and the planet Mars placed side by side; when the pictures were rendered in black and white, it was virtually impossible to tell the difference, save for a wisp of earthly cloud on the horizon of one shot.

Aside from the characteristic red mountains, Khovd also claims a handful of beautiful, eternally snowy 4,000-meter (13,123-foot) peaks, including the country's second and third highest: **Monkhkhairkhan** and **Tsambagarav**. The *aimag* is also part of western Mongolia's Great Lakes basin, and ribbons of river flow through the Altai towards **Khar Us Nuur** and **Khar Nuur**.

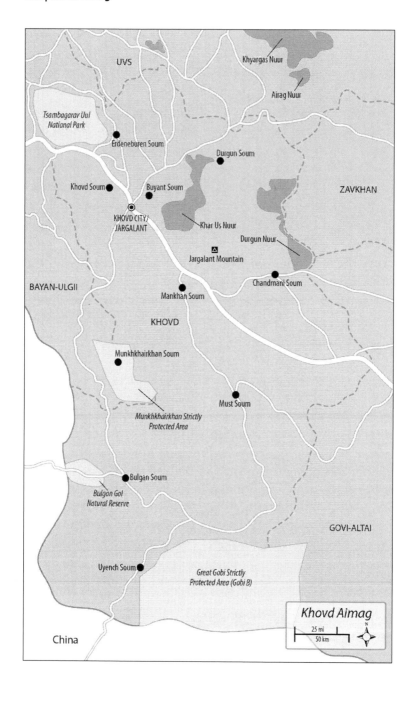

UVS

Khyargas Nuur

Airag Nuur

Tsambagarav Uul
National Park

Erdeneburen Soum

Durgun Soum

ZAVKHAN

Khovd Soum

Buyant Soum

KHOVD CITY/
JARGALANT

Khar Us Nuur

Durgun Nuur

Jargalant Mountain

BAYAN-ULGII

Chandmani Soum

Mankhan Soum

KHOVD

Munkhkhairkhan Soum

Must Soum

Munkhkhairkhan Strictly
Protected Area

Bulgan Soum

Bulgan Gol
Natural Reserve

GOVI-ALTAI

Uyench Soum

Great Gobi Strictly
Protected Area (Gobi B)

China

Khovd Aimag

25 mi
50 km

N

Thanks to these rivers, situated largely in the *aimag's* northern region, Khovd is one of the few major vegetable-producing regions in the country. Aside from the standard carrots, potatoes, and cabbage, Khovd also produces tomatoes, the odd pumpkin, and the watermelon and cantaloupe for which it is famous. A visit to Khovd is best planned for late August or September, when the annual summer mosquito plague begins to pass and the main market in Khovd city is virtually overflowing with small, sweet melons piled on carpets, truck beds, and in the trunks of farmers' cars. Nothing balances the heaviness of the *hoodo* diet on a hot summer day better than a fresh watermelon.

Khovd's diverse nature has also had a very tangible impact on Mongolian culture; the *aimag's* **Chandmani Soum (Чандмань сум)** is the ancestral homeland of Mongolian *khoomii*, or throat singing. Chandmani's residents sing, whistle, and drone to this day, and many will be happy to show off for you. Even better, you might find one to teach you to sing *khoomii* yourself!

# KHOVD CITY (ХОВД)

Officially named **Jargalant Soum (Жаргалант сум)**, the *aimag* capital confusingly shares its commonly used name with both the province and a nearby Kazakh village (Khovd Soum). One of the oldest cities in the country, Khovd was a military post of the western Mongolian Zuungarian kingdom, which also included present day Xinjiang in China, as far back as 1685. The Zuungarians were the last of the Mongols to fall to the Chinese Qing dynasty, fighting until 1757 to maintain their independence. After that, the city was a major Qing frontier outpost, home to a military garrison, the ruins of which can still be seen, and host to Chinese diplomats and merchants.

Today, Khovd is the most developed of the western *aimag* capitals, a bustling town of students, businessmen, and visiting farmers and herders. There is a large number of proficient English-speakers in Khovd, thanks to the presence of two universities and the regional offices for a number of development organizations. Despite this, Khovd's tourism sector is not as well developed as neighboring Bayan Ulgii's, and getting the most out of the *aimag* may require a bit more legwork and patience on the part of the traveler. The experience will be worth it, however.

Flanked by the Buyant Gol and several distinctive mountains, Khovd offers both ample outdoor activities and the conveniences that come with well-populated areas. Khovd has a number of decent restaurants, hotels, and well-stocked shops, making it a good place to stop and rest or restock before the next leg of your journey.

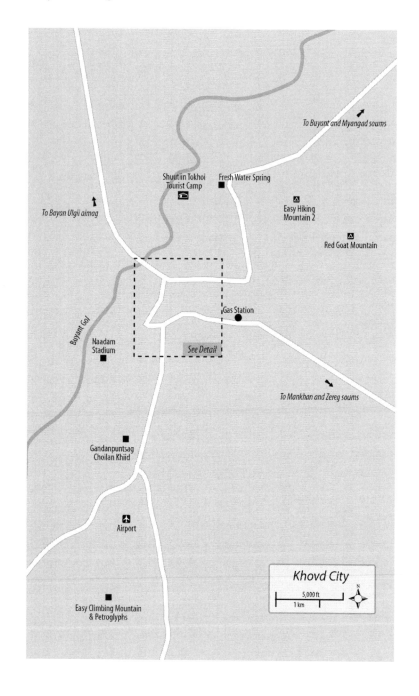

To Buyant and Myangad soums

Shuutiin Tokhoi
Tourist Camp

Fresh Water Spring

Easy Hiking
Mountain 2

To Bayan Ulgii aimag

Red Goat Mountain

Buyant Gol

Gas Station

Naadam
Stadium

See Detail

To Mankhan and Zereg soums

Gandanpuntsag
Choilan Khiid

Airport

Khovd City

5,000 ft
1 km

N

Easy Climbing Mountain
& Petroglyphs

The Guide

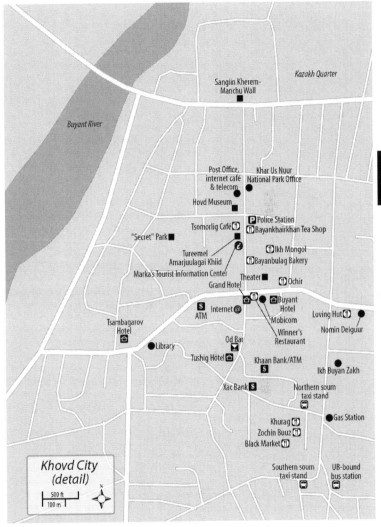

Khovd City
(detail)

500 ft
100 m

Buyant River

Kazakh Quarter

Sangiin Kherem-
Manchu Wall

Post Office,
internet café
& telecom

Khar Us Nuur
National Park Office

Hovd Museum

Police Station

Tsomorlig Café

Bayankhairkhan Tea Shop

"Secret" Park

Ikh Mongol

Tureemel
Amarjuulagai Khiid

Bayanbulag Bakery

Marka's Tourist Information Center

Theater

Ochir

Grand Hotel

Buyant
Hotel

ATM

Internet

Tsambagarov
Hotel

Mobicom

Loving Hut

Winner's
Restaurant

Nomin Delguur

Library

Od Bar

Tushig Hotel

Khaan Bank/ATM

Ikh Buyan Zakh

Xac Bank

Northern soum
taxi stand

Khurag

Gas Station

Zochin Buuz

Black Market

Southern soum
taxi stand

UB-bound
bus station

*More Information Online*

To find the most thorough cache of information about Khovd available in one place, head to www.gohovd.com. The website was created by a team of local Mongolians in cooperation with resident Peace Corps volunteers and covers just about all there is to know about Khovd, from its history to geography and which ethnic groups live in which *soums*.

## GETTING THERE

### By Air

Khovd is served by numerous flights from Ulaanbaatar each week: three on Aeromongolia and daily on Eznis. Mongolian Airlines also has three flights a week. Tickets are expensive, as can be expected for western Mongolia.

The airport is about five kilometers (3 miles) from Khovd's square. Taxis will bring you there for about MNT3,500, although they often ask for more.

### By Land

Buses are the recommended form of land travel to Khovd. For the most part, they are more comfortable than *purgons*. However, they are often tightly packed with people and baggage in the aisle, and you might have an unfortunate soul rest their head in your lap if you have an aisle seat. Ask not to be placed in the two rows of seats in the rear; they are as unpleasant as any *purgon*. Buses average about 40 hours between Khovd and UB. *Purgons* tend to be even slower. The buses generally arrive in the middle of the night and drop passengers off at the square; if it arrives after dawn it will likely go direct to the bus stand by the market. *Purgons* typically drop each passenger off at their respective homes or hotels. A bus ticket will set you back MNT60,000. *Purgons* are a little more.

Buses heading to and from UB leave on Monday, Wednesday, and Friday. In Khovd, the bus departs from a small parking lot near the market. Buy tickets in the small green trailer in the rear corner. Khovd-bound buses leave from the Dragon Center in UB. In either city, it is best to buy a ticket a day or two in advance, although you can get a ticket the day of. Still, the earlier you get a ticket, the better your seat tends to be. In Khovd, you may be able to buy a ticket as much as a week in advance, but the drivers don't all adhere to the same policy on this, and some will tell you to come closer to the departure date.

### By Shared Transportation

*Purgons* heading to UB leave from the same place as the buses in Khovd. To catch a ride from Ulaanbaatar in a purgon, go to the southeast parking lot at Naraantuul Market.

*Purgons* and Russian Jeeps also leave from Khovd to several other western Mongolian destinations on a regular basis. Vehicles travel to Bayan Ulgii daily (MNT20,000) and to Ulaangom in Uvs *aimag* once or twice a week (MNT18,000). Cars headed to Altai in Govi-Altai or Uliastai in Zavkhan can be found at the beginning and end of Khovd University's holidays, when students return to their hometowns (usually in February, early June, and late August). Vehicles to all of these destinations wait for passengers opposite the market's main entrance. Look for the sign in the window to tell you where each car is headed.

## GETTING AROUND THE AIMAG

Shared vehicles travel between Khovd city and the *soums* regularly. The nearest villages have daily drivers while *soums* further afield might send a few cars a week. For *soums* to the north of the city (Buyant, Myangad, Erdeneburen, and Khovd soums), check at the market's main entrance. Drivers don't use signs for these destinations, so you'll have to ask around. For southern *soums*, check on the far side of the market, across the street from the billiard tables.

## WHERE TO STAY

### Hotels

**Tsambagarov Hotel (Цамбагарав)**The lux rooms here live up to the label; they are spacious, airy, and well furnished. The simple rooms (MNT25,000-30,000), which are underwhelming, definitely get less attention. The smaller rooms share a toilet. Finding the bathroom in the maze of hallways could be a challenge during the first night of your stay. The lux rooms (MNT30,000-40,000) have hot water in the evenings. There is also a decent restaurant and a karaoke room on the first floor. *99979858, 99432424*

**Tushig Hotel (Тушиг)** One of the less obvious hotels in town but also one of the nicest, especially for the price. The lux and half lux rooms (MNT25,000) have a few odd Mongolian decorative touches but are otherwise very nice. They also have water heaters in the bathrooms, ensuring hot showers whenever you wish. The standard rooms (MNT16,000) are nothing special but are slightly roomier than most other hotels'. The standard rooms share a toilet, and there is a shower room on the first floor that you can use for MNT1,000. The tiled, vertical layout sets it apart from the stocky communist-built Mongolian hotels and makes it feel more like a South Asian guesthouse. *Ask for Gantuya. 99430044, 95739310; obatzorig99@yahoo.com*

**Buyant Hotel (Буянт)** Probably the most popular hotel in Khovd. It is located in the exact center of the downtown area. Most of the rooms have private bathrooms and showers, although not necessarily hot water. Lux rooms are MNT40,000 while half lux and standard rooms are MNT30,000. There are also dorm rooms with a shared bathroom for MNT10,000-12,000. The restaurant on the first floor is okay;

the Buyant also offers internet access for MNT600 per hour. *99049043; buyanthotel@yahoo.com*

**Grand Hotel** Until recently, this hotel seemed more popular with Mongolians than foreign tourists. However, renovations have increased both the quality and price of the rooms (lux MNT60,000, standard MNT50,000), making this very conveniently located hotel at the edge of the square somewhat more appealing, unless you're a budget traveler. In an effort to provide some real value for your *tugrik*, the Grand now boasts a computer and internet access, along with hot water, in every room. Pretty grand!

## Ger Camps

**Shuutiin Tokhoi Tourist Camp** This camp is just a 15-minute drive down the Buyant Gol from the *aimag* center. Shuutiin Tokhoi is popular among local Mongolians for picnics. It offers a good place to get started hiking on some of Khovd's most characteristic rust-red mountains, and it has facilities for some of the favorite Mongolian team sports, including an outdoor basketball court. The camp can also arrange horse treks, sightseeing tours, and introductions to Mongolian culture. One of the managers, Bayarkhuu, speaks a bit of English. A *ger* with two to four beds is MNT10,000, and the staff will provide you with three meals a day for an additional MNT12,000 per person. *Ask for Bayarkhuu or Nyamdorj. 99438200; bayarkhuu@yahoo.com*

**Khar Sairiin Tourist Camp** Somewhat further afield, this new tourist camp 50 kilometers (31 miles) west of the *aimag* center has accommodations in rugged-looking two- to -four-bed cabins made of stone (MNT15,000). The surrounding area is full of mountains, green alpine pastures, a rushing mountain river, and a waterfall. The owners can organize horse and camel rides, lead you to fishing spots, or introduce you to neighboring nomad families. Be forewarned that the bathroom situation, at the time of research, was quite rustic, and by that we mean there was not yet even an outhouse. *Ask for Otgonbayar. 88439191*

# WHERE TO EAT

## Restaurants

**Loving Hut** The only location of the international, spiritually guided vegetarian restaurant chain in western Mongolia, Loving Hut is a welcome respite from countryside and highway *guanz* food. They make a wide selection of stir-fries and Mongolian standards, using tofu, gluten, and dehydrated soy substitutes in place of meat. Everything on the menu is good, but the *nashaa tsashaa* is especially tasty and has a rare kick of spice. The *tsoivan* proves that traditional Mongolian food doesn't have to be mediocre. As an added bonus in the convenience department, their menu is written in English (although none of the staff speaks any English), and the manager is conversational in German. ₮

**Tsomorlig Café (Цоморлиг)** This café near the museum is small but pleasant and serves good *khurags*. Try the *donna* (донна), ground meat rolled in an omelet—sort of like a breakfast burrito, Mongolian style. ₮

**Bayanbulag Bakery** Although the name would lead you to believe otherwise, Bayanbulag's strengths are the entrees. The *huushuur* is the best in town, and for a cheap but filling fix, the *buudaatai khurag* (stir fried rice) usually has plenty of peppers and other veggies mixed in. ₮

**Ikh Mongol (Их Монгол)** Like the location in Ulaangom, the restaurant seems to try to divert attention from the fact that most of their large menu is unavailable by offering an expansively decorated interior. However, the standard Mongolian options are pretty good when available, and their Chinese dishes are a saucy, tasty way to take a break from straight-up mutton. Ikh Mongol also serves as a bar. ₮₮

**Winner's Restaurant** Below the Grand Hotel, Winner's Mongol-food menu is okay but not spectacular. They do offer a couple decent Korean dishes meant to be shared among friends, and it's a great place to grab a beer or two. ₮₮

**Ochir Restaurant** A relatively new option in Khovd, Ochir is the surefire place to go if you've got a hankering for *schnitzel*, a meat patty fried in an egg batter. They also make good *khurags*. ₮₮

## Guanzes

There is a row of cheap *guanzes* at the market. Not all are created equal. Two of the best are **Zochin Buuz** and **Khurag**.

**Zochin Buuz (Зочин бууз)** This *guanz* serves more than just dumplings as the name might suggest, but the dumplings are as good and cheap as you're likely to find. There are two locations on the strip plus a *khuushuur* house. ₮

**Khurag (Хураг)** Makes good stir-fries and the best *donna* in town. ₮

**Bayankhairkhan Tsainii Gazar (Баянхайрхан цайны газар)** This tiny "tea house" (in actuality, it's more of a tea room) next to the police station is easy to miss, but it serves the best *piroshki* around. ₮

## Grocery Stores

**Black market** At the southeast corner of the city's downtown area, the black market has all the staples, plus a wide variety of locally grown and imported fruits and vegetables.

**Ikh Buyan Zakh (Их буян зах)** A large pink building slightly north of the black market and across from the university dorms, this is a good place to stock up on fruit, especially during winter.

**Nomin Delguur (Номин дэлгүүр)** At the intersection further north from the black and pink markets, Nomin is a grab bag of foreign goods. Supplies are never guaranteed, but come on the right day and you might find peanut butter, real European cheese, Korean marinades, or cake frosting, among other exciting discoveries.

The Guide

# WHAT TO DO IN KHOVD AIMAG

If you happen to be in Khovd during the school year (September-May) on a Wednesday night, a good place to start is the weekly **Monglish event**. This informal bilingual club meets over dinner each week to give foreigners, mainly volunteers and development workers, living in Khovd a chance to practice speaking Mongolian and interested Mongolians an opportunity to speak some English. The Mongolians that attend Monglish range from teachers and students to conservation experts and military officers. It's a great place to meet some locals who speak a little (or a lot of) English and may be willing to help you out during your travels as well as to find out more about life in Khovd. The event is generally held each Wednesday evening at 7:00 p.m. at the Bayanbulag Bakery, but time and place are subject to change. The Buyant Hotel restaurant is a common fallback if the bakery has a special event going on.

Khovd's small **museum** (MNT3,000; open Monday-Friday 8:00 a.m. to 5:00 p.m. with a one-hour lunch break starting at noon) sets itself apart with its exhibit of traditional costumes, representing the many ethnic groups found in the *aimag*. It also has a model of the city during the Manchu period, which may prove interesting to those who spend a bit more time here.

Check in front of the **theater** for signs advertising performances. You may catch a dull variety-show style night of professional, Casio keyboard backed karaoke, or you may be lucky and get to see a night of *khoomii* sung by local masters or spirited Kazakh folk music.

If you walk north from the theater past the museum, you'll eventually run into **Sangiin Kherem**, the ruins of the old Manchu military outpost. The ruins aren't in very good shape these days; no trace of the buildings that once filled the earthen walls remain, and the wall itself is crumbling in many places. If you think for a moment about the era of the Manchu occupation or the state of contemporary Chinese-Mongolian relations, you'll understand why the ruins are in such disrepair. It's worth seeing simply because one day there will be nothing left at this historic site.

The area surrounding the ruins is Khovd's **Kazakh quarter**, and it's worthwhile to take a look around to appreciate this little island of Kazakh culture among the *aimag's* larger Mongolian population. There was a new mosque being built near the post office at the time of research, but there's no saying when it will be completed.

Not to be left out of the religious revival, a new Buddhist monastery, **Gandanpuntsag Choilan Khiid (Гандаппунцаг чойлон хийд)**, was also built in 2009-2010 on the road to the airport. A wall of stupas donated by local and national businesses surrounds the monastery, and the doors in the wall surrounding the courthouse lead to the monks' quarters. Several impressive new temples are within. The whole affair is much larger than the old **Tureemel Amarjuulagai Khiid (Түүрээмэл амаржуулагай хийд)**, which is located near the museum.

While you're checking out the new Gandan monastery, make an afternoon out of it and hike another 4.5 kilometers (3 miles) to the small mountain behind the airport emblazoned with the *soyombo*, Mongolia's national symbol. You'll have to detour towards the river to avoid the airfield. Hike to the backside of the mountain, where, with a pair of sharp eyes, you'll spot some petroglyphs of deer and other animals. After just a few minutes of easy climbing to the top of the mountain, you'll find an *ovoo* and good views of the city and Buyant River.

If you follow the Buyant Soum-Uvs Aimag road northeast out of town for just less than 5 kilometers (3 miles), there is a **fresh water spring**, bubbling up from the middle of a carved stone turtle. Locals claim the water is good for the head, while a spring a few meters off is beneficial for the stomach. While the water is certainly cool and refreshing, we're not sure how much it will actually benefit the traveler's stomach. Across the road from the spring is another **low-slung mountain** that is easy to climb. A round trip from the center of town to the spring and across this ridge should take just about 3 hours plus whatever time you spend hanging out at the spring.

For a more challenging climb, tackle **Red Goat Mountain (Ямаат улаан уул)**, the craggy monolith almost due east from the center of town. The ridge that juts out towards the city is easy to climb and provides a nice enough view, although you'll want to leave a wide berth around the white-walled prison that sits near its base. Follow the ridge towards the main spire, however, and you'll soon find yourself shimmying up a tricky mountain with numerous false peaks. Getting to the top of Red Goat and back will take at least 5 hours, and possibly longer if you choose a more difficult line to the top. A new staircase built into the eastern side of Red Goat Mountain provides a less strenuous approach up.

If you're looking for a walk without an incline, the **Buyant River (Буянт гол)** on the west side of town is a popular spot among locals in all seasons. During summer, though, there is non-stop action there as people picnic and play football near the bridge. Residents of the *aimag* center and nearby Buyant Soum move to camps along the river north of town in summer, dotting the plain with *gers*. Wander through and you very well may be invited to share some tea or a fresh bowl of sheep innards.

## Nightlife

If you're in search of a place to get your dance on, **Od Bar (Од бар)** is the disco of choice among Khovd's university students. The recently renovated bar has a pair of large, aluminum foil-wrapped pillars in the center of the dance floor, making it feel a bit like you're grooving inside a giant robot Halloween costume. The DJ plays hip-hop and Kazakh pop early in the night and gives way to techno as the night wears on.

**Naran Tuv (Наран төв)** has a large nightclub on the second floor, but the place is nearly guaranteed to get sketchy at about 11:30 p.m. Watch out for flying chairs. Both discos close by midnight, so don't spend all evening pre-gaming if you're dying to get funky.

### Shopping

A local English teacher, Marima, recently opened **Marka's Tourist Information Center** (99079485), which includes an internet café and arts shop focusing on Kazakh embroidery. She sells attractive and high quality bags, pillowcases, and tapestries that she and a handful of local Kazakh women make. Her recycled tapestry purses are especially unique. Marima is also a great source of information about sights around Khovd and can help arrange drivers and translators for your trip.

## WHAT TO DO AROUND KHOVD AIMAG

### Munkhkhairkhan Soum (Мөнххайрхан сум)

The *soum* center is a five- or six-hour Jeep drive from Khovd city. There are several routes to get there, but the most interesting and most challenging leads you past Mankhan Soum and along a river through a deep mountain gorge. As you leave the flat plains and journey deeper into the relatively thick wetland forest that covers the gorge's floor, the sense of unknown adventure awaiting you is palpable.

Monkhkhairkhan Soum, nestled along the river at the far end of the gorge, is also home to the Monkhkhairkhan Strictly Protected Area office, where you can pay the MNT3,000 entry fee for the park. The office also serves as a hotel, and it has a couple of beds in a clean, bright room. Like most countryside hotels, there is an outhouse but no running water. The park staff is a great resource and should be able to point you towards the area's geographical highlights, and may be able to help you find a car and driver for adventures further afield if you've taken a shared taxi from the market in Khovd.

**Munkhkhairkhan Strictly Protected Area (Мөнххайрхан уул)** easily rivals Bayan Ulgii's Tavan Bogd in terms of pure, rugged beauty. The area is a virtual treasure chest of snow-capped mountains shimmering like diamonds, sparkling sapphire glacial lakes, and valleys that follow rivers banked by emerald grass and golden rocky outcroppings. The crown jewel is of course Munkhkhairkhan Uul itself,

Mongolia's second tallest at 4,362 meters (14,311 feet). The mountain is a less challenging climb than Tavan Bogd, but you'll still want a guide and some climbing gear for its eternally snowy peak. It shouldn't be too difficult with some asking around to locate Erkhembayar (Эрхэмбаяр), a local resident who has climbed Monkhkhairkhan 44 times and once guided former President Enkhbayar to the top. Erkhembayar will take groups of any size up the mountain for $200.

Travelers who want to climb without the hassle and intensity of the 14,000 foot summit can set off in virtually any direction and find something worth hiking before long, even from the village at **Munkhkhairkhan Soum (Мөнххайрхан сум)** center. The mountains in this area are home to a number of species to keep an eye out for, including wolf, ibex, and the rare snow leopard.

### Tsambagarav Uul National Park (Цамбагарав уул)

Somewhat closer to the *aimag* center than Munkhkhairkhan, other excellent options for serious hiking and climbing are the 4,202-meter (13,786-feet) Tsambagarav Mountain and the surrounding hills. Completing the triumvirate of Mongolia's tallest peaks, Tsambagarav is not a tremendously difficult technical hike, but like its taller mates, it is covered in snow year round and does require climbing gear and due care.

Visible from the main road between Khovd and Bayan Ulgii, it makes most sense to hire a driver in the *aimag* center and head straight for the mountain; the trip should take about three hours. The mountain is, naturally, within the national park that that bears its name, so stop by the national parks office across from the post office in Khovd to pay the MNT3,000 fee before leaving town. The area is entirely worthy of a multi-day hiking trip, but there are no *ger* camps or other accommodations, so bring a tent, warm sleeping bag, and all the food and supplies you'll need.

While it's entirely unnecessary to stop in **Erdeneburen Soum (Эрдэнэбүрэн сум)**, the nearest village, before venturing to the mountain, if you do find yourself in the vicinity, there are some enticing ridges running along the far side of the *soum* that would be great to hike. With the help of some locals, you can find a very popular summer fishing and picnicking spot along the river, where the rapids roar and cliffs rise up from the water like something along the Colorado in the American southwest. The rapids are just beyond an old Soviet-made reservoir about an hour outside of Erdeneburen Soum.

### Khar Us Nuur National Park (Хар ус нуур) "Black Water Lake"

Close enough to the *aimag* center for a day trip, Khar Us Nuur is a major migratory bird sanctuary, a crucial element of western Mongolia's great lakes region, and the second largest freshwater lake in the country. The lake is, in a way, at the envirospiritual heart of northern Khovd Aimag, and it is a feature that many locals will suggest you see. The Khovd River as well as the Buyant River, which provides the *aimag* center, Khovd, and Buyant soums with their drinking and irrigation water, feed Khar Us Nuur.

The lake itself is relatively shallow and has few true beaches; most of the lakeshore is marshland, mud, and muck. As a result, the area is prime real estate for migratory waterfowl in search of summer homes. Khar Us is an excellent destination for birdwatchers, and there is an observation tower for just this purpose on the southwestern side of the lake not far from the main road towards Ulaanbaatar. But be warned that spending prolonged periods of time at the lake during summer may very well lead to insanity. You'll certainly at least appear to have gone off the edge as you flail wildly non-stop to ward off the plague of mosquitoes that also reside by the lake's edge, especially if you've made the mistake of wearing short sleeves, shorts, or neglected to bring a industrial-strength insect repellent. You might want to do as the locals do: bring a hand towel to wear on your neck, and swing at the pests.

Because of the mosquitoes, Khar Us Nuur is not recommended for overnight camping—if you do camp, pay the MNT3,000 fee at the parks office in Khovd—and is perhaps a more popular destination for Mongolians in winter. Once the cold sets in, the whole lake freezes over. The solid surface makes a perfectly smooth roadway, and many nomad families set up their *gers* among the reed beds, where there is ample fodder and easy access to water for the animals. Winter is also the best time for fishing on Khar Us Nuur; during summer the outlying marshes are nearly impassable. Of course, there are no ice-fishing shacks on the lake, so most fishing trips last about as long as birdwatching trips do in the summer, thanks to the cold.

The other feature of the national park that has lodged itself firmly in Khovd's consciousness is **Jargalant mountain (Жаргалант уул)**. Rising to 3,797 meters (12,457 feet) from the flatlands surrounding the lake, Jargalant Uul is impressive; there are no other major peaks to be found for miles. When you see paintings of a mountain in Khovd homes, hotels, and restaurants, chances are it is Jargalant. The mountain should wear a mantle of snow all through summer, but climate change may be changing this. Still, the mountain is an important habitat for wildlife, including snow leopards. Furthermore, a clear ascent makes Jargalant easier to summit than some of the other great mountains in the region.

The best way to approach Jargalant is from the east, meaning you'll have to wrap around the southern slope of the mountain and head back north towards **Chandmani Soum (Чандмань сум)**. Approximately five hours from Khovd, the main Ulaanbaatar road takes you most of the way. Once you've swung off the main road and back towards the mountain, you might as well treat yourself to a bonus stop in Chandmani. Not far from the foot of Jargalant mountain, Chandmani also yields a view of **Khar Nuur (Хар нуур)** and **Durgun Nuur (Дөргөн нуур)**. Best of all, Chandmani is the homeland of Mongolian *khoomii*, known in English as throat singing or overtone singing.

Nearly every male resident in Chandmani can sing at least a bar or two of *khoomii*, and several true masters of the art live there. One is Tserendavaa, a state honored *khoomii* singer. He has toured Asia and Europe to perform, but of the handful or so *khoomii* singers to win Mongolia's top prize for the arts, only Tserendavaa resides permanently in the countryside. A number of foreign musicians and scholars have come to Chandmani to study *khoomii* with Tserendavaa and some of the other great local singers. In 2010, a new *khoomii* palace was built in the middle of the village to hold concerts and promote the art form.

Chandmani doesn't have much in the way of *guanze*s or accommodations, but it does have a few decently stocked shops, and you may be able to score a guest room in a wing of the hospital for about MNT5,000 per person. There is ample space to camp around the *soum* center.

### Mankhan Soum (Манхан сум)

Mankhan *soum*, 80 kilometers (50 miles) south of the *aimag* center, is notable mainly as the home of **Gurvan Tsenkheriin Agui (Гурван цэнхэрийн агуй)**, a series of caves in the mountains outside of the village. The area has been inhabited for tens of thousands of years, as evidenced by the paintings that grace the walls of a handful of chambers in the caves, dating between 12,000 and 40,000 years old. The paintings show a host of animals that captured prehistoric Mongolia's attention, including ibex, camels, and more, all rendered in ochre. The best pictures can be tricky to spot, and of course, the exhibition hall is a dark, unlit cave, so a flashlight is essential and a local guide is recommended.

### Durgun Soum (Дөргөн сум)

Located not on the banks of Durgun Nuur as the name implies but on Khar Us Nuur, Durgun is a quiet village with perhaps the best access to the lake's waters. The trip to the *soum* is nice enough; at one point, when you drop down from the higher surrounding area to the basin that the lake sits in, you have a view of the lake flanked by mountains in a number of shades of white, red, and black. Add in the blue of the water and the green of the grass, and you've got nearly the full spectrum. Sunset

The Guide

along this stretch is always gorgeous as the retreating rays paint the reeds and *gers* in rich, golden light.

There is a small monastery in the *soum* center, although it has seen better days in its short lifespan. If you plan to stay the night, the Durgun Hotel on the edge of town has beds for MNT5,000 per person. The staff will cook you a meal for a few thousand *tugrik* extra.

## Khovd Soum (Ховд сум)

Forty-five kilometers (27 miles) northwest of Khovd city, Khovd Soum is the *aimag's* all-Kazakh village. There isn't much to do there, other than mingle with random locals and pick-a-peak-and-go style hiking, and there isn't much to see. Nevertheless, it is an interesting place to go if you want to get a sense of the impact that emigration to Kazakhstan has had on the local population. Since 1990, scores of families have left this area in search of better opportunities in their "spiritual homeland," and more will leave in the foreseeable future. The result is a village where vacant homes and yards have been taken down, leaving very obvious holes in this small community snuggled into the surrounding mountains.

If you are interested in local Kazakh life, however, a resident by the name of Tilek speaks phenomenal English and will be more than happy to work as your guide and translator in the *soum* or in the countryside around it. He may even be able to track down an eagle hunter or two for you. His home is near the small collection of shops and administrative buildings once you enter the village; any resident should be able to direct you towards it.

## Buyant Soum (Буянт сум)

A quick and easy 25-kilometer (15-mile) drive over a paved road, Buyant Soum is surely one of the most ethnically diverse communities in Mongolia. You'll find a healthy Kazakh population there as well as pockets of all the Mongolian ethnic minorities and a few Tuvans and Uzbeks to boot. If you've somehow made it all the way to western Mongolia and still haven't seen a typical *soum*, Buyant makes a good day trip.

During the summer, most of Buyant's residents move to seasonal camps and vegetable fields upstream in between the *aimag* center and the village. They are responsible for growing a large bulk of the fruits and vegetables that Khovd is famous for,-and the local Kazakhs make a great cantaloupe jam from them.

Buyant makes a great starting point (or destination) for a long, mostly flat day hike to the *aimag* center. We recommend taking a shared taxi from the Khovd market the afternoon before the hike. Taxis leave between 2:00 and 5:00 p.m. and cost MNT3,000. Set up camp along the river, and in the morning, head upstream. After the two small bridges on the main paved road, just be sure to keep the water on your right and the road on your left, and you'll never get lost. After six hours or so of hiking past sparkling river channels and friendly locals working their vegetable patches, you'll be right back in the *aimag* center.

## Must Soum (Мөст сум)
This small village 180 kilometers (111 miles) south of the *aimag* center is home to the surprise of surprises: a small, rural Buddhist monastery run by a lama fluent in English. The lama, named Sansarbat, is the sole caretaker of the temple and welcomes all visitors, tourists included, and exudes positive vibes. He also keeps a large collection of religious scrolls once read by the thirteenth Dalai Lama. This sleepy hamlet may provide the perfect chance to explore Mongolian Buddhism.

## Bulgan Soum (Булган сум)
Bulgan is the largest *soum* in Khovd, due largely to its location on the border with China. If you're looking to get about as far away from anything as possible, this is the place to come. A sliver of the district has been set aside as the **Bulgan Gol Natural Reserve**, incorporated to protect a small population of beavers and a few other

### T. Samdanjigmed

For centuries, Mongolia, its people, and its rugged environment have been nearly inseparable from each other. The culture and temperament of Mongolians has long been dictated by the reality that survival is nature's sometimes begrudging gift to man. In the modern era, planned and then capitalist economies turned Mongolia's focus from the natural balance to the balance of bank accounts, resulting in some unfortunate consequences for the country's environment.

That's where people like Samdanjigmed, known to his friends as Saagii, come in. Since graduating from Khovd University in 2006, Saagii has worked for the Association TAKH, a French organization that partners with the World Wildlife Fund in Mongolia to re-establish *takhi* populations in the wild. *Takhi*, also known as Przewalski's horse, are a wild strain of horse native to Mongolia that went extinct on the steppes in the 1970s. Thanks to the work of the Association TAKH and Mongolian conservationists, there are now several small but steadily growing *takhi* herds in Hustai National Park near Ulaanbaatar and in Khomiin Tal on the border between Khovd and Zavkhan aimags.

Saagii's job isn't simply to keep the *takhi* healthy and protected but also to help area herders preserve the increasingly precarious balance between nature and man, market and ecology. "When I was working as a community development officer, I organized trainings [to] improve livestock practices and develop reliable outlets for livestock products and expand alternative activities to diversify income," Saagii says. "Now as an assistant rangeland officer, I conduct vegetation studies to evaluate pasture health. This research will allow us to implement adaptive rangeland management techniques in Khomiin Tal"—hopefully keeping both animal and man in the balance.

species of large rodents. Otherwise, there is plenty of space for camping and hiking, and several decent hotels for MNT10,000-25,000 per room around the village center.

The trip to Bulgan can be arduous; in the typical Russian Jeep, it's a 12-hour drive at least. But the trip takes you through a fabulous mountain pass where you might be lucky enough to spy some ibex, and you'll pass the **Altai** and **Uyench Soum** centers as well. Uyench in particular has some great camping spots near the river a few kilometers from town.

It is rumored that the Bulgan border crossing into Xinjiang is now open to foreigners. Thus far, it seems like more of a rumor than anything, and there are a few logistical obstacles to enter China—you'd need a Chinese visa to make the crossing, and the border station only works about two weeks out of every month. However, if the rumors prove to be reality, it opens up all sorts of new possibilities for adventure. Try checking with the Chinese embassy in Ulaanbaatar before banking on being able to hop into China from Khovd.

# Khuvsgul Aimag (Хөвсгөл аймаг)

Khuvsgul (pronounced "hooves-ghoul") is the most northern *aimag* and easily one of the most scenic in the country. At 692 kilometers (430 miles) from Ulaanbaatar, it is a land of pristine lakes, icy mountain streams, and soaring lush green taiga. Many travelers come to Mongolia just to get to Khuvsgul Aimag, where they can fish, hike, and ride horses around the **Khuvsgul Nuur**, observe the **Tsataan** or so-called "reindeer people" who live in teepees, or participate in the winter **Ice Festival**. If you're in Mongolia during the summer and enjoy ultra marathons, look up **Toilogt Tour Camp**. The proceeds go to protecting the Khuvsgul park.

In addition to the gorgeous lake, you can see cave paintings and over **100 Deer Stones** dating back to the Stone and Bronze ages. There are also museums, the ruins of **Munkh Khan's palace**, and more contemporary Mongolian history.

Unlike most places in Mongolia, you don't necessarily have to start your trip from UB to reach Khuvsgul, so this could be a good opportunity to hit a few destinations along the way. You can start by traveling from UB to Darkhan (MNT5,000-15,300) and then travel on to Erdenet (MNT4,000-12,000; 6 hours) by train before you come to Khuvsgul. The ride to Khuvsgul from Erdenet (MNT25,000; 10 hours) is especially bumpy the whole way, so even if you don't normally get car sick, you will want to take some Dramamine and do your best to sit facing forward.

Due to the large tourism pull in Khuvsgul, you are more likely to find English-speakers here than in most areas in Mongolia. You can head first to the *aimag* capital Murun. For there, arrange more travel and services with the **Tourist Information Center** located within the local library, with local guesthouses, or with Bob, the founder of the **Khuvsgul Youth Human Rights Association** who donates the majority of his time to helping youth while living off his summer income as a guide.

## MURUN SOUM (МӨРӨН СУМ)

Murun is the *aimag* capital of Khuvsgul and has held the record for being the coldest in the country, though Uvs residents also claim this title. The settlement of Murun was developed around Murungiin Khuree Khiid between 1809 and 1811 on the banks of the Delgermurun Gol. In the beginning of the twentieth century, the population at the monastery peaked at around 1,300 lamas. In 1933, Murun became the administrative center of the *aimag*, and in 1937 the monastery was tragically destroyed.

For today's visitors, the town is mostly just a rendezvous point for traveling to the lake and the *aimag* administrative center.

The Guide

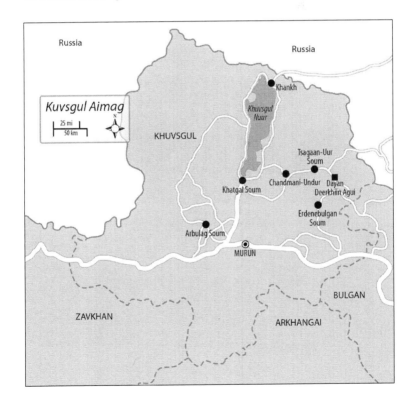

## GETTING THERE

### By Air

EZnis airways flies to Murun three days a week. The MIAT and Air Mongolia companies conduct flights to Murun every weekday and to Khatgal Soum three days a week.

### By Bus

Daily buses from Ulaanbaatar, Erdenet, and Darkhan depart at 12:00 noon. The bus from Ulaanbaatar (MNT26,500) leaves from the Dragon Center. You'll need to buy your ticket one (or sometimes two) days in advance. The trip takes over 24 hours.

### By Shared Transportation

Probably the fastest overland trip is by *purgon* from the Dragon Center. Prices usually run around MNT30,000, making it slightly more expensive than the bus. Moreover, *purgons* are often packed to the gills with people, making the ride less comfortable than the bus. Tickets to UB are booked at Murun's bus station located behind the market.

From Erdenet, a *purgon* costs MNT25,000, takes about ten hours, and is extremely bumpy. Some Dramamine and a forward-facing seat are recommended. Sometimes, you can catch a direct ride from Darkhan (MNT30,000; 16 hours). It's

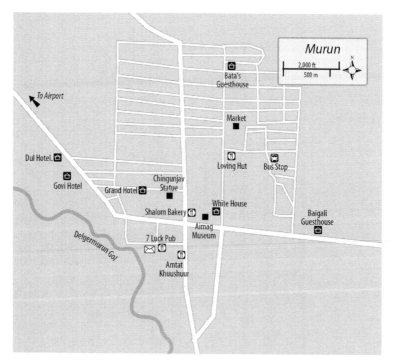

nearly impossible to guarantee a ride from Murun to Erdenet or Darkhan, but it does happen. You can take a chance and ask around at the bus station.

## By Private Transportation

You can make arrangements at the Dragon Center or Narantuul in UB and at the market in Murun. You may want to make these arrangements a couple of days in advance if you can. The prices range anywhere from MNT100,000 to MNT150,000 plus petrol, so you'll need to negotiate to get the best deal, but even that will cost you a fair sum.

## Hitchhiking

Since there is relatively heavy traffic toward Khuvsgul and the lake, hitchhiking is a real possibility if you'll be wandering near the main roads. Remember to negotiate before you get in.

## GETTING AROUND THE AIMAG

You can book much of the travel yourself. From the market, you can hire private drivers or rent a private *mikr*, and, if you go in with a group of other tourists, you can get a pretty good deal even after paying for the driver's accommodations and the petrol fee (approximately MNT100,000 for 20 liters of fuel). Of course, as with most travel in Mongolia, foreigners are quoted higher prices. You could bring a new Mongolian friend to help negotiate a better price; maybe someone you meet at 50° 100° restaurant's English Corner meeting would be willing to help out. Still, there's plenty of transportation to get you where you want to go, whether it's to see the deer stones (MNT10,000; 25 minutes) or to get to Khatgal (MNT70,000; 3 hours), a truly remote and enchanting destination. A private car or Jeep can be rented from the market or taxi station. These vehicles are priced the same as a *mikr*.

## WHERE TO STAY

**Bata's Guesthouse** Next to the market. It is one of the best places to stay and our favorite because of the great staff and low price. This guesthouse consists of two *gers* with five beds each and one house with eight beds. The cost is approximately $4 per night. Breakfast and hot shower are included. Other meals and internet are also available. Additionally, the owner, Bata speaks excellent English and is very friendly. *91387080; bata_guesthouse@yahoo.com*

**Dul Hotel (50° 100°)** In the center of town, this is the fanciest hotel around. The standard, half lux, and lux rooms range from MNT10,000-30,000 per person per night, and all have cable TVs in the rooms. Lux and half lux rooms have a mini-bar. Available services include a billiards room, laundry services, sauna, and a good restaurant. They also run *ger* camps in Khatgal and on the banks of the Delgermurun Gol at the outskirts of Murun, where you can eat traditional Mongolian meals. *013812-22206; www.dul.mn*

**Govi Hotel** Located on the western outskirts of Murun close to the monastery on the way to the airport. They offer standard, half lux, and lux rooms. Prices range from MNT12,000-25,000 per night. You can also choose to stay in a *ger* for MNT8,000-12,000 per night. If you haven't had an opportunity to stay in a *ger* yet, it is a fun experience for a night or two, but this is not the most remote spot. Extra services include VIP karaoke, billiards, laundry, and international phone service. *24509, 99382374*

**White House** Between the circus and the market. White House offers two normal rooms for around MNT6,000 per night. For around MNT15,000, you can stay in one of their seven lux rooms with a shower, TV, and mini fridge. If you are making the trip around the lake, you might want to pay a little extra once you come back to relax, so you can clean up before moving onward and avoid becoming unkempt, stinky foreigner. Extra services include a restaurant, laundry, billiards, and table tennis. *21299, 99388588*

**Baigali Guest House** Located by the Sports Center. Baigali has three *gers* with 15 beds for MNT6,000-25,000. You can cook your own meals and have a shower, and there is a *guanz* on the premises. The staff can also offer assistance with guides and transportation. *9388408*

# WHERE TO EAT

## Restaurants

**50° 100° Restaurant** Located in Dul Hotel. The owner and staff are very supportive of foreign volunteers' efforts and allow Americans to host English Corner there every week. This might be a good place to find Mongolians who speak English and can share with you more intimately about their experience living in Murun. The restaurant serves many good hot dishes and also has a great bakery with the best cinnamon rolls in town as well as other delicious treats. You can even find the occasional cheesecake! The restaurant is conveniently located in the center of town and has a nice, clean, indoor bathroom. ₮₮

**Grand Hotel** The restaurant at Grand Hotel offers great American dishes, including pizza. Like most restaurants in Mongolia, the restaurant does not always have everything on the menu, and if you're interested in pizza, you may have to tell the staff that you can't wait for two hour. Regardless of its limitations, the restaurant always has something that makes the trip worth the effort. It is located behind the police station. ₮₮

**7 Luck Pub** A brand new restaurant. Located next to Chinginjav Square, it is a great place to stop before or after a show. It has a young and friendly atmosphere. You can occasionally help transform it into a little dance spot on Saturday nights as well. ₮

**Шалом (Shalom Bakery)** The friendliest place in town. World Vision helped this Christian bakery get off the ground. They offer several delicious meals as well as great tasty cakes and pastries. On Sunday mornings, they hold church services as well. ₮

### Guanzes

**Цагаан хоол (White Food)** A quaint little *guanz* located next to the market. It serves the best vegetarian meals in town. Unlike some "vegetarian" places in Mongolia, it serves no products containing meat. The service is fast and friendly, and the food is great for the price. ₮

**Амтат хуушуур (Amtat Khuushuur)** Has tasty vegetarian *khuushuur*. You will also find meat *khuushuur* with kimchi and the best milk tea in Murun. ₮

## WHAT TO DO IN MURUN

While you're in Murun, you should visit the *aimag* museum, which houses over 4,000 historical and cultural pieces, including an original shaman outfit and shaman instruments, a mammoth tusk dating back to 100 million years ago, ancient tools and jewelry, Buddhism displays, and much more. Most of the museum is not translated, so you might want to ask at your guesthouse for some help finding a translator.

After the museum, take a walk to visit to the statue of **Davaadorj (Даваадорж)**, one of the most famous soldiers from the area. He earned national honor as a martyr after Chinese soldiers killed him in a Khovd Aimag border incident in 1948. According to the legend, he fought alongside his eight soldiers against as many as 130 enemy troops (perhaps closer to 40, according to some accounts) at the mountain of Baitag Bogd on the western border. He was awarded the posthumous title of "Hero of Mongolia" in 1949. The statue was erected in Murun's main square during a tense time between the two countries in 1968.

Another local hero notable for his military bravado is **Chingunjav (Чингүнжав)** (1710-1757), a nobleman of the Khotgoid clan. His statue, which has stood in front of the circus since 1992, is also a site of interest. As a soldier in the Manchurian army, Chingunjav gained his acclaim in 1756 when he led failed mutinies and popular uprisings in the west against the ruling Manchurian Qing Dynasty. Although his efforts were unsuccessful, 1756 was a year of revolts and riots all over the country, and his legendary rebellions have become part of Mongolian folklore.

Chingunjav was finally captured and brought with much of his family to Beijing to meet with the emperor Qianlong, supposedly for a negotiation. Instead, he and his family were executed, including his 80-year-old mother. His sword and gun were found underneath 13 white *ovoos* close to the center of Arbulag Soum and now reside in the museum in Murun.

The Guide

Continuing on the walking tour of the statues, you can get a feeling for the high status enjoyed by traditional Mongolian wresters in front of the Sport Arena. Though some tourists events and competitions have been organized there since 2002, the main attractions are the statues of three famous Mongolian wrestlers, all from Tsagaan-Uur Soum: Damdin, Tseveenravdan, and Bejin.

**The Uushigiin Uver Deer Stone** is about 20 kilometers (12 miles) to the west of Murun. The site is considered to be one of the most complete and best preserved of all Bronze Age deer stone sites. You can see a complete array of 14 carved standing stones within the remains of sacrificial mounds. On some of the stones you can clearly see exquisite scenes of hunters depicted with bows and arrows, chasing deer, elk, ibex, or argali. The stones even feature entire herds of flying deer, chiseled out in a precise and suggestive style.

# KHATGAL SOUM (ХАТГАЛ СУМ)

Rightfully considered one of the most beautiful places in the country, Khatgal rests at the base of Khuvsgul Nuur and is the most easily accessible from Murun. Though Khuvsgul is often called the "Switzerland of Mongolia," when you pass through Murun, you may wonder who was in charge of the nicknames around here. In Khatgal, however, the moniker fits with just a little imagination. It's a little town nestled amongst rolling hills and patches of evergreen forest with herd animals dotting the green pastures. Years ago, this was a small shipping center between Mongolia and Russia, home to a wool factory and a fuel distribution center with over two hundred trucks. Now, with only around two thousand people living in town, the population is barely a third of what it once was, and only abandoned buildings offer any evidence of its former industry. Since the town is situated at the point where the lake turns into the river, those expecting a lakefront atmosphere may have to travel up the shore a bit, but short hikes along the lake or in the hills offer some wonderful views of the crystalline water.

Since Khatgal is technically part of Khuvsgul Nuur National Park, a few unique restrictions apply to tourists (but are rarely enforced). To enter town you must pass through the park gates and pay a one-time MNT3,000 entrance fee. Camping, horse trips, and fishing require permits, which can usually be acquired through your guesthouse.

There is a surprising lack of options for people who would like to rent a boat— you can try a kayak from MS Guesthouse—but there is the option of taking a two-hour trip on the mighty Sukhbaatar, the as yet unsunk "Titanic of Khuvsgul." It slowly heads north for about 45 minutes, stops, then comes back, but it offers some great views of the lake and may even turn into an aquatic dance party. For tourists, the cost is MNT9,000.

There are a couple places with signs that advertise internet service, and they may actually have access, but the only dedicated internet café in town is on the main road near the school on the south end of the town center. For tourists, it costs MNT1,000 per hour. Access is through a wireless modem, though, so it can get extremely slow when busy.

Definitely make plans to visit the **Ice Festival** held every year sometime after *Tsagaan Sar*. There's skating and fishing, and locals create all manner of fantastic ice sculptures and ice homes. There are also on-ice horse and reindeer sledding competitions and of course lots of sheer natural winter beauty. There are even horseback riding trips along the lakeshore. Occasionally the Tsataan, known for their domestic reindeer herds make an appearance.

### Getting to Khatgal

Cars leave every day except Monday from the back side of the market in Murun (the front of the market is marked by the blaring speakers and large groups of vehicles). Look for the signs on a post or in van windows that says "Хатгал," the *soum*'s name in Cyrillic. Cars usually leave somewhere around 3:00-5:00 p.m., give or take the usual three hours of possible wait time. For tourists it should cost between MNT5,000-10,000, depending on gas prices. For some unexplained reason, getting to Khatgal almost always takes longer than coming from there, but be prepared for a three- to six-hour ride. If you prefer a private car, you can find that at the front of the market; these also typically leave around 5:00 p.m. Private cars are much more expensive and prices vary greatly depending on your negotiation skills.

Going from Khatgal to Murun is much easier. Cars leave from the post office in the morning, between roughly 10:00 a.m. and noon. They can usually pick you up at your guesthouse, too. The trip in, without the fairly common breakdowns and flat tires, can take as little as two and a half hours. Transportation is almost exclusively by *purgons* or microbuses. Some people hitchhike, which seems relatively safe, but it is neither common nor reliable.

### Where to Stay in Khatgal

When you get to Khatgal, you can find many *ger* camps and guesthouses. We recommend you spend the first night in a *ger* camp for around MNT5,000 per person during spring, summer, and fall. The next morning, take the hike to the lake (about two to three kilometers) and find yourself a good camping spot. In the winter, rely on *ger* camps, which are everywhere since it's such an important tourist attraction. We do have a few favorites, though.

**MS Guesthouse** Run by the always capable and gregarious Gambaa, it was one of the first guesthouses in town. *Gers* (MNT7,000 per person per night) and rooms (MNT10,000 per person per night) come with a simple breakfast. The pleasant dining area also offers good Mongolian and some Western food for around MNT3,000 per plate. Laundry is available.

MS shines, however, more for its ability to arrange all sorts of trips, from horseback riding to hiking to even kayaking—two-seat kayaks can also be rented for MNT35,000 per day. Gambaa can get you whatever permits you need as well as arrange plane or bus tickets and private cars to UB. Laundry service (MNT5,000 for a large batch) and hot showers are available. *99796030, 98380366; Lake_hovsgol@yahoo.com*

**Garage 24** Located in a converted factory of sorts. It stands out for its competent staff and its large, pleasant common/dining room. Bunk beds inside or *gers* outside are both $5 per person per night, and both have hot showers. Camping is an option for MNT2,000, though showers are not included (showers are an additional MNT2,000 per person). Food runs from MNT2,000 to 8,000, with basic Mongolian fare to Western options. The service is slow, sometimes up to an hour, since everything is made to order. You can also rent kayaks for about MNT25,000. *011323957, 99118652*

**Nergui's** A small *ger* camp run by the kind, helpful Nergui. It has been under construction recently. Nergui also happens to be a local English teacher, and her English is the best in town. *Gers* are MNT6,000-8,000 per person per night (MNT6,000 if you bring your own sleeping bag, MNT8,000 if not). Hot showers are MNT2,000. Laundry is available, and Nergui's charges by load size. Slow, dial-up internet is available for MNT1,000 per hour. Nergui can also help set up horse trips or anything else you need. Good Mongolian food, including vegetarian options, can be made to order, and there is some Western food, all for MNT2,000-5,000. *99979831, 98189648*

## Where to Eat

There may be one or two places open in the middle of town, serving cheap (MNT1,500-2,500) Mongolian food. If you're lucky, there may even be vegetables with it. In the summer months, there are also a few shacks down by the docks that serve basic fare. If you're really lucky, you may be able to find a temporary *ger* that serves fish *khuushuur*, widely considered the best in town.

For more sophisticated options, try eating at MS Guesthouse for better-than-average Mongolian food for around MNT3,000 per plate. The most upscale eatery in town is Garage 24, which serves a range of options between MNT2,000 and MNT8,000. Though the pizza won't transport you to Italy or New York, the Western options can be a nice change after a few weeks in the countryside.

# WHAT TO DO IN KHUVSGUL AIMAG

The gem of the *aimag* is of course **Khuvsgul Nuur (Хөвсгөл нуур)**, part of the 838,000 hectare, 2,070 acre) Khuvsgul Nuur National Park. "Mother Khuvsgul Lake," or "The Dark Blue Pearl" as it is sometimes called, is not only Mongolia's deepest lake (up to 262 meters or 860 feet deep), but it is surrounded by dozens of mountains 2,000 meters (6,500 feet) high covered in lush forests and pastures teeming with grazing yaks and horses. When you're there, the picturesque setting feels like you're in a movie, the background of which has just been painted around you by an ambitious set designer.

Fed by as many as 111 tributaries, the lake is 2,760 square km (1,715 square mi.), making it the second largest lake by surface area in Mongolia behind Uvs Aimag's saltwater Uvs Nuur. It contains around 380,000 billion liters (100,400 billion gallons) of water, a little less than 2 percent of the world's fresh water. It's the second largest lake in central Asia behind Russia's Lake Baikal to the north, which was created from the same geologic processes and is fed by the Egiin Gol, which flows from Khuvsgul Nurr into the Selenge Gol before reaching Baikal.

Though not as biologically diverse as Baikal, Khuvsgul Nuur is home to taimen, Siberian white fish, Siberian grayling, lenok, umber, Baigali omul, and river perch, making it a fishing paradise. A permit is around $3. You may never be asked to pay unless you're on an organized fishing vessel or tour, but permits can be purchased from guesthouses in Khatgal and the Tourist Information Center in Murun. The lake is also along an important migratory route, so bird lovers may see up to 200 different species, like Baikal teal, barheaded goose, black stork, or Altai snowcock.

Hiking around Lake Khuvsgul is truly stunning and truly difficult, but it's one of the best ways to see the lake and the surrounding mountains. Guesthouses in Murun and Khatgal can give you advice on the best treks given the amount of time you have and will even arrange transport from rendezvous points if necessary. It generally only takes 4 to 5 days to walk around the whole lake if you push it, but you'll need to keep a few things in mind. The near complete thawing of the permafrost terrain in the last few decades often leaves a sloppy marshland surrounding the lake, making it very difficult to maneuver, especially when it rains. Also, the vegetation can be thick at times so you might feel like a modern explorer trailblazing paths that are not always clear or comfortable to trek. When you can, you have to be sure to hug the shoreline as you walk or at least keep your eye on the lake because you can get horribly lost without GPS.

The Guide

The hike is remote, so pack everything you'll need with you and filter your water from the lake. While you are walking, keep your eyes peeled for argali sheep, ibex, bear, sable, and moose that live in the park.

There is a ferry that makes runs between Khatgal on the south and Khankh on the northern shore, which serves as the jumping off point to visit the Tsataan.

**Toilogt Tour Camp** is a nicely furnished tour camp run by Hovsgol Travel and located approximately 30 kilometers (18.6 miles) northwest of Khatgal Soum. There is a smaller lake near Khuvsgul Nuur called Toilogt, which is the namesake of this camp. The company is owned and operated by Mongolians and is dedicated to using creative solutions to protect the environment. In fact, Toilogt is the first camp in Mongolia to use solar energy and every year, the camp organizes the Sunrise to Sunset International Ultra Marathon. All proceeds go to the protection of the national park. They host runners from all over the world who participate in either a full (100-kilometer, 62-mile) or half (42-kilometer, 26.1-mile) ultra marathon. *11460368 (Ulaanbaatar), 98779989, 99115771; info@hovsgoltravel.com; www.hovsgoltravel.com*

## Erdenebulgan Soum (Эрдэнэбулган сум)

Erdenebulgan's *soum* center is located about 115 kilometers (71 miles) or five hours to the northeast of Murun. In 1920, a Danish family settled on this spot and called it "Danish Hill." Close to Danish Hill is a hot spa, which prevents the water of the river from freezing in the winter. Now, there is a small hydropower plant that provides power to the entire village of Erdenebulgan. There are several small but interesting sites around the district. **Tsagaanchuluutiin Ovoo** or "White Rock Ovoo" is about 50 kilometers (31 miles) northwest of the Uushigiin Uver deer stones. This highly unique *ovoo* complex, which has a total of 13 mounds pointing in all four directions, is dedicated to the Mongolian hero Chingunjav.

Erdenebulgan is also home to the ironically small museum of **"Tall Gongor,"** which features information on the giant Undur Gongor, the tallest man to ever live in Mongolia. He measured 2.60 meters (8.5 feet) tall, and you can see pictures of him in the museum.

But the *soum's* most fascinating aspect is the Dukha and Tsataan communities that live far up in the taiga forest. With Mongolian independence, many of the Dukha and Tsataan became part of the independent Republic of Tuva, situated in the far south of Siberia. The Soviet Republic eventually annexed the area in 1944. The Tsataan that now live in Mongolia fled Tuva, the neighboring Russia province, in the 1930s with other groups to avoid being relocated or conscripted by the Russians. At first, the Mongolian government frequently deported them back to Tuva, but in 1956, the groups were granted Mongolian citizenship and resettled near Tsagaan Nuur on the Shishigt Gol.

Now, only 44 Tsataan families remain, comprising between 200 and 400 people. Their lives revolve around the reindeer herds, but since the 1970s, the reindeer population has dropped from near 2,000 to roughly 600 due to changing habitats. No government-supported programs have been able to help the herd numbers, or, in turn, the Tsataan people. Though they have been able to support themselves through tourism, tourism has changed their way of life. Today, it is common for Tsataan families to bring their reindeer and teepees down to tourist sites near the lake. The lichen the reindeer feed off doesn't grow at such southern latitudes, resulting in disease and death.

The Tsataan are not just known for breeding reindeer and living in teepees but are also renowned practitioners of shamanism. They often hold ceremonies and will invite tourists to view for a fee. If you are interested in visiting the Tsataan, it is best to meet with the visitor center in Murun in advance to plan trips with guides that are sensitive to the culture of the reindeer herders while helping to subsidize their income.

The northern *soums* are hard and risky to reach, especially for independent travelers. Though tour companies take travelers through this area, the roads are very difficult in the summer because the ground becomes easily saturated and treacherously muddy. In the winter, the ice road makes traveling smoother, but the ice road is also very dangerous.

## Arbulag Soum (Арбулаг сум)

**Arbulag Soum (Арбулаг сум)** is 60 kilometers (37 miles) northwest of Murun. It was here that **Munkh Khan (Мөнх хаан)** (1208-1258), the eldest son of Chinggis Khan's youngest son Tului and older brother of Khubilai Khan, lived in **Erchuu Palace**. The modest palace was noted by William of Rubruck (Willem van Ruysbroeck) (1210-1270), a Flemish Franciscan monk who wrote the most detailed and valuable accounts of the early Western visitors to the region. On his way to Karakorum to visit Chinggis Khan in his pursuit of converting the Mongols to Christianity, he stopped for a few days to meet with the great khan's grandson and eventual successor (Khubilai Khan) at Erchuu. Now, the ruins include felled walls, towers, and a decipherable basement area. There is also a stone burial mound at the northwest side, along with the remains of a few other buildings that burned to the ground, according to the archaeological evidence. The most valuable find excavated from the site, though, is a statue of Munkh Khan that now stands in Ulaanbaatar's National History Museum. The statue, which was carved during his lifetime, is inscribed with wishes for his long life.

**Khankh (Ханх)** is on the northeastern banks of Khuvsgul Nuur near the border with Russia. There are accommodations in the town, but it's certainly not as tourist-friendly as Khatgal. The 200 kilometer (124 miles) road trip there in the summer can take 10-12 hours. The boat called Sukhbaatar runs from Khatgal to Khankh at varying times, but the best way to reach Khankh is to make a five- to six-day trip on horseback. Contact the MS Guesthouse in Khatgal if you want to plan a tour or stay at their sister camp in Khankh. They can help you book transportation to other northeastern sites as well.

## Tsagaan-Uur Soum (Цагаан-үүр сум)

Northeast from Murun by 180 kilometers (112 miles; 18 hours) on a fairly rough road, Tsagaan-Uur is also a popular horseback destination. A trek there will take five to six days. Tsagaan-Uur is a beautiful town nestled in a densely forested valley where all the houses are made of wood. In the summertime, several different kinds of berries grow and are harvested here for jam, juice, and various tasty desserts. Members of the Buriat ethnic group from eastern Russia make up a large percentage of the town's hard-working population. Of the 18 champions in the history of Mongolian National Wrestling, three of them have come from Tsaagan-Uur. A statue of these three champions stands in front of the circular blue sports palace in Murun.

The most interesting site in the neighborhood is **Dayan Deerkhiin Agui (Даян дээрхийн агүй)**, a cave that was named after a local shaman who fled from Chinggis Khan's soldiers and took refuge here. The cave's many twisting and deep-reaching tunnel branches provided the perfect hide out. To this day, many of the cave's branches remain unexplored. The cave is located on top of a small mountain 50 kilometers (31 miles) southeast of Tsaagan-Uur Soum and only 15 kilometers (9.3 miles) from Dayan Deerkhiin Khiid (N50°26'48.66", E101°53'8.91") along the banks of the Uur Gol. You can expect a brisk 15-minute climb to the cave's mouth, and if you forgot your flashlight or torch, not to worry. There is plenty to see in the front, including more open areas like the stone "*ger*" room. There is no admission fee.

**Chandmani-Undur (Чандмань-Өндөр)** is a quiet town only 5 kilometers (3.2 miles) southeast of Tsagaan-Uur where Chinggis Khan's mother, Oelun is said to have lived. In 1992, a statue of her was placed close to the Arig Gol that follows along the road near the *soum* center (N50°24'59.53", E100°58'31.83"). One of the most famous stories the *Secret History of the Mongols* is the tale of Oelun with her five sons. The boys were always fighting, so she gave each of them an arrow and told them to try to break it. Of course, they did this easily. Then she tied five arrows together and again told them to break the bundle, which, even with great effort, they could not do. In this lesson, she taught her sons about the value of team-work and the fragility of the individual. As a group, they could not be overcome, but any one of them was weak and vulnerable. Thus, the Golden Lineage of Chinggis Khan was built on the strength of alliances.

On the same road, there are six pointed wooden teepees, an *ovoo*, and then six more teepees that represent the 12 signs of the Asian zodiac.

## Bob and the Khuvsgul Youth Human Rights Association

The Khuvsgul Aimag Youth Human Rights Association was founded in May 2010 and has 400 supporting members in the Khuvsgul *aimag* center. Five Mongolian volunteers with educational backgrounds in law, economics, education, and culture run the organzation. These founders are all young people who have returned from UB after graduating from university in order to share their expertise and improve their hometown community.

The mission of this organization is to protect and empower the youth of Khuvsgul Aimag in all areas of their lives through developmental education and to instill a willingness to improve their society through self-empowerment and community service. In April 2011, they opened an office in the apartment complex behind the Dul Hotel. The space is a substance-free location that is open to the public and used to host trainings and events for young people. The organization's members are free to use the space to host any events that benefit the youth of Khuvsgul Aimag.

One of the founders is Byambadorj, also known as "Bob." He graduated with a bachelor's degree in law from the Mongolian National University and is now the director of the Khuvsgul Aimag Youth Human Rights Association. Bob's passion for changing his community and Mongolia is inspiring. He believes that young Mongolians are too concerned with status and making money, which has put the society in a rut. He wants people to work together to increase communication and education with open minds and believes that the spheres of society, economy, government, education, and culture should be the main focus of common work. But he doesn't discount the hard work of individuals to realize their own dreams. Bob hopes to end unemployment by empowering youth to take initiative, saying "If there are no jobs, we should make work for ourselves. There's plenty to do; just do it." He wants young people to employ their energy and creativity not only to help themselves but to empower those around them, young and old, to work toward a common, prosperous future with dignity and pride.

Bob works throughout the year on a strictly volunteer basis and saves money to support his own living costs by working as a translator and guide in the summer. If you come to Khuvsgul, look up Bob (99782520, 93138378; byambaa.bob@gmail.com).

The Guide

# Orkhon Aimag (Erdenet) Орхон аймаг (Эрдэнэт)

This *aimag*, formed in 1994 from a part of Bulgan Aimag, is essentially just the mining city of **Erdenet**, and you would be hard pressed to find anyone referring to it as Orkhon Aimag. It sits 410 kilometers (255 miles) northwest of Ulaanbaatar and is accessible by train and bus from Ulaanbaatar as well as Darkhan Aimag. In 1967, joint exploration with Russian and Czechoslovakian geologists led to the discovery of copper and molybdenum, an element that can withstand extreme temperatures and is useful in the making of aircraft parts, electrical contacts, and filaments. Since 1974, the Erdenet Mining Company has been mining the ores and feeding the development of the surrounding Soviet-planned town. The sole purpose of Erdenet was to house miners, but it has grown up as Mongolia's second largest city behind only Ulaanbaatar.

A walking tour around the town starting from the **Barilagchidin Talbai**, the taxi and bus stand on the east end of town, and a small hike to a nearby mountain make for a fun day taking in what is arguably Mongolia's nicest city. Erdenet is cleaner and safer than Darkhan or Ulaanbaatar, and its residents are used to seeing foreigners. You might also want to pick up a carpet **Erdenet Carpet**, one of Mongolia's largest companies and its largest carpet manufacturer.

Erdenet is a required stopping point for travel to the more rustic and rural Bulgan Aimag.

## ERDENET (ЭРДЭНЭТ)

Sometimes called the "Paris of Mongolia," Erdenet is an urban enclave city with a population of around 100,000. The Erdenet Mining Corporation, which was founded in 1974, is now a jointly owned Russian (51 percent) and Mongolian (49 percent) venture. Not only is the mine still the largest employer in the area, but it produces over 13 percent of the total Mongolian GDP, and since they pay comparatively good wages to local employees, Erdenet is the wealthiest city in Mongolia.

Because of its relative wealth, Erdenet's hotel, restaurant, and entertainment choices are fairly good, though because the city was strictly built for the mine, there are not many cultural or sight-seeing opportunities. Restaurants are springing up every month, and menus and services are becoming more and more Westernized.

The Guide

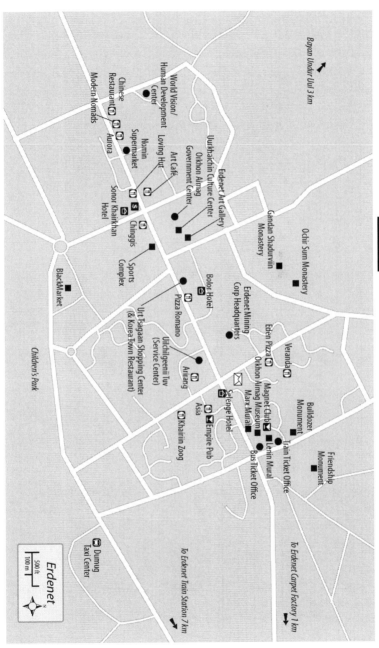

Bogan Undur Uul 3 km

World Vision/
Human Development
Center

Chinese
Restaurant

Modern Nomads

Nomin
Supermarket

Aurora

Art Café

Loving Hut

Orkhon Aimag
Government Center

Uurkhaichin Culture Center

Erdenet Art Gallery

Gandan Shaduvriin
Monastery

Ochir Sum Monastery

Sonor Khairkhan
Hotel

Chingis
Complex

Sports
Complex

BlackMarket

Children's Park

Bolor Hotel

Pizza Romano

Erdenet Mining
Corp Headquarters

Urt Tsagaan Shopping Center
(& Korea Town Restaurant)

Uilchilgeenii Tuv
(Service Center)

Ariang

Eden Pizza

Veranda

Magnet Club

Orkhon Aimag Museum

Marx Mural

Selenge Hotel

Asia

Khairin Zoog

Empire Pub

Lenin Mural

Bus Ticket Office

Bulldozer
Monument

Train Ticket Office

Friendship
Monument

Dumug
Taxi Center

Erdenet

500 ft
100 m

N

To Erdenet Train Station 7 km

To Erdenet Carpet Factory 1 km

While Erdenet lacks deep ties to Mongolian history, it is still heavily influenced by its cross-cultural communist past. The city is extremely compact, which makes walking everywhere very easy. You can also take a taxi anywhere in the city for MNT800. It is also extremely safe, with police officers patrolling all the time and a vibe that is much less tense than that of UB or Darkhan. Feel free to explore and don't be surprised if someone strikes up a conversation with you, though it might be in Russian.

Today, the Russian population in Erdenet is around 1,000, a mere shadow of the tens of thousands that once lived there. Because the top mining engineers are Russians living there with their families, if you are Caucasian, more often than not, it will be assumed that you are Russian, especially by the older people in town. However, the younger generation can generally tell Europeans and Americans from Russians.

## Erdenet Carpets

Erdenet Carpet (Эрдэнэт хивс) is Mongolia's largest rug and tapestry manufacturer and one of the country's ten largest companies. Founded in 1981, Erdenet Carpet now employs over 900 people in their factory and distributes its wool wares, including slippers, dolls, and other souvenirs made from the byproducts, throughout the country. It also exports to the USA, Sweden, Russia, China, Australia, Italy, and Kazakhstan. The rugs are renowned for their Mongolian designs that pull in traditional patterns and symbols, but they also have modern designs for full rooms (up to several million *tugriks*) and even small squares (around MNT15,000-30,000).

# GETTING THERE

## By Bus

There are six daily buses from Ulaanbaatar (10:00 a.m., 11:00 a.m., 12:00 noon, 2:00 p.m., 3:00 p.m., and 4:00 p.m.) from the Dragon Center. The six-hour trip costs MNT12,000 and arrives at the Barilagchidin Talbai bus station on the east end of town.

From Barilagchidin Talbai, there are five buses to UB per day (10:00 a.m., 11:30 a.m., 1:00 p.m., 2:30 p.m., and 4:00 p.m.). Tickets (MNT12,000) must be bought from the bus ticket office in the small building across from the parking lot in front of the Lenin mural. The office is open daily 8:00 a.m.-8:00 p.m.

## By Train

Trains from Ulaanbaatar to Erdenet (MNT6,800-20,300) leave daily at 7:00 p.m. and take about 12 hours, traveling overnight.

Trains to Ulaanbaatar leave at 7:40 p.m. every evening and take about 12 hours, arriving the next morning. You can also book a hard seat ticket for the 5.5-hour trip to Darkhan for around MNT2,000.

In Erdenet, the ticket office (open daily 9:00 a.m.-12:00 noon and 2:00 p.m.-7:00 p.m.) is in the building with the Lenin mural on the side facing the parking lot. It is also possible to buy tickets at the train station, but for first or second class, it's better and easier to buy in advance at the office in town. The train station is about 10 kilometers (6 miles) east of town; if you arrive by road you'll pass it on your way in. Taxis will be waiting for train travelers to arrive in the morning (MNT2,000 to any place in town). To get to the train station from town, ask a taxi driver for the *wokzal* (вокзал) or listen for that cry from microbuses around the sports palace or Barilagchidin Talbai. They shuttle people to the station between 6:00 and 7:00 p.m. for MNT800.

### By Shared Transportation

You can book a *mikr* to and from Ulaanbaatar's Dragon Center for MNT11,000 per person. Shared taxis to and from Ulaanbaatar start at MNT20,000 per person. Both leave when they're full, but they leave regularly starting in the morning.

Shared taxis and microbuses arrive and leave all day from the Barilagchidin Talbai bus parking lot, but they also leave from in front of the sports complex and *dumug* (дөмөг) taxi center on the southeast edge of town. You might have to check at any one of these spots to find your ride, depending on the time of day.

You can also find shared vehicles to Bulgan (MNT4,000; 1 hour), Murun in Khuvsgul Aimag (MNT25,000; 10 hours), Tsetserleg in Arkhangai Aimag (MNT25,000; 7 hours), and Uliastai in Zavkhan Aimag (MNT45,000; 20 hours) from any one of the taxi and *mikr* stations.

### Private Transportation

A private car will cost at least MNT50,000 plus fuel and meals for the driver (possibly as much as MNT200,000). However, a private car gives you the flexibility to stop at Amarbayasgalant Khiid in Selenge Aimag or other sites you find or plan along the way.

## WHERE TO STAY

Erdenet is arguably the nicest city in the country. However, considering it isn't a top tourist destination, there is a lack of affordable guesthouses among the 300 beds spread across 25 hotels. But why not live a little once in a while? Still, there are some more affordable options, too.

**Selenge Hotel** Across from the post office and telecom center. With 25 beds, it's a medium-sized hotel with good accommodations and the biggest hotel in Erdenet. Standard rooms come with kettle and tea, half lux rooms have multiple beds and some furniture with a mini-bar, and the lux twin is a little more intimate. All rooms come with cable TV with international channels and free WiFi. The hotel has room service, a restaurant, and a sauna. *Standard $25, half lux $32, lux twin $35. 99353521, 0135222624*

**Sonor Khairkhan Hotel** Around the corner from the Khan Bank on the main street. It's a smaller hotel, but the staff can help you book taxi, train, or bus tickets. Also, the hotel has a laundry service and a small restaurant. The eight rooms go for between $13 and $43, but the accommodations at the higher end are not significantly better than at the lower end, so do your best to inspect and negotiate for the best price. *135228120, 99352280*

**Bolor Hotel** On the lower end of the hotel spectrum. If you're looking to save your money for Khuvsgul, Darkhan, or Bulgan excursions, this is your place. It is located in building IV-16, just behind Urt Tsagaan shopping center. Go through the opening near Korea Town restaurant. The hotel is about 25 meters back on the right hand side. Rooms go for $8-15 per person per night. They have a small *guanz* and almost no other frills. *99354435, 0135225361*

# WHERE TO EAT

## Restaurants

**Korea Town** The cheaper of the Korean restaurants in the city and overall one of the best restaurants overall. Korea Town has a large menu with a few vegetarian options, and many entrees are large enough to split. Located in the Urt Tsagaan "strip mall" in the middle of the city. ₮₮

**Veranda** Has a Western-style menu at competitive prices, though you can expect to pay MNT10,000 for an entree and a beer. Very nice décor and good coffee drinks. Located in the first district. ₮₮

**Arirang** The more expensive Korean restaurant in town and more upscale in presentation and quality. You can split dishes to save money, but don't expect to get out of there for less than MNT15,000. The food is excellent and the restaurant is extremely popular for company parties and other celebrations, which sometimes monopolize the whole dining area during holidays and special occasions. ₮₮/₮₮₮

**Asia** A very nice restaurant with extremely professional wait staff. It's next door to Empire Pub in the first district but is slightly more upscale. The food is so good you won't want to split it, but the portions are generous enough that you could if you wanted to. ₮₮/₮₮₮

**Chingiss** On the fourth floor of the Nomin department store. It is fairly new and very busy around the winter holidays when companies rent out the restaurant for parties. The chicken dishes here are very good, but expect to spend around MNT15,000 for an entree and a beverage. ₮₮/₮₮₮

**Aurora** Near Nomin, it is one of the newest of the Western restaurants—and hopefully, it will be around for a while. It has an excellent chicken club sandwich and the French fries actually resemble McDonald's. The great decor and live music on Friday nights makes it a fun and interesting place to visit. Diners are usually treated to free popcorn while they wait for their food, and the dessert menu is extensive. ₮₮/₮₮₮

**Modern Nomads** Next to Aurora, it is the Mongolian chain restaurant that caters to the less adventurous traveler and eater. The club sandwich is good, and the steaks (from cows) are the best thing to order because they can be cooked to preference. The menu is in English, and the staff can communicate fairly well in English. ₮₮/₮₮₮

**Pizza Romano** A pretty good pizza place, and it delivers. We recommend the cheese and pepperoni pizzas (medium MNT11,000, large MNT14,000). You get a 1.25-liter bottle of Coca-Cola with every pizza order. ₮₮/₮₮₮

**Eden Pizza** Also delivers, but we recommend the spaghetti or fried chicken instead of the pizza. Also, beware that if you order a cheeseburger, chances are it will be mutton instead of beef, which can be a fun switch if you're in the right mood and disappointing if you're not. The prices are good, especially for the location. ₮/₮₮

## Guanzes

There are many *guanzes* around town where you can find cheap Mongolian food, though the menus are all in Mongolian, but there are a few we can recommend if you want something a little bit out of the ordinary.

**Art Café** Halfway between a *guanz* and a good restaurant. It's a good place to eat if you're low on cash but want a pretty decent meal. They have English on their menus, and the staff usually speak a few words of English. They have the standard Mongolian *buuz*, *khuushuur*, and *tsuivan*, but the quality is good. ₮/₮₮

**Loving Hut** The popular Ching Hai vegan restaurant, located in the basement of the office building next to Khan Bank. It's predictably cheap and healthy food. If your pockets are light, go for either the *peroshki* or *mantuun buuz*. They are ready fast and two should fill you up for about MNT300 each. Plan for lunch rather than dinner, as they usually close the doors by 6:00 p.m. ₮

**Khairiin Zoog** A local vegan restaurant about 200 meters southeast of the post office. Veggie *huushuur* is the standard cheap item (MNT300), and most other dishes run MNT1,500-2,500. Though the food and atmosphere are quite similar to Loving Hut's—the "Supreme Master" channel is often on the TV—Khairiin Zoog is much smaller and is getting more popular, so tables aren't always available. You can, however, take food to go for a hot picnic. ₮

# WHAT TO DO IN ERDENET

## Erdenet Self-Guided Walking Tour

The best way to see the city is by taking a self-guided walking tour. The big clockwise loop should take about two hours and an hour more if you continue up and back from the Bayan Undur Mountain. You can start at the beginning or pick it up at any point of interest.

The best place to start is the **Barilagchidin Talbai (Барилгачидын талбай)** or "Builders' Square" bus and taxi stand because it is near several worthwhile sights. If you arrived by train and haven't seen the bus stand yet, it is next to Government Building 3 (*Zakhirgaanii guravdugaar bair*, Захиргааны гуравдугаар байр).

Immediately north of the bus and taxi parking lot is the **Friendship Monument**, an impressive hilltop statue, resembling Ulaanbaatar's Zaisan, which features the Russian and Mongolian words for friendship across its base. The long set of steps and plateaus (about 150 meters or 500 feet long) leading to the monument start from the edge of the parking lot. A climb up the stairs yields a view across the city, and if you turn around you'll see a large Buddha statue to the north (still under construction as of spring 2011). After descending, check out the old bulldozer across the street, which is now a monument commemorating the construction of Erdenet in 1974.

Heading back toward the bus stand, you'll see a **mural of Vladimir Lenin** (1870-1924) composed of pieces of iron nailed into a brick wall facing the main street. Lenin was the head of the Bolshevik Red Army and founder of the USSR, and he supported Mongolian independence from China in the 1920s. As a philosopher and theorist, his agrarian interpretation and application of Marxism became known as "Leninism" and was emulated in Mongolia before the more extreme and violent Stalinist regimes. Ironically, the Lenin profile is located on a building that now houses the Chamber of Commerce and Industry.

On the side of the next building over you'll notice the German philosopher and political theorist **Karl Marx** (1818-1883) along with a message declaring the strength and truth of his ideas most famously outlined in his *Communist Manifesto*, a document describing a capitalist and materialistic struggle between the haves (the bourgeois) and the have-nots (the proletariat) that he argued naturally leads to the exploitation of the everyman. His philosophy, Marxism, aimed to empower the common folk through the confiscation of private property for the equal benefit of the masses, which he believed would eventually lead to a classless communist society.

In between the two murals is the **Orkhon Aimag Museum** (admission MNT1,500; open weekdays 8:00 a.m.-4:00 p.m.), which has culture, history, and nature exhibits all crammed into its small space. There is practically nothing in

English, but you don't need language to enjoy the two-headed calf and the array of artwork celebrating the copper mine.

Continue westward along the main street and you'll pass through a park in front of Erdenet Mining Corporation. On the next block is **Urt Tsagaan** ("Long White"), Erdenet's strip mall with various cheap lunch options inside. For something relatively upscale, try the Korean restaurant, Korea Town.

Past the Urt Tsagaan is the center of town, where the Orkhon Aimag government offices are located. Next to it is the **Uurkhaichin Cultural Center (Уурхайчин соёлын ордон)**. The so-called "Miner Cultural Palace" is the town civic center, which houses community events. It got its name and financial backing from Erdenet Mining Corporation. Ceremonies commemorating holidays, elections, and other events are held either on the square or inside the culture center, so you may get lucky and have a chance to see a performance of *morin khuur* players, singing, dancing, or contortion.

The Guide

## Human Development Center

Erdenet's Human Development Center (*Khunii khugjiliin tuv*, Хүний хөгжлийн төв) was founded in 2009 with support from World Vision Mongolia. Its mission is to provide training and support services for local children and adults. The center is composed of several partnered organizations sharing World Vision's building on the western edge of the city's fifth district. The groups include a technical club where kids learn engineering concepts and build model vehicles, a family counseling center, a library and internet access room, Eternal Springs café and youth center, which offers various dance and music lessons, Mongol Designer, which offers classes on clothing design and other textile skills, and the Eye of Wisdom school, which features classes in English, mathematics, and computers.

Each of the HDC's organizations usually operates during regular business hours, so on any given day there may be various trainings and educational activities taking place with participants of all ages. While World Vision continues to provide rent-free space in their central office building, the organizations otherwise sustain themselves through fees for their services. There are about 25 staff members among them, 15 of whom work for World Vision. Altogether, the HDC organizations serve more than 2,000 people in the area each year. They do this despite sharing a building with only one room capable of accommodating more than about a dozen people.

Chimgee, the director of the HDC's Eye of Wisdom school, taught English at another school in Erdenet for three years before starting her own private school. She also occasionally does translation work for other projects happening around the community, such as the 2011 effort to bring water pipes to Erdenet's *ger* neighborhoods. Chimgee has worked with several English-speaking volunteers in Erdenet. If you are traveling through Erdenet and you want to volunteer, she and the Human Development Center welcome your skills, expertise, and enthusiasm. You can contact her directly at 95959598 or chimgee_eyeofwisdom@yahoo.com or call the office at 0135225821.

Across the street from the cultural center on the south side is the large **Sports Complex** with one of Mongolia's only Olympic sized swimming pools (for members only). This is a good place to venture off the main road because south of the sports building is the **Black Market**, which is worth passing through to peruse the stalls for souvenirs. There are a number of great shops where you can find cheap gifts and one religious store selling Buddhist idols, copperwares, and incense.

Continue beyond the market for a visit to the **Children's Park**. When the weather is warm enough for the park to open, you can ride the Ferris wheel for MNT1,000 or partake in a variety of other carnival-style games like shooting at balloons. If you come in the winter, there are numerous outdoor ice skating rinks and a ski hill (with rope pull) in town.

Make your way back toward the main street and continue westward to **Nomin Supermarket**, which has a section featuring **Erdenet Carpet** products in the front. Some of Erdenet's nicer restaurants are also located on this block. Aurora (mostly American food) and Modern Nomads (a mostly upscale Mongolian chain) are in one building, and Chinese Restaurant is in the next. If you're not ready for a meal, circle back later but for now continue past the restaurants and turn right at the steeple-topped Mormon church on the edge of the commercial strip. Up the street you will pass the World Vision building on your right, which contains the **Human Development Center** (see previous box).

If you are interested in a short hike, continue straight (off the road) toward **Bayan Undur Uul**. The top of this mountain is a great spot to get an aerial view of the city. Go around to the left side for a gentler incline.

Get back to the road and follow it as it loops back to the east. You'll see two temples, **Gandan Shadurviin** and its smaller neighbor, **Ochir Sum**, about two-thirds of the way back to the bus stand. The temples are not remarkable compared to others in the country, but they're the only ones you'll find in the middle of Erdenet. They're good landmarks to help you find your way back. From the temples you can see the main part of town and can make your way back to the main street and the majority of the food, shopping, and lodging. If you haven't seen the Friendship Monument and Soviet murals, continue along the back road and it will curve around to take you there.

## Nightlife

**Magnet** The largest discotheque in town. It is near the center of town by the bus station. It has Western music, fog machines, and lasers to enhance your dance and invite booty shakers out onto the floor. Its two-story seating is usually packed on Saturday nights, so come early. Don't be too shy to join in on the group circle dance.

**Empire Pub** This is where you can grab a reasonably priced drink and talk with friends. The music isn't loud, and you can usually find Johnny Walker if you've had too much vodka. The pub has a low-key evening feel (i.e., no circle dancing). If you find you've had a few too many Altan Govi beers, they have typical Mongolian pub food and English on the menu. The staff can usually figure out what you want even if you don't speak Mongolian. We recommend the potato salad.

# Selenge Aimag (Сэлэнгэ аймаг)

Selenge (pronounced "sill-ing") is in Mongolia's northern-central region on the border with Russia and on the train line. Selenge is considered the breadbasket of Mongolia, as it produces about half of the nation's grains. The *aimag* center, **Sukhbaatar**, has a relatively well-developed infrastructure, including a healthy flour manufacturing industry. The *aimag* center is easy to get to, as it is located on the train line and connected to a web of paved roads running to and from Ulaanbaatar and Darkhan as well as to the neighboring villages.

Selenge is famous for its beautiful trees, which used to support a now defunct lumber industry at the convergence of the **Orkhon Gol** and the **Selenge Gol** just outside of Sukhbaatar. The Selenge Gol, the largest river in Mongolia, flows into Lake Baikal in Russia and eventually connects to the Arctic Ocean. To get a good look at the river and the Russian border, get to **Saikhani Khutul**, a hilltop park.

With its northern geography and confluence of major waterways and tributaries,

The Guide

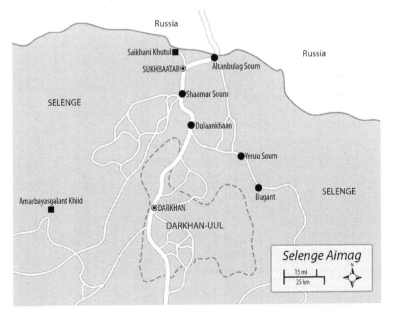

this *aimag* has a harsher winter than the Gobi. The landscape, with numerous evergreens and rolling hills, still makes it a worthwhile place to visit even in winter because of the picturesque views, and if you have your own skates, you can whirl around the skating rink in downtown Sukhbaatar.

**Altanbulag Soum**, an important site in Mongolian's struggle for independence from China and the site of the *aimag's* museum, is on the border mirroring the Russian city of Kyatkha, but without a visa you can't cross it.

The pride of the *aimag*, though, is the famous **Amarbayasgalant Khiid**, its most popular tourist attraction and one of the largest and oldest monasteries in Mongolia.

## SUKHBAATAR SOUM (СУХБААТААР СУМ)

Sukhbaatar is a charming town undergoing a bit of a renaissance on the border of Mongolia and Russia. The colorful pastel buildings on its main road near the train station seem to offer a welcoming salutation. The city was founded in the 1940s and named after Damadiin Sukhbaatar, the "Red Hero" who teamed with the Bolsheviks to overthrow the waning Qing Dynasty and for whom Ulaanbaatar, Ulaanbaatar's main square, and Sukhbaatar Aimag are named. The population here is about 20,000. Administrative districts are spread out over 11.5 kilometers (7.25 miles), making it a decent sized town in Mongolia. It is the first Mongolian stop on the Trans-Mongolian track and a good place for travelers to get their first taste of the country.

Because the eastern *aimag* is also called Sukhbaatar, be sure you're going to "Selenge Sukhbaatar" and not Sukhbaatar Aimag, whose capital is Barrun Urt. It can be confusing sometimes. If you're on a bus to Sukhbaatar, you've done something wrong because no buses come to Selenge's capital.

## GETTING THERE

### By Train

Trains depart from Ulaanbaatar twice a day. They take about 9.5 hours and cost MNT6,000-18,000 depending on which compartment class you choose. The day train departs UB at 10:30 a.m. and arrives in Sukhbaatar around 8:00 p.m. The overnight train leaves UB in the afternoon at 4:20 p.m. and arrives in Sukhbaatar at 6:10 a.m. The return train leaves for UB at 9:05 p.m. every night. You can buy your tickets only after 6:00 p.m. on the night that you leave. The train is by far the safest and easiest way to get to Sukhbaatar. The overnight train is also a two-for-one deal: you travel overnight with a place to sleep. The train is slow and makes frequent stops, but you're not likely to be disturbed in a first class room. The overnight train does get in before most things are open, but you can usually still find a taxi and most tourist hotels and guesthouses are within walking distance.

## By Bus

No buses run to Sukhbaatar Soum these days. You can take a bus to Darkhan (MNT6,000) and then take a *mikr* or taxi from the Darkhan station (MNT9,000).

## By Shared Transportation

It is extremely difficult to book travel directly to Sukhbaatar unless you get lucky at Narantuul or know somebody who's going. Instead, the best way to get there is to make your way to Darkhan. Microbuses to Darkhan (MNT5,000) leave daily from the taxi center in the Sukhbaatar market and are best caught in the morning around 10:00 a.m. The numerous transportation options to Ulaanbaatar from Darkhan give you the perfect opportunity to plan a visit to Amarbayasgalant Khiid on your way to or from Sukhbaatar.

## Private Transportation

You might be able to find a Selenge-bound car at Naraantuul Market in Ulaanbaatar, but it's not entirely likely. From Sukhbaatar, it is possible to book a driver to Ulaanbaatar, but you will have to pay to rent the whole vehicle. A private car to Ulaanbaatar can be approximately MNT30,000, but since they aren't very common and you're a foreigner, you might end up paying more. Jeeps are not common and not necessary as there are mostly paved roads in Selenge.

## Hitchhiking

Hitchhiking is fairly common up and down the paved road. Speeds are higher on this road than most other places around the country, so you want to be especially careful who you ride with. At the very least, make sure the driver isn't drunk.

# GETTING AROUND THE AIMAG

In Sukhbaatar, microbuses to UB and *aimag* attractions are available every day at the taxi center and outside the train station. The taxi center is in the middle of the market by the Russian shop. Microbuses to Ulaanbaatar do not leave frequently. You will be better off arranging a trip through a private driver, breaking the trip up by going via Darkhan, or using the train.

You can also catch a ride to nearby Shaamar and Altanbulag *soums* from the taxi center. They leave only when someone asks for them or a vehicle fills up. Prices vary depending on how far you are going and should be no more than MNT6,000 per person for a 20-minute ride to the neighboring *soums*. Taxis are coming in and going out all the time, but the best time to catch one is between 12:00 noon and 4:00 p.m. Taxis to Darkhan are easier to get in the morning.

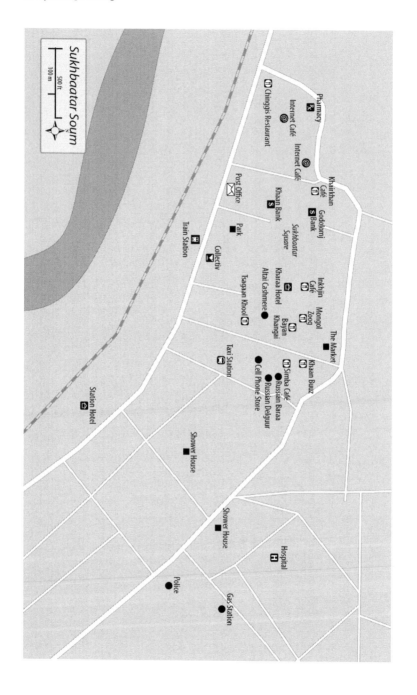

Sukhbaatar Soum

500 ft
100 m

Chinggis Restaurant
Pharmacy
Internet Café
Internet Café
Khairkhan Café
Godolomj
Post Office
Khaan Bank
Bank
Park
Sukhbaatar Square
Train Station
Collectiv
Inkhjin Café
Mongol Zoog
Altai Cashmere
Kharaa Hotel
Tsagaan Khool
Bayan Khangai
The Market
Taxi Station
Simba Café
Khaan Buuz
Russian Baraa
Cell Phone Store
Russian Delguur
Station Hotel
Shower House
Shower House
Hospital
Police
Gas Station

# WHERE TO STAY

**Station Hotel** Adjacent to the train station. It's about MNT5,000 per night per person for a small room with a toilet. Station Hotel is a great price, but keep in mind there is no laundry, kitchen, or hot shower.

**Kharaa Hotel (Хараа)** Next to the town square behind the monastery. It is approximately MNT10,000 a night per person for a single, and MNT25,000 for a double. This hotel also has no laundry or kitchen.

# WHERE TO EAT

**Tsagaan Khool (Цагаан хоол)** Makes all the Mongolian classics but with no meat. The food and service are both very good, too. The vegetable *buuz* and *khuushuur* are highly recommended. The employees speak some English, and their location within the market is super convenient. Sadly, this favorite is closed during the winter months. ₮₮

**Khairkhan Café (Хайрхан кафе)** Just behind Khadgalamj Bank. It is very nice, but the service is almost always slow. It's a great place to go if you are not in a hurry and just want to be in a quiet place with a classy atmosphere. It also says "hotel" on the sign outside, but rumors are that it doesn't serve as a hotel anymore. Perhaps, it is worth inquiring. ₮

**Simba Café (Симба кафе)** Serves Russian food, making it a favorite among Russian travelers coming through on the main road or the train. The café might also benefit from being easy to find, as it is located at the opening of the market just past the Russian store. The restaurant serves huge portions at great prices, and the food is good. The service is usually very fast. ₮

**Bayan Khangai (Баян хангай)** Where you will probably find the best Mongolian food. It is located between the town square and the market. The service is usually relatively slow. It plays contemporary American pop music and is very clean. Sometimes it also has fried chicken. ₮

**Chinggis Restaurant (Чингис)** Has high quality food and even fried or broiled chicken. Chinggis Restaurant has excellent and friendly service, but you will definitely pay for it. It is good for get-togethers thanks to its large, open space. There is a draft system for beer, but the restaurant doesn't always have the actual kegs. The restaurant is just a quick walk west from the town square past the post office. ₮₮₮

## Guanzes

**Khaan Buuz (Хаан бууз)** National fast food chain. It is snuggly located just inside the market. You can always get Mongolian food, not just *buuz*. It also has *tsuivan*, soups, and other food, so if you're hungry and just looking for a quick bite, this is the place. ₮

**Inkhjin Café (Инжин кафе)** Has some vegetarian options like egg salad and bread but mostly just typical Mongolian food. It is very close to the market, just northeast of the town square. The people who work here in the summer speak English and are friendly. ₮

**Mongol Zoog (Монгол зоог)** Between the town square and the market. Mongol Zoog offers typical Mongolian food at cheap prices. Look for cheap, hot *khuushuur*. ₮

# WHAT TO DO IN SUKHBAATAR

You can do some hiking in the countryside surrounding the town center. On top of a mountain on the edge of town, you can see all of Sukhbaatar as well as Russia. It's quite a beautiful site! It about an hour's hike northwest from the center of town.

**Sukhbaatar Square**, like the one in UB, is the main parade ground in front of the government building where you can find a statue of the great Sukhbaatar himself. Next to it, there is a cute, tiny park that looks beautiful no matter the season. During New Years, people gather here to light fireworks.

**Khutagt Ekh Datsan Buddhist Temple** is a very nice looking temple, but it is small. It is along the main road and surrounded by a white fence. Interestingly, it is run by a female lama.

Hiking around the local hill and mountains is one of the best ways to see the Orkhon and Selenge Gol. Head west on the road and over the hill toward the big Buddha statue. Follow that path through the district called Korpus. On the western edge of the district is a white archway that leads to an abandoned lumber mill. If you continue on the road that leads around the plant, it will lead you to the convergence of the two rivers and give you some nice cliff-side views along the way. There is a great camping area on the western bank, and you'll often find fishermen angling and tourists relaxing in the cool water. Mongolians frown upon swimming in the river. Drownings, usually of locals, who tend to be novice swimmers, occur every year. We suggest caution after a big rain.

## Shopping

**Russian Delguur** A store that sells many Russian goods and also some American goods. This is your best bet if you're looking for higher quality products. You may be able to shop for necessary items here rather than in UB if you are coming from the north.

**The Market** In the center of town east of the main square. Because of Sukhbaatar's location, you will find a few miscellaneous items you wouldn't find elsewhere, but for the most part it's a typical Mongolian bazaar. It is particularly famous for delicious smoked fish from the Selenge River, and you can buy your own basic pole and tackle for cheap if you'd like fresh fish. The large loaves of white Buriat bread are the softest and tastiest in the country, and buying one is an absolute must. Top it with urum (өрөм), a thick milk cream, and honey or sugar.

**Duty Free** Inside the train station there is a duty free shop for international travelers such as yourself. The station mostly sells liquor and cigarettes, and it is open during regular business hours, not necessarily when international trains arrive.

**Altai Cashmere** Not only do they sell cashmere, the vegetarian Buddhists who run Altai also operate a tiny vegetarian café in the back. The staff are very nice, and the food is always good!

**Russian Baraa (Ороос Бараа)** Where you'll find a lot of household items as well as souvenirs and Russian dolls. There is also Russian candy and food. If you are going camping, this could be a good place to shop for your supplies.

## Nightlife

**Collectiv** Has decent music and decent vibes. The club is mainly frequented by Russians. It is on the main road. It tends to be rather loud and sloppy here.

**SS Club** Probably a better bet than Collectiv, especially because the music selection is better. It has a good atmosphere, but be careful because the revelers can get a bit sloppy and rowdy as the hours tick away. SS Club is frequented by soldiers and border guards, some of whom speak a little bit of English. In case you're wondering, it has no connection to the Nazi SS in any way.

# WHAT TO DO AROUND SELENGE AIMAG

The Selenge-Orkhon Forest Steppe is an ecoregion characterized by spotty forests at higher elevations and wide mountain valleys in the Orkhon and Selenge river basins. The open steppe vegetation is a combination of pine and aspen along with steppe flora. The area contains rodents such as mountain hare, Korean field mouse, and squirrel. If you are interested in birdwatching, you can see many species including the Dalmatian pelican, white spoonbill, and black stork. The lower valleys of the Selenge basin are used widely for agriculture, hay making, and livestock harvesting. Sadly, there are numerous threats to this area: heavy settlement by herders, widespread animal husbandry, pressure from the railways, roads, and industrial processing. There are several smaller protected areas within this region, but there is no broad protection for the ecological integrity of this area.

### Amarbayasgalant Khiid (Амарбаясгалант хийд)

Nestled in the Ivon Gol Valley at the foot of the Burenkhan Mountains rests Mongolia's largest and most celebrated monastery, Amarbayasgalant. Since the eighteenth century, the monastery has enjoyed two hundred years of prosperity, endured fifty-four years of neglect, and now benefits from a modern revival. Currently there are sixty resident novice and ordained monks living and studying at the monastery, ranging in age from 12 to 60.

In the early eighteenth century, the Manchurian Chinese Emperor Enkh-Amgalan Khan established the monastery to honor the spiritual leader Undur Gegen Zanabazar (1635-1723), the seventeenth century Mongolian leader famous for his sculptures, paintings, poetry, and medical practices. He spread Buddhist teachings across Mongolia and founded a plethora of temples and monasteries.

Construction of Amarbayasgalant began in 1726 and was completed in 1736. At its peak, the monastery held 3,000 monks living and studying Buddhism.

Outside the actual monastery, there are two huge statues atop enormous hills that overlook Selenge. At the foot of the mountains on the far side of the valley sits a row of stupas, which make a great destination for a short hike. The scenery in this isolated valley, cut by ribbons of river, is truly divine.

The monastery itself was built without one copper nail (only wooden nails) and has stood for almost 300 years! Visitors may watch the monks reciting prayers at 9:00 a.m. and 4:00 p.m. daily.

Drivers can be booked to Amarbayasgalant from Darkhan. The best way to reach Amarbayasgalant is by going to the Darkhan bus station or black market and talking to the drivers hanging out there. Rates for the trip should be about MNT50,000 per day. While the monastery is accessed easily enough from the main Darkhan-Erdenet road, it does take a few hours to get there. We highly recommend spending at least one night at Amarbysgalant, both because it makes the travel time worth it and because camping in this magical monastery's valley is one of the most serene and exquisite experiences to be had in Mongolia.

The head monk at Amarbayasgalant is named Olonbayar; his English is amazing. He's in his late twenties and is a really remarkable guy. The monastery can be contacted at the phone numbers and email addresses listed below. There is no mobile reception at the monastery, so when Olonbayar is there, his phones won't work, and he doesn't check email all that often. (11322529, 99124006, 99011818; amarbayasgalant@gmail.com, gerlee@amarbayasgalant.org; http://www.amarbayasgalant.org)

The **Selenge Gol** is a gorgeous, narrow strip of waterway. It is the largest river in Mongolia, measuring 992 kilometers (616 miles) long, of which 593 kilometers (368 miles) flows through Mongolian territory. Several other large rivers, including the Orkhon, Yeroo, and Tamir, all drain into the Selenge before it runs straight to Lake Baikal in Russia. The area near the Russian-Mongolian border is one of the top places to fish in Mongolia. The best fishing happens between September and October. If you can't make it out there to fish for yourself but have access to a kitchen, be sure to stop by the market in Sukhbaatar city to buy some genuine Selenge fish.

**Saikhani Khutul (Сайхаиы хөтөл)** is a fantastic place to have a picnic and one of our favorite views in all of Mongolia! It's a mountaintop park on the northern border that overlooks the forested rolling hills stretching into Russia as well as the winding Selenge Gol. You're likely to find Mongolians resting, praying, drinking, and eating up there when they're not climbing on the various concrete statues of animals.

Before you go, you need to get a permit from the border patrol office in the Sukhbaatar police station. The office you're looking for is *tsirignii angi*. Ask for a permit (*zuvshuurul*, зөвшөөрөл) to go to *saikhani hutul*. You can say, "*Bi saikhani hutul ruu yawmaar baina*," or do your best miming and map pointing.

To get there, you can either walk the 10 kilometers (6 miles) or find a taxi in Sukhbaatar Soum and ask them to take you to the park. You can find taxis during normal business hours to take you to the border for about MNT4,000-7,000 round trip. Once there, you will show the border troops your passport and the permit.

## Altanbulag Soum (Алтанбулаг сум)

Altnabulag is a peaceful and quiet border town just 24 kilometers (15 miles) from Sukhbaatar, but the town itself is not as attractive as its Russian Orthodox Cathedral. The town was established as a free trade zone to invite tax-free national and international investment, but it hasn't quite worked out as planned. Instead, it is little more than a trading town, and it still looks a bit like a ghost town with many abandoned buildings.

The Russian Cathedral is at the edge of town even closer to the border, but you'll need a Russian visa to actually go to it. In fact, the border with Russia is within walking distance, and although Mongolians can typically pass freely, you should be careful not to go too far outside the edge of town because you might set foot in "no man's land." As a rule of thumb, the hill closest to the edge of town is okay to walk on, but you should not go any further than that (where the trees are).

The most interesting thing about Altanbulag is its significant role in Mongolian independence, which is inseparably connected to its counterpart across the border, Kyakhta. Mongolian and Chinese representatives signed a treaty there in 1915 to grant limited Mongolian autonomy with the backing of Bolshevik dignitaries. When Chinese troops began re-invading Mongolia in 1919, they violated the treaty and forced Mongolian revolutionaries into exile in Kyakhta on the other side of the border from Altanbulag. The exiled Mongolian Revolutionary People's Party leaders formed the People's Provisional Government of Mongolia there in 1921, and Sukhbaatar was named the defense minister. The battle fought in Altanbulag later caused the defeat of the Manchurian Army and led to Mongolia independence in

The Guide

1924. Sukhbaatar, whose name means "Axe Hero," became the hero of the communist or "red" revolution. Mongolia's capital, Ikh Khuree, was renamed *Ulaanbaatar*, "Red Hero," in his honor.

**Selenge Aimag Museum**, in Altanbulag, has a very heavy communist aura, reinforced by the watchful statues of Sukhbaatar and Lenin. It is small but has some of Sukhbaatar's personal effects, including his gun, boots, and desk. It opens from around 10:00 a.m. to 5:00 p.m. and is closed between 1:00 p.m. and 2:00 p.m. for lunch. Entrance is MNT3,000. If you're already in the area you should stop by, but don't make a special trip to Altanbulag for the museum.

## Boldbaatariin Bayan

Bayan comes from a rural Sukhbaatar district called Korpus, 2.5 kilometers (1.5 miles) northwest of the center of town. His family lives in a wood and brick house that he, his sister, and his parents built together when he was in his teens. Now in his early 30s, he lives in South Korea temporarily working in a factory to make money.

Bayan trained as a cameraman. For a time, he freelanced for most of the big TV stations in UB and Darkhan while intermittently commuting back and forth to be with his young daughter in Selenge, but he wasn't making enough money. Single parent households are common in Mongolia, and grandparents are often very involved. However, Bayan's parents are raising his daughter because the mother is out of the country, also in South Korea. She and Bayan have separately joined the estimated 33,000 other Mongolians who live there (70 percent of which are believed to be working in South Korea illegally), which makes South Korea's Mongolian population the largest international Mongolian population in the world. In fact, the South Korean government estimates that half of the urban households in Mongolia have a family member working there, mostly in the industrial sector.

Bayan's father is a proud, retired Mongolian army soldier who spent many months traveling back and forth to Moscow during and after Mongolian communism. Now he works part time as a security guard for a Sukhbaatar bank and drives a taxi every other day of the week. He loves to sing and is also a macho handyman, always tinkering with his car. Bayan's mother worked at the lumber factory on the edge of town that shut down when the government support stopped in the early 1990s. Now her main duty is to look after the family's four cows. Every morning she wakes up early to milk the cows and then turns them loose outside the family's compound, or *khashaa*. From the milk she will make *urum*, a heavy, solidified cream spread on bread with sugar or honey or mixed with milk tea. Every day during the summer, she will make a fresh batch of yogurt, which is eaten as a cool evening snack. What the family does not use, she sells to a local shop, which freezes the yogurt in small containers and sells them.

There is no telling when Bayan will make it back to Mongolia or how his relationship with his family, especially his daughter will be affected. But for now, she is an excellent student, happily participating in a group of young cadets—perhaps, she will follow in her grandfather's footsteps—and she dutifully helps her grandmother herd the family's cows.

## Yeruu Soum (Ерөө сум)

The stunning Yeruu Gol flows from a quiet, lush area southeast of Sukhbaatar. The main attraction is **Bugant (Бугант)**, a remote yet surprisingly urban village in the mountains surrounded by trees. The town, about 66 kilometers (41 miles) from the *soum* center, was built as a gold mining town and had a flourishing lumber mill, though neither trade seems to be thriving these days. One option for a day's journey would be to follow the river upstream through the Khentii Mountain Range on horseback, if you can. You could also hike, but if you go wandering through the forest during the hunting season, please be careful and remember to wear bright colors to avoid being mistaken for an animal.

## Shaamar Soum (Шаамар сум)

The *soum* is extremely beautiful and serene, whether it is winter or summer, and it's even smaller than Altanbulag. It's far from the border so you will not have any trouble with border troops or off limit areas. You can hike in any direction as far as your eye can see and your motivation will carry you.

One village in Shaamar is **Dulaankhaan (Дулаанхаан)**, 62 kilometers (38 miles) south of Sukhbaatar. This tiny village is home to Mongolia's only bow and arrow factory where some of the last Mongolian bow makers ply their trade. In the last few generations, apprenticeships for the arts have decreased dramatically, so it is difficult to find trained artisans who know how to make a traditional Mongolian bow. In fact, there may be only 10 of these artisans left in the country. They make the bows and arrows from a variety of materials, including animal bones and fish. Remarkably, they take about four months to complete, so only 30 to 40 sets are made every year. You can usually buy a set for about $200.

**Mother Tree (Ээж мод)** is 3 kilometers (1.8 miles) from the center of Shaamar *soum* west off the main road. There is a small wooden sign pointing to the site. The Mother Tree is a spiritual site where Mongolians worship the spirit of the tree. This practice is rooted, pardon the pun, in shamanism. The tree has been struck by lightning, but it still holds a sacred place in the Mongolians' hearts. Typically, people offer rice, vodka, candy, and milk to the tree; you will notice a distinct smell of rotting milk as you approach. Most noticeably, you will see the tree covered in thousands of *khatags* (scarves). You are likely to see people placing blue ones on the tree in order to gain favor with the tree's spirit.

The Guide

# Sukhbaatar Aimag (Сүхбаатар аймаг)

Sukhbaatar Aimag (not to be confused with Selenge Aimag's capital by the same name) is located in the wide-open eastern steppe, where the grasslands meet the Gobi Desert. You can walk minutes outside any village to see unobstructed views that stretch until the earth curves away into the horizon. The sunsets are beautiful, the wild white gazelles are plentiful, and kind Mongolian people can be found at every turn. There is a large population of the Dariganga (pronounced "dari-gaan") ethnic group, who live throughout the *aimag*.

This area is developing very quickly and has a growing English-speaking community, especially in **Baruun Urt**. Coal and zinc mining throughout the *aimag* brings in revenue that supplements traditional animal husbandry. Much of the *aimag* is covered by mining licenses and is under exploration by various companies looking for the next big mineral strike.

Across the *aimag*, there are 220 dead volcanoes, 20 natural springs, and a rich white antelope population, which resembles a flowing yellow wave as the animals gallop together in the distance. The southern part of the *aimag*, especially in **Dariganga Soum** with its expansive natural park, is the *aimag's* main attraction and the location of most developed tourism infrastructure. At the intersection of the Gobi and the steppe are the sand dunes, including the **Moltsog Els**, many of which are topped by vegetation. The park extends throughout most of the district and is about a 6-hour drive from Baruun Urt on a good day, but the trip can be up to 12 hours on muddy spring and summer days after a soaking rain.

The Sukhbaatar Government has established a **Tourist Information Center** where you should be able to find drivers and guides and get help booking hotels, *ger* camps, and trips. Visit the center's website at www.thesukhbaatarexperience.com or email the staff at sukhbaatartourism@gmail.com. The Tourist Information Center has been operating temporarily out of the museum, but e they should soon be permanently moving to a new building behind the government building on the north side of the main square.

## BARUUN URT (БАРУУН УРТ)

The *aimag* center, whose name means "Eastern Range," is a friendly little town in the far east of seemingly nowhere, 557 kilometers (346 miles) from Ulaanbaatar. Despite its remoteness, it's amazingly full of shops and international restaurants that you wouldn't expect. It's not a major metropolitan area, that's exactly its charm. Most attractions in the capital are within a five-minute walk from the center of town, and other activities like horse and camel riding in the countryside and wild gazelle watching are within thirty minutes to an hour outside the city via car.

## HOW TO GET THERE

### By Bus

Buses from Ulaanbaatar's Bayanzurkh bus station (MNT21,500; 11 hours) leave at 8:00 a.m. and arrive in Baruun-Urt, Sukhbaatar in the early evening. Tickets can be purchased up to a week in advance from either Bayanzurkh Bus Station or the Dragon Center, but must be purchased at least one day in advance of travel. The bus station in Baruun Urt is in the town center, where you can buy your ticket back to UB.

### By Shared Transportation

You can book a *mikr* from the Narantuul parking lot or possibly from Bayanzurkh station. It's the same price and time in the *mikr* as in a bus, so just take the bus; you'll be way happier in your own personal seat. The advantage of the *mikr* is that you can generally find one leaving that day, but it will be leaving with umpteen other people and all their precious cargo.

### Getting Around the Aimag

Vehicles are available from the middle of town and by the bus station throughout the day, but especially in the morning. Notifying drivers the day of a trip to a *soum* center is perfectly fine since there are plenty of Jeeps, cars, and SUVs willing to travel

The Guide

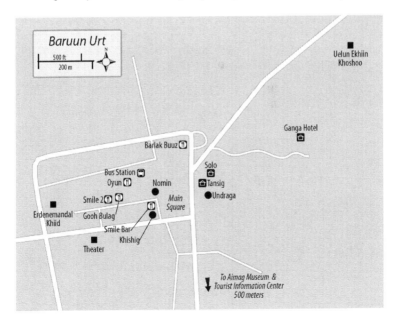

with no advanced notice. For a multi-day tour of the *aimag*, some advance notice may be necessary, although some drivers will likely be willing to move out by the end of the afternoon if the price is right.

# WHERE TO STAY

**Ganga Hotel (Ганга)** Near the Mother Mongolia Monument. The single rooms (MNT10,000) and double rooms (MNT18,000) are clean and basic with a shared central toilet but no shower. The hotel charges for laundry services by the kilo, and the staff will help you book transportation to *aimag* sites. Its restaurant is among the nicest in town and has karaoke rooms available to rent. *0151221515, 99794213, 99512088*

**Tansig (Тансиг)** A little nicer and little more expensive that Ganga but also a little smaller. It does not have a shower. It's located close to the government square, and it has a restaurant on the first floor. Rooms ($16-35) are suites with living rooms and en suite toilets. Services include laundry, massage, internet, transportation booking, and a very nice restaurant. *0151222444, 99112001, 99516357*

**Solo** Located just off the east side of the main square behind Tansig. Single rooms (MNT10,000) and double rooms (MNT30,000) have separate bathrooms. The clean, nice restaurant on the first floor has a limited menu, but what they have is good.

## Ger Camps

There are *ger* camps at Shiliin Bogd Uul and Taliin Agui.

**"Wood House" Resort** One of the newest resorts in Sukhbaatar Aimag. It's located just outside the Erdentsaagan *soum* center, about 250 kilometers (155 miles) southeast of Baruun Urt. It is a very nice resort offering Mongolian food and art, herder visits, and photo and hunting trips. Consisting of both a large hotel building and some *gers*, its capacity will be 100 people when fully complete, with 40 beds in the main building and 60 in *gers*. Prices range from MNT25,000 to MNT60,000 per night for basic or lux rooms. The *gers* will be large luxury *gers* with up to six beds. *99080424*

**Nuudelchin Khuree Burd Camp** Situated on the Ongon Els sand dune, the camp is 90 kilometers (56 miles) northwest of the Dariganga *soum* center and 120 kilometers (75 miles) from UB. It can hold 50 guests in five *gers* and 20 hotel rooms for about MNT5,000 per bed. The camp offers camel and horseback riding, herder visits, Mongolian food and folk art, volleyball, basketball, billiards and table tennis, and photo safari trips. *95851129*

# WHERE TO EAT

## Restaurants

**Ganga Hotel Restaurant** The best Chinese restaurant in town (though it may not be the most authentic you've ever had). It's a nice place with good service, and it's especially well suited for big groups. With Mongolian, Chinese, and European menu selections, it's overall one of the best places in town. It used to be one of the only restaurants in town with chicken, and while the competition has been catching up, Ganga still has the best chicken nuggets. Vegetarian *khuushuur* and *tsuivan* are sometimes available by special order, but you won't find them on the menu. ₮₮/₮₮₮

**Tansig Hotel Restaurant** One of the fancier places in Baruun Urt, and though more expensive by about MNT1,000 per plate than Ganga, the quality is high. The restaurant makes a concerted effort via presentation to feature the chef's take on standard Mongolian and European-style dishes. ₮₮/₮₮₮

**Oyun** Centrally and conveniently located next to the bus station. Oyun has both Mongolian and Chinese foods and a friendly staff. ₮₮

**Gooh Bulag Restaurant** A small restaurant with Chinese dishes and good Mongolian food including the best *khuushuur* in town. It's just down the street from Nomin, 500 meters west of the square. ₮₮

**Smile Bar** On the western side of the square. It has good Mongolian and Chinese food at moderate prices, especially compared to the nicer restaurants in town. The staff is friendly, and you might be able to get some vegetarian *tsuivan* and *khuushuur*. ₮₮

**Smile 2** Typical Mongolian menu with excellent soup and friendly staff. It's the little sister to the Smile Bar and one of our favorites because it's cheap and quick. ₮/₮₮

### Guanzes

**Barlak Buuz** Has the best milk tea and robust, albeit not spectacular, *khuushuur* and vegetarian *tsuivan*. ₮

### Groceries

**Undraga** A locally owned supermarket chain that is well stocked with food and sundries. The main location is on the east side of the main square.

**Nomin** The rival national franchise has camping and fishing gear and usually the cheapest beer. It is located on the north side of the square next to the government building.

**Khishig** An import shop with expensive favorites like trail mix and cheese. Khishig is located just east side of the square.

# WHAT TO DO IN BARUUN URT

**Sukhbaatar Aimag Museum** is on the edge of town. It's about an eight-minute walk south from the square, but it is actually a very good museum compared to those in other *aimags*. The taxidermy section isn't great, but their artifact collection is, especially the displays of artisanal silver wares, examples of traditional formal dress from the area, and the collection of carvings from a well-known Mongolian sculptor and silversmith, M. Baldan-Osor. They also have the *ger* and personal effects of the "Red Hero" Damadiin Sukhbaatar, for whom the *aimag* was named. Unfortunately, there's not much in the way of English information in the museum, and although they do not speak English, the curator and other staff members are happy to give tours, so it is worth trying to find a translator to bring with you.

**Erdenemandal Khiid (Эрдэнэмадал хийд)** is a medium-sized monastery with about a dozen monks located west of the square. They have irregular hours, but if the door is open, you are welcome to walk in. It's customary to approach the alter, light some incense, and leave a few *tugriks*.

**Uelun Ekhiin Khoshoo (Өэлүн эхийн хошоо)**, also known as the "Mother of Mongolia Statue," sits atop the hill overlooking the town. It makes for a short, fun hike, and it presents a nice view of the city and a place to just hang out for a bit. The statue, which was commissioned in 2006 to commemorate the 800th anniversary of Mongolia, features baby Temujin (the young Chinggis Khan before he was given the title of king) in the arms of his mother, Oelun. It's charming to remember that the legendary leader and controversial conqueror was once an innocent child cradled by his adoring mother.

### Nightlife

**Great Mountain** is the place to go in the evenings to bust a groove with the local university crowd. Located about a kilometer west of the square. The DJ leaves a bit to be desired, but the food is pretty decent. It doesn't get too rowdy, though you may run into a few wrestling matches spilling out into the streets around midnight when the bar closes.

## WHAT TO DO IN DARIGANGA SOUM (ДАРЬГАНГА СУМ)

With hundreds of domestic and international tourists each year, Dariganga is the most well known destination in Sukhbaatar Aimag. Despite its popularity, there aren't any hotels or much in the way of restaurants in the *soum* center yet, though there is a *guanz* and a few small shops. Because of this, you should plan to bring most of your food with you. The spring just south of the town provides cool water that is safe to drink.

While there are over 60 twelfth century statues scattered around Sukhbaatar, four are close to the Dariganga *soum* center. Three of them are very nearby on the north-northeast side of the town. The "king and the queen" or "mother and father" is one pair. There is also the "prince/son" about 20 meters south of them, while the "wife/daughter" is about a kilometer east of them. Each one is about a meter tall and weather worn, but you can still see the carvings and tie your *khatag* to the fence around them. Traditionally, locals visit the "parents" for good luck. Men seeking a wife visit the wife statue, and if a mother is hoping for a son or daughter, she'll go to the corresponding statue as well.

On the western edge of town and farther in the countryside, there are some perennial *ger* camps with restaurants that operate in the summers. There is a campground and *ger* camp on the south edge of the town as well, and the school dormitory has rooms open in the summer if you're in a pinch. However, it's often difficult to find the caretaker of the school, especially without speaking Mongolian. If you're interested in staying in Dariganga, you should inquire with the travel center in Baruun Urt.

**The Dariganga Natural Park (Дарьганга байгалийн газар)** includes the dunes, lakes, and dead volcanoes around Dariganga Soum. **Altan Ovoo (Алтан овоо)** is a dead volcano overlooking Dariganga *soum* center that has been worshipped since the seventeenth century. The peak is capped by a large, fancy golden-topped *ovoo*. The steep five-minute climb is certainly worth it for the tremendous, expansive view, but it's a man-only mountain—sorry, ladies. Traditionally, men would climb to the top while women would walk all the way around it, though these days you don't see too many women doing so. Instead, there are shrines and stupas for women and men alike at the base of the mountain. Near the mountain are the so-called marble king, queen, and bride *balbals*.

Not far south of the *soum* center is the northern edge of the **Moltsog Els (Молтсог элс)**, a range of dunes that extends 248 square kilometers (96 square miles) separating the steppe from the Gobi. It's interesting to check out, though these are mostly small waves of vegetated dunes, unlike the big, bare, sweeping dunes of Khongoriin Els in Umnugovi Aimag or the Mongol Els of western Tuv Aimag. Still, the dunes and the park extend all the way past **Ganga Nuur (Ганга нуур)** to **Dagshin Nuur (Дагшин нуур)** and are flanked by the lakes **Kholboo (Холбоо)**, **Erdene (Эрдэнэ)**, and **Duut (Дуут)**, all of which host migrating cranes and other birds during autumn, which is the best time to be here. You also may run across one or more of the 60 broken and scattered deer stones in and around the park.

**Shiliin Bogd Uul (Шилийн богд уул)** (N45°28'22.99", E114°35'7.63") is about 60 kilometers (37 miles) east of Dariganga Soum, a two- or three-hour drive. The mountain is one of three "energy centers" in Mongolia—the others are in Dornogovi Aimag near the Danzanravjaa Khamariin Khiid and in Umnugovi Aimag's Khanbogd Soum. At 1,778 meters (5,833 feet), it is the highest peak in the *aimag,* but it only takes about ten minutes to walk to the top. From the base, it's a little bit steep (though not too difficult since even all the elderly Mongolian *emees*, grandmothers, seem to make it up there just fine), but the view from the top is stupendous. From there you can see all the 10-15 million year-old dead volcanoes scattered around it. You can also see China's Inner Mongolia to the south. To get the full impact of the spiritual energy of the mountain, locals suggest you be on the peak at sunrise (as early as 3:30 a.m. in June!). Loads of domestic tourists take annual trips to the mountain for good luck, and natives of Sukhbaatar Aimag often go more frequently. If you come to the *aimag*, you can't leave without a trip to the top.

**Shiliin Bogd Ger Camp** is open year round and costs only MNT5,000 per bed

## B. Aldarmaa and "Awesome Sukhbaatar"

B. Aldarmaa grew up in a *ger* in the countryside of Sukhbaatar Aimag outside of Baruun-Urt. Now as a professional adult who has dedicated her life to teaching and intercultural exchange, she is actively focused on promoting education in the aimag to improve the economic development and growth of Baruun-Urt.

After excelling as an English teacher at a local school and subsequently at a university for 12 years, Aldarmaa is now the foreign language specialist for all of the schools in Sukhbaatar Aimag. Not surprisingly, she was also selected as the representative from Mongolia to participate in an embassy-sponsored trip to the United States along with other educators from around the world.

As someone who enjoys developing partnerships and new opportunities, Aldermaa can often be found meeting with other English speakers and talking about her family, her country, and the many new ideas she has for Baruun-Urt. Two programs she is particularly hopeful to see through are a homestay program for travelers and an English resource center for Mongolian students.

When Aldarmaa is not traveling around the aimag working with the English and Russian teachers, you can catch her teaching English on the local SB Television network or spending time with her two sons and husband.

Aldarmaa is not alone in her dedication to helping the up-and-coming provincial center retain its small town spirit while striving to encourage its development. She and other community members are engaged through Awesome Sukkhbaatar, a chapter of the worldwide Awesome Foundation (www.awesomefoundation.org). Aldarmaa is the chairperson, or "dean," of this ten-person group that aims to help Baruun-Urt retain those qualities they think make it a wonderful place for their children and future generations. Each member contributes a small monthly due, and then the group reads small proposals submitted by local students and adults. The group selects a project, and they award their combined dues to one person or team who then makes their "awesome idea" happen. Aldarmaa and the other members of Awesome Sukhbaatar have a truly exciting task ahead of them as they work to inspire and empower students and members of the community to turn ideas into realities.

Awesome Sukhbaatar also has several international members that help to support the club, primarily former Peace Corps Volunteers that want to retain close connections with this tight knit community. If you're interested in meeting with the members of Awesome Sukhbaatar while you're in Baruun-Urt to get an idea of the new initiatives taking place in the community or to learn more about Awesome Mongolia, the countrywide organization heading up the Awesome groups in the country, contact hi@awesomemongolia.com.

per night. It offers Mongolian food, horse riding, herder visits, folk art, and a souvenir shop. It can hold 40 to 50 guests. Call the camp at 99033140.

**Lkhachinvandad Uul Natural Reserve** is the area surrounding Shilin Bogd Uul. It sits along on the border with China, 200 kilometers (120 miles) and six or more hours south of Baruun Urt. The reserve is comprised of lush grassland that remains thick and tall because herders aren't allowed to graze their cattle there. It is also home to a cool freshwater lake where the Gobi meets the steppe.

**Taliin Agui (Талын агуй)** (N45°35'25.55", E114°30'3.64") is a frosty cave located a short 15 kilometers (9.5 miles) northwest from the Shiliin Bogd Uul. It is pretty cold in there even in the summer, and if you visit there, you might have the impression that you are in a walk-in refrigerator. The entrance is a squeeze, so larger people might not be able to get into it, but most people shouldn't have too much of a problem in the summer after much of the ice covering the entrance has melted. After that you have about three meters (10 feet) where the ceiling is only about 1.25 meters (4 feet) high before the cave opens up into three main caverns, 4.5 meters (15 feet) high and 9 meters (30 feet) in diameter. Blue *khadags* hung by previous visitors adorn the walls.

In the summer, the **Taliin Agui Ger Camp** operates near the entrance of the cave. It has basic accommodations and food for about MNT5,000 per night. If you forgot your flashlight (torch), you may be able to borrow one here. It's about 60 kilometers (37 miles) northeast of the Dariganga *soum* center. It includes a lodge and 10 *gers* that can hold up to 100 people. The camp serves Mongolian food and offers folk art, horseback riding, volleyball, table tennis, and basketball. Call the camp at 99261659.

# Tuv Aimag (Төв аймаг)

Named for its location, Tuv Aimag or "Center Aimag," surrounds Ulaanbaatar, though it lies slightly north and east from the center of country. The western part of the Khentii Mountain Range and the Tuul River make the landscape interesting and provide important resources for UB and for tourists. It is home to roughly 100,000 people spread over 27 *soums*, some of which blend seamlessly into Ulaanbaatar's outskirts.

The crown jewel of the *aimag* for tourists is **Gorkhi-Terelj National Park** (or simply **Terelj**). If you're short on time in Mongolia and you want to visit the country-side without getting too remote, Tuv Aimag, and more specifically Terelj, is where you should go. It's one of Mongolia's bigger provinces, but most travelers who step off the Trans-Siberian railroad in Ulaanbaatar with only a few days to experience Mongolia

The Guide

find themselves in the park pursuing all things traditional. The *ger* camps with showers (and other more remote ones), horse and camel riding, and eagle displays offer tourists a quick way to check Mongolian must-do's off their list before they head back across the border. Guesthouses in UB can almost always book or help you book a cheap, interesting time here, often with family members or friends of theirs who live in the area. There are also luxury hotels with Western-friendly amenities for the less adventurous, and golf courses that are more adventurous than you might expect.

The **Khustain Nuruu National Park** is host to a stable and flourishing Takhi (Przewalski's) horse population due to a successful reintroduction program that began in the early 1990s. The park is only about 100 kilometers from Ulaanbaatar, making it both accessible and affordable to reach if you're short on time.

The ruins of **Manzshir Khiid** are a nice walk from the *aimag* capital, **Zuunmod**, which is itself a cheap *mikr* away from UB. Or you can reach the monastery ruins by a brisk day hike over the **Bogd Khan Uul** south of UB by the Zaisan Monument.

## GETTING THERE

### By Bus

There are no buses that go to Zuunmod, but there are UB city buses that reach into certain portions of Tuv Aimag overlapping into the city. However, these aren't especially useful for tourists. These buses cost a little over the normal fare but are still very cheap if you just want to hop on a bus and see the city from a different vantage.

One daily bus makes the round-trip journey to Terelj and back. You can find it on the south side of Sukhbaatar Square. The 2.5-hour trip leaves around 4:00 p.m.

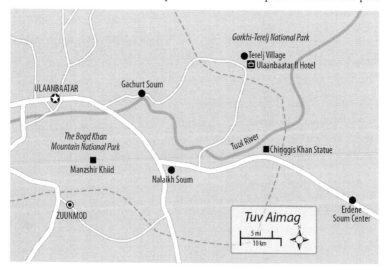

The bus coming back leaves around 7:00 p.m. Tickets costs around MNT2,000 each way and are purchased on the bus. Look for "Тэрэлж" on the front of the bus.

## By Shared Transport

Microbuses to Zuunmod leave regularly from the Teveerin Tovchoo, a short walk from BD's Mongolian Grill on Seoul Street in UB. Look for a sign in the front window that says "Зуунмод." It should cost you around MNT1,500, but some drivers may try to ask you to pay more depending on capacity and whether you look like a foreigner. You will be dropped off in the center of Zuunmod at the taxi stand. You can find your return trip from here as well. As with all microbuses, they leave when they're full (and overfull) and often pick up passengers along the way, but this is the cheapest and easiest way to Zuunmod.

Sometimes in the summer, drivers will stop on the rural road to buy a bottle of *airag*. If you're looking for a taste of the famous drink, this would be as cheap and authentic as it gets. If you want them to stop, try calling out *"Zocks-or-ray! Airag awmaar ben."*

## Private Taxi

UB taxis will gladly take you all the way to Zuunmod, but they will charge around MNT30,000. If you have five passengers and you're in a hurry to get out there, it's an option. Don't let the driver charge you for the return fare unless you're actually in the car with him.

# ZUUNMOD (ЗУУНМОД)

The capital of Tuv Aimag has a quaint feel to it with a grassy park in the center and a few pretty good places to eat. The name means "100 Trees," but there are certainly more than that. Because of its proximity to UB, it has a bit of a bedroom community or suburb feel.

There are many new brick houses and paved streets, and a few people speak more than a little English. In the surrounding countryside, herders raise their animals in more permanent settlements than you might expect, complete with barns and stables. During the summertime, it can be a bit of a ghost town, as folks retreat farther out.

There used to be a textile factory that employed much of the town, but it didn't survive the transition to capitalization. It now sits awaiting investment. If you know somebody who'd like to invest, stop by the local Chamber of Commerce office next to the taxi stand.

## WHERE TO STAY

**Governors Hotel** Located on the left side of the government building, the first floor is a big restaurant. The rooms are on the second floor, and they cost MNT10,000-25,000. The lux rooms have a single king bed and en suite toilet while the regular rooms have multiple beds and a shared toilet. No shower or laundry, but the shower house is close by. Look for the little yellow sign that says "Hotel & Café" in English.

**New World Hotel** The first floor is a little disco bar with cheap Borgio and a *guanz* with Chinese and Mongolian food, but it's not the fanciest looking joint. The rooms are on the second floor, and they cost between MNT15,000-25,000. The lux rooms have big sofas and bigger beds, TV, and en suite toilets, but the standard rooms have a shared toilet and a little shared "VIP" dining room where you can eat your own food. There is no shower or laundry, but if you need some fresh clothes in a pinch, the waitress at the restaurant can do it for you overnight. The sea green building is topped with a big red sign that reads "New World Hotel" on the top.

## WHERE TO EAT

### Restaurants

**Duluun (Долөөн)** Located on the left side of the central park, it is a Korean restaurant that doubles as a karaoke room. We recommend the spicy Korean noodle soup, which is cheap, though the real great choices will set you back close to MNT10,000. They also have the usual Mongolian dishes, which are by far the more reasonably priced choices. The karaoke room costs MNT5,000 per hour. ₮₮

### Guanzes

**Turleg (Түрлэг)** This is the cheapest and easiest to find place for food in Zuunmod. Located next to the taxi stand, you can order a few *khuushuur* and a *suutei tsai* (milk tea) for under MNT1,000. Add a little *salat* and make a meal of it. ₮

## WHAT TO DO

**Gorkhi-Terelj National Park**, or simply Terelj, was founded in 1993 to protect the area from the sprawling development of UB. The national park is home to herders, tour companies, two golf courses, a ski lodge, and many *ger* camps catering to tourists. There is also a small village settlement with shops at the terminus of the daily round-trip bus from UB.

The park has become the one-stop Mongolian countryside theme park for travelers looking to get a quick glimpse of Mongolia outside UB. It also provides a haven for city dwelling Mongolians to take refuge by communing with nature without having to go too far. Many of the services there are luxurious compared to what you will find elsewhere in the country, like *gers* with toilets or windows sitting on concrete slabs, restaurants with Western-style food, and accessible horse, camel, and yak rides.

In the summer, the alpine landscape, with its evergreen forests and running mountain streams, makes the park a peaceful retreat. You may even remember the park from an episode of the American travel competition show, "The Amazing Race," which featured Terelj in the second episode of its tenth season in the fall of 2006.

There is also the legendary **Turtle Rock (*Melkhi Khad*)** (N47°54'26.50", E107°25'21.67"), a rock formation so named because it looks, with very little imagination, like a giant turtle. The reptiles have been considered sacred throughout Asia for centuries and represent long life. This huge rock has become the iconic symbol of the park and is quite interesting, for being a giant rock. There are numerous ger camps within the park.

The cheapest way to get there on your own is to take the bus, which leaves around 4:00 p.m. from Peace Avenue on the south side of Sukhbaatar Square, headed east. Look for the name "Тэрэлж" on the front of the bus, which also goes through Nalaikh Soum on the outskirts of UB, technically located in Tuv Aimag. It costs around MNT2,000 for the ride, which terminates near the Ulaanbaatar II Hotel, home of the best golf course. You should get off at Turtle Rock or thereabouts and spend some time walking throughout the park. It's a great place to take a picture and hike about before continuing by foot down the road toward the dinosaur park, which is also located on the main loop. You should be able to approach any of the *ger* camps along the way and find a place to sleep for the night, arrange for a horse or camel ride, or get your picture taken while holding an eagle or hawk. Or you can head into the pasture behind turtle rock to find a herder to squat with for the night—or at least pull up a patch of ground for your tent. The bus leaves in the morning along the same route. Ask around for the bus's approximate time of departure wherever you end up or just hitch with a car headed toward UB.

You could also arrange a pretty fun time through your guesthouse in UB. UB guesthouses often have family or friends who are herders in the area, and they can drive you out to the huge silver **Chinggis Khan Statue** near Erdene Soum. A driver for the day will cost you about $45, and a tour of Terelj with accommodations around $30-80. We recommend tours from the Mongolian Steppe Guesthouse, UB Guesthouse, or Khongor Guesthouse.

**Manzshir Khiid (Манзшир Хийд)**, founded in 1733, housed a large population of monks and lamas until the late 1930s when the purges leveled the grounds. Now, all that can be seen of the 20 buildings is a terraced hillside topped by one reconstructed temple. This acts as a museum dedicated to telling the story of the monastery and the 300 monks who lost their lives during its forced demise. Some of the museum is in English, and the staff couldn't be friendlier.

If you hike there from Zuunmod, you may want to stay overnight in the *ger* camp, which has a small restaurant. You could also pitch a tent nearby or make your way back to Zuunmod for the night. It is also possible to take a taxi to Zuunmod and then a microbus to UB. You can certainly make the monastery into a day trip from the capital.

## The Bogd Khan Mountain National Park

Marking the southernmost sprawl of Ulaanbaatar, near the Zaisan Memorial, is the Bogd Khan Mountain. It has been a protected area since 1778 and is considered a sacred site. As the story goes, the mountain, which was said to be directly connected to Tibet, began to grow up from the steppe. It was angry because it had not been acknowledged with a proper name, as all mountains should be. Finally, the Bogd Khan or "sacred king" named it after himself, and it suddenly stopped its skyward ascent, calmed by the great honor.

On the side of the mountain facing Ulaanbaatar is the face of Chinggis Khan, laid out with white rocks to commemorate the 800th anniversary of his unification of Mongolia in 1206. There was a huge countrywide celebration, as you can imagine.

## Ulaanbaatar-Zuunmod Hike (Via Manzshir Khiid)

With Zuunmod, the center of Tuv Aimag, only about 20 kilometers (12 miles) away from Ulaanbaatar, it is quite possible to hike between the two. The venture is a great way to get out of the hustle and bustle of the city. The walk can be completed in a day if you're willing to push hard, or you can make it a more leisurely overnight hike. As an added bonus, the entire duration of the hike is located in the very pleasant and relatively lush conifer forests of the Bogd Khan National Park. Zuunmod is very nearly directly south of UB, with Manzshir Khiid just a few kilometers further east.

Hiking up and over Bogd Khan doesn't take a great deal of skill, but it does require awareness of time and adherence to the buddy system. If you're going to hike this route, we strongly advise doing so with a partner, sharing your plans with a friend or your guesthouse staff, and taking a compass or GPS unit that you can use confidently.

Even the main trail is not marked as well as it perhaps could be, and navigating can be a mix of luck and direction-by-sight at times (although, unlike the treeless mountains of, say, western Mongolia, the forest here makes it considerably more difficult to rely on sight to tell you where to go).

Weather is another risk factor, as the area is known for abrupt changes in conditions, generally for the worse. Things are usually calmer during the summer, but even then fast-moving thunderstorms, fog, or freak snowstorms of spring and autumn may pop up. In 2010, a young American hiker died after tiring on this route and getting caught in freezing overnight temperatures. Some months later a British expat on his way to Manzshir got lost as well. After a search team found him and took him to a Mongolian hospital for hypothermia, the man apparently refused treatment and fled the facility, which made for one more bit of gossip for the Mongolian blogosphere's running discussion on how weird foreigners are. But back to the fun stuff:

To hike from UB, take the bus or a taxi to Khoroo 11 behind the Zaisan Monument. By taxi, bear right where the main road heading south forks and follow it to the end. If you go by bus, the final stop is in front of a large walled complex, a prison, incidentally. Get off there (you'll have to) and head south along the path on the west side of the prison. When possible, head west to meet back up with the paved road, then follow it to the end where the **Bogd Khan National Park** shares a gate with a *ger* camp popular among local Mongolians. Hike up the road towards **Bogd Khan Uul** and through the camp. You'll have to pay the standard MNT3,000 park fee.

Walk through to the back of the camp, where you will see a trail that heads up the hill. Follow that trail as it works its way up the hill, keeping an eye out for yellow tags, which will keep you more or less on the main trail. The trail generally leads in a southerly direction and is fairly well beaten until you get to a meadow where you will begin to descend. It is a fairly long descent, and a road will cut across your path at one point. At the bottom of the descent you will start to see some buildings on the other side of the valley; before you reach them there is a low saddle heading up to the left. Climb up to that saddle and start following the ridge in a southeast direction. This will take you over a couple of smaller ridges and eventually you will drop down to Manzshir Khiid. From the monastery there is a road and a small creek that can be followed back to Zuunmod. You may also drop into the meadow that is one ridge to the west, which also has a road that leads back to Zuunmod. Following the meadow and creek will bring you to a paved road on the right, just after a factory. Following the road west and then taking the second paved left will put you on the main street of Zuunmod. The road that turns right after the government building and square will take you to the bus stop at the edge of town.

If you choose to depart from Zuunmod and trek back to UB, the trail is slightly more difficult to find simply because it blends in with the surrounding forest. From

Manzshir Khiid, head northwest up the ridge around the monastery. If you continue in a northwest direction over a couple small ridges, you will drop down into the long meadow mentioned above. Working your way up the meadow and up the hill, you will eventually get to the top where the trail picks up again. It takes a bit of hunting, but from here you should be heading roughly north. Going in this direction, you don't have the advantage of being able to see the city once you've made it over the spine of the mountain. Head slightly northwest and drop down into the *ger* camp near UB. Descending too soon and too far east can get you in trouble with the legion of guards protecting the presidential palace, so do your best to keep to the yellow-tagged trail.

The hike as a whole should take between eight and ten hours depending on your speed and hiking crew. Along the way, you may see the logs attached to long wooden legs resting against trees; these are battering rams used by pine-nut harvesters. Otherwise, there are few signs of mankind along the route, despite the close proximity to sprawling Ulaanbaatar.

## Khustain Nuruu National Park (Хустайн нуруу)

The Khustain Nuruu Nature Reserve was established in 1993 to preserve and reintroduce Mongolia's wild *takhi* (pronounced "takh") horses and their habitat. The *takhi* is also known as the Asian wild horse, the Mongolian wild horse, and most often as Przewalski's horse after the Polish-Russian Nikolai Przewalski, a nineteenth century geographer and explorer who is credited as the first European to describe the wild horse. Today the horse is probably the most recognized symbol of Mongolia and its wildlife. The horses used to roam free in great herds before poachers, livestock overgrazing, and habitat reduction withered their numbers in the 1960s, and all but rendered them extinct. Thanks to captive breeding programs in zoos in Germany and the Netherlands, the *takhi* were reintroduced into specially protected areas in the 1990s, though they were never domesticated. The park, which is supported by the Dutch Foundation for the Preservation and Protection of the Przewalski Horse in conjunction with the Mongolian government, is now home to hundreds of *takhi* that survive in and around wolves, gazelles, lynx, and other animals that benefit from the protected habitat.

To see the horses, you must be accompanied by a guide; you can book a guide at the Takhi Information Center inside the park. The guides only travel on worn paths to minimize their environmental impact. It is also possible to hike or go horseback riding inside the park, but fishing must be booked separately with private transportation (usually through a tour company). You must also purchase a fishing permit (MNT10,000).

The best way to reach the park is from Zuunmod, but you would do better to hire a Jeep in UB for the trip. You can negotiate a rate of about $80 round-trip. You can take the UB-Kharkhorin bus and get off at the turn off toward the park, where a sign indicates that it is 10 kilometers to the entrance, and then walk to the Takhi Information Center inside the park. From there, you might be able to book lodging at the Moilt Ger Camp (MNT23,000) that sits on the border of the park, but there is no camping inside the park. You might also wrap this trip into a tour heading to Kharkhorin booked through a guesthouse or agency. Entrance to the park is about MNT6,000.

### Chinggis Khan Statue Complex (Tsonjin Boldog)
Outside of Erdene Soum on the road toward Khentii Aimag stands an enormous silver statue of Chinggis Khan atop a horse (N47°48'26.05", E107°32'7.59"). Begun in 2004 and completed in 2007, it stands several stories above the otherwise completely

The Guide

## Enkhtuul Chimedtseren

Enkhtuul Chimedtseren or Tuul (pronounced like "toll", not "tool") is an affable and smiley English teacher in her 20s from Zuunmod. She is named after the river that flows north to south through UB and Tuv Aimag and has a personality almost as big. Her story has inspired many travelers to be on their best behavior.

As a small girl, she saw a white guy walking along the street by her apartment building. With wide eyes, she hung her body half way out the window and waved enthusiastically as she screamed hello to the stranger. The stranger turned around, looked up, smiled, and said his hello with a wave in return. At that moment, she knew she wanted to be an English teacher because she just had to connect with more people like this.

Nearly every volunteer and traveler can tell a similar story from their opposite perspective. We've all heard the complaint, "I walked down the street and all these kids were yelling 'Hi!' It was really annoying." From Tuul's window, though, she saw the English-speaking outside world in this one smiling stranger and wanted to connect.

When Tuul was in the fifth grade, her cousin's family moved to UB, and her cousin lived with Tuul's family in order to finish school in Zuunmod. That year she taught Tuul some English letters and a few words. The next year, Tuul began to study English at school, receiving much praise and encouragement from her teachers for her hard work and success, which emboldened her efforts. She took computer and English courses at the State University of Education, and four years later, she returned to her secondary school as a computer and English teacher. On preferring to teach English to computers, she quipped with a big smile, "I don't know why. Maybe it's because computers don't talk with me." She's now in India taking computer classes, and she is able to use her English in this phase of her career and personal growth.

Her story offers a good reminder that travelers are ambassadors. People are constantly watching your every move and attaching how you behave with how all Americans or Australians or white women or black men or Russians or non-Russians behave. Be on your best behavior . . . they're taking notes.

wide-open landscape. It is intended to be the Eiffel Tower of Mongolia, but as there is no reliable transportation to it, getting there isn't easy. The best way to get to it is by hiring a driver, usually with a Terelj tour, who can take you there. The cheapest way to get there is to take a microbus from Teevriin Tovchoo to Erdene Soum, and then walk to the statue or find a local taxi driver to take you. The easiest way to see it from a distance is by enjoying the view from your bus on the way to Khentii or Sukhbaatar Aimags.

Currently, there is no museum or interpretive center at the statue, so stopping there isn't so interesting (a theme park is planned for the surrounding area), but you can climb to the top of the statue for a view of the massive Mongolian plains. It seems that every Mongolian you meet has a picture in their house with this statue, though, so if you want to impress your friends back home with how authentically Mongolian your experience was, you might want to hang this picture on your wall. If you have Mongolian friends visit you, this is likely to get you instant street credibility.

# Umnugovi Aimag (Өмнөговь аймаг)

Umnugovi is the largest and least populated province in Mongolia at a population density of 0.28 persons per kilometer (0.17 per mile). The *aimag*, whose name means "South Gobi," is widely known for the discoveries of dinosaur bones and eggs that have been found throughout the desert dating back to the 1920s when the first Western explorers began poking around. It is one of the more explored tourist areas, which means it has a lot of infrastructure compared to other parts of the country, but the *aimag's* western region contains "The End of the World" as described by explorer Roy Chapman Andrews. If you're in the country for a week or less and you want to see the famous Gobi Desert, Umnugovi should be on your agenda.

The premiere Gobi destination is **Gurvan Saikhan National Park** or "The Three Wonders Park." It stretches from the border with Bayankhongor Aimag to the outskirts of Dalanzadgad and includes the **Yolin Am**, an excellent location for birding, and the majestic **Khongorin Els (Khongor Sand Dunes)**. This part of the Gobi is a magical place where some of the most important dinosaur discovers were made, including the first full fossilized skeleton. Just outside the park is **Bayanzag (Flaming Cliffs)**, the first place dinosaur eggs were discovered.

The **Danzanravjaa Demchigiin Khiid** energy center and monastery in **Khanbogd Soum** is a popular destination for monastery fans because of its special historic location.

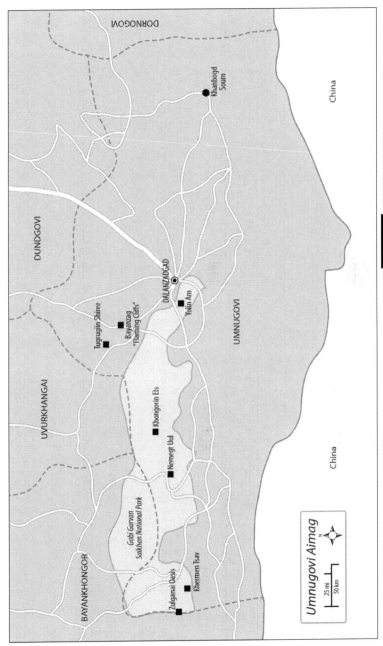

The Guide

Umnugovi Aimag

25 mi
50 km

DORNOGOVI

China

Khambogd Soum

DUNDGOVI

DALANZADGAD

Yolin Am

UMNUGOVI

Tugrugiin Shiree

Bayanzag
"Flaming Cliffs"

UVURKHANGAI

Khongorin Els

Nemegt Uul

China

Gobi Gurvan
Saikhan National Park

BAYANKHONGOR

Zulganai Oasis

Khermen Tsav

The *aimag's* mountains reach an altitude of 2,825 meters (9,268 feet) and support a diverse range of wildlife, including the extremely rare snow leopard, which you are unfortunately rather unlikely to spot. You are much more likely to see the black-tailed gazelle darting across the open landscape, and since the *aimag* is home to one quarter of the country's domesticated camels, you're likely to not only see some but to ride some, too.

## GETTING THERE

### By Air

EZnis airways has regular flights to Dalanzadgad year round. You are able to view flight schedules and book flights online. Prices vary but should be around $150 each way. Visit eznisairways.com for more information. The airport is nearly in town, less than a kilometer from the center. You can arrange for transportation to outlying *ger* camps ahead of time, and they will pick you up from there.

### By Bus

The bus to Dalanzadgad (MNT22,000) leaves daily at 8:00 a.m. from Bayanzurkh in Ulaanbaatar. The return bus leaves from the bus station in Dalanzadgad at 8:00 a.m.

There is a bus that goes to Khanbogd that also leaves from Bayanzurkh on Mondays at 8:00 a.m. for around MNT23,000. The return bus to UB leaves on Wednesday at 8:00 a.m.

## The Story of the Weeping Camel

Umnugovi is famous not just for fossils. It is now known for being featured in the independent German film "The Story of the Weeping Camel," which was nominated for Best Documentary at the 2004 Academy Awards. In the film, a herder helps one of his camels through the painful delivery of a rare white colt that is then rejected by the mother. The herder and family employ many tricks trying to get the calf feeding and bonding with the mother, eventually even employing the services of Buddhist lamas who perform blessings. After all else fails, two of the sons set out on camels toward the *aimag* center where they summon a *morin khuur* (horse-head fiddle) player who they hope can help with his music. He agrees and accompanies the boys back to their countryside home. Remarkably, as the player strums his special song on the ornate two-stringed instrument and the mother of the family sings along, tears begin streaming from the eyes of the mother camel. When the song is finished, the mother camel incredibly allows the calf to feed from her for the first time. It's an inspiring movie you should see if you haven't already. There are subtitles for the Mongolian, but there is little dialogue in the movie.

In addition to dinosaur bones, tourists, and camels, Umnugovi is rich in mineral deposits, including massive deposits of coal and gold, coveted internationally and accounting for a large portion of the country's GDP.

### By Shared Transportation
You can book a *purgon* or *mikr* for about the same price as the bus (MNT23,000-25,000), but the bus is more comfortable and more convenient.

From Dalanzadgad, *mikrs* depart daily for UB and local *soums* from the front of the Everyday Supermarket. Check with your hotel because they should be able to help recommend and arrange drivers.

### Getting Around the Aimag
Jeeps depart from in front of the Everyday Supermarket building, and taxis to the airport and around town depart from the taxi station (MNT500-1,000).

## DALANZADGAD (ДАЛАНЗАДГАД)

Dalanzadgad, pronounced pretty much like it looks, is the capital of the *aimag*. This city, 553 kilometers (344 miles) from Ulaanbaatar, is a growing city thanks to tourism and mining. You can hire a Jeep or a *mikr* to all major tourist attractions from here, but there really isn't much to do in town besides visit the museum or perhaps see a movie. It mostly just functions as a stopping point for traveling to and from UB.

## WHERE TO STAY

There are a few hotels in Dalanzdgad where you can lay your head very cheaply if you're traveling through, but you should get out into the countryside toward the Gurvan Saikhan National Park as soon as you can. Because the reserve is such a popular tourist destination, there are some "luxury" *ger* camps and tours close to the *aimag* center, while the budget options are found in the *aimag* center.

### In Dalanzadgad

**Dalanzadgad Hotel** Located north of the town center, on the paved road on the way to the airport. It is a little bit on the high end, but it's the best place in town. A lux room has a double bed for MNT90,000 per room. Half lux comes with a double bed and costs MNT60,000 per room, and the standard is a twin bed for MNT40,000 per room. There is a small tourist store on the first floor, and the hotel can help you book travel and other services. A fun feature (although it's a little outdated) is the big map of the town inside the hotel. *01532-24455, 99877613, 99732864*

**Mazaalai Ger Camp** A small *ger* camp located directly across from the bus station in Dalanzadgad. At $6-15 a night, the nine *gers* on the grounds are a good bet for a cheap overnight stay. The camp has a decent restaurant and bar, shower, laundry, and billiards, and the staff can help you book trips to the attractions. *01532-23040, 99847411*

**Erkhec (Эрхэс)** No big extras or perks. This is your best budget option. It is located next to the Oyu Tolgoi Office and across from Gandirs Tower, which houses the

Everyday Supermarket. A lux room is MNT30,000, the four-bed room is MNT48,000, a two-twin bed room goes for MNT26,000, and the standard one-bed room, which is perfect for two people, is MNT18,000. You can usually book when you arrive.

## Ger Camps in the Countryside

**Three Camel Lodge** (N43°53.603', E103°44.435') Named among National Geographic's top 50 eco lodges in the world in 2009. The lodge is located about 65 kilometers (40 miles) outside of Dalanzagdad, which puts it in the middle of the countryside and about 30 kilometers (18.6 miles) from the Flaming Cliffs and 125 kilometers (78 miles) from Khongorin Els. Not only is it a luxurious camp ($175-300 per night, including meals and excursions and $50-75 for lodging), but it is also a base for scientific research and wildlife monitoring. The operators of the lodge actively fight against animal poaching and the unauthorized removal of dinosaur fossils from paleontological sites, and they work with residents and business to dissuade them from using plastic bags in an effort to clean up the Gobi. If you're a lover of conservation and responsible eco tourism, this is your place. *11313396; info@ThreeCamelLodge.com; www.threecamellodge.com/*

**Juulchin Gobi Tours** (N43°45.236', E104°07.578') Offers specialized group tours for birding and fossil hunters. However, the tours are not especially cheap ($150-$170 per day, including meals and travel). The camp is located about 55 kilometers (34 miles) from the Flaming Cliffs and 30 kilometers (18.6 miles) northwest of Dalanzadgad. Their accommodations ($40 for lodging) are nice, the food is good, the grounds are plain yet substantial, and they have a second camp at the Khongorin Els. It's a good place to meet and swap stories with other travelers, some of whom spend up to six or more nights at the camp. The staff speaks Russian, Japanese, German, and Swedish. The camp also has an airstrip, so you can park your jet. *99074355, 88084959, 99852645, 95144470; info@juulchingobi.com; www.juulchingobi.com*

**Tovshin Ger Camps** (N43°45.841', E104°02.838') A little more of a lower end option compared to the others, though the price suggests otherwise (lodging $45, large discounts for groups of five or more). The surroundings and the camps offer no real frills, but they do have hot water, toilets, and restaurants. Tovshin 2 is more rural (27 kilometers or 17 miles from Gurvan Saikhan) and focuses on nomadic lifestyle exploration. Tovshin 1 is bigger and has more of a camp feel; it even includes a telescope. It's 40 kilometers (25 miles) from Dalanzagdad and 40 kilometers (25 miles) from Gurvan Saikhan. *11463251, 99114811, 99114810, 99097824; nomadicurtuu@magicnet.mn*

**Gobi Discovery** Has been around since 2003. Gobi Discovery offers summer and winter tours including winter camel treks and customizable summer trips to the main western attractions from their two camps. The South Gobi camp is about 40 kilometers (25 miles) from Dalanzagdad (N43°46.636', E104°04.100'). It has 90 beds and a restaurant. The Khongor camp (N43°46.495', E102°20.307') is on the Khongorin Gol near the Khongorin Els. It has 100 beds ($20 per night), a European-style restaurant (three meals for $25), and trips to oases and other remote attractions in the western part of the aimag. *11312769; gobidiscovery@magicnet.mn; http://www.gobidiscovery.mn/*

The Guide

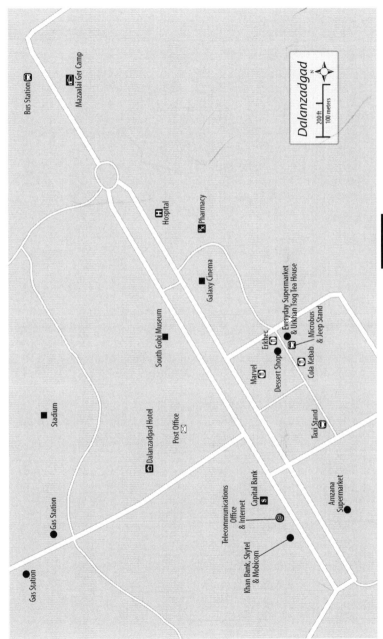

Dalanzadgad

200 ft
100 meters

Bus Station

Mazaalai Ger Camp

Hospital

Pharmacy

Galaxy Cinema

South Gobi Museum

Everyday Supermarket
& Urkhan Tsog Tea House

Erkhec

Marvel

Dessert Shop

Cola Kebab

Microbus
& Jeep Stand

Stadium

Dalanzadgad Hotel

Post Office

Taxi Stand

Gas Station

Telecommunications
Office
& Internet

Capital Bank

Gas Station

Khan Bank, Skytel
& Mobicom

Amzana
Supermarket

# WHERE TO EAT

## Restaurants in Dalanzadgad

**Marvel** Has very interesting decorations that you will have to see for yourself. The food is also good especially for the price. The restaurant serves spaghetti and a meaty goulash, and the Korean-style soups are a real treat. ₮₮

**Bayanburd Restaurant** Inside the Dalanzadgad Hotel. This is the best bet for vegetarians; it even serves a green salad. The restaurant has the most European-style selections in town. Be on the lookout for the corn soup, stuffed chicken roll, and chicken with pineapple. The Mongolian fare is also high quality, especially the *khuushuur*. ₮₮

**Эрхэс (Erkhec)** Your standard Mongolian restaurant focusing on Mongolian cuisine. It's neither a fine dining experience nor a tea house, but the price is alright for the food selection. ₮₮

## Guanzes

**Urkhan Tsog Tea House (Урьхан Цог цайны газар)** In the same building as Everyday Supermarket. If you want an inexpensive quick meal, this place has some of the best *peroshki, buuz, and tsuivan* in town and you can't beat the price. ₮

**Cola Kebab** One of the newer restaurants in town. This place is uncommonly good for Dalanzadgad, and it serves a variety of Chinese-style dishes. ₮/₮₮

## Groceries

**Amzana Supermarket** The place to go when in you're in Dalanzagdad and you want some wine. You should try some Mongolian wine, though you might want to buy a back up of something else. This supermarket has vegetables and a very good selection of toiletries.

**Everyday Supermarket** With the best selection of hard liquor in town, it's your place to explore the world of spirits before you while away the evenings stargazing in the countryside or in Dalanzadgad. It carries a lot of Western items including cereal, Pringles, and pretzels, and the store also has a great selection of wine.

**Dessert Shop** An amazing little shop that focuses on groceries of sorts, especially produce. The prices for produce are the best you will find in town. Not only is it usually well stocked, it also has the best selection and prices for ice cream.

# WHAT TO DO IN DALANZADGAD

The **South Gobi Museum** (MNT2,000; 9:00 a.m.-6:00 p.m. Monday-Friday) on the main street, just off the square, doesn't have much as far as dinosaur bones and eggs go, but it does have a huge stuffed vulture, the namesake creature of Yolin Am in Gurvan Saikhan National Park. There are also Buddhist paintings and artifacts here. It's not the main attraction of the *aimag*, but it is a good way to pass an hour while getting to know the area.

**Galaxy Cinema** is a nice, new cinema that you wouldn't expect to find in this remote city. It usually has an American movie playing with Mongolian subtitles. If you've been traveling for a while and need a touch of Western culture, it can be a welcome respite from long overland travel before heading out for another long haul day.

## WHAT TO DO AROUND UMNUGOVI AIMAG

**Gobi Gurvan Saikhan National Park (Говь гурван сайхан байгалийн цогцолбор газар or "The Three Gobi Beauties Park")** spans from the border of Bayankhongor Aimag to the outskirts of Dalanzadgad. The name describes the attractive qualities of the eastern, central, and western mountain ranges that cut across the eastern part of the park. The park itself (entrance MNT3,000) runs along the northern part of the *aimag* and contains a variety of wildlife sustained by mountain runoff. Two of the most famous *aimag* attractions (Yolin Am and Khongorin Els) lie within the park, but you can also make your own extreme fossil-hunting hiking expeditions through the central and southern areas.

**Yolin Am (Ёлын Ам)** (N43°29'7.34", E104°4'18.94"), whose name means "The Mouth of a Bearded Vulture," sometimes also goes by the names Ossifrage Valley, Lammergeyer Valley, and Eagle Valley because of the many birds found there. It is a gorge more than 10 kilometers (6 miles) long that is filled with ice in the winter that can get up to 10 meters (33 feet) thick. In the past, the ice rarely melted in the summer, but now it usually melts by sometime in June and is dry by August. It is part of the Zuun Saikhanii Nuruu (the Eastern Beauty Range), about 46 kilometers (29 miles) west of Dalanzadgad.

The site, which is a habitat for several vulture species including the Lammergeier, Ossifrage, Himalayan, and Eurasian Griffon and the occasional Oriental Honey Buzzard, is great for birdwatchers, and the walk through the gorge can be enchantingly good fun. Look up for a chance to glimpse the vultures or look along the winding path of the narrowing channel for Sulphur-bellied warblers, beautiful rose finches, white-winged snowfinch, and Kozlov's accentor. The peculiar wallcreeper is probably the coolest Mongolian find. It can be fun to watch as it flits and lurches its way along, probing the crags.

**Khongorin Els (Хонгорын элс)** (N43°46'34.28", E102°11'32.44") are sand dunes that stand around 300 meters (985 ft) high, 12 kilometers (7.5 miles) wide, and 100 kilometers (62 miles) long. These are some of the largest, most spectacular, and perhaps the most visited dunes in the country. They are also known as the

The Guide

"Singing Dunes" or Duut Mankhan because of the way the sand grinds as it slides around. Do yourself a favor and climb the dunes at dusk, slide down the soft sides listening for the eerie humming that give the dunes their name, and watch the spectacular sunset. You'll notice the sand change color as the sun melts into the horizon. The Khongoriin Gol runs along the northern edges, enabling lush green grass to grow, contrasting beautifully with the yellows of the dunes.

There are great spots for camping nearby, and there are also a few *ger* camps (Gobi Discovery, Juulchin Gobi 2) where you can ride camels and horses. You can climb to the top of the dunes to have wonderful views of the desert and then slide back down if you have plastic bags handy.

Birdwatchers should keep their eyes peeled on the way to Khongorin Els for MacQueen's bustard in the taller grasses and Henderson's ground-jay scooting through gravel washes. There is water and greenery at the foot of the dunes, so be on the lookout for the steppe grey shrike, desert wheatear, desert warbler, greater sand plover, Mongolian finch, and Palla's sandgrouse.

**Nemegt Uul (Нэмэгт уул)** (N43°39'53.30", E101°31'29.30") is in the heart of the reserve, 400 kilometers (250 miles) west of Dalanzadgad. It is known for the fossils, similar to those in Bayanzag, that have been found among its red cliffs. If you're looking for a remote and rugged hike, tour Jeeps do come through here, so you could get a ride here and work your way through the Nemegt Canyon (нэмэгт ам). The south of the mountain is where you might head if you want to look for fossils. Remember to only look and don't touch unless you're on a registered archeological dig—unless your name is Indiana Jones.

Laid out below the mountains is the wide and dinosaur fossil rich Nemegt Basin or Badlands, which are so harsh and isolated that even herders don't live there. Many of the most famous digs have taken place around the badlands and in the canyons, but it's very, very remote. If you plan an expedition through here alone, you'll need a lot of water until you can reach the Zulganai Oasis (зулганай) (N43°34'11.18", E99°29'47.22"), a far western oasis.

**Khermen Tsav (Хэрмэн цав)** (N43°28.006', E99°49.976') was named "The End of the World" by Roy Chapman Andrews because of the collection of fossils found there and because of the area's general aura of extreme remoteness from civilization. In fact, the first full skeleton of a dinosaur was found here, not to mention the many other miscellaneous bones and fossilized eggs. It is a canyon 6 kilometers wide (3.7 miles) and 15 kilometers long (9.3 miles) full of cliffs up to 30 meters (98 feet) high in a region that was sea bottom about 200 million years ago.

**Bayanzag (Баянзаг or "Flaming Cliffs")** (N44°8'9.33", E103°43'21.84") are well known for the dinosaur bones and eggs that have been found in the area. In 1923, American explorer Roy Chapman Andrews made some of the most significant discoveries in paleontology here, including the first dinosaur eggs, which confirmed that dinosaurs came from eggs rather than by live birth. His expedition also found mammal skulls from the Cretaceous period, proving that mammals and dinosaurs did exist at the same time. He coined the area the "Flaming Cliffs" because of the enchanting red rock formations sticking up from the flat steppe, though the Mongolian name describes a rich stand of saxual bushes, which are low-growing, wind-gnarled trees stretching just above the otherwise barren landscape. Most people visit the red cliffs for the fossil hounding, but birders go targeting the Saxaul sparrow, an unassuming denizen of the saxaul "forest." It is a strange and peaceful place, and even the landscape around the area is gorgeous. It is only accessible by private car.

## Mining in Umnugovi

Because of Umnugovi's advantageous position near China, the largest consumer of coal in the world, Mongolia has played an important role in China's booming economy and its hunger for coal to fuel industrial growth, particularly because China lacks huge oil and natural gas reserves.

But the business of minerals is more complicated than the single interests of one booming country. There are two main companies digging for coal in Umnugovi: SouthGobi Resources and Oyu Tolgoi. Both are owned by Ivanhoe, a Canadian company that shares ownership of the latter with Rio Tinto, a British-Australian multinational mining and resources group with headquarters in London and Melbourne.

Fifty seven percent of SouthGobi Resources is owned by Ivanhoe Mines, but China's sovereign wealth fund is also a main investor. One of their mines, Ovoot Tolgoi, is also about 40 kilometers (25 miles) north of the border with China in Khanbogd Soum. A direct rail line to the Chinese side of the border has been constructed, but the Chinese government had to scrap additional planned rail lines in Mongolian because of a breakdown in talks with the Mongolian government. Instead the Chinese are planning a road that will be cheaper in the short term.

Oyu Tolgoi, the world's largest undeveloped copper and gold project, is 80 kilometers (50 miles) north of the Mongolia-China border. Sixty-six percent of it is owned by Ivanhoe Mines, and the Mongolian government owns the minority thirty four percent. When it's fully operational, the mine is expected to account for more than 30 percent of Mongolia's GDP, which has made for widespread accusations of corruption since the gold and copper ore was discovered in 2001. By 2003, heavy exploration began, and in 2009 tense negotiations for mineral rights and taxation ended in a successful deal for all parties.

Not only will the tax benefits help support the developing economy, but as of October 2010, Minerals and Energy Minister D. Zorigt reported that 63 percent of the 5,700 employees at the mine were Mongolian and that there were 2,400 registered Mongolian companies that supplied services and products to the project, worth nearly $240 million for private companies.

The Guide

Just 22 kilometers (13.5 miles) northeast of Bayanzag is Moltsog Els. These dunes are smaller than the premiere Khongorin Els, but they are closer to the Flaming Cliffs and are a popular spot for tourists who don't want to trek the tough 125 kilometers (80 miles) to the southwest to the bigger brother dunes. Tours often also venture to Tugrugiin Shiree (N44°16'59.45", E103°29'11.92"), the site of the famous "Fighting Dinosaurs" of the Cretaceous Period that were discovered during a joint Polish and Mongolian dig in 1971. Two dinosaurs, a flesh-eating velociraptor and a well-armored protoceratops, were fossilized for 80 million years together, locked in a deadly battle. The fight ended with a velociraptor claw in the neck of the protoceratops, which had bitten the arm of his attacker. These finds are traveling the world on exhibit and replicas are sold as learning aids for classrooms, but don't expect to see much besides the oasis-like saxual forest at the present-day site.

### Demchigiin Khiid (Дэмчигийн Хийд)

Located in Khanbogd Soum (N43°07.711', E107°07.668'), the monastery is in the same district as the Oyu Tolgoi Mine. Just 9.5 kilometers (6 miles) southwest of the Khanbogd village itself, it is an energy center known for its alkaline granite and one of five monasteries built by the mystic monk of Dornogovi Aimag, Danzanravjaa.

## Roy Chapman Andrews

Roy Chapman Andrews was a man responsible for some of the most groundbreaking discoveries of his time. Born in Beloit, Wisconsin in 1884, Andrews was an explorer, adventurer, and eventual director of the American Museum of Natural History. Some claim the fictional character Indiana Jones, a history professor and globetrotting archeologist portrayed in four films by Harrison Ford, is based on him.

Chapman has been primarily celebrated for a series of expeditions that he led through China and into Mongolia in the 1920s, in which he and his team discovered the first-known fossil dinosaur eggs, the "Fighting Dinosaurs" locked for eternity in mortal combat, and a veritable wealth of dinosaur fossils including the first complete skeleton. Before many of these discoveries, it wasn't known for sure whether dinosaurs were live-born or born from eggs, and there was still some question about their diet of either plants or meat. As any second grader can tell you now, dinosaurs came from eggs, and some ate plants while some ate other dinosaurs.

Andrews's adventures to Mongolia involved driving a fleet of cars westward from Peking, China in 1922 to Mongolia's Gobi Desert. Over the course of Andrews's four Mongolian expeditions, his findings included oviraptor eggs and a mammal skull that dated back to the Cretaceous period, proving that mammals existed alongside dinosaurs. We like to think that Mongolia, and Umnugovi in particular, was as instrumental in these landmark scientific discoveries as Andrews was, so make sure you make both the explorer and his dinosaur pals proud by seeing it. As you will discover, not much has changed in scenery or transportation in the past nine or so decades, so you too may feel like an intrepid explorer. But unlike Andrews and his team, you are not authorized to take your discoveries out of the park.

The monastery was destroyed in 1937 and is now undergoing a major renovation. In the surrounding mountains there are petroglyphs, but you may need to consult an experienced guide in order to find them.

# Uvs Aimag (Увс аймаг)

Uvs Aimag is, without a doubt, western Mongolia's diamond in the rough, or perhaps simply its roughest diamond. Incredibly remote despite its location on the Russian border, few foreigners make it to Uvs, which lends it a delightfully unexplored aura. The nature here is diverse and impressive, featuring salty **Khyargas Nuur** and the vast **Uvs Nuur**, the largest lake in Mongolia by surface area, **Kharkhiraa Mountain**, a glacial 4,000 meter peak, sand dunes, and large tracts of desert and much more. Uvs is known as the coldest *aimag* in the nation; winter temperatures of -50° C (-58° F) are not uncommon.

Uvs was once part of an all-encompassing western province that also included Khovd and Bayan Ulgii aimags. In the 1930s, it was briefly called Durvud Aimag, after the largest ethnic group in the province. Today, Durvud Mongols make up somewhere around half the population, while other ethnic groups including Khalka, Bayad, and Khoton round out most of the rest. The Khoton are one of the more intriguing ethnic groups to be found in western Mongolia. Residing almost exclusively in Tarialan (Тариалан) *soum*, the Khoton are a Turkic group imported by a Zuungarian king in the seventeenth or eighteenth centuries to cultivate wheat, since the nomadic Mongols wouldn't do it themselves. The Khoton are largely Mongolized at this point. They wear *deels* and speak Mongolian, but they have retained their Islamic roots, and Tarialan Soum is perhaps the only "Mongolian" *soum* in the country with an active mosque.

The Durvud speak a distinct dialect of the Mongolian language, which can prove a challenge even for native Mongolian speakers. Thanks to its remoteness and distinct dialect, Uvs suffers from a reputation as a backwater that is somewhat akin to that of the American deep south. A surprising number of Ulaanbaatar taxi drivers seem to hail from Uvs.

Despite the bad rap, Uvs has produced a number of notable Mongolians, including a veritable stable of today's most popular contemporary folk pop singers, like Javkhlan, as well as **Yumjaagiin Tsendenbal** and **Jamiin Batmunkh**, the communist leaders in power from 1953 to 1990.

For those intrepid enough to do a circuit of the west, Uvs is a good place to start. It is easier to find a car heading from Uvs to Khovd than vice versa, and almost no traffic goes between Uvs and Bayan Ulgii. Thus, starting in Uvs and heading south to Khovd and then west to Bayan Ulgii makes a good deal of sense.

The Guide

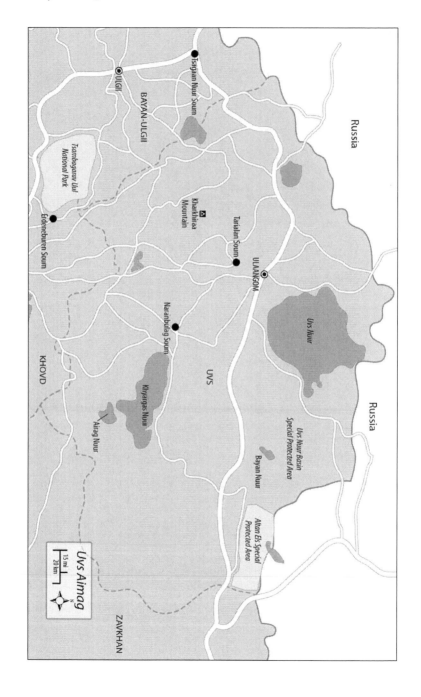

# GETTING THERE

## By Air

Aeromongolia flies between Uvs and Ulaanbaatar (with a stop in Murun) three days a week. EZnis Airways makes two flights per week during summer. Expect one-way tickets to be in excess of $300. Both airlines have offices in Ulaangom.

## By Land

Buses and *purgons* leave from the Dragon Center in Ulaanbaatar several times a week for around MNT51,000. Heading towards Ulaanbaatar, buses and *purgons* depart from the bus stand in front of the market, generally taking the northern route passing through Tosontsengel in Zavhan province. The northern highway (unpaved like all the rest) is beautiful, especially along the Zavhan-Arhangai border, but it is particularly arduous. Average travel time between Uvs and Ulaanbaatar is probably around 50 hours.

Shared *purgons* sometimes travel between Khovd and Uvs. From either *aimag* center, vans to the other are found in front of the main entrance to the market in the town. Look for the sign stating a bus's destination in the window. The cost is MNT18,000.

## Hitchhiking

Thumbing it out here is not recommended due to Uvs' remoteness. Tosontsengel in Zavkan Aimag, which is itself about as remote as it gets, is the only logical place to hitch a ride.

# ULAANGOM (УЛААНГОМ)

Ulaangom is a slightly sleepy *aimag* center with a decidedly rustic feel. Small rivers and tracts of trees, which give the *ger* districts a welcoming aura, ring the outskirts of the city. There are relatively few apartment blocks, and horses and horse carts are far more common in the streets than in the other Western *aimag* capitals. One foreigner, a longtime resident of western Mongolia, says that Ulaangom today is at the same level of development that Khovd's center was ten years ago.

The town may see the occasional Russian pass through, but almost no other tourists visit it. Perhaps because of this, the residents of Ulaangom seem to keep their distance a bit more than in other regions, although you can be sure they are watching you with well-disguised interest. When Mongolians do approach you, they are more likely to be courteous and interested in your story, which can be a welcome change if you've spent some time in more jaded parts of the country.

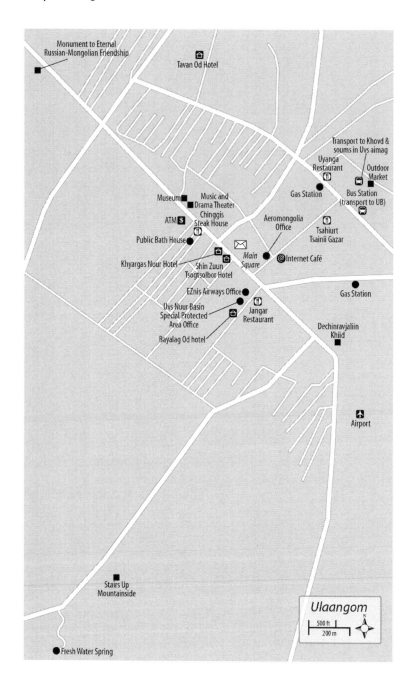

Monument to Eternal
Russian-Mongolian Friendship

Tavan Od Hotel

Transport to Khovd &
soums in Uvs aimag

Uyanga
Restaurant

Outdoor
Market

Gas Station

Bus Station
(transport to UB)

Museum

Music and
Drama Theater

Chinggis
Steak House

Aeromongolia
Office

ATM

Tsahiurt
Tsainii Gazar

Public Bath House

Khyargas Nuur Hotel

Main
Square

Internet Café

Shin Zuun
Tsogtsolbor Hotel

EZnis Airways Office

Gas Station

Uvs Nuur Basin
Special Protected
Area Office

Jangar
Restaurant

Bayalag Od hotel

Dechinravjaliin
Khiid

Airport

Stairs Up
Mountainside

Ulaangom

500 ft
200 m

N

Fresh Water Spring

# WHERE TO STAY

**Khyargas Nuur Hotel (Хяргас Нүүр)** The hidden gem of Ulaangom accommodations. One- and two-bed rooms are MNT15,000-20,000, depending on the size of the room. A three-bed *ger* is also available for MNT15,000. To find someone on staff at this small, family run hotel, go through the hall to the courtyard behind the hotel and give a hearty, "Hun bain uu?" ("Is anyone here?"). Rooms are clean and bright, and each has a TV and water kettle. The biggest drawback is that all rooms share a bathroom, although it's very clean compared to many others. The main worker here is Tungaa, who happens to be the only English-speaker employed by any of Ulaangom's hotels. She is very willing to help travelers, and the hotel offers a range of services including Jeep rental with driver. Tungaa also operates a foreign language training school attached to the hotel, and you may be able to negotiate cheaper room rates in exchange for teaching a few lessons of spoken English. *99065691, 99065691*

**Tavan Od Hotel (Таван од)** Located a bit outside of the center of town. Two-, three-, and four-bed rooms are MNT18,000-25,000. The half-lux (MNT30,000) and lux (MNT35,000) rooms are the nicest in town and have their own bathrooms with water heaters, meaning hot water all year round. The other rooms share a bathroom. The rooms are well kept and nicely furnished, but the cheaper rooms are not always available. The hotel also has a sauna, a restaurant, and billiards.

**Shin Zuun Tsogtsolbor Hotel (Шинэ зуун цогцолбор)** Conveniently located directly across from the square, this hotel didn't even have a sign on the building last time we were there. Singles and doubles with a bathroom are MNT17,000-20,000. A half lux is MNT20,000, and a lux room is MNT30,000. The rooms are adequate, if the toilet isn't broken, but not exactly pleasant, and sometimes the staff will tell you that the cheapest rooms are unavailable even though the rest of the hotel seems deserted.

**Bayalag Od hotel (Баулаг од)** No more pleasant than the Tsogtsolbor Hotel. This is still the place to go if you're on a budget and the Hyargas Nuur Hotel is full. Simple rooms start at MNT15,000. Half lux rooms are MNT20,000, and lux rooms are MNT25,000. At least the simple rooms have attached bathrooms.

# WHERE TO EAT

**Chinggis Steak House** The best in town for quality and variety. The *byaslagtai beefshteiks* is a winner, as is the meatless *tsuivan* from the menu's small vegetarian section. Chinggis has an outdoor seating area in summer. The menu is in both English and Mongolian. ₮₮

**Ikh Mongol** Like its sister location in Khovd, the interior decorating is intricate. If only they paid as much attention to the food. It's decent, if you can get it. The restaurant wasn't serving on most days we tried to eat here. On one trip, when the restaurant finally did serve us, the staff only had variations of the ground meat-and-egg theme; on another they only had Chinese food—Mongol style, of course. ₮₮

The Guide

**Uyanga Restaurant (Уянга ресторан)** A good place to go grab a meal if you're waiting around at the market for your *purgon* to leave. The service is fast, and most of the menu's extensive offerings are available. The *khuurgas* tend towards the fatty side, though. ₮

**Jangar Restaurant (Жангар ресторан)** This recently renovated restaurant, in a structure built to look like a *ger*, serves tasty *khuurgas*. There are a few vegetarian options on the menu, including *khuurgas* with dehydrated soy meat. Jangar seems popular with the locals, and has some very, very cool Mongolia-inspired blacklight posters that you'll wish were for sale. ₮₮

## Guanzes

**Tsahiurt Tsainii Gazar (Цахиурт цайны газар)** This small *guanz* near the internet café serves the best *tsuivan* in the world, provided that you operate on the philosophy that the best *tsuivan* is the one that you've got in front of you. ₮

# WHAT TO DO IN ULAANGOM

Uvs has several nice walking destinations located just outside the city center. Follow the main road northwest from the square 2 kilometers (1.25 miles) to the edge of town, and just after the bridge you'll find the **Monument to Eternal Russian-Mongolian Friendship (Мөнх найрамдал)** set near a small river and cow pastures.

Just over 3 kilometers (2 miles) south of the square are a pretty **fresh water spring** and an *ovoo* revered by locals. We drank the water with no ill effects, but travelers who have recently arrived in the country may want to play it safe. Walk down the street past the Bayalag Od Hotel and Jangar Restaurant until it ends, bear left, then turn right onto the dirt road that heads south next to the rust colored mountain. The spring is on the far side of the mountain, which itself offers an easy climb—there are even stairs to the top towards the middle of the mountain—and a good view of the city.

The local **museum** (MNT3,000; open 9:00 a.m.-6:00 p.m. Monday-Friday) has the usual collections of taxidermy and historical artifacts as well as a wing devoted to hometown "hero," Marshal Yumjagiin Tsedenbal, the head of Mongolia's communist government for some 40-odd years between World War II and the 1980s. The museum director, Begjav, is one of the most engaging and interesting rural historians you're likely to meet, and he is not afraid to discuss elements of Mongolian culture borrowed from China and other pre-Mongolian societies. You'll need a translator to understand his broad-ranging discussion of western Mongolian history, but scheduling a tour of the museum with him is well worth it.

On the eastern edge, near Ulaangom's airport, you'll find the **Dechinravjaliin Khiid (Дэчинравжалийн хийд)**, a small but friendly monastery that is merely a shadow of its former glory. A 300-year-old, 2,000 lama strong monastery was destroyed in the Stalinist purges of the 1930s, and this monastery was built to replace it about 20 years ago. A dozen or so monks now practice here. The head monk is quite friendly and happy to answer questions.

The **Music and Drama Theater** (Хөгжмийн драмын театр) is somewhat active and may have a concert while you're in town. Advertisements are usually posted in front of the theater the day of the event.

---

## The Reddest Aimag
Countryside Mongolians often vote MPRP, but Uvs takes the red cake. Typically 80-90 percent of their votes are cast for Mongolian People's Revolutionary Party (the former communist party, now named the Mongolia People's Party) candidates, and Uvs residents are proud that both legendary communist leaders hail from there. Yumjaagiin Tsedenbal ruled Mongolia from Choibalsan's death in 1953 until 1981. Jamiin Batmunkh took over and presided until hunger strikes in 1990 broke the government.

---

# WHAT TO DO IN UVS AIMAG

## Uvs Nuur (Увс Нуур)
This enormous lake—at 3,423 square kilometers (11,230 square feet), Mongolia's largest by surface area—is located just an hour's drive from Ulaangom. Uvs Nuur was once a much larger inland sea, and it still appears like one. From some parts of the lake, the opposite shore is invisible. The lake is said to be five times saltier than the ocean, although a taste test didn't quite prove this to be true. You still wouldn't want to drink it, however. The lake is uniformly shallow and is fine for wading, but doesn't offer much of a swimming spot. The lake is part of one of the largest UNESCO World Heritage sites in the world and also belongs to the **Uvs Nuur Basin Special Protected Area (UNBSPA, Увс нуур дархан цаазат газар)**. As such, you will need to pay a MNT3,000 entrance fee either at the Uvs Nuur Strictly Protected Area offices in Ulaangom or upon meeting a park ranger at the lake.

Uvs Nuur is a major stop for migrating birds, and a couple hundred different species can be found there at varying times of year. The Protected Area's staff can help give you information about what you'll be able to see during your visit.

Unfortunately, the lake is also home to clouds of vicious mosquitoes that lurk anywhere there is vegetation. Locals say that late August is the best time to visit. Day trips from Ulaangom are recommended; ask at the Khyargas Nuur Hotel to arrange a driver. Camping there earlier in the year will probably result in being driven temporarily insane by the bloodsuckers. However, there is a *ger* camp open to tourists at the most commonly visited end of the lake.

### Altan Els (Алтан элс) "Golden Sand"

A wide tract of sand dunes expands from the southeast corner of Uvs Nuur. Known as Altan Els or, alternatively, as **Buurugiin Els (Бүүргийн элс)**, the dunes nearly surround a small lake, **Bayan Nuur (Баян нуур)**. The Uvs Nuur Basin Special Protected Area office claims that these are the northernmost sand dunes in the world. You can easily get to the sand dunes from Zuungov Soum (Зүүнговь су), but if you go much further east, you'll enter the **Altan Els Special Protected Area (Алтан элс дархан цаазат газар)**, for which you'll need a permit (MNT3,000), which you can purchase at the UNBSPA office.

### Khyargas Nuur (Хяргас нуур) "Kyrgyz Lake"

Khyargas Nuur is Uvs' second largest aquatic attraction. Smaller and less salty than Uvs Nuur, it nevertheless offers a somewhat more dynamic experience. Khyargas Nuur is the temporary home to large numbers of bird species and far more fish than Uvs Nuur. Because of its greater distance from Ulaangom, you may want to travel by a shared vehicle to **Naranbulag Soum (Наранбулаг сум)** and hire a driver from there if traveling alone.

Towards the northwest corner of the lake is a fresh water spring. Mongolians claim it has medicinal powers, and wooden troughs have been set up to direct the water into the cups and bottles people bring, each labeled with the body part their water benefits. There is a summer camp of the Soviet-style (housed in wooden cabins and fairly uninteresting) near the spring.

On the southeast side of the lake is **Hetsuu Khad (Хэцүү хад** or **"Difficult Rock")**. This cliff rises unexpectedly from the middle of the lake and is colonized by large flocks of migratory cormorants each summer. A *ger* camp named after the rock is also nearby.

Khyargas Nuur, as well as the much smaller, freshwater **Airag Nuur (Айраг нуур)**, is located within the **Khyargas Nuur National Park (Хяргас нуур байгалийн цогцолборийн газар)**, which is subject to the usual MNT3,000 fee, payable at the parks office in Ulaangom or upon running into a park ranger.

### Tarialan Soum (Тариалан сум) "Grain Soum"

Tarialan is the headquarters of Uvs' Khoton population. The Khoton are an ethnic group of Turkic origin brought to Mongolia during the Zuungarian period to cultivate wheat and vegetables when the local Mongolians would not. The Khoton mainly speak and dress like Mongolians these days, but many continue to practice Islam. The *soum* has a small mosque, which is in good shape. Tarialan is about 30 kilometers (18 miles) from Ulaangom; shared taxis travel between the two daily for just a few thousand *tugriks* one-way. Taxis leave from the market in Ulaangom.

Tarialan is located as the mouth of the **Kharhiraa River (Хархираа гол)** valley. Heading west from the *soum* center along the river, you will find excellent riverside camping spots in the forested canyon beyond the small dam. It's probably best not to stay here when it rains, as the canyon could flood. The mountain on the *soum* side of the river is a good day hike; heading further upstream another 50 odd kilometers (30 or more miles) will bring you past **Harhiraa (Хархираа)** and **Turgen (Түргэн)** Mountains, 4,037 and 3,978 meters (13,245 and 13,051 feet) tall, respectively, to **Khotgor Soum (Хотгор Сум)**.

### Javkhlan

Javkhlan, who is in his early 30s, sings about traditional countryside life and is especially known for his song about his mother's boiled milk tea in "Eejing Chansan Tsai." Each of his music videos shows him in a *deel* and other traditional wear in the open air near rivers and animals. This conservative romanticizing of Mongolian steppe life is a common theme, not just in Javkhlan's music but also in the Mongolian contemporary folk pop that dominates the radio. His anthems are sung on every car and bus trip. You no doubt will hear him at some point during your stay in Mongolia, even if you never leave the train station or airport.

## Uvurkhangai Aimag (Өвөрхангай аймаг)

Uvurkhangai is loaded with history and with several notable attractions, and it can be one of the most interesting places to visit in Mongolia. It features the **Orkhon Valley Cultural Landscape**, a UNESCO World Heritage site near modern-day Kharkhorin. It is also home to **Erdene Zuu Monastery**, the oldest surviving Buddhist monastery in the country, which is adjacent to the ancient city of **Karakorum,** which served as the capital of the Mongol Empire for 40 years under Uguudei Khan before Khubilai Khan moved it to what is now Beijing, China. **Khar Bulgas**, in a more remote location, was the seat of the Uighur Empire between the eighth and tenth centuries, and there are numerous other spots marking former civilizations that ruled the steppe from this valley.

The **Khangai Mountain Range** runs across the northwest and the **Altai Mountain Range** across the southwest, but the majority of the *aimag* is steppe.

For spa lovers, **Khujirt Soum** houses a spa with water renowned throughout all of Mongolia for its healing properties, and the pilgrimage destination of **Tuvkhun Khiid** is a popular site for monastery enthusiasts. The 24-meter (79-foot) high **Red Waterfall** on the Orkhon River is a major tourist attraction, especially for travelers moving on toward Arkhangai Aimag or up to Khuvsgul Aimag.

The road from UB is paved most of the way, and this has cut the travel time to about six hours to Arvaikheer (the capital) and Kharkhorin (near the ancient Karakorum ruins).

Arvaikheer is an interesting little town to experience, full of colorful rooftops and colorful people. You can find reliable transportation to all points in the province from there for MNT10,000-13,000, though you can also travel directly to many points of interest from UB. You won't miss too much if you skip Arvaikheer in favor of Kharkhorin, especially if you're short on time, but as the transportation infrastructure improves, so does Arvaikheer. In fact, some people believe it will grow to the size of Darkhan in the next decade.

## GETTING THERE

### By Air
EZnis usually has one-hour flights to and from Kharkhorin's single dirt runway during the summer. Check www.eznisairways.com for booking information. No airline offers flights to Arvaikheer, but there is a runway you can use to land your private jet.

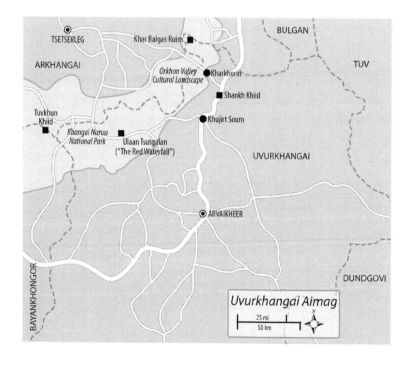

## By Bus

Buses leave twice daily (8:00 a.m. and 2:00 p.m.) from the Dragon Center in Ulaanbaatar to Arvaikheer. A ticket costs MNT14,000 for the six-hour ride, but make sure to get your tickets at least a day in advance.

Buses to Kharkhorin leave from the Dragon Center every day at 11:00 a.m.

Khujirt has a plethora of regional travel options and regular transport directly from the Dragon Center in UB, also for MNT14,000.

Return bus tickets to UB can be booked a day ahead at the bus stop in Arvaikheer or at the posts office in Kharkhorin and Khujirt.

## By Shared Transportation

*Mikrs* and *purgons* leave from both the Dragon Center and from Narantuul Black Market. They run MNT15,000, and won't leave until they are full, which is usually in the late afternoon. Additionally, they make frequent stops. Khujirt and Kharkhorin have direct *mikrs* from Ulaanbaatar as well.

You can find return travel from Arvaikheer's bus station on the edge of town or at the market in the center of town.

## By Private Transportation

You can easily hire a driver with a private vehicle from the market in Arvaikheer or Kharkhorin for the "standard" rate, which after some negotiating should be between $40 and $50 a day.

## Hitchhiking

Thumbing it is not recommended from UB, but you may have some success getting to points of interest inside the *aimag*. Because vehicles rarely leave Ulaanbaatar empty, you are better off hopping into a *mikr*, *purgon*, or bus unless you are already outside of city and on the way. You might also want to stop at **Khugnu Khaan Uul Nature Reserve** (Хөгнө хаан уул), which takes up the southern tip of Bulgan Aimag. The park is just north off the road from Ulaanbaatar, but it is only accessible from the south along this road. If you do take this route, hire a *mikr* or *purgon* to the turnoff for the park and walk the 12 kilometers (7.5 miles) if you can't find a ride from there. The reserve is not that well known or visited, though it is a great place to explore with a backpack and a tent because of the interesting convergence of taiga and steppe landscapes. The main attraction is a destroyed Zanabazar monastery. Since the main road to and from UB is so close, you could easily find a ride if you wanted to stay a few days and then hitchhike on toward Arvaikheer or Kharkhorin. See page 190 for transportation from Bulgan Aimag.

From Uvurkhangai, the buses only go to UB and back, but you can try to jump on the bus to Bayankhongor at one of the two gas stations on the main road to UB just outside of town. It stops there for about 15 minutes to refuel. Folks with home-made *buuz*, *khuushur*, and snacks attack the bus when it stops around 1:00 or 2:00 in the afternoon. Approach the bus driver (who won't speak English) with an offer. The drivers not supposed to pick up extra non-ticket passengers, but the cash goes in his pocket, making him a lot more willing to let you sit on top of the pile of luggage in the middle aisle.

# ARVAIKHEER (АРВАЙХЭЭР)

Especially if you have been traveling in the countryside for a few days already, Arvaikheer is a great town to stop for a rest. It is 10 kilometers (6.2 miles) from the geographic center of Mongolia and 420 kilometers (261 miles) from UB.

Arvaikheer, whose name means "field of couch grass" (a strong grass that spreads rapidly by its underground stems), is named after a famous horse called Arvagarkheer (Арварархээр). Just outside of town, continuing on the main UB road away from the city, is the **Morin Tolgoi** monument celebrating the famous horse. With its wide open plains, Arvaikheer is a good place for horses and races, but this also makes it one of the windiest *aimag* centers in Mongolia. It gets hit especially hard during the spring dust storms.

You can set up travel to the more touristy spots from here, enjoy getting to know the local vegetarians at the **Loving Hut** restaurant, check into the *aimag* museum, or meet Baatar at the **Gandaan Khiid (Monastery)**.

**Ayush Hero's Square (Аюуш баатрын талбай)** is the town center, where the *aimag* government headquarters are located. On the south end of the square on the median strip stands a sculpture of Ayush himself. He is venerated for his heroics during the Second Sino-Japanese War. You may notice that he appears as if he is about to rifle-whip someone on the ground. Across the street behind Ayush is the communications center, which contains a small gift shop, a post office, telephone booths with international phone cards, and two internet cafés.

# WHERE TO STAY

**Kharaa (Хараа) Hotel** One the better of the hotels in town. Lux rooms have a big bed, a shower, and mini-bar with mini-bar prices, and breakfast is included. Half lux rooms have two small beds, a shower, and included breakfast. Regular rooms include one small bed or two beds. Laundry and snooker on site. *Lux MNT30,000; half-lux MNT30,000; double MNT24,000; single MNT16,000. 0132226020, 99329695*

**Time Hotel** Located near the main square. Lux rooms include a big bed, TV, and a shower. Half lux rooms have either three small beds or two small beds with a shower and a TV. Regular rooms include either two small beds or one big bed. It's also close to the disco. *Lux $35; half-lux $17; single or double $15. 0132222866/7*

**Bayanbulag Hotel** A small hotel with friendly staff. It is a block away from the main square, next to the MobiCom building. It has half lux rooms with minbar, shower, and TV as well as standard rooms. The restaurant serves mostly Mongolian food but some European-style dishes as well. *Half-lux MNT25,000; standard MNT17,000. 01322-23374, 99329677*

# WHERE TO EAT

## Restaurants

**The Loving Hut** Part of the chain of vegetarian and vegan restaurants operated by devotees of the spiritual leader Ching Hai. The shop offers pretty good vegan pizza, some killer donuts, and a few surprisingly tasty vegetarian versions of Mongolian

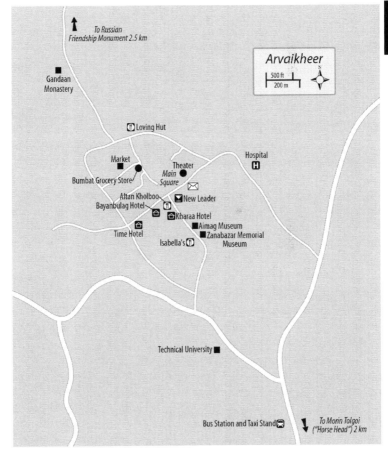

standard fare. It is a bit of a walk from the square, but it's our choice for the best in town, especially given the price, despite the fact that it doesn't have a toilet. The owner, Oyunchimeg, is an English teacher and a complete doll. ₮/₮₮

**Isabella's** Has some Korean food and chicken dishes. The walls feature pictures of celebrities including Tom Cruise and Brad Pitt. Standing dividers offer some privacy and a little ambiance. The pepper beef hot plate (MNT8,000) is one of the best options. ₮₮/₮₮₮

**Altan Kholboo** Next to the Kharaa Hotel is an interesting little place. It looks a bit like something out of an old spaghetti Western with its step-up booths. If you like to mix singing or table sports with your refreshments, the restaurant has karaoke and snooker. Depending on the cook and availability of food, the options are fewer than at Isabella's, but the French fries (*sharsan tums*) are better than any other place in town. ₮₮/₮₮₮

## Groceries

**Bumbat Grocery Store (Бумбат)** A smaller shop with a few aisles of food and sundries. Prices are good, and the staff is friendly.

# WHAT TO DO IN ARVAIKHEER

**Gandaan Monastery**, about 1 kilometer (.5 miles) from the center of town, is a point of interest for travelers with a lama fascination. Listen for the clanging of bells announcing the calls to prayer throughout the day, and stop in to meet with Bataar. He studied Buddhism in India and considers himself a teacher, though he doesn't work there full time. His English is great, and he can answer any questions you might have about the monastery and Buddhism. If he's not there, you might ask for his phone number or his wife Ishe's number and give them a call.

**The Arvaikheer Aimag Museum** (entrance MNT2,000) has the usual stuffed animals from the mountains and desert that may or may not still roam in the wild. Because the *aimag* is composed of desert, mountains, and steppe, there is a wide variety. It also has some ancient handicrafts, carvings, and Karakorum artwork. There is a **Zanabazar Memorial Museum** around the corner that houses religious artwork by the Mongolian icon and master artist, but it has been mostly closed lately. If you're interested, check with the caretaker at the *aimag* museum. She speaks English and even has a stack of item descriptions translated into English by local students.

**The Morin Tolgoi or "Horse Head" (Морьин Толгой)** is a monument celebrating a famous horse that won an important race against a thousand horses in the eighteenth century. Located 10 kilometers (6.2 miles) west of town, the monument commemorates the horse and the town of Arvaikheer with a mix of Buddhist reverence and civic pride. The memorial is a colorful and spectacular semicircle surrounded by 108 stupas, each of which contains white and gold relief sculptures of horses. The complex surrounds a painted statue of Arvagarkheer, the famed champion of the thousand-horse race. Each stupa also has two sides carved with eight auspicious signs from Buddhist iconography (a pair of golden fish, a victory banner, a white umbrella, a conch shell of melody, a sacred vase, a *dharma* wheel, an endless knot, or a white lotus of honesty) in gold leaf.

Facing the semicircle of columns that encloses the statue of Arvagarkheer is a famous mountain called "Aav Khairkhan." In Mongolian oral folklore Aav Khairkhan, or "Father Mountain," is the site of a Robin Hood-esque bandit's rescue from certain imprisonment. The story features a do-gooder bandit who stole sheep and goats from the rich. He redistributed them to the poor and was being chased through the Arvaikheer Valley by a local police force on horseback. When he reached a wide and violent river at the center of the valley, he realized he could go no farther. The police were approaching fast, but try as he might to ford the river, the bandit's horse was too afraid of the rapids to cross. Desperate to escape, the bandit invoked the name of the big brown mountain swelling out of the land across the river: "Aav Khairkhan, take me to safety!" Just like that, his horse rose into the air and flew him across the water to the top of the mountain, and he escaped the authorities to continue stealing from the rich and giving to the poor.

**The Wishing Tree** is an interesting spot if you're in the mood for a hike. Located in the hills on the northwestern edge of the town, the Wishing Tree was erected in late august of 2008 by local monks as a place for the people of Arvaikheer to pray for good fortune. Visitors will typically circumambulate the tree clockwise three times while making their wish, and often they will tie a bolt of sacred colored cloth to the branches. The tree is now totally covered in strips of green, blue, red, yellow, and white cloth, and it makes for a gorgeous picture against the backdrop of the town and the steppe to the south.

**The Russian Friendship Monument** is a concrete sculpture of the hind legs of a horse arching towards the sky. Positioned at the very top of Underleg, the largest of the hills directly above Arvaikheer, the monument was apparently erected as a symbol of friendship with the Russian government in the early 1990s. Proud students from the town like to tag the statue with their class numbers, and sweethearts have also covered it with hearts bearing their names. It's a surprisingly strenuous walk to the top, but the view is well worth the climb. To the north are the rolling hills of the Khangai range, and to the south is a stunning view of the green and red rooftops of Arvaikheer sliding into the steppe.

The Guide

**Paleolithic Cliff Drawings** cover the northward side of the slightly taller mountains directly behind Underleg (where the Russian Friendship Monument is located). Wind your way down the backside of Underleg and scramble up the taller mountain behind until you reach the top. Then, follow a path to the right until you reach a second (and much smaller) monument. Just on the other side of this monument, you will find dozens of ancient cliff drawings featuring elk, deer, livestock, hunters, and even mammoths. The presence of the mammoth art would date the images to at least 12,000 B.C.E.; some experts, however, have estimated that analogous drawings in other parts of Mongolia may be up to 40,000 years old. These are definitely worth the hike, particularly if you have an interest in prehistory.

### Nightlife

**New Leader** The town's most respected night club. It is huge, with plenty of space to flail about or join in on the circle dancing. The strobe and disco lights give off the visual equivalent of the pounding dance beats. There is seating around the edges of the room, though the music is so loud, you won't find yourself lounging or chatting

---

## Uuganaa of Arvaikheer

Uugantsetseg Gantuumur, or "Uugana" for short, is an incredibly good connection to have when visiting Arvaikheer. She is the founder and caretaker of Arvaikheer's public English Library and Youth Development Center. The facility, aptly named "Nomiin Gur" (Mongolian for "Book Bridge"), is part of an ongoing community project to extend English language learning tools to the youth of Arvaikheer. Peace Corps volunteers and members of the community help her teach classes, run movie clubs, and engage in a variety of youth social programming at the NGO, and she always appreciates a helping hand from any English-speaking visitors.

Outside of Nomiin Gur, Uugana spends much of her time preparing high school students for upcoming standardized English exams and teaching at the local university, Shuutiis. She is widely regarded as the best English teacher in the region, and it shows in her students' devotion to learning. Inspired by her success. Many of them have even gone on to study abroad in America and Europe.

Uugana has been working with development and social work organizations throughout Mongolia for over a decade. She has been extremely active with Scouts and has taken groups of students from Arvaikheer to Germany and Thailand on several occasions. She has also done extensive peer facilitation work in HIV-AIDS education with the Red Cross, held English language classes for disabled children through World Vision, and rounded up record attendance at English speaking clubs in local schools. Her boundless energy and passion for community development have made her an indispensible part of youth education in the province.

If you want to stop by and help the kids practice their English, read a good book, or even just meet Uugana and her wonderful son and daughter (both of whom speak English pretty flawlessly), you can find the Nomiin Guur NGO in the teal Children's Center building across from the Merged Complex school in the middle of town.

much. The place does get a bit rowdy, so the later you stay, the more fights you'll likely have to wade through. Ladies might want to use the buddy system, and it would be best to have a male friend with you. Vodka is available by the bottle. The squat toilets in the back are pretty gross. There is another club around the corner, but it's a much younger crowd (mainly adolescents) and pretty sketchy.

## Shopping

The market is in the center of town about 200 meters from the main square. It contains both indoor shops and outdoor stalls selling everything from food to pots, clothes, sundries, and appliances. You can find taxis and transportation to other locations on the north side.

# KHARKHORIN SOUM (ХАРХОРИН СУМ)

Near the site of the original Mongol palace, **Karakorum**, modern Kharkhorin is 360 kilometers (223 miles) from UB. The village's main industry, along with agriculture, is tourism. Still, it is a small town of under 9,000 people and has next to no luxuries. You may prefer to camp, but you can also stay in a *ger* or sleep in a small hotel with hot showers.

Kharkhorin sits in a wide, open plain, and many of the important sites are within hiking distance when the weather is good. There are plenty of taxis and guides available for hire, too.

Food around town is good for the size of the town, and even though most people here don't speak much English, they are used to accommodating tourists.

# GETTING TO KHARKHORIN

## By Bus

From UB you can take a bus directly to Kharkhorin (MNT13,000) from the Dragon Center. The bus leaves at 11:00 a.m. The ride generally takes about five to seven hours.

It's easy to find cars and taxis headed for Kharkhorin at the market in Arvaikheer. Vehicles usually leave in shifts during the morning hours around 9:00 a.m. and in the afternoons between 1:00 and 2:00 p.m. Vehicles leave when they are full or the driver has arranged enough passengers. If you have a mobile phone, you can give your number to the driver and arrange for pick up someplace within the city or just wait around nearby until he's ready to leave. The usual price is MNT10-13,000.

# WHERE TO STAY

There are many local guesthouses and *ger* camps, some coming and going with each tourist season. Because it is so competitive, the prices remain low and the competition for lodgers is high. Often during the tourist season, guesthouses will greet passengers as they get off the bus, looking to pick up lodgers. This is a good way to get a deal because you can bargain a bit.

**Morin Jim** On the main road behind the market just past the green Khan Bank. It is generally only open during tourist season (approximately May through September) but is a great restaurant with a very friendly staff. It is also a guesthouse with about four *gers* available, complete with a shower available for guests and non-guests to use for a nominal price.

**Anar Ger Camp** A permanent camp 5.5 kilometers (3.4 miles) west from the center of Kharkhorin, near the Great Imperial Map Monument. It has fifty individual *gers* with three to five beds for $25-30 per night. There are two enormous *ger* restaurants, toilets, showers, and electricity. The location on the Orkhon River is amazing. *96663761; anura@magicnet.mn*

**Blue Eternal Heaven** Located 2 kilometers (1 mile) west of Kharkhorin near the banks of the Orkhon river. With 18 *gers* and 50 beds, the camp is medium-sized, but it is also the cheapest around ($20-50). The staff can arrange horseback riding, archery, and drivers. *99119163, 99143742; mongolievoyages@magicnet.mn*

**Kharakhorum Tour Company** A small *ger* camp of 11 *gers* and 44 beds 3 kilometers (2 miles) east of Kharkhorin. *Gers* are $30-40 per night. They have traditional performances and games, visits to real herder families, and horseback riding. *99119163, 99143742; altandul@magic.mn*

# WHERE TO EAT

**Дзон** Located right along the main road that cuts through town, just behind the market. It is on the second floor of the building. This restaurant has a lot of different Mongolian dishes as well as some Korean-style options with kimchi, various meat and vegetable mixes, and soups. There are a few good vegetarian options, too, including our favorite, the vegetarian *tsuivan*. The restaurant also offers a vegetable and potato dish and some salads. Drinks are usually limited to milk tea, lipton tea, and a few different juices. If you want something cold, bring your own juice or water. No English-speakers work there, but the menus have a basic English translation. It's open year round with a nice atmosphere, and sometimes (heavy emphasis on sometimes) there is a computer with working internet available for use. ₮/₮₮

**Morin Jim** A restaurant and guesthouse on the main road behind the market, just past the green Khan Bank. It is generally open only during tourist season (approximately May through September), but it is a great restaurant with a very friendly staff and very friendly atmosphere. There's even some outdoor patio seating when weather permits. The breakfast, lunch, and dinner menu includes both meat and vegetarian options, and of all the restaurants in town, it is the one that caters most to a Western diet, though there are traditional Mongolian dishes available as well. It is one of the only places in town with chicken on the menu and regularly available, Morin Jim also has an extensive beverage menu. A few members of the staff speak English, as well as French and a little German. The bill generally adds up to more than at Дзон, though that's mostly because you're more likely to grab a drink and a piece of cake for dessert. ₮₮

**Bakery (Бэйкери)** Also located on the main paved road, between Khaan Bank and Morin Jim. This place is very popular with locals and with non-English-speakers. It is a better place for a small meal or snack than for a full lunch or dinner, but it does have some great options for soup and Mongolian-style salads. Best of all, there is a variety of inexpensive pastries and tasty breads to have with your tea or coffee. ₮

# WHAT TO DO IN & AROUND KHARKHORIN

**The Orkhon Valley Cultural Landscape** is a UNESCO World Heritage site near modern-day Kharkhorin that contains the ruins of several empires that once ruled the steppe. It would be nearly impossible for you to see all the sites where ruins exist, so we have picked the ones you'll mostly likely to be able to find.

Empires that have been seated here include the Xiongnu or Khunnu (400s-300s B.C.E.), whose raids of China forced the Qin Dynasty to connect and fortify the Great Wall to keep them out, the Xianbei or Tunghu under rule of the Chinese Han Dynasty (207 B.C.E.-220 C.E.) that consisted of non-Han peoples who became an important part of the burgeoning silk road across the steppe, the Rourans (330-555 C.E.), who were the first people to use the titles "Khagan" and "Khan" for their emperors, and the Goturks or "Celestial Turks" (552-747 C.E.), who were the first to write using the Orkhon script that can be seen on scattered relics. They were conquered by the Uighurs of Khar Bulgas (742-848 C.E.), who transformed the Orkhon script into the characters that were later adapted to fit the Mongolian language becoming what is the now traditional Mongolian script first used by Chinggis Khan around 1204.

**Khar Bulgas Ruins** (N47°53.262, E103°53.685) are north of Kharkhorin by about 28 kilometers (17.4 miles). This site was the capital of the Uighur Empire. The ancient civilization abandoned the capital in 840 C.E. and fled the area for Xinjiang Province in China after an invasion by the Kyrgyz of southern Siberia. The cost of traveling to the ruins with a private car can be expensive. The 28 kilometer (17.4 mile) trip costs MNT50,000. The more people you have, the better the deal, since cost is per ride and not per person. Buses don't go directly there, but if you're up for the adventure, it's possible to ride on the bus to Tsetserleg and then hike the 2 kilometers (1 mile) north from the road.

**The Khunnu Remains** are another set of ruins in the area that is worth seeing. Who knew the Khunnu, and not Chinggis Khan had perhaps the first Mongolian state? It's certainly up for debate, but the Khunnu (*Xiongnu* in Chinese) people in the fourth to third centuries B.C.E. united various clans under the ruler Tumen, who is credited with being the first to use the cavalry system in units of tens (1,000, 100, 10 soldiers), which was later perfected by Chinggis Khan. The territory of the Khunnu was vast, stretching from Lake Baikal to the Great Wall of China and Korea and nearly to Iran. The Khunnu grew wheat and millet and possibly baked breads. Soldiers, who were talented archers and horsemen, ruled the massive Khunnu military state. When the empire broke down, some fled toward the Ural Mountains and the Caspian Sea. Atilla the Hun likely came from this group of refugee Khunnu.

Situated about 10 kilometers (6.2 miles) outside Kharkhorin are five Khunnu graves and a **Man Stone** (*Khunii chuluu*, Хүний чулуу) located in the Munkhdagiin Am (Мөхданийн ам). If you'd like to see it, it's best to hire a driver and have him lead you there.

After the death of Chinggis Khan, his son Uguudei set up a permanent settlement and palace on the banks of the Orhkon River at **Karakorum**. He received countless ambassadors and tribute in the form of goods from all over the Mongol Empire. This more sedentary lifestyle was contrary to the template of success that his

---

## Karakorum – Mountains, Highway, Mongol Palace City

A mountain range, a highway, and an ancient town all share the name *Karakorum*. They are separate entities with separate origins, kind of.

Today, the town next to the site of the original palace city is called "Kharkhorin" by Mongolians, a derivation on the ancient Turkish *Qara Qorum* (or, alternatively, *Carachoran, Caroccoran, Karakorum, Kharakhorum*). The word for "mountain" in ancient Turkish was *qorum*, which literally means "rolled stone" or "boulder," and the word *qara* meant "black," similar to *khar* in Mongolian. The name Kharkhorin moved toward the "kh" sound because words in the Mongolian language do not start with the "k."

The names *Kharakhorum, Kharkhorin,* and *Karakorum* are virtually interchangeable and considered by Mongolian scholars as referring to crumbly volcanic stone like those at the dead volcano of the Orkhon Waterfall about 150 kilometers (93 miles) away. In fact, Paul Pelliot, an early twentieth century French sinologist, also wrote that the name is based on the rocky mountain where the Orkhon River takes its headwater. The name predates Chinggis Khan.

Karakorum is the name of the mountain range that holds the famous K2 and other glaciated peaks lining the border between Pakistan, India, and China. The Karakorum Highway connecting east and west through China and Pakistan atop the Karakorum Range is the highest paved international road in the world. The words also mean "black stone" in Kyrgyz and other Turkic languages but are not directly linked to the Mongolian mountains of the same name.

father had established, however, resulting in the eventual collapse of the empire. As strongholds in the empire began to lag in sending their tribute, the empire ultimately unwound over time.

The site is now a mere specter of the legendary Karakorum, which in itself was not a grandiose estate. There is next to nothing to see except for some stones that represent part of the outline of where the palace city once was. In the last ten years, researchers have uncovered possible new evidence of the walls of the city, but there is still much speculation about the actual dimensions of the city.

**Melkhi Chuluu (Мэлхий чулуу or "Turtle Rocks")** are among the most notable remnants of Karakorum. The turtle rocks mark the boundaries of old Karakorum, and there is one very close to Erdene Zuu Monastery. Follow the path from the entrance to the northwest. In the distance, about 300 meters (330 yards), you'll likely see a gathering of cars and people, and if you head for them, you'll find the ancient turtle.

Another turtle rock stands 25 kilometers (15.5 miles) southeast of Kharkhorin, where an old stone craftsmen's workshop was located on the banks of the Orkhon when the river used to flow directly through this part of the valley. It now stands unguarded in the middle of the field, surrounded by a scattering of other stone fragments cut in the thirteenth century, when the craftsmen's branch of Karakorum stood here marking the edge of Uguudei Khan's palace city.

**Erdene Zuu Khiid (Эрдэнэ зуу хийд)**, which means "One Hundred Treasures Monastery," is Mongolia's oldest surviving Buddhist monastery. It is a walled complex on the edge of modern Kharkhorin that dates back to 1586. The four 420-meter (1378-foot) walls containing the museum and religious grounds are topped every few meters by pristine white stupas. In 1792, Erdene Zuu held 62 temples and 10,000 monks. In its current, post-communist incarnation, it contains 54 monks and 13 colorful but weathered temples. The Lama Temple, the only one currently used for worship, has the typical white plaster exterior and is adorned with upturned eaves. Some of the complex was made from the ruins of the Karakorum capital city of Chinggis Khan and Uguudei Khan. Miraculously, the monastery was not destroyed in the late 1930s by the order of Joseph Stalin, who wanted to preserve it and Ulaanbaatar's Gandan Khiid for foreign tourists. After a 1944 visit from American vice president Henry Wallace, the government created further protections for the site and created a small budget to keep it as a state museum. From 1938 to 1990 there were no religious activities at Erdene Zuu because it was illegal, especially for communist party members.

The Guide

Erdene Zuu's current head monk, Kh. Baasansuren, speaks English well and was profiled in a January 2011 New York Times article, "Bringing a Monastery Back to Life." In the article, he explains the monastery's growing ambitions in the community, including a community center that needs capital investment.

The Dalai Lama Temple, a red brick building nearest the main gate, was built in 1675 to mark Altan Khan's trip to Tibet, which reinvigorated Buddhism in Mongolia. Ceremonies are held each day around 11:00 a.m. in the Lavrin Temple in the northwest corner of the grounds.

There are three main temples. The West Temple is dedicated to Buddha, including Sakyamuni (historic Buddha), Sanjaa (Buddha of the past), and Maitreya (Buddha of the future). It also contains *balin*, decorated ornaments made from dough and fat. Also look out for the eight auspicious symbols: lotus flowers representing purity and enlightenment, the endless knot or *mandala* representing harmony, a pair of fish representing conjugal happiness and freedom, the victory banner representing a victory in battle, the wheel of *dharma* representing knowledge, a treasure vase representing inexhaustible treasure and wealth, the parasol representing protection from the elements, and conch shells representing the thoughts of the Buddha.

The Central Temple is guarded at its entrance by Gongor (Sita Mahakala) on the left and Baldan Lkham (Sridevi) on the right. The center statue is a child Buddha next to the Otoch (Manla) Buddha of medicine. To his left is Amida (Amitabha), the Buddha of infinite light. The artwork includes *tsam* masks and art from Zanabazar.

The East Temple holds a statue of an adolescent Buddha. The statue on the left is Tsongkhapa, the founder of the Yellow Hat sect of Buddhism, and on the left there is a statue of Janraisig, the Buddha of compassion, who is the current fourteenth incarnation of the Dalai Lama.

In front of the temples are the gravestones of Abtai Khan (1554-1588) and his grandson Tusheet Khan Gambodorj, the father of Zanabazar.

**Er Khunii Beleg Erkhtenii Chuluu (Эр хүний бэлэг эрхтэний чулуу or "Male Sex Organ Rock")** is about 1 kilometer (.6 miles) from Kharkhorin just up the road from Erdene Zuu Monastery. It is a phallic monument to chastity in the shape of an enormous penis. Look for the corresponding shape drawn on signs along the road to point you in the right direction. As the story goes, a monk who should have been attending to other things was engaging in an unsavory romantic rendezvous with women, which led to his castration. To remind the lamas to avoid a similar fate, a monument in the shape of the male organ was erected. Oddly, or perhaps appropriately, it is one of the only Mongolian monuments with a barrier around it. Relax and allow your gaze to follow the pointing tip out toward the horizon and behold the so-called "Vaginal Slope Mountains" that also may have given rise to the phallic formation. Local vendors sometimes camp out next to the cock rock to sell phallic trinkets, including penis-shaped snuff bottles.

**Great Imperial Map Monument** (N47°10'50.91", E102°47'59.35") is 2.5 kilometers (1.5 miles) from the center of town in the opposite direction of the Orkhon River and Erdene Zuu. It is a good site to visit at the end of the day, especially if you're staying at the Anar or Blue Eternal *ger* camps. The mosaic stone and brick circle was finished in 2004. It sits unassumingly outside the southwest corner of town as a tribute to the area's great empires throughout history.

**Shankh Khiid (Шанх хийд)** (N47°03.079', E102°57.236'), founded in 1647 by Zanabazar, is one of the oldest and most important monasteries in Mongolia. Also called West Monastery, it was the most important in the area and housed over 1,500 monks that served the religious, medical, and educational needs of the region for almost 300 years. It is located 25 kilometers (15.5 miles) southeast from Kharkhorin.

The monastery was closed in 1937 and the temples burned in the purges. Most monks were either killed or shipped off to Siberia. Impossibly, and at great risk, five monks who are now in their 70s but were boys at the time of the purges kept the monastery underground in a *ger* until 1990. Of the three largest temples, they have since been able to restore one main temple.

The underground lamas lacked teachers, so in 1993 the Dalai Lama sent three Tibetan monks from the Namgyal Monastery in Dharmsala, India, to help foster a renaissance of Buddhism in Mongolia. One of those monks was Tenzin Yignyen, who taught at Ganden Monastery in Ulaanbaatar from 1993 to 1995. He holds a degree of "Master of Sutra and Tantra" studies from the Namgyal Monastery and taught Tibetan Buddhism, art, and language at a Namgyal branch monastery in Ithaca, N.Y. for three years. His sand *mandalas* are displayed throughout the United States, at the Cleveland Museum of Art in Ohio, The Natural History Museum of Los Angeles, the Rochester Memorial Art Gallery, and the Asia Society in New York City.

## KHUJIRT SOUM (ХУЖИРТ СУМ)

Khujirt is a quiet, small town renowned for its mineral hot springs and health spa. Most foreign travelers pass by it on their way to the Red Waterfall, but it is a well known and popular destination for Mongolians.

**The spa at Khujirt** or *rashaan* (also sometimes referred to as "sanatorium") is a little outside of the town on the northeast side, close to a holy mountain. There are

The Guide

showers there, and a couple hotels. The spa rooms are shared with groups. Though the rooms are not uncomfortable, to stay at the spa you do have to be receiving treatment, which may include mud baths, massages, alkalines, hydrogen sulfide, water pressure treatments, and other various "healthy" gadgets. The prices vary, and foreigners are charged extra.

The lodging for the village is mainly at the spa. Rooms are around MNT15,000 a night, and there are restaurants and *guanzes* in and around the hotels at the spa as well. In the town itself there are a few attractions to see, including the Gandan Piljeling Khiid in the very center of town. The town central square is where you will find a lot of stores and businesses with souvenirs and other goods you may want to

## Local Kharkhorin Tourist Services

There are plenty of tour companies and tour guides in UB that bring tourists to Kharkhorin, but there isn't a good system for finding what you need if you just wander into town. There are a few options, however. To find them, we recommend making a visit to Tuya or Soyombo.

**Tsarandorjiin Tuyatsetseg, "Tuya,"** (88841466; zuch_20@yahoo.com) is not necessarily a tour guide. She's more of a free travel agent for tourists. She has been donating her services to the community for eight years and has helped over 500 tourists find their way. Along with personal stories and personal contacts, she has brochures and books she's eager to share with travelers.

Tuya began her love affair with travel as a university student in Russia from 1978-1984, when she studied the Russian language. Not only did she pick up a few friends and fluency in Russian, but she found her knack for hospitality. Nowadays, after teaching herself English with the help of volunteers, she runs a free tourism service to help link tourists with local sites around Kharkhorin.

The loveable 50-year-old grandmother sets up shop in the most welcoming junkyard you're likely to find anywhere, behind and to the right of the telecom building as you cross the bridge over the aqueduct. In typical Mongolian fashion, she's the quintessential doting host who won't send you on your way without at least some tea and a good conversation. If you can, you should meet up with Tuya to get a lay of the land and hear her stories about living and studying abroad.

**Ts. Mandakhsoyombo "Soyombo"** (99914132; info@thetravelmongolia.com; http://www.thetravelmongolia.com) is a local tour guide with Veranda Tour Company, which he brought to Kharkhorin from UB in 2008. He has a degree in tourism management, has been certified by the Tourism Management Institute as a guide, and speaks English well. Now in his late 20s, he has been giving tours on and off since 2004, and he has worked with World Vision's Uvurkhangai Area Development Program for two years.

Soyombo's conscientious company offers many different tours around the country, so travelers can "take only photo, leave only foot print." His offerings include specialized tour packages featuring horseback riding, fishing, and customizable tours.

Since he's been in Kharkhorin, he has learned the art of cattle herding and breeding with small-time herders who also receive random tourists throughout the year. To help herders reliably supplement their income by hosting and providing an interesting time to their guests, Soyombo and his colleagues at Veranda attempt to link the herders to tourists.

take with you. There are some nearby deer stones, including one near the spa and one on the mountain.

**Tuvkhun Khiid (Төвхөн хийд)** (N47°00.7772', E102°15.362') is inside the Khangai Nuruu National Park (entrance MNT3,000), high in the mountains. It is 60 kilometers (37 miles) from Kharkhorin and accessible from Khujirt on the way to the waterfall. You can make the steep, one-hour walk from the parking area, or you can rent a horse. The retreat was founded by Zanabazar in 1653, and he lived there intermittently for 30 years. It was here that Mongolian Buddhism was truly developed, along with such innovations as the Soyombo script. In fact, much of the art that is now in the Zanbazar Museum in UB came from this site. The monastery was destroyed in 1937 but rebuilt in the 1990s. Several pilgrimage sites have emerged around it, including the caves where you can supposedly see Zanabazar's boot imprint.

**Ulaan Tsutgalan (Улаан цутгалан or "The Red Waterfall")** on the Orkhon River is one of the main attractions in the area. The river has brought life to the arid area for many centuries. It flows north 1,120 kilometers (696 miles) to the Selenge Gol, another of the most famous and important rivers in the country. The waterfall, which was formed around 20,000 years ago by volcanic eruptions and earthquakes, is exciting and majestic when it's fueled by a soaking summer rain, but it can be dry much of the year. Almost without warning, the earth just opens up below your feet as you approach the waterfall. One path down is very steep and direct, but an easier path comes around at more tolerable grade. You can rent rubber rafts in the pool at the bottom and ride directly under the water for a small fee.

## Getting to Khujirt

There is a bus from the Dragon Center in UB (MNT14,000) that goes directly to Khujirt on Mondays, Wednesdays, and Fridays and back to UB on Tuesdays, Thursdays, and Saturdays. The ride takes 7.5 to 9 hours, using the same road to Arvaikheer and veering off the pavement about an hour before reaching Khujirt. The pick-up and drop-off point is conveniently located at the spa a few kilometers from the town center. Tickets for the bus to and from UB need to be bought the day before travel. In Khujirt, purchase tickets at the post office on the east side of town.

There is also a bus that runs back and forth from Arvaikheer and Kharkhorin twice a week (Tuesdays and Thursdays) and stops off at Khujirt. It is the only viable way to get to Kharkhorin and back from Khujirt without having to first travel down to Arvaikheer.

The Guide

You can always find daily transportation to UB by *mikr* at the town square and from UB straight to Khujirt at Narantuul. The *mikr* is overcrowded and more expensive, but it's there if you need it.

From Khujirt, there are *mikrs* to Arvaikheer every day, leaving between 12:00 noon and 2:00 p.m., but you should start looking before 10:00 a.m. *The mikrs* return to Khujirt from the market in Arvaikheer around 4:00 to 6:00 p.m. Start looking around 1:00-2:00 p.m. The other buses and *mikrs* can typically be paid for upon arrival at your destination. Even though it's closer than Arvaikheer, there are almost never private rides to or from Kharkhorin, and if you want to hire a taxi, it can cost about MNT25,000.

# Zavkhan Aimag (Завхан Аймаг)

Zavkhan is famous for two things: being the coldest province in Mongolia and being the home of **Otgontenger Uul**. Zavkhan's reputation for being cold is certainly justified, but all of Mongolia gets cold, and the capital, **Uliastai**, is only slightly colder than Ulaanbaatar most of the time. The coldest and more eye-catching places lie in the north of the province, which most tourists do not see. More surprising, and sometimes annoying, is the tendency for unexpected cold snaps to come through Zavkhan, especially in the summer. The winter in Zavkhan starts in October and ends in late April, but it's not unheard of for there to be a snow in July. **Tosontsengel**, the second-largest city in the *aimag*, is known for being the coldest *soum* in Mongolia.

Traveling in Zavkhan is extremely difficult if you don't know Mongolian well and don't have a translator. Very few Mongolians in the *aimag* speak English, even in Uliastai, and there are very few foreigners living there. Every summer, some brave Europeans travel there, but it's extremely confusing and difficult. This is a great place to break up a trip from Khovd toward UB. You'll be glad you took a rest, but Uliastai is probably your only real point of interest on a trip like that, and you can see it in a day.

## GETTING THERE

### By Bus

There's only one bus that goes through Zavkhan. It goes between Uliastai and the Dragon Center in UB, and the schedule varies seasonally. It leaves from the bus ticketing office in Uliastai three times a week during the summer. The ride takes anywhere from 24 to 36 hours and costs between MNT33,000 and MNT36,000. The ladies at the bus ticketing office don't speak English, so put your miming hat on and be patient to work out the details for day, time, and seat.

## By Shared Transportation

There's a *mikr* stand near the traffic circle in the middle of town where drivers wait for passengers to fill their vehicles. A *mikr* to UB costs about MNT30,000, but drivers will try to get foreigners to pay much more. Do you best to hold your ground. There is usually one *mikr* to Erdenet and one *mikr* to Govi Altai.

## By Private Transportation

Private cars and Jeeps are few and far between. There are advertisements on local TV for cars and Jeeps going to UB looking for more passengers. Hiring a private car or Jeep to go anywhere is extremely expensive, though. The cost of gas alone will make almost any trip over MNT100,000. You can hire one at the same place you can hire a *mikr*, but drivers generally don't speak English.

## Hitchhiking

There are gas trucks that go between Uliastai and Ulaangom, the capital of Uvs Aimag. Inquire at either the big red gas station or the big blue gas station next to the *mikr* stand. It should cost about MNT30,000 one-way, but the drivers will try to overcharge foreigners. Usually, no one at either gas station speaks any English. Getting to UB is the most reliable route, since other routes may have very few cars on them. Vehicles leave and arrive at capacity, so if you thumb it, it's likely you will be in one of the *mikrs* or cars trying for the "most people ever in one vehicle" game. And though you might not win this game, it's not going to be comfortable.

## Getting Around the Aimag

There are other *mikrs* that go to certain *soums* in Zavkhan (usually Aldarkhaan, Dorvoljin, and Ider) from the *mikr* stand near the traffic circle.

# ULIASTAI (УЛИАСТАЙ)

Uliastai means "with aspen trees," which were once prominent around here, but you won't see many these days. Most of them were cut down for firewood during the electricity shortages that followed the collapse of Communism. Uliastai is one of the most interesting provincial capitals in Mongolia in terms of its appearance. Its cottonwood-lined main street, at the right angle, might remind you of a small town in the American Midwest. Seriously—try it.

The town used to be a regional seat of government during the Manchurian-led Qing Dynasty. These feudal times in Mongolia are still resented by Mongolians, who were happy to see the Chinese leave. You can see virtually nothing to suggest the nearly 270 years of Manchurian influence, but the Soviet influence is undeniable.

The town is situated in a valley with two rivers running lazily through it. They form colorful deltas during wetter times, which you can see from the stupa hill. Because of the layout of the city and because the population used to be much larger, Uliastai feels like a sprawling city, but it also has a quaint, small-town feel. Its remoteness, and the difficult roads leading to it, means it's relatively free of foreigners.

## WHAT TO DO IN ULIASTAI

The main attractions in Uliastai are the nature, the history, and the stupa hill. You won't need too much time to take them in.

**The Nine White Shrines** is the row of nine white stupas on a hill overlooking the town. Each stupa honors a notable former resident of Zavkhan. Going up to visit the stupas is the only "must" for any visitor to the city. The stupas themselves aren't very interesting, but the view from the top of the hill is definitely worth the climb. Look in a grocery store for the vodka named after it called Nine White Shrines. Mix with juice and enjoy, or share shots with some new friends.

**Zavkhan Aimag Museum** (open 9:00 a.m.-1:00 p.m., 2:00 p.m.-6:00 p.m., Monday-Friday) is located on the main street close to the theater and the Fish Eye Pub. Inside, you can find a few treasures among the usual taxidermy animals that may or may not still be found in the region. If you're interested in Mongolian history during the Manchurian-led Qing Dynasty, you'll enjoy a peek at the silk tapestries on the second floor with brightly adorned soldiers. The tapestries show scenes of everyday feudal life, and there are visually provocative depictions of torture and oppression that shed some insight on the ill feelings modern Mongolians harbor toward the Chinese. Most residents of the city aren't interested in the museum, and many foreigners may find it underwhelming as a whole, but the tapestries are worth the price of admission. Though you'll be on your own to interpret the exhibits, a guide may lead you through the winding rooms, turning the lights on and off as you go. Admission for foreigners is MNT4,000.

Probably the best way to have fun in Uliastai, though, is to have a picnic by one of the rivers. Grab some groceries and a beverage, and follow either river out of town. Within just a few minutes, all you'll hear is the wind and trickling water. Put down a cloth, make a sandwich, and relax. This is also a good camping spot. Take your trash with you, please.

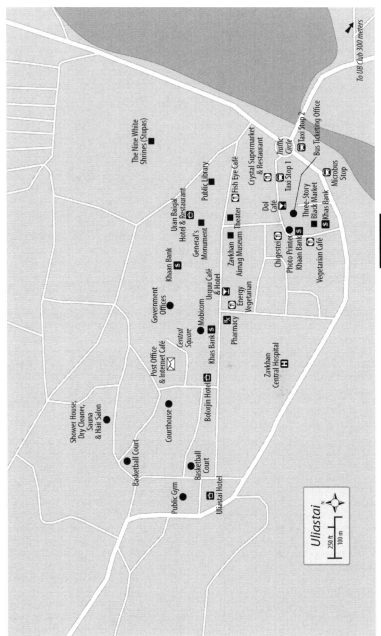

The Nine White Shrines (Stupas)

To UB Club 300 meters

Taxi Stop 2

Bus Ticketing Office

Traffic Circle

Taxi Stop 1

Microbus Stop

Crystal Supermarket & Restaurant

Public Library

Fish Eye Café

Three-Story Black Market

Khas Bank

Uran Baigal Hotel & Restaurant

Dol Café

Genetal's Monument

Zavkhan Aimag Museum Theater

Khaan Bank

Chigestei

Photo Printer

Khaan Bank

Vegetarian Café

Government Offices

Urguu Café & Hotel

Energy Vegetarian

Mobicom

Central Square

Pharmacy

Post Office & Internet Café

Khas Bank

Zavkhan Central Hospital

Bolorjin Hotel

Shower House, Dry Cleaner, Sauna & Hair Salon

Courthouse

Basketball Court

Basketball Court

Public Gym

Uliastai Hotel

Uliastai

250 ft

100 m

The Guide

For more adventurous day hikers, choose any of the mountain peaks and take a walk for some ridiculous vistas. At the top, grab a rock and add it to an *ovoo* or make your own by stacking up a few rocks. Also feel free to give small offerings of food and milk to these shamanistic mounds. If you leave in the morning, you should not have trouble returning before dark, but do return before dark. It gets pretty cold up there when the sun goes down.

While you're in town, if you're looking for a game, go to one of the several outdoor basketball courts, especially by the apartments on the west side of town. Bring a soccer ball or basketball and start a game with local children. They tend to have their own versions of games, so take notes and play along. It's a fun way to interact without sharing a language. Still, there should be a couple of kids ready to try out their English on you.

Frisbees are a novelty, so you might have to play teacher for a few minutes. If you're traveling with someone else, just start throwing near some idle kids. In no time, you should have some pretty fun company.

## Shopping

**Crystal Supermarket** The friendliest store in Uliastai for foreigners, and the only store where you can pick out your own items and then check out at a cashier. All other stores require you to ask the shopkeeper to give you the items from behind the counter. The selection of fruits and vegetables is limited, but you will find all the dried goods and beverages you'll need.

## Nightlife

**UB Club** The only club in town. The atmosphere looks legit, but the music isn't the greatest. Stop in for a beer and meet some new friends between spurts of disco dancing. The staff speaks some English. Cover is MNT2,000.

**Dol Café (Дол кафе)** Doesn't serve food. However, it does have cheap vodka and beer and a karaoke room for rent.

**Urguu Café (Өргөө кафе)** Under a small hotel. It has a nice karaoke room. Bond with some folks over the sounds of Jakhvlant and shots.

**UB Pub** In the Uliastai Hotel. It has a nice lounge atmosphere, but drinks are the same price as everywhere else. It's more of a place to relax than to shake your money maker.

# WHERE TO EAT

## Restaurants

**Fish Eye Café (Загасан нүд кафе)** The best thing on the menu, and in the town as a whole, is the fried fish. The menu has pictures but no English. The second floor has dancing, and there is a karaoke room in the hallway between upstairs and downstairs. ₮

**Chigestei Restaurant (Чигэстэй ресторан)** The oldest restaurant in Uliastai. The fried chicken is good. There are no pictures or English on the menu. The owner, Tuya, speaks some English. ₮₮

**Energy Vegetarian Restaurant (Энэрги цагаан хоол)** Look for the "SOS" on the sign. It serves vegetarian versions of Mongolian dishes. The menu has pictures but no English, and everything on the menu is pretty good. ₮

**Uliastai Restaurant (Улиастай ресторан)** In the Uliastai Hotel. The atmosphere is nice, but the food isn't any nicer than at any of the other restaurants. This is the best-stocked bar in town. Some staff members speak a little English. ₮₮

### Guanzes

**Vegetarian Café (Цагаан хоолны кафе)** Menu changes daily and has no English or pictures. The food can be somewhat bland, but the vegetarian *piroshkis* are very good and cheap. ₮

# WHERE TO STAY

**Uliastai Hotel (Улиастай)** Really nice, new hotel with 30 rooms. The nicest rooms are MNT100,000 and include a private bath with a hot shower. The cheapest room is a single with a shared bath for MNT20,000. The staff speaks some English. There is a sauna, pub, restaurant, and Khan Bank ATM inside.

**Bolorjin Hotel (Болоржин)** Has five rooms and two bathrooms. The doubles with a shared bath are the cheapest at MNT13,000. The most expensive is a single room with a queen-sized bed and private bath at MNT25,000. Both bathrooms have hot showers.

**Uran Baigal Hotel (Уран Байгаль)** The hotel's name is in Mongolian Script. Just look for the big red sign that says Hotel behind the General's Monument across from the theater. The cheapest bed is MNT8,000 in a dorm room with shared bath. The cheapest single with a private bath is MNT15,000. A two-bed room with a private bath is MNT20,000. Bathrooms have hot showers.

# WHAT TO DO AROUND ZAVKHAN

Because of the difficulty of traveling to Zavkhan, there is little tourism infrastructure. That's not to say that it's not worth experiencing, especially if you enjoy being alone.

### Tosontsengel Soum (Тосонцэнгэл сум)

This *soum* in the north of Zavkhan is the second-largest in Zavkhan. There are hotels and plenty of restaurants there, and you should be able to find some English-speakers. During the summer there are horseback tours through the area, which offers some of the most majestic country in all of Mongolia. Look to www.mongoliatravels.com to help book your adventure.

The Guide

The big attraction outside of Uliastai is the sacred **Otgontenger Uul** (**Отгонтэнгэр уул**), whose picture is on the back of a 10 *tugrik* note. Every four years, there is a large, semi-religious festival at Otgontenger, during which people from around the world come to visit and honor the mountain, though climbing Otgontenger is forbidden by law. The festival occurs in late June, before the yearly *Naadam* festival.

It is roughly 60-70 kilometers (37-43 miles) east of Uliastai, and although it is by far the tallest mountain in the region, it can't be seen from Uliastai unless you hike to the top of the tallest mountain in the city. The walk takes at least six hours, and unfortunately no *mikrs* go out there. You will have to negotiate a price with a private driver, which can get pricey. The nearest village to Otgontenger is Otgon Soum. Your best bet is to arrange something through the same tour company as transportation and accommodations are extremely limited.

---

## Mandy, Zavkhan's Rising Sun

Mandakhnar, or "Mandy," is a 36 year-old Zavkhan native. She was born in Zavkhanmandal, a small village northwest of Uliastai, and she grew up in her father's hometown of Santmargaz, where her father was a veterinarian and her mother worked at a dormitory for the children of herders. She moved to Uliastai after graduating from a university in UB and took a job as a teacher at a local secondary school. Currently, she is the local representative of GTZ, a German semi-governmental aid organization. Her job responsibilities include providing logistical and administrative support to GTZ projects in the area, translating the monthly newsletter into English, and occasionally translating for visiting subject matter experts. As of January 2011, she is the only permanent local employee of GTZ. During her summers, Mandy works as an interpreter for a horseback riding trek for tourists here in Zavkhan and has been doing so since 2002. You can see more information about the horse trek at www.zavkhan.co.uk.

In her free time, Mandy, whose name means "Rising Sun," enjoys playing ping-pong and volleyball like most residents of Uliastai. She also enjoys going to the countryside to live the traditional Mongolian lifestyle, including milking cows and riding horses. When asked about her city, she said she likes most things about Uliastai. She adds, "Our city is very nice and beautiful. It is surrounded by high mountains and forests. Uliastai is a very beautiful place because we can see Gobi [Desert landscapes] and Khangai [Mountains] in Zavkhan *aimag*. We are proud of Otgontenger Mountain, which is the second highest mountain in Mongolia. Also, the people in Uliastai are very kind, friendly, and, hospitable. My city is peaceful enough to live in, and it is developing day by day."

Her advice to travelers is to dress warm. If you are going into the mountains at any time of the year, bring warmer clothes, since the temperatures at high altitudes can be significantly cooler than the temperatures in Uliastai. She also encourages travelers to consider buying a *deel*, the traditional Mongolian silk robe. They're not cheap, but they make an excellent souvenir. In general, Mandy highly recommends Mongolia as a travel destination because of relative safety of travel, the beautiful landscapes, and the friendliness of the people. And perhaps nowhere else in Mongolia embodies all of those qualities to the extent that Zavkhan does.

# Language Reference

## ENGLISH IN MONGOLIA

Despite its location far from the West and the fact that few people outside the capital use English in everyday life, English is an official second language of Mongolia. According to the Ministry of Nature and Tourism, between 400,000 and 450,000 tourists have been welcomed to Mongolia in each of the last five years. Many of them have come from neighboring China and Russia for trade, but nearly half have come from South Korea, Western Europe, the United States, and Australia, fueling the drive for English-speakers. In fact, around 7,500 students attend tourism courses at 56 universities and institutes. Most travel companies and foreign-oriented companies employ English-speakers to help you plan your travel, sometimes even in the countryside, but most people above the age of about 35 will have learned Russian as a second language. Even with language gaps, Mongolians on the streets of Ulaanbaatar and in remote villages are generally eager to communicate with and help tourists, even if it involves an impromptu game of charades instead of speaking.

## RUSSIAN IN MONGOLIA

During most of the twentieth century, the main second language of Mongolia was, unsurprisingly, Russian. In the 1940s, Cyrillic became the new writing system replacing the vertical Mongolian script. Students learned the language and the script in schools, and it was the language of science, technology, and the arts. All the intellectuals, leaders, party bosses, and their children studied in Russia at some point, and many school children attended summer camps around the Soviet Union. Russians lived and worked in mines and in many provincial capitals in various capacities, often involving the military or factories. Consequently, anyone over the age of about 35-40 can speak at least a little Russian and can read it even better.

New styles of dress were introduced through the language so modern suits, skirts, dresses, T-shirts, and other clothing not only stayed in fashion but also remained in the Mongolian language. Many fruits and vegetables, even when they have Mongolian names, are referred to by the Russian word. You might also hear folks toss out a *"poka"* (goodbye) as they part ways. Most prominently, unfortunately, Mongolian has borrowed expletive from Russian. Mongolians don't have many truly dirty words, but the Russian vulgarity for lady parts (*pizda*) is commonly heard everywhere from the playgrounds to casual adult conversions.

## THE MONGOLIAN LANGUAGE

Here is a quick crash course on what to expect from the Mongolian language and how to use the it when you're traveling. It's best to quickly learn hello, thank you, and goodbye. You may need a little more to get around depending on where you go but not too much more. Read the alphabet and familiarize yourself with the pronunciations. If you can't learn to say a phrase in the guide below, you can even hold it up and point to the phrase you want; the same goes for the glossary. Remember, you don't have to be fluent in the language to communicate as 70 percent of language is in the body gestures, tone, and facial expressions you can manage without knowing a single word.

### Knowing Your A, Б, B's is Easy as Neg, Hoyor, Gurav

The Mongolian Cyrillic alphabet is not a perfect phonetic representation of the language, and as most languages are, Mongolian is usually written a bit differently than it is spoken anyhow. There are also some regionalisms, of course. Regardless, this guide should help you read and pronounce new words in Mongolian through the Cyrillic script, which is much easier to decipher than the traditional Mongolian script, which looks a lot like Arabic written vertically.

| Mongolian letter | Transliteration | Sounds-like survival guide |
|---|---|---|
| Aa | Aa | ah, doctor, clock |
| Бб | Bb | baby |
| Вв | Ww | way, vote |
| Гг | Gg | go (at the beginning or middle of words) or kick (at the end of words) |
| Дд | Dd | dog |
| Ее | | ye |
| Ёё | | yo |
| Жж | Jj | judge |
| Зз | Zz | dz, adds |
| Ии | Ee | street, feet |

| | | |
|---|---|---|
| Йй | | (combined with other vowels to make diphthongs or double "И") |
| Кк | Kk | ketchup |
| Лл | Ll | lamp (more lateral than in English; Sometimes called a "wet L") |
| Мм | Mm | mom |
| Нн | Nn | night |
| Оо | Oo | hot, bog |
| Ѳѳ | Oo, Uu | boat or push (in American English) |
| Пп | Pp | pop (often interchangeable with "Ф") |
| Рр | Rr | pero (rolled "R" as in Spanish) |
| Сс | Ss | stop |
| Тт | Tt | table |
| Уу | Ou ou | source (sound comes from the back of the throat) |
| Үү | Uu | oops |
| Фф | Ff | far (often interchangeable with "П") |
| Хх | Kh kh or H h | German Bach, Scottish loch (not like "kit") |
| Цц | Ts ts | cats |
| Чч | Ch ch | chair |
| Шш | Sh sh | shoe |
| Щщ | Sh-ch sh-ch | cash-check |
| Ъъ | | (hard sign; turns "Я" into "И" sound at the end of words) |
| Ыы | | (soft sign; no sound) |
| Ьь | | (soft sign; no sound) |
| Ээ | Ii | bin, in |
| Юю | You you | you |
| Яя | Ya ya | yard |

| Diphthong | Transliteration | Sounds-like survival guide |
|---|---|---|
| Ай | Aa | bat, cat, sat (rarely, like "eye") |
| Эй | Ay ay | pay, may, day |
| Иа | Ia ia | miat, fiat (quickly sliding across both sounds) |

| Ио | Io io | sen<u>io</u>r |
|----|-------|---------|
| Иу | U u | <u>u</u>nion |
| Ой | Oy oy | b<u>oy</u> |
| Уай | Oy oy | w<u>o</u>nder |
| Үй | Ui ui | w<u>ee</u>k |
| Үй | Oo oo | h<u>oo</u>t, t<u>oo</u>t |

| Doubled vowels (stressed when doubled) | Transliteration | Sounds-like survival guide |
|---------------------------------------|-----------------|----------------------------|
| Аа | | c<u>a</u>r, t<u>a</u>r |
| Ээ | | r<u>ai</u>n, c<u>a</u>ne |
| Ий | | t<u>ea</u>m, tr<u>ee</u> |
| Оо | | cl<u>o</u>ck |
| Өө | | b<u>u</u>rn, t<u>u</u>rn (at the beginning of a word); b<u>o</u>ne, <u>o</u>wn (at the end) |
| Уу | | b<u>o</u>ne, <u>o</u>wn |
| Үү | | s<u>oo</u>n, b<u>oo</u>n |

To help you wade through how to interpret the characters inside words, you need to know a few of the rules.

Words are stressed on the first syllable unless the vowels are doubled making the doubled vowels stressed instead. Diphthongs (combinations of vowels) are not stressed, and the second vowel is usually not spoken at all. So, the summer festival, *Naadam*, is stressed on the first syllable only, the word for information (*medeelel*) is stressed in the center, and the capital of the country, Ulaanbaatar, is stressed twice in the center of the word. Here is an example:

N<u>aa</u>dam sounds like "NAA-dm"

Med<u>ee</u>lel sounds like "mid-DAY-lil"

Ul<u>aa</u>nb<u>aa</u>tar sounds like "o-LAHN-BAHtr"

Additionally, vowels that end a word are not pronounced but instead written to show how to pronounce the final syllable of a word. For the word *baina* ("to be"), the final "A" is silent, making the word sound like "ban" not "banaa." Words ending with a "N" by contrast, are pronounced with an "ng" sound like "si<u>ng</u>" as in the word *tsagaan* ("white"), which that sounds like "tsagaang."

Example:  "Saina baina uu?"

"Saina. Saina baina uu?"

"Saina."

Sounds like:  "San ban o?"

"San. San ban o?"

"San."

Combining forces to make it nearly impossible to recognize, the silent "A," the rolled "R," and the wet "L" meet in the word *bayarlalaa* ("thank you"). It can be pronounced a few different ways including "buyer-laa" and "buyer-shlaa." As with all the words, you'll have to practice with a Mongolian to really get a good feeling for it.

Finally, there are two sounds for the "G" character. If it comes at the beginning or middle of the word, it sounds like "go," but at the end of a word, it has a "K" sound as in "ki<u>ck</u>." Sometimes when translated the word *tugrug* ("money") is written "tugrik" (as it is in this guide) to show the difference in pronunciation between the two.

---

## Pronunciation Notes

Please, take note in the alphabet chart that "O" is pronounced more like "ah" as in "clock." There are three different "U" characters (Уу,Үү, Өө) with distinctive sounds, and the "X" in Mongolian might sound a bit like clearing your throat. The "R" in Mongolian is rolled as in Spanish, though the "L" has a distinctive, unvoiced wet sound. It is pronounced with a flat tongue against the top of the mouth like a lisp. One difference Russian speakers should particularly note is that the diphthong "ai" is pronounced more like the "A" in "apple" in Mongolian rather than like "eye" as it is in Russian.

## Helpful Phrases

Greetings in Mongolian are not about conveying real information but are meant to satisfy social convention. If someone asks how you are, you say "good." If someone asks how you slept, you say "great." Always.

| Mongolian phrase | Survival sounds-like guide | English |
|---|---|---|
| Сайн байна уу?<br>Sain baina uu? | San ban o | Are you good? (Respond "San.") |
| Баярлалаа<br>Bayarlalaa | Buyer-shlaw | Thank you |
| Баяртай<br>Bayartai | Buyer-tay | Goodbye |

| Mongolian phrase | Survival sounds-like guide | English |
|---|---|---|
| Уучлаарай<br>Uuchlaarai | Ohch-laray | Sorry/excuse me |
| Миний нэр _____ гэдэг<br>Minii ner _____ gedeg | Mini nearr _____ gidik | My name is _____ |
| Сайхан амраарай<br>Saikhan amraarai | Sakhin amraray | Rest well |
| Сайхан амарсан уу?<br>Saikhan amarsan uu? | Sakhin amr-snow? | Did you rest well? (Respond "saikhan.") |
| дараа уулзъя<br>Daraa uulziya | Daraa uldzie. | See you later./Meet you later. |
| Чиний/Таны нэр хэн бэ?<br>Chinii/Tanii ner hin be? | Chini/Tani nir him bay? | What's your name sir/madam? |
| Сайн яваарай!<br>Sain yavaarai! | San yowr-ay! | Please, have a good journey! |
| Энэ Ямар үнэтэй вэ?<br>Ene yamar unetei we? | In yamr oontay way? | How much does it cost? |
| _____ байгаа юу?<br>_____ baigaa you? | _____ bag-uh you? | Do you have any _____? |
| Энэ авъя.<br>Ene awiya. | In ow-ie. | I'll take this. |
| Ямар ямар хоол байна?<br>Yamar khool baina? | Yamr hall ban? | What food is here? |
| Дахиад нэг _____.<br>Dakhiad neg _____. | Dakh-et nick _____ ow-ie. | I'll have another _____. |
| Зөөгчөө!<br>Zuugchuu! | Dzoke-CHUH! | Oh, waiter! |
| Тоцоо хий.<br>Totsoo khii. | Tot saw he | Check, please |
| Хаашаа явах вэ?<br>Khaashaa yawakh ve? | Hasha yowk way? | Where are you going? |
| Хамт яваж болох уу?<br>Khamt yavaj bolokh uu? | Hamt yowch ballk-hoe? | May I ride with you? |
| Болох уу?<br>Bolokh uu? | Ball-khoe? | May I? |
| Хэдэн цаг борж байна?<br>Kheden zag borj baina? | Hidden dzahk borj ban? | What time is it? |

## Mongolian is Agglutinative

Mongolian is an agglutinative language, which means there are base words to which speakers add certain particles to show relationship, ownership, proximity, etc. The main advanced particles to learn (or just hear) are the double vowels showing relationship, adding "tai" to show you have something, and the "please" ending added to verbs. Remember, Mongolian observes vowel harmony, meaning only certain vowel sounds can appear in each word.

By attaching a repeated double vowel sound to the end of a word, you show a sort of relationship. If you don't know someone's name, they are "brother of mine" or "sister of mine" and you can always address a driver by his title "driver of mine."

| Example: | Brother | Akh | Ax |
|---|---|---|---|
| | My brother | Akhaa | Axaa |
| | Sister | Egj | Эгч |
| | My sister | Egjee | Эгчээ |
| | Driver | Jorloj | Жорлоож |
| | My driver | Jorlojoo | Жорлоожоо |

To show that an item has something, attach "tai" to the end to show it "is with" something.

| Example: | Soup with vegetables | Nogoo<u>toi</u> shul | Ногоо<u>той</u> шөл |
|---|---|---|---|
| | Khuushuur with potatoes | Tum<u>stui</u> Khuushuur | Төмс<u>төй</u> хуушуур |
| | With friend(s) | Naiz<u>tai</u> | Найз<u>тай</u> |

When you put those two endings together at the end of the base word, you can say "to be with my friend" all in one word.

| Example: | Friend | Naiz | Найз |
|---|---|---|---|
| | My friend | Naiz<u>aa</u> | Найз<u>аа</u> |
| | With a friend | Naiz<u>tai</u> | Найз<u>тай</u> |
| | With my friend | Naiz<u>taigaa</u> | Найз<u>тайгаа</u> |

Conjugating a verb in Mongolian is not so much about the subject as it is about the state of the verb. Endings attached to the verb tell the time, and since there is no real word in Mongolian to say "want" or "please," you need to conjugate the verb to do it for you. If you know the infinitive of a verb, you can change it get your meaning across.

| Examples: | To eat | Идэх | Id<u>ekh</u> |
|---|---|---|---|
| | Eating (now) | Идэж байна | Id<u>ej</u> baina |

| | | |
|---|---|---|
| Ate | Идсэн | Id<u>sen</u> |
| Will eat | Идэнэ | Id<u>ene</u> |
| Want to eat | Идмээр байна | Id<u>meer baina</u> |
| I'll eat | Иды | I<u>di</u> |
| Please eat | Идээрэй | Id<u>eerei</u> |
| | | |
| To buy | Авах | A<u>wakh</u> |
| Buying | Аваж байна | Aw<u>aj baina</u> |
| Will buy | Авана | Aw<u>ana</u> |
| Bought | Авсан | Aw<u>sen</u> |
| Want to | Авмаар байна | Aw<u>maap baina</u> |
| I'll buy | Авья | Aw<u>iya</u> |
| Please buy | Аваарай | Aw<u>aarai</u> |

## Pronouns

There are no genders in Mongolian, but elders and unacquainted people use "Ta" to address each other. If someone is younger or a close friend, they are addressed as "Чи."

Here is a chart of the pronouns you might need to communicate with your new Mongolian friends and they with you. Remember, you don't have to master the language to get your point across.

| English | Transliteration | Cyrillic |
|---|---|---|
| I | Bi | Би |
| You | Chi<br>Ta | Чи (informal)<br>Та (formal) |
| He | Ter | Тэр |
| She | Ter | Тэр |
| It | Ene | Энэ |
| We | Bid | Бид |
| You (to elder)/(plural) | Ta nar | Та нар |
| They | Ted | Тэд |

| English | Transliteration | Cyrillic |
|---|---|---|
| My | Minii | Миний |
| Your | Chinii/Tanii | Чиний/ Таны |
| His | Tuunii | Түүний |
| Her | Tuunii | Түүний |

| English | Transliteration | Cyrillic |
|---------|-----------------|----------|
| Its | Tuunii | Түүний |
| Our | manai | Манай |
| Your | Ta Narnii | Та Нарны |
| Their | Tednii | Тэдний |
| Parker's | Parkernii | Паркерны |

## Question Words

| English | Transliteration | Cyrillic |
|---------|-----------------|----------|
| Where? | Khaana? | Хаана? |
| Where to? | Khaashaa? | Хаашаа? |
| When? (pronounced "hid-zay") | Khezee? | Хэзээ? |
| Who? (pronounced "hing") | Khen? | Хэн? |
| What? | You? | Юу? |
| Why? | Yagaad? | Ягаад? |
| How? | Yaj? | Яаж? |
| Which? | Yamar? | Ямар? |

## Numbers

Because of the exchange rate, most prices are in the thousands and tens of thousands. Numbers are built pretty simply in Mongolian, but they are pronounced a bit differently than they are written.

Most merchants use calculators to show you the price, so don't stress if you can't pick up the numbers too quickly. And don't forget to use your hands either. When you count on your fingers, start with the thumb and then add the pointer finger (like a gun) to show the number two.

| Numeral | Mongolian | Transliteration | Survival sounds-like guide |
|---------|-----------|-----------------|----------------------------|
| 1 | Нэг | Neg | Nick |
| 2 | Хоёр | Khoyor | Hoyer |
| 3 | Гурав | Guraw | Gore-oh |
| 4 | Дөрөв | Duruw | Doo-roo |
| 5 | Тав | Taw | Tau |
| 6 | Зургаа | Zurgaa | Dzore-GAH |
| 7 | Долоо | Doloo | Doll-AH |
| 8 | Найм | Haim | Name |
| 9 | Ес | Yes | Youss |
| 10 | Арав | Araw | Are-oh |

| Numeral | Mongolian | Transliteration | Survival sounds-like guide |
|---------|-----------|-----------------|---------------------------|
| 11 | Араван Нэг | Arawan neg | Are-oh-in nick |
| 12 | Арван хоёр | Arawan hoyor | Are-oh-in hoyer |
| 13 | Арван Гурав | Arawan guraw | Are-on-in gore-oh |
| 20 | Хорь | Hor | Hore |
| 21 | Хорин нэг | Horin neg | Hore in nick |
| 30 | Гуч | Guch | Gooch |
| 40 | Дөч | Duch | Dooch |
| 50 | Тавь | Tav | Tav (like "tack") |
| 60 | Жар | Jar | Jar |
| 70 | Дал | Dal | Doll |
| 80 | Ная | Naya | Nigh |
| 90 | Ер | Yer | Ear |
| 100 | Зуу | Zuu | Dzoh |
| 1,000 | Мянга | Myanra | Myunk |
| 10,000 | Арван мянга | Arwan myanga | ARE-oh-in myunk |
| 100,000 | Зуун мянга | Zuun myanga | DZONE myunk |
| 1,000,000 | Сая | Saya | Sigh |

## Pronunciation Reminders

– Unless the last letters are doubled, don't pronounce the last vowel sound, only the consonant.

– Words ending in "N" are pronounced like "NG" as in "drinking" or "eating."

– Roll the "R" to be better understood.

## Mongolian-English Glossary

| English | Transliteration | Cyrillic |
|---------|-----------------|----------|
| After | Daraa | Дараа |
| Air | Utaa | Утаа |
| America, American | Amerik | Америк |
| Area, administrative office, place | Gazar | Газар |
| Arrow, bullet, church | Sum | Сүм |
| Australia, Australian | Australi | Австрали |
| Authentic | Jinkhene | Жинхэнэ |
| Ax(e) | Sukh | Сүх |
| Bad | Muu (pronounced "Moe") | Муу |
| Ball | Bumbug (pronounced "boom-book") | Бөмбөг |

| English | Transliteration | Cyrillic |
|---------|-----------------|----------|
| Basketball | Sagsan bumbug (pronounced "saksin boom-bk") | Сагсан бөмбөг |
| Be, to become (used for asking permission) | Bolokh | Болох |
| Bear | Baavgai | Баавгай |
| Bed | Or | Ор |
| Beer | Pivo (pronounced "peeve") | Пиво |
| Before, north | Umnu | Өмнө |
| Beverage, sometimes carbonated beverage like soda | Uundaa | Уундаа |
| Big | Tom | Том |
| Bird | Shuuvuu (pronounced "show-whoa") | Шуувуу |
| Black | Khar | Хар |
| Blissful, content, happy | Jargaltai | Жаргалтай |
| Blue | Tenger | Тэнгэр |
| Bone | Yas | Яс |
| Book | Nom | Ном |
| Boots | Gutal (pronounced "go-tl") | Гутал |
| Border | Khil | Хил |
| Boss | Darga | Дарга |
| Bread | Talkh | Талх |
| Bread pocket that is leavened and filled with meat and rice | Peroshki | Пирошки |
| Bread pocket that is not leavened and filled with meat | Khuushuur | Хуушуур |
| Broken | Evdersen | Эвдэрсэн |
| Buddhist beings (See p43) | Bodhisattva (pronounced "bo-dee-sat-va") | Бодхисаттва |
| Buddhist Tibetan scarf (see p146) | Khadag | Хадаг |
| Buddhist Tibetan beads that are small and red | Suren | Сүрэн |
| Building, house | Baishin | Байшин |
| Bus in UB running along a few major routes tethered to an overhead electrical grid | Trolley | Троллейбус |

| English | Transliteration | Cyrillic |
|---|---|---|
| Bus, carriage | Autobus | Автобус |
| Butter | Maslo (pronounced "masl") | Масло |
| Cabbage | Baitsaa | Байцаа |
| Café, bistro, tea shop, tea house, diner, hole-in-the-wall restaurant that serves a few main staple meals | Guanz | Гүанз |
| Cairn or pile of stones, usually accompanied by blue scarves signigying a special place, usually on the top of a mountain or hill | Ovoo | Овоо |
| Camel | Temee | Тэмээ |
| Camera | Apparat | Аппарат |
| Canada, Canadian | Kanad | Канад |
| Candy, sugar, sweet | Chikher | Чихир |
| Capsicum, sweet peppers | Chinjuu | Чинжүү |
| Carrot | Luuwun | Лууван |
| Cat | Mur | Мөр |
| Center | Tuv | Төв |
| Cheese | Byaslag | Бяслаг |
| China | Khyatad | Хяатад |
| Chocolate | Shokolad | Шоколад |
| Clean, pure | Tsever | Цэвэр |
| Clothing worn by herders, traditional Mongolian robe | Deel | Дээл |
| Cloud | Uul | Үүл |
| Coal | Nuurs | Нүүрс |
| Coffee | Kofe (sometimes pronounced "copy") | Кофе |
| Cola | Kola | Кола |
| Cold | Khuiten (pronounced "hootng") | Хүйтэн |
| Come, arrive | Irekh | Ирэх |
| Communications center, Telecom centrum | Kholboo | Холбоо |
| Computer | Kompyuter | Компьютер |

| English | Transliteration | Cyrillic |
|---|---|---|
| Condom | Belgevch | Бэлгэвч |
| Cookie fried in butter | Boortsog | Боорцог |
| Country, state | Uls | Улс |
| Countryside | Khuduu, khudoo (pronounced "who-dough") | Хөдөө |
| Cow | Ukher | Үхэр |
| Daughter, girl | Okhin | Охин |
| Day | Khonog | Хоног |
| Desert, semi-desert | Govi | Говь |
| Difficult | Khetsuu | Хэцүү |
| Diner | Zoogin gazar | Зоогийн газар |
| Dirty, ugly | Muukhai | Муухай |
| Dish of food, almost always bits of meat with something sometimes on a cast iron hot plate (exception: Budaatai huurga is like tsuivan with rice instead of flat noodles) | Khuurga | Хуурга |
| Dislike | Duurgui | Дуургүй |
| District or village | Sum or soum (pronounced like "soap") | Сум |
| Doctor | Emch | Эмч |
| Dog | Nokhoi | Нохой |
| Dress | Palaaj | Палааж |
| Dried meat | Borts | Борц |
| Drink (verb) | Uukh | Уух |
| Driver | Jorlooj (pronounced "jar-lotch") | Жорлоож |
| Dumplings | Buuz | Бууз |
| Dumplings, small and usually part of a soup | Bainsh | Байнш |
| Dung | Baas | Баас |
| Eagle | Burged | Бүргэд |
| Ear | Chig (pronounced "cheek") | Чиг |
| Earing | Eemeg | Ээмэг |

| English | Transliteration | Cyrillic |
|---|---|---|
| Eat | Idekh | Идэх |
| England, English, British, Briton | Angli | Англи |
| Eternal | Munkh | Мөнх |
| Europe, European | Yevrop | Европ |
| Evening | Oroi | Орой |
| Eye | Nuud | Нүүд |
| Family | Ger bul | Гэр бүл |
| Fast | Khurdan | Хурдан |
| Fat | Uukh | Өөх |
| Father | Aav | Аав |
| Female; medicine | Em | Эм |
| Fence, family compound | Khashaa | Хашаа |
| Field, steppe, plot | Tal | Тал |
| Fire | Gal | Гал |
| Flash drive, thumb drive | Flash | Флаш |
| Flour | Guril | Гурил |
| Flower | Tsetseg | Цэцэг |
| Fly (verb), airport | Nisekh | Нисэх |
| Foot, leg; far | Khol | Хол |
| Football, soccer | Khol bumbug (pronounced "hall boom-bk") | Хол бөмбөг |
| Fox | Uneg | Үнэг |
| France, French | Frants | Франц |
| Friend | Naiz | Найз |
| Full, sated, satiated, stuffed | Tsadsan | Цадсан |
| Garlic | Sarmis | Сармис |
| Gasoline, petrol, benzine | Benzin | Бензин |
| Gazelle | Oono | Ооно |
| Germany, German | German | Гэрман |
| Gift | Beleg (pronounced "bilik") | Бэлэг |

| English | Transliteration | Cyrillic |
|---|---|---|
| Glass | Shil | Шил |
| Glasses, spectacles | Nuudnii shil | Нүүдний шил |
| Go | Yavakh | Явах |
| Goat | Yamaa | Ямаа |
| God, deity | Burkhan | Бурхан |
| Gold | Alt | Алт |
| Good | Sain | Сайн |
| Goodbye | Bayartai | Баяртай |
| Grandchild | Ach khuu | Ач хүү |
| Grandfather, old man | Uvuu | Өвөө |
| Grandmother, old woman | Emee | Эмээ |
| Grass | Uvs | Өвс |
| Great, extremely good | Saikhan | Сайхан |
| Green | Nogoo | Ногоо |
| Hair | Uus | Үс |
| Hand, arm | Gar | Гар |
| Hat | Malgai | Малгай |
| Head | Togloi | Тоглой |
| Help, please | Tuslaarai | Туслаарай |
| Herder | Malchin | Малчин |
| Here | End | Энд |
| Hero | Baatar | Баатар |
| High, great, much, extreme | Ikh | Их |
| Homosexual person | Gomo | Гомо |
| Horse | Mori | Морь |
| Horse-head fiddle | Morin khuur | Морьн хүүр |
| Hospital | Emneleg | Эмнэлэг |
| Hot | Khaluun (pronounced "hall-OWNg") | Халуун |
| How? | Yaj? | Яаж? |

| English | Transliteration | Cyrillic |
|---------|-----------------|----------|
| Husband | Nukhur | Нөхөр |
| Ice | Mus (pronounced "moose") | Мөс |
| Ice cream | Zairmag | Зайрмаг |
| Information | Medeelel | Мэдээлэл |
| Inside | Dotor | Дотор |
| Internet | Internet | Интернет |
| Ireland, Irish | Irland | Ирланд |
| Japan | Yapon | Япон |
| Juice | Juus | Жуус |
| Ketchup | Kechup | Кечуп |
| King | Khaan | Хаан |
| Korea, Korean | Solongos | Солонгос |
| Koumiss, fermented mare's milk | Airag | Айраг |
| Lake | Nuur | Нүүр |
| Laptop computer | Nuutbuuk | Нөөтбүүк |
| Left | Zuun | Зүүн |
| Light, torch, flashlight | Gerel | Гэрэл |
| Like | Duurtai | Дууртай |
| Lion | Arslan | Арслан |
| Livestock, herd | Mal | Мал |
| Lock | Tsooj | Цоож |
| Lost | Tuursun | Төөрсөн |
| Lunar New Year, White Moon, White Month | Tsagaan Sar | Цагаан Сар |
| Makeup | Goo Saikhan | Гоо сайхан |
| Male | Er | Эр |
| Meat | Makh | Мах |
| Meatballs | Teftel | Тефтель |
| Metal | Tumur | Төмөр |
| Microbus | Mikro (pronounced "mikr") | Микро |

| English | Transliteration | Cyrillic |
|---------|----------------|----------|
| Milk | Suu | Сүү |
| Minute | Minut | Минут |
| Mixture | Khormog | Хормог |
| Monastery | Khiid | Хийд |
| Mongolian money | Tugrug or tugrik | Төгрөг |
| Monk, lama | Lama (pronounced "lam") | Лама |
| Monkey | Mich | Мич |
| Moon, month | Sar | Сар |
| Morning | Ugluu | Өглөө |
| Mother | Eej | Ээж |
| Mountain | Uul | Уул |
| Mountain (a flowery word sometimes used to describe a mountain of special importance) | Khairkhan | Хайрхан |
| Mountain range, spine | Nurru | Нүрүү |
| Mouse | Khulgana | Хулгана |
| Mouth | Am | Ам |
| Movie | Kino (pronounced "keeno") | Кино |
| Much, extreme | Mash | Маш |
| Nature, environment | Baigal | Байгал |
| Near | Oilkhan | Ойлхан |
| Necklace | Zuult | Зүүлт |
| New Year, celebrated January 1 | Shine Jil (pronounced "shin jeel") | Шинэ жил |
| New Zealand | Shine Zeland | Шинэ зеланд |
| Nice, beautiful, pretty, awesome, cool | Goye | Гоё |
| Night | Shunu | Шөнө |
| Ninja miner, an artisinal miner | Ninja | Нинжа |
| No, nope | Ugui, gu | Үгүй, гү |
| Noodle dish with bits of meat, fat, and vegetables | Tsuivan | Цуйван |
| Noodles | Goimon | Гоймон |

| English | Transliteration | Cyrillic |
|---|---|---|
| Nose | Khamar | Хамар |
| Now, soon | Odoo | Одоо |
| Number | Too (pronounced "tah") | Тоо |
| Oasis | Shar burd | Шар бурд |
| Ocean | Dalai | Далай |
| Older brother | Akh | Ах |
| Older sister | Egch | Эгч |
| Onion | Songino | Сонгино |
| Outside, Foreign | Gadaad | Гадаад |
| Palace | Ordon | Ордон |
| Pants | Umd | Өмд |
| Paper | Tsaas | Цаас |
| Parliament, committee | Khural | Хурал |
| Pastry, usually fried, sometimes lightly sweetened | Boov | Боов |
| Pen, honey | Bal | Бал |
| Pepper | Perets | Перец |
| Permit | Zuvshuurul | Зөвшөөрөл |
| Person | Khun | Хүн |
| Person who is younger, usually any family member or close friend | Duu (pronounced "doo") | Дүү |
| Phone, "hand phone," mobile, cell phone | Gar utas | Гар утас |
| Phone units | Negj | Нэгж |
| Picture, photo, painting | Zuraga (pronounced "zork") | Зурага |
| Pink | Yagaan | Ягаан |
| Plane or boat | Ongots | Онгоц |
| Police | Tsagdaa | Цагдаа |
| Post office | Shuudan | Шуудан |
| Power, electricity | Tog (pronounced "tahk") | Тог |
| Price | Une (pronounced "oon") | Үнэ |

| English | Transliteration | Cyrillic |
|---|---|---|
| Province, province center | Aimag | Аймаг |
| Przewalski's horse | Takhi (pronounced "takh") | Тахь |
| Purple | Yagaah khukh | Ягаан хөх |
| Purse, bag | Tsunkh | Цүнх |
| Queen | Khatan | Хатан |
| Rain | Boroo | Бороо |
| Rainbow | Solongo | Солонго |
| Ray, beam of light | Tuya | Туя |
| Red | Ulaan | Улаан |
| Reindeer | Tsaa buga | Цаа буга |
| Repair | Zasvar | Засвар |
| Rice | Budaa | Будаа |
| Right | Baruun | Баруун |
| Ring | Bugj | Бөгж |
| River | Gol | Гол |
| Road | Zam | Зам |
| Rock, stone, avenue | Chuluu | Чулуу |
| Sacred | Bogd | Богд |
| Salad | Salat (pronounced "sal-AT") | Салат |
| Salt | Daws | Давс |
| Sandals, flip-flops | Sandaal | Сандаал |
| Sausage | Khyam | Хям |
| School | Surguuli | Сургууль |
| Seat | Suudal | Суудал |
| Secret | Nuuts | Нууц |
| Sex | Seks | Сэкс |
| Sheep | Khoni (pronounced "hon") | Хонь |
| Shirt | Tsamts | Цамц |
| Shop, kiosk, store | Delguur | Дэлгүүр |

| English | Transliteration | Cyrillic |
|---------|-----------------|----------|
| Shower | Khaluun us | Халуун ус |
| Silver | Mungu | Мөнгө |
| SIM card | Sim kart | Сим карт |
| Sing | Duu | Дуу |
| Skirt | Yubka (pronounced "you-bk") | Юбка |
| Sky | Tsenger | Цэнгэр |
| Slippers, house shoes | Tapochki (pronounced "tahw-chk") | Тапочки |
| Slow | Udaan | Удаан |
| Small | Jijig | Жижиг |
| Snow | Tsas | Цас |
| Snuff bottle | Khuuraga | Хуурага |
| Socks or boot inserts | Olms | Олмс |
| Son, boy, child, dude, chap, fella, guy | Khuu | Хүү |
| Soup | Shul | Шөл |
| South | Khartsaga | Харцага |
| Soy | Shar Buurtsgiin makh | Шарбуурцгийн max |
| Soy sauce | Tsuu | Цуу |
| Star | Od | Од |
| Stool, chair | Sandal | Сандал |
| Stop! | Zogs! | Зогс! |
| Stop, please | Zogsooroi | Зогсоорой |
| Strong | Bat | Бат |
| Student | Suragch | Сурагч |
| Sugar | Saakhar/Chikhir | Саахар /Чихир |
| Summer sports festival | Naadam (pronounced "Naaadm") | Наадам |
| Sun | Nar | Нар |
| Sun glasses | Narnii Shil | Нарнйи Шил |
| Surely, certainly | Shuu | Шүү |

| English | Transliteration | Cyrillic |
|---|---|---|
| Sweety, lover, baby, honey | Amarag | Амараг |
| Table tennis, ping-pong | Tennis | Теннис |
| Tall or great | Undur | Өндөр |
| Tea | Tsai | Цай |
| Teacher | Bagsh | Багш |
| Team, district, group | Bag (pronounced "bahg") | Баг |
| Teeth | Shuud | Шүүд |
| Thank you | Bayarlalaa | Баярлалаа |
| This | Ene (pronounced "in") | Энэ |
| Throat, gorge | Khooloi | Хоолой |
| Throat singing | Khuumii (Khoomii) | Хөөмий |
| Tiger | Bar | Бар |
| Time, hour | Tsag | Цаг |
| Tired | Yadarsan | Ядарсан |
| Tobacco, cigarette, snuff | Tamikh | Тамих |
| Today | Unuudur | Өнөөдөр |
| Tomato | Pomidor | Помидор |
| Tomorrow, later | Margaash | Маргааш |
| Tongue, language | Khel | Хэл |
| Tourist | Juulchin | Жуулчин |
| Train car, wagon | Vagon | Вагон |
| Train station | Voksal | Вокзал |
| Tree, wood | Mod | Мод |
| Turnip | Manjin | Манжин |
| United Kingdom | Kholboot vant uls | Холбоот вант улс |
| United States of America (USA) | Amerikiin negdsen uls | Америкийн нэгдсэн улс (АНУ) |
| Van with 4x4 | Furgon, purgon | фургон, пургон |
| Vehicle | Machine | Машин |

| English | Transliteration | Cyrillic |
|---|---|---|
| Vest worn on top of a deel for special occasions or alone with jeans and high heels by women | Khantaz | Хантаз |
| Vodka | Arkhi | Архи |
| Volleyball | Gar bumbug (pronounced "gar boom-bk") | Гар бөмбөг |
| Wait | Baijie (pronounced "BAY-jee") | Байжие |
| Waiter | Zuugch | Зөөгч |
| Wall | Khana | Хана |
| Water | Us (pronounced "oh-s") | Ус |
| Welding | Gangnuur | Гангнуур |
| Wet | Noiton | Нойтон |
| What? | You? | Юу? |
| Wheel, tire | Dugui | Дугуй |
| When? | Khezee? (pronounced "hid-zay") | Хэзээ? |
| Where? | Khaana? | Хаана? |
| Where to? | Khaashaa? | Хаашаа? |
| Which? | Yamar? | Ямар? |
| White | Tsagaan | Цагаан |
| White food, vegetarian food | Tsagaan khool | Цагаан хоол |
| Who? | Khen? (pronounced "hing") | Хэн? |
| Why? | Yagaad? | Яагаад? |
| Wife | Ekhner | Эхнэр |
| Wolf | Chono | Чоно |
| Yak | Sarlag | Сарлаг |
| Year | Jil | Жил |
| Yellow | Shar | Шар |
| Yes, yup | Tiim, ti | Тийм, Ти |
| Yesterday | Uchigdur | Өчигдөр |
| Yogurt | Tarag | Тараг |
| Yurt, felt tent, home | Ger | Гэр |

# KAZAKH LANGUAGE

The Kazakh language is spoken by roughly 8 million people worldwide, and a sizable portion of this number resides in Mongolia. Not surprisingly, the approximately 200,000 Kazakh-speakers in Mongolia live in the far western regions that are closest to Kazakhstan, mostly in Khovd and Bayan Ulgii aimags. Like Mongolian, Kazakh belongs to the Altaic language family, is agglutinative, and employs vowel harmony. In Kazakhstan and Mongolia, the Kazakh language is written in the Cyrillic alphabet, but Kazakh speakers in China use script that closely resembles Arabic and is similar to what is used to write Uighur. Kazakh diasporas in Turkey use a modified Latin alphabet.

In Kazakh Cyrillic, there are 42 characters, nine of which are specialized for the Kazakh language (Ә, Ғ, Қ, Ң, Ө, Ұ, Ү, һ, І). Formerly, they were written at the end of the alphabet, but now they are next to the similar sounds. Of these, 11 sounds are not used in native Kazakh words, and seven are only used in Russian loan words.

| Cyrillic | Transliteration | Survival sounds-like guide |
|---|---|---|
| A a | A a | father |
| Б б | B b | bed |
| В в | V v | very |
| Г г | G g | got |
| Ғ ғ | Ğ ğ or Gh gh | (backlingual glottal "g") |
| Д д | D d | day |
| E e | Ye ye or E e | yes |
| Ё ё | Yo yo | yawn |
| Ә ә | Ä ä | apple |
| Ж ж | J j or Zh zh | Measure |
| З з | Z z | zone |
| И и | Ii iy | feet |
| Й й | Y y | (diphthong, used with other vowels) |
| І і | İ i | till |
| К к | K k | kind |
| Қ қ | Q q | (lingual glottal fricative "k") |
| Л л | L l | element (hard), limo (soft) |
| М м | M m | main |
| Н н | N n | not |

| Cyrillic | Transliteration | Survival sounds-like guide |
|---|---|---|
| Ң ң | Ñ ñ or Ng ng | so<u>ng</u> |
| һ h | H h | <u>h</u>at |
| О о | O o | h<u>o</u>t |
| Ѳ ѳ | Ö ö | <u>ea</u>rly |
| П п | P p | <u>p</u>ark |
| Р р | R r | (rolled as in Spanish) |
| С с | S s | mi<u>ss</u> |
| Т т | T t | <u>t</u>en |
| У у | Ww, UW, uw | s<u>ui</u>t |
| Ү ү | Ü ü | p<u>oo</u>l (with tip of the tongue high to the front) |
| Ұ ұ | U u | f<u>u</u>ll |
| Ф ф | F f | <u>f</u>our |
| Х х | X x | lo<u>ch</u>, Ba<u>ch</u> |
| Ц ц | C c | i<u>ts</u> |
| Ч ч | Ç ç | <u>ch</u>eck |
| Ш ш | Ş ş | <u>sh</u>ip |
| Щ щ | Şş şş | ca<u>sh ch</u>eck |
| Ъ ъ | " " | (Russian only; hard sign) |
| Ы ы | I ı | <u>u</u>nder |
| Ь ь | ' | (Russian only; soft sign) |
| Э э | E e | <u>e</u>nd |
| Ю ю | Yu yu | <u>you</u> |
| Я я | Ya ya | <u>yah</u> |

## Helpful Phrases

| Kazakh phrase | Survival sounds-like guide | Meaning |
|---|---|---|
| Амансыз ба? <br> Amansyz ba? | Aman ciz ba? | Hello, *literally, "You good?"* (Respond "Aman.") |
| Рахмет <br> Rakhmet | Rockmet | Thank you |
| Сау болыныз <br> Sau bolyniz | Sau bolengiz | Goodbye |

| Kazakh phrase | Survival sounds-like guide | Meaning |
|---|---|---|
| Ғафу етіңіз<br><br>Gafu etiniz | Gafu entiniz | Sorry/excuse me |
| Менің атым _____.<br><br>Menyn Atim _____. | Min-ing atim _____. | My name is _____. |
| Жақсы демалдыңыз ба?<br><br>Zhaksy demaldiniz ba? | Jaksa ma? | Did you rest well? (Respond "Jacksa.") |
| Жақсы демалдыңыз<br><br>Zhaksy demaliniz | Jacksa demalingz | Rested well |
| Кездескенше сау тұрыңыз<br><br>Kez bolgansha sau turiniz | Kizdeskenshe sau turunguz | See you later/meet you later. |
| сенің атің кім?<br><br>Cening ating kim? | Sining ating kim? | What's your name? |
| Жолыңыз ашық болсын<br><br>Zholyniz ashyk bolsyn | Joloungoz ashok bolson | Please, have a good journey |
| неше сом?<br><br>Neshe som? | Neshe som? | How much does it cost? |
| Сізде _____ бар ма?<br><br>Sizde _____ bar ma | Sizde _____ bar ma? | Do you have any _____? |
| Бұны алғым келеді.<br><br>Buny algym keledi. | Bun algom keleda. | I'll take this. |
| Қандай тамақтар бар?<br><br>Khanday tamak bar? | Konday tamaktar bar? | What food is here? |
| Тағы нарсе алайын _____.<br><br>Tagy narse alayin _____. | Tago narce alaion _____. | I'll have another _____. |
| Оффицант!<br><br>Offytsyant! | Offetsant! | Oh, waiter! |
| Төлем жасайын.<br><br>Tolem jasayin. | Tolem jasaeon. | Check, please. |
| Қайда барасың?<br><br>Khayda barasyn? | Kyeda barasin? | Where are you going? |

| Kazakh phrase | Survival sounds-like guide | Meaning |
|---|---|---|
| Сізбен бірге жүрсем бола ма?<br><br>Syzben byrge jursem bola ma? | Cizben birgay jurcem bola ma? | May I ride with you? |
| Б ола ма?<br><br>Bola ma? | Bola ma? | May I? |
| Неше сағат болды?<br><br>Neshe sagat boldy | Neeshe sagat bolda | What time is it? |

## Kazakh-English Glossary

| English | Kazakh transliteration | Cyrilic |
|---|---|---|
| Airport | Aeroflot | аэрофлот |
| Bed | Tosek | Төсек |
| Bird | Khus | Құс |
| Cell Phone | Telefon | Телефон |
| Cold | Suik | Суық |
| Come, arrive | Kelu | Келу |
| Communications Center | Tele Kommunikatsya Ortaligi | Теле коммуникация орталығы |
| Cow | Sear | Сиыр |
| Day | Kun | Күн |
| Dislike | Unamau | Ұнамау |
| Doctor | Dariger | Дәрігер |
| Drink (verb) | Ishu | Ішу |
| Driver | Shoffeur | Щофер |
| Eagle | Burkit | Бүркіт |
| East | Shigis | Шығыс |
| Eat | Zheu | Жеу |
| English | Agilshin | Ағылшын |
| Evening | Kesh | Кеш |
| Family | Semiya | Семия |
| Fast | Zhildam | Жылдам |
| Fire | Ot | От |

| English | Kazakh transliteration | Cyrilic |
|---|---|---|
| Fly | Ushu | Ұшу |
| Friend | Dos | Дос |
| Full, sated, satiated, stuffed | Toly | Толы |
| Gift | Syilik | Сыйлық |
| Go | Juru | Жүру |
| Good | Zhaksy | Жақсы |
| Goodbye | Sau Bol | Сау бол |
| Green (color) | Jasyl | Жасыл |
| Green (vegetable) | Jemis | жеміс |
| Happy | Kuanyshti | Қуанышты |
| Hawk | Kharshyga | Қаршыға |
| Here | Bul | Бұл |
| Hospital | Aurukhana | Аурухана |
| Hot | Istyk | Ыстық |
| Hour | Sagat | сағат |
| How? | Khalay? | Қалай? |
| Information | Zhanalyk | Жаналық |
| Lake | Kol | Көл |
| Like | Unatu | Ұнату |
| Livestock | Mal | Мал |
| Lost | Zhogalu | Жоғалу |
| Meat | Et | Ет |
| Monastery | Meshyt | Мешіт |
| Morning | Tan | Таң |
| Mountain | Tau | Тау |
| Near | Jakyin | Жақын |
| Nice, beautiful | Ademy | Адемі |
| No | Zhokh | Жоқ |
| North | Soltustyk | Солтүстік |
| Now | Khazyr | Қазір |
| Person | Adam | Адам |

| English | Kazakh transliteration | Cyrilic |
|---|---|---|
| Phone units | Telefo | Телефон |
| Picture, photo, painting | Suret | Сурет |
| Please, help | Komek | Көмек |
| Please, stop | Toktatyniz | Тоқтатыныз |
| Police | Polytsiya | Полиция |
| Power, electricity | Elektyr | Електір |
| Price | Baga | Баға |
| Repair | Zhondeu | Жөндеу |
| River | Ozen | Өзен |
| Road | Zhol | Жол |
| Seat | Taktay | Тақтай |
| Shop | Duken | Дүкен |
| Shower | Dush | Душ |
| Slow | Akyryn | Ақырын |
| Small | Kyshkene | Кішкене |
| Soon | Keshykpey | кешікпей |
| South | Ongtustyk | Оңтүстік |
| Tea | Shay | Шай |
| Thank you | Rakhmet | Рахмет |
| This | Bul | Бұл |
| Time | Uakhyt | Уақыт |
| Tired | Sharshau | Шаршау |
| Today | Bugyin | Бүгін |
| Tomorrow | Erteng | Ертең |
| Tongue, language | Tyl | Тіл |
| Tourist | Turyst | Турист |
| Traditional Mongolian robes | Ulttyk | Ұлттық |
| Tree | Terek | Терек |
| Vegetarian food | Jemysti | Жемісті |
| Waiter | Offisyant | Оффицант |
| Water | Su | Су |

| English | Kazakh transliteration | Cyrilic |
|---|---|---|
| West | Batys | Батыс |
| What? | Ne? | Не? |
| When? | Khashan? | Қашан? |
| Where? | Khayda? | Қайда? |
| Where to? | Khayda? | Қайда? |
| Which? | Khay? | Қай? |
| Who? | Kaysy? | Кім? |
| Why? | Nege? | Неге? |
| Wood | Agash | ағаш |
| Yes | Yaah | Ия |
| Yesterday | Keshe | Кеше |
| Yurt | We | Үй |

**Contact us at**

**www.otherplacespublishing.com**


**info@otherplacespublishing.com**